THE REALIST GUIDE TO RELIGION & SCIENCE

THE REALIST GUIDE TO RELIGION & SCIENCE

PAUL ROBINSON

GRACEWING

First published in England in 2018
by
Gracewing
2 Southern Avenue
Leominster
Herefordshire HR6 0QF
United Kingdom
www.gracewing.co.uk

No part of this publication may be reproduced, stored in a retrieval system, or transmitted in any form or by any means, electronic, mechanical, photocopying, recording or otherwise, without the written permission of the publisher.

The right of Paul Robinson to be identified
as the author of this work has been asserted in accordance
with the Copyright, Designs and Patents Act 1988.

© 2018 Paul Robinson

ISBN 978 085244 922 6 paperback
ISBN 978 1 78182 013 1 cased

Typeset by Gracewing

Cover design by Bernardita Peña Hurtado

*Sedi Sapientiae, Reginae coeli et terrae, Matri universae
a servo filioque suo amanter dedicatus est hic liber.*

CONTENTS

ACKNOWLEDGEMENTS..................................xi

ABBREVIATIONS...xiii

FOREWORD..xv

PREFACE..xix

I. REASON..1

1 - THREE WITNESSES..3

2 - FOUR CAUSES...33

3 - THREE KNOWLEDGES.................................71

II. RELIGION..111

4 - PAGAN PANTHEISM..................................113

5 - CATHOLIC CREATIVITY.............................155

6 - MUSLIM MONOTHEISM...........................199

7 - PROTESTANT BIBLICISM..........................233

III. SCIENCE..**307**

8 - SCIENCE SUICIDE.....................................309

9 - GODLIKE UNIVERSE.................................349

10 - INORGANIC LIFE....................................393

11 - UNSPECIFIED SPECIES...........................433

EPILOGUE..497
BIBLIOGRAPHY..505
INDEX OF NAMES..511
GENERAL INDEX..515

ACKNOWLEDGEMENTS

GOING CHRONOLOGICALLY, MY first thanks are owed to three people who encouraged me to write a book: Doug Korfhage, the tile man from my home town, Guy Finnie, our Holy Cross Seminary cook, and Fr Joseph Azize, the erudite Maronite priest. Father added to his encouragement, throughout the composition of this book, helpful guidance drawn from his own experience as author of several works.

I would next like to extend my gratitude to the many who provided constructive criticisms and timely suggestions during the writing of the book: Gil Garçon, who edited the book and, in doing so, provided instructions in style at the same time, Dr Dennis Bonnette, who scrutinised the more philosophical parts with his professional eye, Fr Daniel Themann, my superior who carefully read and corrected one of the last drafts, James Forsee, my stepfather, whose remarks led to my conception of the epistedometer, James Vogel, who assisted me throughout the work, Br Joseph Xavier, who meticulously proofread the entire text, Fr Robert MacPherson, Michael Baker, and Dr Jakub Taylor.

Others provided much needed encouragement during the long months of composition by reading one or more of many draft copies. Their support was appreciated, and they include Stephen Dunne, John McGrath, Cindy Carroll, Carmel Attard, Fr Thomas Onoda, Fr Jordie Stephens, and Fr Ludger Grün.

Lastly, at the publication stage, I am beholden to Rev. Dr Paul Haffner for accepting the book for publication, for patiently addressing my many questions during the preparation process, and for kindly writing the book's foreword, and also to Michael Sestak for his excellent work in rendering professionally the book's images.

ABBREVIATIONS

Abbreviations for the works of Thomas Aquinas

ST	*Summa Theologiae*
SCG	*Summa Contra Gentiles*
In Met.	*In duodecim libros Metaphysicorum Aristotelis Expositio*
In Phys.	*In octo libros Physicorum Aristotelis Expositio*

Notes on usage

- The word *billion* throughout the text, is used to refer to a thousand million (10^9), while *trillion* refers to a million million (10^{12}).
- The numbering for the Psalms follows the numbering of the Septuagint version of the Old Testament.
- References to works of Aristotle follow the Bekker pagination numbers. Those numbers correspond to the page number, column, and line number of the given citation of Aristotle in the Prussian Academy of Sciences edition of the complete works of Aristotle.
- Similarly, for Plato, references follow the Stephanus pagination numbers, which are based on a 1578 edition of Plato's complete works published by Henricus Stephanus in Geneva. The numbers give the page and section of the given citation of a Platonic dialogue, as found in one of the Stephanus volumes.

FOREWORD

I WARMLY COMMEND this book by Fr Paul Robinson highlighting the importance of the realist perspective in the dialogue between Science and Religion. Realism is the metaphysical bridge which guarantees the true relation between the mind and reality and is thus the right approach to link reason with Christian belief in God. An access to the true nature of the universe is needed in order to reflect properly on God's handiwork. Reality is rather like a mine in which understanding, like precious metal, has to be quarried at the cost of great effort. Or, in the analogy of Fr Robinson, it is like a hike into a high mountain range with all the challenges that this enterprise involves.

Christian tradition has always held that man is truly capable of understanding creation and gradually uncovering its meaning, within a realist perspective. In the prelude to his monumental profession of faith, Pope Paul VI stated:

> It is of the greatest importance to recognize that over and above what is visible, the reality of which we discern through the sciences, God has given us an intellect which can attain to *that which is*, not merely the subjective content of the 'structures' and developments of human consciousness.[1]

Pope John Paul II lay firmly in the realist tradition.[2] For him acceptable systems of philosophy must share the metaphysical realism of St Thomas Aquinas, including his position on the natural knowability of the existence of God:

> It is the Church's duty to indicate the elements in a philosophical system which are incompatible with her own faith. In fact, many philosophical opinions—concerning God, the human being, human freedom and ethical behaviour—engage the Church directly, because they touch on the revealed truth of which she is the guardian. In making this discernment, we Bishops have the duty to

be "witnesses to the truth", fulfilling a humble but tenacious ministry of service which every philosopher should appreciate, a service in favour of *recta ratio*, or of reason reflecting rightly upon what is true.[3]

Pope Benedict XVI gave a Christological foundation to his realism:

> The real novelty of the New Testament lies not so much in new ideas as in the figure of Christ himself, who gives flesh and blood to those concepts—an unprecedented realism. In the Old Testament, the novelty of the Bible did not consist merely in abstract notions but in God's unpredictable and in some sense unprecedented activity. This divine activity now takes on dramatic form when, in Jesus Christ, it is God himself who goes in search of the 'stray sheep', a suffering and lost humanity.[4]

Pope Francis has also affirmed that realities are more important than ideas, and this flows from the doctrine of the Incarnation.[5]

Reality speaks to us, communicating its message through the senses of our human nature, shaped from flesh and spirit. A realist approach to the cosmos is essentially based on the Thomist axiom: 'the being of a thing, not its truth, is the cause of truth in the intellect.'[6] Common-sense realism involves a true partnership between man as a knower and the world and contrasts with nominalist, positivist, pragmatist, idealist and nihilist positions. Realism affirms the existence of universals against nominalism. Against positivism, realism proposes that reality extends beyond that which the natural sciences can measure. It affirms the validity of objective truth in its own right against a merely pragmatist or utilitarian view. Realism affirms against idealism that the external world is not simply the projection of the mind. Against nihilism, realism teaches that the world makes sense and has meaning.[7]

Moderate realism is the 'cement' in any synthesis of faith and reason; it stipulates the real existence of the external world independent of the mind of the observer, yet with a mutual relation between the mind and reality. This helps us to understand better the beauty of the cosmos as inspired by the words of the great Doctor of the Cappadocian School, St Gregory of Nyssa:

> As painters transfer human forms to their pictures by means of certain colours, laying on their copy the proper and corresponding tints, so that the beauty of the original may be accurately transferred to the likeness, so I would have you understand that our Master also, painting the portraits to resemble His own beauty, by the addition of virtues, as it were with colours, shows in us His own sovereignty.[8]

Fr Robinson succeeds in leading his reader into the highlands of truth concerning the relations between science and religion, and invokes many masterly figures like Fr Stanley Jaki, G. K. Chesterton and Étienne Gilson. He does so with skill but also in way which should enable the ordinary reader to engage this quest with relative ease; his use of diagrams and tables should help the more visual generations in this respect. It is my hope that this book will help many people to understand better the importance of the dialogue between Christian faith and the natural sciences.

Rev. Dr Paul Michael Haffner
President, Stanley Jaki Foundation
Rome, 10 January 2018,
Feast of St Gregory of Nyssa

Notes

[1] Pope Paul VI, *Credo of the People of God* (30 June 1968), 5.
[2] See A. Dulles, 'The Metaphysical Realism of Pope John Paul II' in International *Philosophical Quarterly* 48/1 (March 2008) pp. 99-106.
[3] Pope John Paul II, *Fides et ratio*, 50.
[4] Pope Benedict XVI, *Deus Caritas est*, 12.
[5] See Pope Francis, *Evangelii Gaudium* (24 November 2013), 231–233.
[6] St Thomas Aquinas, *Summa Theologiae*, I, q.16, a.1: '... esse rei, non veritas eius, causat veritatem intellectus.'
[7] See my book *The Mystery of Reason* (Leominster: Gracewing, 2001) pp. 12-19.
[8] St Gregory of Nyssa, *De Hominis Opificio*, 5.1.

PREFACE

The most profound evil of our times consists in the lack of realism.

Gustave Thibon

AT THE BEGINNING of his New York Times bestseller *The Greatest Show on Earth*, atheist biologist Richard Dawkins tells of a psychological experiment in which he participated. He and some others were to watch a short video clip of some young people passing basketballs to one another. While watching, they were to carefully count how many times the balls were passed during the duration of the video. After the video was over, the experimenter collected the individual tallies of the participants and asked the general audience the question: 'How many of you saw the gorilla?' Dawkins tells us:

> The majority of the audience looks baffled: blank. The experimenter then replays the film, but this time tells the audience to watch in a relaxed fashion without trying to count anything. Amazingly, nine seconds into the film, a man in a gorilla suit strolls nonchalantly to the center of the circle of players, pauses to face the camera, thumps his chest as if in belligerent contempt for eye-witness evidence, and then strolls off with the same insouciance as before. He is there in full view for nine whole seconds—more than one-third of the film—and yet the majority of the witnesses never see him.[1]

The point that Dawkins makes is that indirect evidence received through scientific instruments is often more reliable than eye-witness evidence. There is, however, another, bigger point to be made from this example: we often only see what we are looking for, and Dawkins is a prime example of that intellectual disposition.

On the other side of the scientific fence is Stephen Meyer's bestseller *Darwin's Doubt*. Interestingly, in chapter 19, he makes a very similar observation to that of Dawkins. He mentions his puzzlement at the mountain of evidence pointing to intelligent design in nature on the one hand, and the refusal of many brilliant scientists to accept that evidence on the other. In the midst of pondering on this question, he read a Chesterton short story entitled 'The Invisible Man.'

In Chesterton's tale, a murder has been committed in an apartment complex that is carefully guarded by four honest men. There is only one entrance to the room where the murder was committed and all four men swear that no one went up the stairs. Fr Brown, however, is not convinced. He sees a 'stringy pattern of grey footprints' on the snow covering the outside entrance. The four guards believe they were made by an invisible man, but Fr Brown realises they were made by the postman. The guards, who were on the watch for a suspicious looking man with an evil motive, did not think of reporting the harmless looking man with the ordinary motive. And so, they saw the postman without seeing him, that is, they did not consider him as a possible suspect. Consequently, they completely factored out his coming and going in the commission of the murder.

Meyer reflects, 'The theme is a favorite of detective-story authors: the obvious possibility missed by the experts, because their assumptions prevent them from considering what might otherwise seem to be an obvious possibility.'[2]

I must concur with this unexpected agreement between Dawkins and Meyer. The human mind is quite capable of falling short in its knowledge of reality by missing evidence, by not reasoning with sufficient care and effort, or by relying on false presuppositions. On the other hand, when it is correctly oriented in its relationship to reality, the mind's ability to learn about the world is simply astounding.

This book attempts to prove that there is only one 'reality mentality' that is sane, safe, and successful for the human mind.

Preface

It is called *realism* and it indicates the precise way in which humans know and so also the precise way in which they relate to reality. The reason that a case needs to be made for realism is that humans, by an abuse of their free will, can choose other reality mentalities than the one which is theirs. Doing so, they restrict and even break off their inherent ability to know the world around them. Reality becomes washed out, the mind's eye becomes feeble, gorillas and postmen pass by without being noticed.

When reason goes wrong, when an unhuman worldview is chosen to replace the human one, usually religion or science is at fault. Much ink has been spilled about the incompatibility of religion and science. Whenever they are incompatible, however, it is not because they are incompatible with one another, it is because one or the other of them is incompatible with reality.

This book will reconcile religion and science, but it will not do so through religion or science. It will do so by reconciling the human mind to reality. It will do so through the guidance of realism. If, as a realist viewpoint indicates, there is but one single source of the entire universe, then reality is a unified whole. Moreover, if that single source, in creating humans, gave them the capacity to grasp reality as such, then there is no reason why a person's perception of reality should not also be a unified whole. I aim to show that you can, and indeed should, have a single unifying vision of reality, where there is room for God *and* for God's creation, without the two of them coming into conflict, but rather with them co-existing in separate but not ontologically exclusive realms.

Perhaps more importantly, religion and science become *more* rational and hence more credible to the degree that they are harmonised. Since they are both needed to fill out a coherent, sane picture of reality, they mutually assist one another when they occupy their proper places in that picture. When science rests in the realm of empirical fact and religion in the fabric of reality underpinning empirical fact, they hold one another in place, as it were. On the other hand, when science is stretched into a religion or religion is used to patch over science, reality's fabric becomes torn, leaving a void of contradiction and incoherence.

Thus, this book aims to detail a reality mentality wherein both reality and human reason are given their full rights and, as a result, religion and science co-exist in maximal harmony. Because my purpose is to achieve their union in the mind, based on my conviction that they cannot be opposed in reality, then I must make use of an arbitrator that stands outside of both of them. That arbitrator, as I have mentioned, is realist philosophy.

'Philosophical realism' in today's intellectual climate invariably conjures up images of mailed knights, pensive monks, dusty manuscripts, and Gothic cathedrals. It speaks of a world in which modern science cannot possibly seem to fit. The West has assumed for nigh on 500 years that the common sense philosophy of the Middle Ages was exceedingly naive, and so it is of no use for our advanced age. Wasn't all that philosophy completely overthrown by the subtle attacks of Hume and Kant?

On the contrary, not only has realism not been overthrown, it remains to this day the only philosophical mentality that can provide an account of human reasoning that does not fall into rank contradiction. It holds the modest position that *the things we perceive are really, objectively there*, that reality is real, *and that our faculties of sense and intellect enable us to know it*. While this would seem to be an obvious stance to take, unfortunately it has not seemed obvious to many cultures and thinkers in human history. On the contrary, as we will see, realism has been a minority position in human thought and currently has residence in the philosophical dog house, on a long term, self-renewing contract. It is high time that realism be restored to a world in desperate need of objectivity.

I do not hesitate to state that my inspiration came from the writings of the late, great Fr Stanley Jaki, physicist and theologian, herculean researcher, and prolific writer. From the early 1960s until his death in 2009, he applied his rapacious and capacious mind to exhaustive research into the history of science. The sheer

Preface xxiii

volume of first hand sources from the past as well as contemporary works that he read, assimilated, and synthesised seems to justify his magisterial tone, forceful invective, and adamant insistence, all wrapped in a sophisticated and obscure prose. Jaki packs a punch.

One of Jaki's main contentions is that realism is needed to do religion rightly and to do science rightly.[3] To do religion rightly means to provide it with a rational foundation, by means of realist philosophical proofs for the existence of God and His attributes. To do religion wrongly is to base it upon an irrational emotion or a sacred text read irrationally. To do science rightly is to require that its theories match empirical evidence and conform to the world as we know it, that is, that it be realist. To do science wrongly is to cook up theories which do not serve hard fast evidence, but rather serve some preconceived notion of the way that the universe ought to be. What is the mentality behind right religion and right science? Realism. What is the mentality behind wrong religion and wrong science? Either idealism or empiricism.

Such is Jaki's contention, and he threw the entire weight of his training into proving his point. As physicist and historian, he turned to the history of mankind, looking carefully to see how science developed or failed to develop in the various world cultures. What he found was that the 'mentalities' of which I just spoke were the single most important factor for determining whether or not cultures and individuals were able to make scientific progress or, for that matter, do science at all. Realism made for success; idealism and empiricism made for failure.

I myself will be taking up the same thesis, but I will broaden it and approach it from a different angle. I hope to provide a more solid philosophical foundation for the thesis, as well as make it clearer. In doing so, I am also seeking to solve two difficulties that readers might have with Jaki's approach and writing style.

The first difficulty is the density of Jaki's writings. Going through his books can be like reading by the light of fireworks, to adapt a comment made by A. R. Orage about G. K. Chesterton's works. Brilliant phrases, clever diction, and studied complexity are the standard fare in Jaki's prose. In the words of one of his reviewers, 'Every sentence is so loaded with meaning that it is hardly possible to absorb it at the first or even the second read. Jaki tends to assume in his readers a breadth of knowledge similar to his own.'[4] Thus, while Jaki's work is stunning and impressive, it is also fairly inaccessible.

The second difficulty is that Jaki writes more as an historian than a philosopher. For this reason, he focuses much more on events and individuals than on ideas. Here too, his books resemble a fireworks show. An historical episode or detail flashes by with an apt quotation and a most incisive comment by Jaki. Then he quickly passes on. Your interest is piqued by your glimpse of the intellectual framework underlying Jaki's argument, but you are not allowed to enjoy it, for it was only a flash, and soon you are viewing the next Roman candle from Jaki's immense arsenal. Jaki's brilliant mind was often content to make a point, while seeing little need to develop it.

Fr Paul Haffner, who wrote an excellent overview of Jaki's writings, notes that Jaki did not give any systematic exposition of the philosophy underpinning his arguments: 'For the purpose he had set himself, Jaki did not have to go into minuter details of [realism]. His purpose was to uncover the major features of the intellectual landscape which is the philosophical interpretation of the history of science.'[5] Jaki himself admits that 'A speculative study of natural theology is not my specialty.'[6] He did not write as a scholastic philosopher, but as a scientific historian. For this reason, we easily miss the full weight of Jaki's arguments.

What I propose to do in this book, then, is to remedy both of these difficulties. On the one hand, I have aimed for clarity above all else. This book is meant to be a well-guided tour of realism's take on religion and science disputes. On the other, I have focused on ideas, more than on persons or events, as I want to display as fully as possible the rich and extensive backdrop that lies behind Jaki's fireworks show. I write as a philosopher more than a

Preface

historian, drawing from my own particular training and decade of experience in teaching various branches of Thomistic philosophy.

To accomplish its task, this book sets forth a general principle about human knowing, and then illustrates that principle by looking at the history of religion and science, as follows:

- **General principle**—realism is the human way of relating to reality and so is the default basis for all the knowledge of it that humans acquire
- **Religion as example of principle**—religion is reasonable when realist and becomes irrational to the degree it is not
- **Science as example of principle**—science is reasonable when realist and becomes irrational to the degree it is not

These three bullet points correspond to the three sections of the book. First, we have to know reality using realist eyes; second, we have to see how religion is reasonable when realist and unreasonable when not; third, we must do the same for science.

The first section, then, explains what philosophical realism is, then provides a picture of what the whole of reality looks like when you are a realist, and finally situates religion and science in that realist picture. These ideas are presented in three separate chapters:

- what realism is, in opposition to idealism and empiricism—chapter 1
- what realism has to say about the whole of reality, all that exists—chapter 2
- where religion, philosophy, and science fit in realism's view of reality—chapter 3.

The second section considers pre-modern cultures where religion set the tone of human thought. Among such cultures, there were instances of religion assisting science. Much more often, however, religion impeded it. The reason why religions were an aid or hindrance to intellectual progress, I claim, was their possession or lack of realism. Part two considers the following cultures and religions:

- pre-Christian cultures: the Indians, Chinese, and Greeks—chapter 4
- Catholicism—chapter 5
- Islam—chapter 6
- Protestantism—chapter 7.

The third and final section looks at the scientific perception of reality that developed after the Scientific Revolution. Scientists have made incredible discoveries in the past four centuries by effective use of the scientific method. Many of them, however, have fallen into irrationality by reducing the whole of reality to the scope of their discoveries. This would not have happened if they had remained realist, as I attempt to show in the four chapters of third part:

- The departure from realism in the age of science—chapter 8
- scientific findings about the universe—chapter 9
- scientific findings about life—chapter 10
- scientific findings about evolution—chapter 11.

In covering these topics, I have not wanted to over-simplify the issues at stake, and so I do not hesitate to delve into some intricacies of philosophy and science, in order to expose clearly whether a given reality mentality is either driving minds to a deeper understanding of reality or driving them to irrationality.

At the same time, I do not assume any previous knowledge on the part of the reader. Throughout, I seek to break down difficult concepts and illustrate them with concrete examples, as well as indicate sources that might be useful for further study. There are tables, flowcharts, and even a reality mentality meter that are gauged both to maintain the reader's interest and guide him in the understanding of the material. In this way, the book attempts to combine a popular style with academic content, so as to make the work accessible to as many as possible. Chances are that if you are comfortable with the content and style of this preface, you will find the rest of the work easily digestible.

I do feel the need to issue a caution, however. You might pick up this book and quickly turn to the controversial parts—those on creationism, evolution, and the Big Bang—just to see whether you agree with them or not. You might flip through to have a glance at the illustrations, flowcharts, and tables, while thinking that the book requires a bit more focus than you are willing to invest. But except you, dear reader, patiently read from start to finish, you will not pluck the real fruit which has been prepared for you: a single, unifying view of the universe—intellectually satisfying and coherent—wherein religion and science are in harmony without being mutually exclusive.

Is it really possible to have such integrity of mind in this day and age? Can we aspire to that wisdom so desired by the ancients, whereby one knows the highest things, and sees all other things in their light? Can the mind's eye be single, even in this fragmented twenty-first century?

You will see that we can answer 'yes' to those questions as you read. Any other answer would be one of despair. The realist is also an optimist.

Notes

[1] R. Dawkins, *The Greatest Show on Earth* (New York: Free Press, 2009), pp. 14–15.
[2] S. Meyer, *Darwin's Doubt* (New York: HarperOne, 2013), p. 383.
[3] This is the subject of his book *The Road of Science and the Ways to God* (Port Huron, Michigan: Real View Books, 2005). See also his words on this topic in *A Mind's Matter* (Grand Rapids, Michigan: William Eerdmans Publishing Company, 2002), p. 93; in *Bible and Science* (Grand Rapids, Michigan: William Eerdmans Publishing Company, 1996), pp. 199–200; and in *Lord Gifford and His Lectures* (Edinburgh: Scottish Academic Press, 1986), pp. 31–32.
[4] Cited in P. Haffner, *Creation and scientific creativity* (Leominster, England: Gracewing, 2009), p. 162.
[5] *Ibid.*, p. 181.
[6] *The Road of Science and the Ways to God* (Port Huron, Michigan: Real View Books, 2005), p. 324.

I Reason

1 THREE WITNESSES

Whatever may be the meaning of faith, it must always mean a certainty about something we cannot prove. Thus, for instance, we believe by faith in the existence of other people.

G. K. Chesterton

Mount Everest, standing as it does at 29,029 feet, makes for a difficult climb. To reach the top, you must have stamina, endurance, strong lungs, good guides, and high quality equipment. The good guides are the Sherpas, the Nepalese natives who are well acclimated to the extreme conditions in the Himalayas. The equipment includes goggles, gloves, thermals, ice axe, harness, trekking poles, and oxygen.

While careful planning and rugged determination are important, they do not guarantee success. Over 250 have died on the slopes of Earth's highest mountain. Some were buried in avalanches coming down from the treacherous Khumbu Icefall. Some slipped and fell. Most perished in the 'death zone', the area above 26,000 feet where low atmospheric pressure means that only a third of a human's normal oxygen intake is available.

In this first section of the book, we need to climb to the top of reality. At the top, we will be able to see where religion and science reside, and how they co-exist in harmony. That vantage point will also enable us to determine why so many perished on the way up, that is, fell into the abyss of irrationality. For some, it was religion that caused the avalanche—we will consider them in section two. For others, science caused the brain cells to freeze—we will consider them in section three.

Our guides up the slopes of reality will be Aristotle, St Thomas Aquinas, Etienne Gilson, Stanley Jaki, and others. Our equipment will be our human faculties for knowing. The climb will be undertaken by philosophising, that is, using our knowing faculties in their most abstract capacities to attain an understanding of everything.

Our ascent will not take place until the next chapter, after which we will locate religion and science in chapter three. The first thing that we need to do, in this chapter, is examine our equipment carefully. We must understand what it does and how to use it. Otherwise, we cannot expect to make it safely to reality's apex.

The technical word for this examination of human knowing equipment is *epistemology*, literally the study of knowledge. This word will appear quite often as we go along, and it involves a consideration of:

- the ability of humans to understand reality, and
- the validity of human knowledge.

We can speak of a person's epistemology, what I referred to as a 'reality mentality' in the preface.[1] By that, I mean a person's position on:

- whether truth can be attained
- how truth is known
- to what degree truth can be known
- the tools used in reaching truth

The task immediately ahead of us is to present a certain epistemology called *realism*, for it alone has a proper understanding of our knowing equipment. Only as realists will we be able to get to the bottom—I mean, the top—of reality.

How we know

Humans are equipped with two types of faculties which enable them to *know*, that is, perform an internal activity which unites the knower at some level with the thing known.[2] One type of knowing faculty, the *senses*, comes from our body, while the other, the *intellect*, is rooted in our soul. Besides exercising these knowing powers directly on the outside world in order to understand it, each of us can also gain knowledge indirectly, by having other human knowers teach us about what is. This makes for three different types of equipment available to us for conquering reality:

- the senses, external and internal,
- the intellect, and
- authority.

An epistemologist investigates these tools for knowledge and takes a stance on whether or not they provide a true grasp of reality and to what degree they do so. Let us then examine the realist position on each type of equipment.

The senses, external and internal

By the senses, I mean the material organs of our *body* that are designed to capture a particular aspect of external reality. Eyes assimilate light, the ears sound, the nose smell, the tongue taste, and the skin feelings. These sense organs are able to take in their respective objects, providing us immediate contact with the world around us. Through them, data from the real world, reality, enters us. Having crossed the threshold of our being, sense data does not fade away but rather comes under the influence of internal sense faculties which we call instinct, memory, common sense and imagination. These faculties interpret, retain, collate and image the data provided by the external senses.

Realism takes for granted that:

- the data which we receive from the outside world is real,
- our perception of it is real, and so
- we are connecting with reality at the moment of sensation.

These statements cannot be proven, but let someone try to deny them and then live life. They would have to become 'solipsists', those who deny all external reality and hold themselves to be the only ones who exist. While one can call oneself a solipsist, one cannot live as a solipsist. When you do not consider the food in front of you to be real, for instance, you stop eating.

This fact that the senses connect us with reality highlights the radical need we have of them. We are so constructed that we look outwards, not inwards. Our senses, the external ones at least, are on our outside, while our intellect is on our inside. Since reality is outside of us, our intellect cannot get to reality directly. It must rely upon the senses to make the connection with the external world. If we had no senses, our intellect would not be presented anything to penetrate and understand.

These reflections bring us to another fundamental realist principle: *all knowledge has its starting point with sensation of the outside world*. Thomas Aquinas remarks on this fact as follows:

> According to its manner of knowing in the present life, the intellect depends on the sense for the origin of knowledge; and so those things that do not fall under the senses cannot be grasped by the human intellect except in so far as the knowledge of them is gathered from sensible things.[3]

Fast on the heels of this realist principle is the following corollary: *knowledge is dependent upon reality, and not reality upon knowledge*. Phrased another way, 'if there were no things, there would be no knowledge'.[4] We do not make reality, we learn from it. We must come into contact with reality in order to attain truth; otherwise, our supposed knowledge is just make believe, a raw construction of subjective thought that corresponds to nothing other than itself. We humans need truth. But to attain truth, we need reality. Thus, we must not seek for 'truths that serve us but a truth we may serve'.[5]

In his book *The Science Before Science*, Anthony Rizzi gives a good illustration of our need of the senses to know, an illustration which I adapt here.[6] Consider what it would be like if a man with sight goes to an isolated land where all are blind. When he arrives, does he find anyone that has a notion of colour? And if he tries to explain colour to the natives, how does he go about it? The people would have no concepts corresponding to words like 'appearance', 'hue', 'shades', 'red', 'green', 'blue.' The reason they would have no such concepts is that such concepts are only formed by the mind once it has received data from the sense of sight.

Chesterton provides us another example, illustrating the fundamental role of sense data in all learning: if you do not speak to children, they do not learn language.

> You may indeed 'draw out' squeals and grunts from the child by simply poking him and pulling him about ... but you will wait and watch very patiently indeed before you draw the English language out of him. That, you have got to put into him.[7]

Thus the senses, while having the ability neither to think nor to know truth, yet provide our intellect with data from which concepts can be formed. They are what philosophers would call a *material cause* of understanding, because they provide the intellect with the actual matter to be understood. In this way, they are the basis or gateway to all intellectual knowledge.[8]

Another epistemological question to consider about the senses, beyond the assistance they provide to the intellect, is the nature of their own knowledge. What sort of data from reality do they grasp? To answer this (using Aquinas's reasoning in ST, I, q.85, a.1), I must begin by stating that sensation is the activity that corresponds to bodily organs, such as our eyes, ears, and brain. And bodily organs, being material, can only take in material data, such as colour, sound, and image. Thus, sensation must grasp material data. But material data is radically individual. Thus, *sensation grasps that which is individual and unique*. This is why Wuellner defines sensation as the 'consciousness of singular, concrete, material objects by means of one of the sense powers and organs in a material way'.[9]

The following syllogism is another way to argue the same point:[10]

Everything actually existing is individual and singular.[11] But sensation connects us with what is actually existing. Therefore, sensation provides knowledge of what is individual.

Let us take an example to illustrate. You *look at* a photograph of a group of people taken on 5 March 2015, at 3:47 p.m. The snapshot shows what they were wearing at that precise moment, how they were standing, the expressions on their faces, and so on. Your eyes, as external sense organs, can and do channel to your brain the colours of the photo, but just the colours and nothing more. The brain's internal senses can in turn distinguish shape and distinct, individual beings. No internal sense, however, is capable of forming ideas about the figures represented, ideas such as 'people', 'humans', 'Australians'.

The intellect

The starting point of knowledge is some radically particular fact grasped directly by the senses. That is like the base of Mt. Reality. From there, one's perception of 'what is' must climb higher, becoming more universal in scope, leaving behind specific facts to comprehend entire regions of reality at once from a more elevated vantage point. To reach this universal perspective, humans must have a faculty other than the senses, one that is not tied to a single, specific material aspect of reality, as eyes are bound to light and the ears to sound. There must be a power capable of relating to any object whatsoever. This additional faculty is the intellect, the highest power of the human *soul*.

Jaki describes the intellect's activity as follows:

> While our eyes see only a particular stone, the mind notices the universal features in that stone and forms a noun which relates to a large variety of hard pieces. Armed with that noun the mind can correlate a multitude of different stones, or rather hover over each and every one of them.[12]

Thus, the mind has the ability to read into the data of sense and form a concept from that particular data that corresponds to all instances of the phenomenon to which it testifies. Philosophers refer to our concepts as 'universals', because they unite many individual instances into a generic notion that contains only what is common to those individuals and nothing of what is particular to any one of them. Just take the definition of almost any noun in your dictionary, such as 'abbot' or 'abacus' or 'abalone'. The definitions indicate only what is true of all instances of the noun.

Both intellect and sense are able to receive reality and correctly reflect it with their respective powers, but the way in which they do so is different. The intellect reflects the common or universal aspects of reality with its concepts, while sensation reflects the particular aspects of reality with its internal sense images. In this reflective capacity, both sense and intellect act like mirrors of the outside world.[13]

The intellect, however, can go a step further in its knowledge. It can not only know in the manner of a mirror, but also be aware that it knows and make assertions about reality from its knowledge. For instance, when the internal senses form an image of a mountain that is being seen and the intellect forms the concept 'mountain' from that image, both senses and intellect are acting like a mirror of reality. The intellect, however, can also *realise* that it is reflecting an aspect of reality in its knowledge of mountains. Because of this awareness, it can proceed to make a conscious relation between its knowledge and reality, by passing a judgement such as, 'Mountains are high.'

When the intellect forms such a judgement and that judgement is correct, then it has attained truth in the truest sense of the word.[14] Truth occurs, in its essence, when the mind affirms a correct proposition about reality, aptly joining a subject and predicate by the concept 'is'. 'Is' expresses real being; it is the assertion of something really existing outside the mind. When the mind says 'Mountains are high', reality has not just connected with the mind; the mind has also connected with reality.

The intellect's judgements about reality are acts of a different order from the knowing acts of the senses. The senses can take reality in, but they cannot reflect it back out by means of an intellectual judgement. Without the intellect, we could receive sense information from reality, as the animals do, but we could not relate to reality as it is in itself. We could not conceive any notion of existence nor form its corresponding word 'is'. We could not have a two-way commerce with the outside world. For that, it is necessary to both form a concept from reality and construct some mental statement about it asserting something to really exist.

Consciously connecting with reality through such judgement assertions is the essential perfection of our intellective faculty, as Josef Pieper remarks:

> In the tradition of Western philosophy, the capacity for spiritual knowledge has always been understood to mean the power of establishing relations with the whole of reality, with all things existing ... *Spirit*, it might be said, is the power and capacity to relate itself to the totality of being.[15]

Realism does not just affirm the ability of the human intellect to acquire knowledge from reality; it also affirms the intellect's ability to know that it knows, and so also the ability to say what reality is. We all do this so automatically that we tend to take it for granted. It is obvious to us that when we say things like 'Mountains are high', we intend to indicate something actually existing outside of our minds. We believe that we speak truly, because we believe that we know something about what is.

These reflections provide us two more key principles of realism:

- the senses know what is particular, the intellect what is universal[16]
- the intellect's highest act is the attainment of truth by the formation of a correct intellectual judgement about reality.

Authority

Lastly, we come to the witness of authority. Human beings have the gift of language, by which we are able to communicate truths one to another. This communication is a process that demands a realist epistemology. The reason is that words, being material sounds that represent immaterial ideas, combine in themselves both the testimony of sense and that of intellect.

Because the individual scope of our activity, experience, and life span is so limited, we are able to acquire only a narrow range of knowledge through our contact with nature. To broaden our minds, we must undergo instruction. Indeed, the vast majority of propositions we hold to be true have come to us through words. We only have to go back through the paper relics of our past education to see the degree to which we have relied on the knowledge of others to build up that of our own mind. For instance, how do we know that the country of Cambodia exists? Unless we have travelled there, we are accepting it to be real on the authority of our atlas.[17]

Realism summary

In summary, we need the senses to know particulars, the intellect to know universals, and authority to know extensively. The senses begin knowledge, the intellect achieves it, and authority supplements it. I call these three resources 'witnesses' because, in addition to our mind, we also possess the faculty of free will, by which we make choices. Whenever our senses, our intellect, or our friends provide us knowledge of reality, we are not bound to accept that knowledge with our will. 'I can't believe my eyes', we might say, or 'That just can't be true.' All knowing involves some acceptance from us, some *trust*; there is no truth here below that so presents itself to us that we cannot possibly deny it, at least with our lips. Such is the context of the quote from Chesterton at the head of this chapter (found in his *Heretics*, chapter 12). Or, as he says in another place:

> It is idle to talk always of the alternative of reason and faith. Reason is itself a matter of faith. It is an act of faith to assert that our thoughts have any relation to reality at all.[18]

This is not to say that all knowledge as such is doubtful. On the contrary, human beings cannot avoid knowing—and knowing with certainty—basic truths. Aristotle quotes a Greek proverb that illustrates this: 'no one misses the door',[19] meaning that everyone can find the entrance to a house. Our knowing faculties become one with reality, at a certain basic level, whether we want them to or not.

Thus, just by a child of ten hearing his mother's voice calling, his senses will register the sound and his mind will form a concept from the sound, by their natural functioning. These acts of knowing are immediate, automatic, intuitive, and so their having taken place is no less certain than that the child exists with functioning senses and mind. At the same time, however, the child has another faculty, his *will*, which can choose consciously and maliciously to refuse what his faculties unconsciously understood, because he does not want to answer the call of his mother. He cannot change that the knowing took place, but he may deny that it did. He is not able, in such a case, to prevent his functional faculties from knowing, but he is able to reject what they know.

Realism asserts that reality is real, and it also holds that *the human faculties of sense and the intellect both connect human beings with reality*, according to their respective roles. This stance leads it to give a positive answer to two fundamental epistemological questions:

1. Is there objective reality outside of us? Yes.
2. Do human faculties of sense and intellect provide objective knowledge of that objective reality? Yes.

The realist will always seek to give the senses and the intellect their full due. He will not deny with his will what he has known immediately through sense and intellect. He will not restrict reality, compress it, refuse it, spin-doctor it, and so on. Rather, he will leave it as is, as it is presented to him by his knowing faculties, without excluding the evidence of either. In short, he will always keep his epistemology well-tempered, a state which I will illustrate throughout this book by means of the 'epistedometer'.

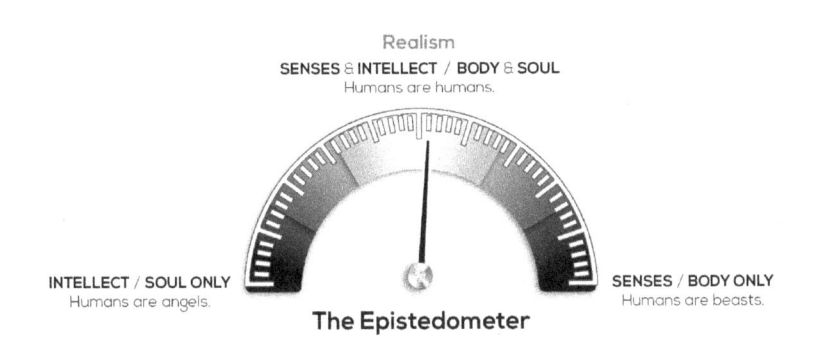

Realism
SENSES & INTELLECT / BODY & SOUL
Humans are humans.

INTELLECT / SOUL ONLY
Humans are angels.

SENSES / BODY ONLY
Humans are beasts.

The Epistedometer

The peg pointing straight up indicates a realist, one who does not deny any immediate evidence from reality provided to the senses or the intellect. Such a one will find reality shot through with light and will be best situated to draw knowledge from it.

The peg at right of centre indicates one denying evidence of the intellect and over-emphasising evidence of the senses, a position which reduces humans to a mere body. The more one is entrenched in such a denial, the further the peg slips from the vertical position and the more obscure reality becomes, as represented by the dark shading on the epistedometer.

The peg at left of centre indicates one denying evidence of the senses and over-emphasising intellectual concepts, a position which turns humans into a disembodied soul. As with the gauge deviating to the right, so too with it deviating to the left, reality becomes more obscure for the mind. This is likewise represented by dark shading on the left of the meter.

Someone driving on the highway must be careful not to drive too slowly, allowing the speedometer to drop down on the left side; nor to drive too quickly, pushing the speedometer too far to the right. Similarly, when the gauge of the epistedometer drops away from the vertical position, to the left or right, the human mind is in trouble. Different from the speedometer, however, the epistedometer is not meant to indicate how fast the mind is thinking! Rather, it is only meant to indicate a mind's reality mentality and the degree to which that reality mentality favours or disfavours understanding reality.

Authority does not, of itself, enter into the epistemological equation and so is not included in the epistedometer.

Let us take an example of a realist accepting the reliability of the three witnesses—senses, intellect, and authority—to connect him with reality.

I am sleeping soundly and wake up suddenly. Is it day yet? I open my eyes and see light streaming through the window. My eyes are testifying to the presence of sunlight. Thus, in wilfully accepting the testimony of the eyes, I judge it to be true that presently it is day.

Then, I look at the clock and see that it is 5:00 in the morning. I remember that I had not intended to wake before 5:30, and my mind performs a mathematical operation, telling me that 30 minutes remain before my intended waking time. Thus, in accepting the testimony of my mind, I judge it to be true that I can safely sleep for another 30 minutes.

But, before falling back to sleep, someone knocks at my door, telling me that a poor soul is dying at the hospital and is asking for the last sacraments. Thus, in accepting the testimony of the person at the door, I judge it to be true that I need to rush to the hospital to provide priestly care for the dying person.

Or, to shift the example from me to you, your eyes are now testifying to the shape and darkness of the letters on this page, your intellect to their meaning, and I to their truth. But the choice is yours whether to accept each of these inputs as real.

Let us turn now to consider the two epistemologies, which are to the left and right of the realist balance on our epistedometer.

Denying our faculties

On the playground as children, many of us made the vain boast that we could do such and such with 'one hand tied behind our back.' The point of the brag was to illustrate the ease of the challenge facing us. It was so easy that we would have to handicap ourselves in order to make the challenge interesting. Some mountaineers have become so acclimated to high altitudes that they take no oxygen into the 'death zone' and actually make it to the top of Mount Everest and back down without the assistance of a tank.

A similar thing occurs when certain philosophers form their epistemologies. They examine the human equipment available for knowing reality—senses, intellect, and authority—and decide that this or that tool is useless. Tossing it aside, they begin their ascent of reality without it. Unlike the hardy mountaineers, however, they don't make it to the top. In fact, they don't make it anywhere.

Why would they sell short their human faculties? Aristotle provides a reason in his *Metaphysics*.[20] He notes that our customs or habits exercise a very powerful influence on us in our pursuit of truth. We can become so accustomed to a certain form of knowing, so confident in that form, and so attached to it, that we legislate to reality that we will only accept communication from it in our preferred way. It is like being so impressed with our mountain climbing thermals that we decide we have no need of boots or ice pick. Similarly, some thinkers love their senses so much that they refuse the intellect's ability to know truth, others are infatuated with abstract ideas and hold sense data to be illusory, while still others only trust their own minds and refuse all truths presented by outside authorities. These are three different epistemological stances deviating from realism, and they must be considered in turn.

The idealist

One epistemology, called *idealism*, mistrusts the senses, holding the intellect alone able to provide true knowledge about reality. In some works, you will find idealism referred to as 'exaggerated realism' or 'Platonic realism',[21] as opposed to our position, which is referred to as 'moderate realism' or 'scholastic realism'. To avoid muddying the waters, I will only refer to those denying sense data as *idealists*.

Generally, idealists bring forward two reasons why we should not trust our senses:

- Firstly, the senses can present true data that is yet deceiving, such as mirages in deserts or bent sticks in ponds.
- Secondly, the information of sense is constantly changing, such that what is presented as reality at one given moment does not hold true in the next.

Focusing on these two limitations of sense, the idealist takes a suspecting attitude towards the physical world. It seems to be a source of illusion, a mere shadow of truth, which must be consistent and unchanging if it is to hold. Hence, the idealist concludes, the senses are not a valid reference point for truth.

Meanwhile, the idealist is keenly aware of the power of the intellect to establish the truth, especially in the realm of mathematics. There, all concepts are sharply defined and conclusions are reached by a strictly deductive logical process that leaves no room for error. This is the way the idealist wants all knowing equipment to work. Meanwhile, the intellect is not able to prove the reality of the data of sense. No syllogism, for example, can establish that you have an ingrown toenail; its reality can only come to you by immediate experience.

REALISM
Senses & Intellect

IDEALISM
Intellect Only

EMPIRICISM
Senses Only

Idealism

And so, if someone is unwilling to hold as true that which cannot be established by a deductive syllogism, he will not accept his senses.

In the end, it is impossible that we have demonstrative certainty without assuming that sensation provides true knowledge. Augros points this out perfectly:

> To have perfect certainty about anything (which is what *proof* implies), we would first have to be sure that our senses and brains are trustworthy organs of knowledge bringing us real information about real things, and we would have to come to this knowledge without relying on our senses and our brains, which is impossible.[22]

The idealist, then, takes the opposite stance towards reality from the realist. For the realist, it is reality that makes for knowledge; for the idealist, it is knowledge that makes for reality. Realism is based on a knowledge, which is the knowledge of an object, but idealism 'derives from the analysis of a thought'.[23] The idealist thinks he has to relate to himself by an act of knowing before he can relate to reality. Once he has performed an act of knowledge, then he sets out on the task of proving that reality exists. The whole reason that he lays down such a procedure for himself is that he does not trust his senses in telling him about reality. By denying the validity of the senses, he has cut off his only bridge to reality, and so must make reality himself.

An obvious consequence of the idealist stance is that truth becomes a wholly personal affair, that is, there is not one truth that is true for all knowers, but rather each knower determines his own truth. Sense data provide the basis for human knowing, but they are also the basis for uniting the community of human minds in the understanding of reality. We are all able to use the word 'colour' in conversation with the same meaning, because we have each experienced colour. But if we are to reject sense experiences as unreliable and form concepts in some other way, what is the single objective source from which we will form like concepts? We will all be left the task of creating our own ideas and imposing them on reality. Meanwhile, the words that correspond to our ideas will be useless tools of communication, for they will not be able to form a bridge between one mind and another. They will represent what one mind thinks, not what many think. The consistent idealist, then, has no reason to make use of words, and so logically should remain silent.

The empiricist

At the other extreme of epistemological stances are the *empiricists* or *materialists*, who refuse, to a greater or lesser degree, the concepts and principles of the intellect. For them, ideas are discontinuous, static, and symbolic, while reality is continuous, dynamic, and actual.[24] For instance, the idea 'justice' is an abstraction that has no exact equivalent as such in the extramental world. There are people who give to others what is owed them, courts deciding that certain behaviours are just and others are not, but no living, tangible justice, some personification of the concept 'justice'. Isn't it foolish, then, to claim that ideas like justice can supply any true knowledge of concrete reality? Sense data imposes its truth upon us by its immediacy, but the cold realm of the intellect is unable to get us into touch with the outside world.

This epistemology is impressed by the vividness and sheer impact of sense life, and wants the life of the intellect to impose itself on us with the same force. 'If you are real, hit me!' demands the sensualist of his thinking faculty. The mind, however, being wholly spiritual, does not of itself exercise any material effect. Thus, it is impossible for it to 'prove' itself to us in such a way.

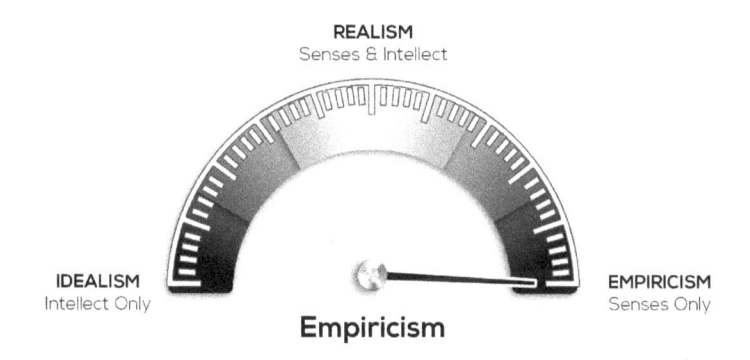

REALISM
Senses & Intellect

IDEALISM
Intellect Only

EMPIRICISM
Senses Only

Empiricism

To deny completely the ability of the intellect to provide truth, one must refuse what are called the 'first principles'. These are self-evident truths, the basic propositions that must hold true for any reasoning to be valid, propositions that are grasped and held to be certain by the intellect by its very nature. The first principles include the following:
- the principle of non-contradiction: 'It is impossible for a thing to be and not-be at the same time, in the same respect.'[25]
- the principle of identity: 'A thing is what it is.'

- the principle of sufficient reason: 'A thing must have a sufficient reason for its existence either in itself or in another.'
- the principle of causality: 'Every effect has a cause.'

Someone asserting that 'there is no such thing as absolute truth', for instance, is implicitly denying the principle of non-contradiction. He is proposing as a truth that truth does not exist; he is effectively saying, 'Truth is and is not at the same time.' This position in turn undermines all reasoning processes, which seek to establish that something is or is not. 'Is' has to be 'is' and completely separate from 'is not' for a statement using one of them to be valid. A person denying the principle of non-contradiction, then, must logically:

- conclude that the intellect is useless for knowing reality, and
- leave off seeking to find truth by means of it.

A more anti-intellectual position can hardly be imagined.

It might be a surprise to find that the empiricist is as much of a subjectivist as the idealist.[26] He insists that only hard, factual data are to be accepted as true: the brightness of the sun, the green of the grass, the smell of the smoke. Meanwhile, he claims that the *ideas* which we form about those facts are pure inventions of the mind: they don't correspond to reality and so are not true. We cannot, however, keep ourselves from forming ideas about things and using those ideas as the basis for what we consider to be true about reality. Thus, the empiricist is forced to say that each of us have our own ideas and our own truth, that is, he is forced by the logic of his position to be a subjectivist.

Empiricist materialists likewise destroy the value of words. Words are signs of ideas, and if ideas say nothing about reality, then words seeking to express ideas to others are useless. This is why materialists end up questioning the value of words themselves, as Bertrand Russell did constantly in his famous 1948 debate with Fr Copleston on the existence of God. Empiricists attempting to communicate would be more consistent to howl, grunt, or snarl.

The empiricist, in short, like the idealist:

- leaves each person to form his own subjective ideas about reality
- renders words useless by his epistemology, and so
- has no justification to communicate through language.

The individualist

Lastly, there are *individualists* who refuse to accept the testimony of authority. They are unreasonably sceptical about the abilities of their fellow humans. Even the greatest figures of the past, they say, were mistaken in many respects, holding ideas which are totally rejected now. Moreover, according to this law of intellectual history, today's ideas will no doubt be debunked in the near future, and so we must not listen to our contemporaries. Furthermore, if we allow our thoughts to be shaped from the outside, we will lose our own creative capabilities and we will not be able to bring our full talent to fruition. Much better it is, then, to be an independent thinker, each of us preserving our individuality.

Such a perspective places great faith in the individual, while having no faith in the group of individuals which is society. It tends to deify the individual, while demonising institutions. Since humans are not born ready-made geniuses, however, but rather must achieve their intellectual development through hard work, those who refuse to be educated begin and end in ignorance.[27]

Table 1.1 The Three Witnesses

Witness	The witness provides	Rejecting the witness leads to	He who denies the witness is a
Sense	Particular data of reality	Subjectivity and Irrationality	Idealist
Intellect	Universal concepts of reality	Subjectivity and Irrationality	Materialist
Authority	Extended scope for knowing	Ignorance	Individualist

By looking at the false epistemologies of idealism and empiricism, we are able to obtain a clearer view of realism. Realism does not mistrust the abilities of our senses or intellect to attain their own proper objects of knowledge, and in this sense it is optimistic. Meanwhile, it gives objective reality priority over our faculties of knowing. By taking these two stances, realism validates both the source of true knowledge (reality) and the powers of knowing (sense and intellect). It holds that there is a natural bridge between the two, and that without such a bridge, no knowledge would exist. In the words of Chesterton, 'Either there is no philosophy, no philosophers, no thinkers, no thought, no anything; or else there is a real bridge between the mind and reality'.[28] This is his way of saying that either realism is true or nothing is true. At the end of the day, empiricism and idealism are utterly unable to account for a person knowing anything true about reality. This makes realism not only an obvious choice for one's epistemology, but even absolutely necessary if one wants to claim to know anything about reality and be coherent in that claim.

Table 1.2 Epistemological Viewpoints

Epistemology	Senses are	Intellect is	Path of knowledge	Analysis of the Epistemology
Empiricism	reliable	unreliable	reality → senses ↛ ~~intellect ↛ reality~~	Humans obtain information from reality but cannot form ideas about it.
Realism	reliable	reliable	reality → senses → intellect → reality	Humans obtain information from reality, which they use to form true ideas about it.
Idealism	unreliable	reliable	~~reality ↛ senses ↛~~ intellect → reality	Humans form ideas about the reality outside themselves, without having information about it.

The bare minimum

Before I wrap up this first chapter, I must solidify that last point, namely, that realism is the absolutely necessary epistemology for every human being, because:

1. Only realism matches the way that human beings know: by way of both senses and intellect.

2. Only realism can account for human beings actually having knowledge of reality.

Realism alone corresponds to humans' particular construction as knowing beings. It links the marriage in humans of sense and intellect, of body and soul, to the marriage of matter and spirit in reality, of physical principles that fall under the senses and of immaterial principles that are perceived by the intellect.

Up to this point, I have made my case on the one hand by putting forth a *negative* argument for realism, and on the other hand a *positive* one. The negative argument shows what happens when one denies realism by wilfully choosing to refuse the knowledge of the senses or intellect: one falls into incoherence and cannot justify his own speech. This shows that epistemologies that are *not* realist are absurd. The positive argument points out that realism and only realism *affirms* the automatic, intuitive way in which humans gain the foundation of all their knowledge, via the mind forming concepts from sense data.

Now, I will seek to seal the positive argument definitively by showing that the most basic concept possible, that of 'being' or 'what exists', a concept which is in play whenever we think or speak, can only be formed by use of the senses and intellect. Our argument runs syllogistically as follows:

1. If we are to have any true knowledge of reality whatsoever, we must know 'being'.
2. But we can know 'being' only by an intuitive, automatic use of both senses and intellect.
3. Therefore, only by trusting the abilities of sense and intellect can we claim to have any knowledge of reality.

It is the second statement that I must establish, and I will do so by means of an image.

You are sitting at your desk one day and God suddenly creates a grown man, Bob, who stands before you. God commands you to educate Bob. How? Where do you begin? So you push your laptop over to Bob and say 'this is a computer'.

But you quickly realise that even the most basic propositions of human language include several layers of meaning. Before Bob can understand 'computer', he must understand the notions that the word presupposes, the first of which is 'being'. A computer, after all, is a certain type of existing thing. 'This is a computer' can only be understood if several other propositions are already understood, namely, 'A computer is a type of being', 'Beings are things that exist', and 'This thing here //is a being//[exists]' are also understood. By expressing these presupposed notions, you come to a deep philosophical insight into the very foundation of thought.

The insight is this: when language is broken down into its bedrock components, 'being' is always at the bottom level. Unless the mind can identify things, outside of it, as separate entities that really exist and are distinct from others, that is, 'beings', then it cannot move to establish relations between those entities, as is done with every proposition, such as 'this is a computer.'

So, to teach Bob, this new Adam, you must start by giving him a notion of 'being', that which is not nothing, the really existing, that which is. Okay, so you are going to explain 'being' to him. You start searching for the right words, but you quickly realise that it is going to be impossible. Communication between humans is only realised through words, and words depend on concepts, and concepts all in the end depend on the notion of 'being'. How do you instruct someone that a 'being' is something that is, when you must make use of the notion that you are trying to explain? 'Bob, 'is'. Yes, 'is'! 'Is' is 'is', you see! 'Is' is what is, d'ya get it?' Every mental step you take towards that project leaves you flummoxed. Quite simply, the notion cannot be taught.

It was for this reason, among others, that St Thomas held that the notion of being is formed automatically, as it were, with the very first rational act of the human mind working on the data of sense. For if the notion of being cannot be taught and yet we all have that notion, then it must be formed by the mind itself, intuitively, as the first and most basic inference of the mind working on sense data.[29]

Someone might object by saying that humans are born with ideas already in their minds, but in a state of forgetfulness. It only remains to reawaken those ideas, and such is the work of education. This was the opinion held of old by Plato and maintained today by those who believe in reincarnation. If this were the case, however, then blind men would know colour without having to learn of it from their eyes.[30] Our reliance upon our senses to know teaches us that we are not born with knowledge, but we gain it by contact with reality.[31]

To recap, a true notion of being is required for all knowledge and communication. The notion of being is not formed by instruction, but automatically by the mind working on sense data. Thus, both sense data and mind must be held to be reliable, if we are to give any real value to our knowledge and communication. If you do not make use of both pieces of equipment, not only will you not make it to the top of reality, you will not make a single step on your journey.

For this reason, one who claims either that sense data is false (idealist) or that our intellectual notions do not match up with reality (empiricist) has no right to speak at all! Every use of speech assumes that the speaker has grasped real being. One person sends forth a material sound, which represents an immaterial concept in his mind. Another receives the vibrations of the air made by the first into his ear and understands from them an immaterial concept. Without both legs of our path to knowledge, sense and intellect, the entire edifice of rational thought crumbles. An epistemologist who denies either has only to speak to refute himself, and if he will not, he has reduced himself to a plant, as Aristotle remarks.[32]

The proof of realism that I have presented here is an *indirect* one, i.e. one showing that realism is the only philosophy of knowledge or *epistemology* which can be correct, and that any rival position must be deficient. First, I explained that there are three and only three epistemologies to choose from: one accepting sense data and intellectual concepts as providing true knowledge of reality (realism); one denying sense data but accepting intellectual concepts (idealism); and one accepting sense data but denying intellectual concepts (empiricism). Second, I showed that those choosing idealism or empiricism have no logical basis for engaging in speech (which assumes the validity of senses and intellect) or justifying knowledge of the concept 'is' (which can only be formed by an intuitive act of the mind working on sense data). Third, I offered the following alternative: either choose realism or abstain from speaking.

If I could have used a direct proof of realism, I would have. No such proof exists, however, because you have to *assume* knowledge in order to prove how knowledge is obtained. No epistemology can be proved directly. What I *have* shown you is that if we do not accept realism, then we can never claim to know anything—and that would be absurd.

Chapter summary

In this chapter we looked at various epistemologies, or theories about human knowledge, about human equipment for penetrating reality. We saw that, objectively, human beings know reality through their senses and intellect. They use another faculty, the will, to choose an epistemology by accepting or rejecting human knowing equipment as able to do its job. Those who take reality—and human capacities for knowing it—as they are, are called 'realists.' Some of the principles which they hold are the following:

- the data which we receive from the outside world is real
- our perception of the outside world is real
- we connect with reality at the moment of sensation
- all knowledge has its starting point with sensation of the outside world
- knowledge is dependent upon reality, and not reality upon knowledge

- the senses know what is particular, the intellect what is universal
- the intellect's highest act is the attainment of truth by the formation of a correct intellectual judgement about reality
- the human faculties of sense and the intellect both connect human beings with reality, according to their respective roles
- the first principles of all knowledge are grasped immediately, intuitively, and with absolute certainty by the mind working on sense data.

We are Realists.

Besides setting forth these principles, I also argued that realism is the only coherent epistemology, the only one that can make a consistent claim that humans can know truth and communicate it. One reason for this is that the most basic of concepts, 'being', cannot be formed unless the senses and intellect each connect with reality, according to their complementary roles.

Moreover, realism matches with the architecture of the human being. It is simply a common sense statement on the way we live our rational lives. Quite simply, we are made to be realists; it is the natural default position for everyone. No one has stated this better than Gilson:

> The first step on the realist path is to recognize that one has always been a realist; the second is to recognize that, however hard one tries to think differently, one will never manage to; the third is to realize that those who claim they think differently, think as realists as soon as they forget to act a part. If one then asks oneself why, one's own conversion to realism is all but complete.[33]

Similarly, Chesterton says of realism that 'it is the only working philosophy. Of nearly all other philosophies it is strictly true that their followers work in spite of them; or do not work at all'.[34] In the same place he says, 'God made Man so that he was capable of coming in contact with reality; and those whom God hath joined, let no man put asunder.'

Both innovative scientific discoveries and the proofs for the existence of God that are at the basis of reasonable religion are underpinned by realism.[35] The Bible is realist,[36] everyday life and common sense are realist, and it is impossible that human communication can rest logically on any other epistemological paradigm.

Thus, the choice of an epistemology has serious consequences. Only realists are able to be fully human. Our proper operation—what differentiates us humans from all others in the material cosmos—is our ability to know reality as such. As we are made to understand reality, by our nature, it is knowing that fulfils and perfects us on the natural level.[37] Being born into life as a blank page, a *tabula rasa*, with our minds empty of concepts,[38] we are meant to progressively delve deeper into the realities of life in their complete richness, ever pursuing that highest of natural attainments, the possession of wisdom or the understanding of the first principles of all reality.

A realist is able to use his faculties at the apex of their innate powers, embrace all of the material means for attaining knowledge, and make a careful discernment of information provided him to judge accurately that which is true and that which is false. Idealists and empiricists, however, constrain their knowing powers, shying away from paths to deeper truths, refusing to accept the testimony of a certain class of evidence presented to their judgement.

So throughout this book, we will be realists. We will not commit wilful intellectual suicide, purposely seal ourselves off from the outside world by a false epistemology, flee from truth as from some fearsome spectre. Instead, we will try to allow reality its full rights, by accepting whatever it communicates to us via sense and intellect. We will get our epistedometer out, carefully calibrate it, and try hard not to allow it slip in the direction either of empiricism or idealism.

Now, having taken stock of our knowing equipment, we are ready to start our climb to the upper reaches of reality.

Three Epistemologies

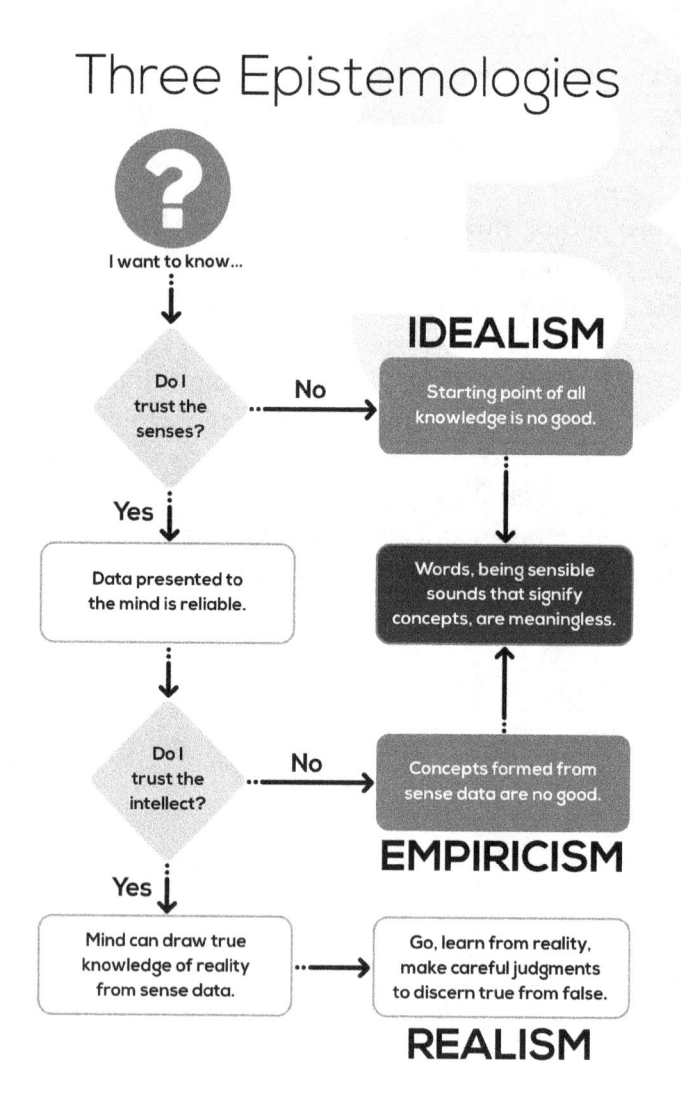

I want to know...

Do I trust the senses? — No → **IDEALISM**: Starting point of all knowledge is no good.

↓

Words, being sensible sounds that signify concepts, are meaningless.

Yes ↓

Data presented to the mind is reliable.

↓

Do I trust the intellect? — No → **EMPIRICISM**: Concepts formed from sense data are no good.

Yes ↓

Mind can draw true knowledge of reality from sense data. → Go, learn from reality, make careful judgments to discern true from false.

REALISM

Notes

1. See p. xviii.
2. See Aquinas, ST, I, q.14, a.1.
3. Aquinas, SCG, Book I, chapter 3, paragraph 3. See also Aquinas, ST, I, q.12, a.12; *De Veritate*, q.12, a.3, ad 2; *In De Trinitate*, q.6, a.2; Aristotle, *Topics*, 100a10.
4. E. Gilson, *Methodical Realism* (San Francisco: Ignatius Press, 2011), p. 53.
5. J. Maritain, *Degrees of Knowledge* (London: Geoffrey Bles, 1959), p. 4.
6. A. Rizzi, *The Science before Science* (Baton Rouge: IAP Press, 2004), p. 38. See also Aquinas, SCG, Book II, chapter 83, paragraph 26.
7. G. K. Chesterton, *What's Wrong with the World* (London: Cassell and Company, 1910), p. 201.
8. See Aristotle, *On the Soul*, 432a5.
9. B. Wuellner, *Dictionary of Scholastic Philosophy* (Fitzwilliam, New Hampshire: Loreto Publications, 2012 reprint of 1956 edition).
10. Wuellner, in *Ibid.*, defines 'syllogism' as 'an argument consisting of three propositions so connected that if the first two are posited, the third necessarily follows'.
11. See Gilson, *Methodical Realism*, p. 57.
12. S. Jaki, *Impassible Divide* (New Hope, Kentucky: Real View Books, 2008), p. 97.
13. For the difference between sense and intellectual knowledge, see W. Wallace, *The Modeling of Nature* (Washington, DC: The Catholic University of America Press, 1996), pp. 120, 132–133.
14. See *Ibid.*, p. 151.
15. J. Pieper, *Leisure, the Basis of Culture* (Indianapolis: Liberty Fund, 1952), p. 133, emphasis in original. See also Aquinas, *De Veritate*, q.1, a.3; ST, I, q.16, a.2.
16. See Aquinas, *In De Anima*, Book 2, lesson 5, number 6.
17. In his *The Modeling of Nature*, p. 266, Wallace states, 'Most of what the normal person knows about geography and history, or what an investigator accepts as data from collaborators, or what the average scientist knows about fields other than his own, is known by simple faith—as facts that are certain'.
18. G. K. Chesterton, *Orthodoxy* (London: William Clowes and Sons, 1908), p. 56.
19. *Metaphysics*, 993b4.
20. 994b32.
21. See E. Feser, *Neo-Scholastic Essays* (South Bend, Indiana: St. Augustine's

Press, 2015), p. 32.

[22] M. Augros, *Who Designed the Designer?* (San Francisco: Ignatius Press, 2015), p. 184, emphasis in original.

[23] Gilson, *Methodical Realism*, p. 89.

[24] See F. J. Sheen, *God and Intelligence in Modern Philosophy* (New York: Longmans, Green and Co., 1925), chapter 2.

[25] Aristotle, *Metaphysics*, 1005b18.

[26] See Br. Benignus, *Nature, Knowledge, and God* (Milwaukee: The Bruce Publishing Co., 1947), pp. 11–12.

[27] See Hesiod quoted by Aristotle (*Nicomachean Ethics*, 1095b10): 'Far best is he who knows all things himself; / Good, he that hearkens when men counsel right; / But he who neither knows, nor lays to heart / Another's wisdom, is a useless wight' (translation R. McKeon, *The Basic Works of Aristotle* (New York: Random House, 1941), p. 938).

[28] *St. Thomas Aquinas* (London: Hodder & Stoughton Limited, 1933), p. 177.

[29] See Aquinas, SCG, II, Book 83, chapter 31; ST, I, q.5, a.2.

[30] See Aquinas, ST, q. 84, a.3.

[31] For technical philosophical arguments against reincarnation, see Aquinas, SCG, Book II, chapters 83–84.

[32] *Metaphysics*, 1006a11.

[33] *Methodical Realism*, p. 93.

[34] *St. Thomas Aquinas*, p. 221.

[35] See S. Jaki, *A Mind's Matter* (Grand Rapids, Michigan: William Eerdmans Publishing Company, 2002), p. 93.

[36] *Ibid.*, p. 156.

[37] Aquinas, *In Met.*, paragraphs 2–4.

[38] Aristotle, *Posterior Analytics*, 99b30.

2 FOUR CAUSES

Science is certain knowledge through causes.

Aristotle

As one climbs higher up a tall mountain slope, the landscape starts to change. At first, there are thick clusters of trees. These slowly disappear to be replaced by bushes and scrub brush. Finally, one reaches the snow line, the terrain which remains so cold throughout the year that snowfall never melts. The permanent snow on Everest's cap adds an extra four metres to its already towering height.

The snow on mountain tops is beautiful to look at, but dangerous for the eyes viewing it. Fresh snow reflects 80 per cent of the ultraviolet rays coming from the sun. Moreover, there is more UV to reflect the farther one rises above sea level. UV radiation increases by four percent every thousand feet mountaineers climb, as the atmosphere thins.

This double dose of UV reaching the eyes of humans perched on the heights of the world sometimes leads to *photokeratitis*, also called 'snow blindness'. About one quarter of those mounting Everest suffer its effects: haemorrhages in the retina and impairment of eyesight. In some cases, blindness results, but most retain their sight and are healed within a few weeks after descending to lower altitudes.

What we must avoid at all costs, as we ascend to the apex of reality, is a blindness resulting from false epistemologies that cause haemorrhages in the mind's eye. Since we want to see our way all the way to the top, we have carefully set our epistedometer and put on realist glasses, which block Unhealthy Views from impairing our intellectual vision. So equipped, we are ready to take a close look at the whole of reality, trusting that we will be able to ascend its heights without missing anything.

Causes, professional knowledge

As realists, we must start at the bottom of the mountain with the senses. They provide particular data, from which we can ascend to higher levels of understanding. This way of proceeding is called *a posteriori* or 'after the fact' reasoning. We emphatically don't use *a priori* or 'before the fact' reasoning, starting with some idea not taken from reality and then drawing from it a conclusion about reality. Rather, we begin with reality in order to form correct ideas about reality. We don't assume that reality must be this way or that way, but allow it to show us what it is.

So, we start with sense data. What does it reveal to us? That it is contingent, that is, that it is dependent on another for its existence, that it is a not self-existing thing.

> Since [sense data] are born, last for a time, and disappear to be reborn once more, it follows that their existence is not in itself necessary. It equally follows that their existence depends on something other than themselves—on something which *causes* them to be born and to exist; stops producing them and they disappear; produces them again and they reappear. In a word, *their manifest contingency obliges us to look for a cause.*[1]

From our beginning in sensation, we quickly realise that we must go further, and going further means finding the cause of that sense data. We start with an effect revealed by sensation and we move to the cause of the effect by a process of thinking (effect → cause). We ask questions, and their answers provide the *reasons* for the effects we have observed. Such is the human mode of knowing, moving from effect to cause.

For instance, you remark that you have been sneezing more than usual, and you ask yourself: why so? The effect is your sneezing and the question demands the cause of the sneezing for its answer. Then, you remember that your friend has invited you over for a glass of wine the past two nights and that you sneezed immediately after taking a drink. From this memory, your mind assigns a cause as a reason for the effect: I am allergic to that vintage Cabernet Sauvignon.

Aristotle, who was the first known professional realist, was also the first to identify causes as the source of professional knowledge. By 'cause', he means 'that from which a thing comes to be', not cause in its scientific meaning of 'what is predictable by physical law'.[2]

Aristotle does not say that only causes provide knowledge. We have already seen that knowledge is gained through the senses, which do not know causes. What he does say is that causal knowledge alone can provide *certainty*, that it alone can assign the *reason* for this or that, that it alone fits us to *teach* others, that it alone us enables to *make progress* beyond the knowledge of the senses. As such, he gives that knowledge a special name, *science*. For Aristotle, causal knowledge is higher than sense knowledge, and the highest possible knowledge is the knowledge of the highest causes. With them, one knows everything, the whole of reality.[3]

Causes act like footholds as we climb up the mountain of reality, or the ropes that are used to guide mountaineers on Everest. They represent stages on the way, real advancements in the process of understanding the world around us.

It turns out that the changes presented by sense data cannot be accounted for by a single type of cause. For instance, there is much more to be said about sneezing besides its being caused by an allergic reaction. We could also say that the body is seeking to expel something harmful, that sneezing is a sudden and violent forcing of breath, that it contains certain body fluids. In the end, several categories of explanation are needed to indicate all of 'that from which a thing comes to be'. How many such categories are there? Aristotle famously reduced all possible causal explanations to four types:[4]

1. **material cause**—that *out of which* something is made, its *matter*
2. **formal cause**—that *into which* something is made, its *form*

3. **efficient cause**—that *by which* something is made, its *maker*
4. **final cause**—that *for the sake of which* something is made, its *purpose*

These four causes 'are the answers that Aristotle gives to four questions that can and should be asked about the changes with which we are acquainted in our common experience'.[5] Take, for instance, the construction of an aeroplane. Its material cause is all of the components from which it was assembled—wheels, wings, windows, and so on. Its formal cause is a flying machine. Its efficient cause, what made the thing, is Boeing or some other company. It final cause or purpose is flying.

Of these four causes, the one most likely to be misunderstood is the formal cause. We must be extremely careful not to understand a thing's *form*, in the word's philosophical meaning, as that thing's *shape*. Form here has nothing to do with a thing's material body; it has everything to do with an immaterial principle giving a thing to be a certain type of being. When your mind wants to locate the form of the object before you, the most helpful thing to do is say what the thing is and then add to that word the suffix '-ness'. We could say that the form of our aeroplane, for instance, is 'aeroplaneness'.

Take any thing. Look for its material components, its form, its maker, and its purpose. When you find them, you will have gained at least a partial knowledge of the ultimate principles which combine to constitute the being of the thing.

Aristotle arrived at these four categories of causes by studying real beings very closely. He was seeking to understand the ultimate principles that must be in place to constitute those beings, that is, to make beings be beings. His conclusion was that these four causes and only these four make the beings around us (effects) be what they are. Furthermore, because these four causes make a being what it is *in reality*, then these four causes must also be sought *by a mind* wanting to gain a complete knowledge of a being. If Aristotle's realism is correct, then we have two important conclusions from his insights:

Four Causes　　　　　　　　　　　　　　　　　　　　　　　　　　37

1. **Material Reality:** every being in the material universe must be a composite effect of the four causes, that is, made up of the four causes in its very ontological structure, in its structure as a being
2. **Knowing Reality:** to know a being is to know what constitutes it; since the four causes are what constitute material beings, then knowing them means knowing their four causes

These four causes—material, formal, efficient, and final—will be crucial as we proceed in the book, and so it is important that we get to know them better. Our current task is to provide evidence that Aristotle was right that there are only four causes for material beings, and so also that the four causes deliver the highest, most complete knowledge of material beings. This is not something that I can prove directly, but I can show that no alternative makes any sense. I will do so by having us constitute some material beings ourselves.

Writing science fiction

Imagine that you decide to sit down and write the next science fiction blockbuster, a work you determine will be completely unique in that it will not include in it any living being known to us on Earth. All of the creatures in your novel are going to be the product of your own imagination.

Staring at your blank sheet of paper, you wonder if you will be able to supply such great resources of creativity. Perhaps after getting the first creature done, the others will be easier. What will you call it? After mulling around for a bit, you settle on a 'plasmata'. Well, then, what will it be? I would ask you at this point to stop reading, close your eyes and really think about what you require to piece your creature together, before reading the next paragraph.

Okay, so you realise from thinking about this first of your new beings that several items are going to have to be determined for it:

- **matter:** What sort of body will it have, for instance, how many arms, legs, eyes, and so on? What will it be made of: bones, slime, dirt, stone? → material cause
- **form:** What type of thing will it be and what corresponding abilities will it have? Is a 'plasmata' a plant, an animal, a humanoid? If it is an animal, what manner of animal? For instance, how does it move: does it walk, run, fly, slide, swim, jump, hop, and so on? → formal cause
- **maker:** What made it? Where did it come from, or what process brought it into existence? Did it hatch from an egg or drop out of a cloud? → efficient cause
- **purpose:** What will be its specific purpose? Will it be to reproduce its own kind, build bridges across streams, sing lyrical melodies? → final cause

Once you have answered all of these questions for the 'plasmata' and in great detail, you are able to insert it into your story and have it behave throughout most consistently. Notice that you are allowing for the use of *concepts* that come from our common experience, as plant and animal, but you stipulate that those concepts are to be pieced together in a way that does not correspond to anything living on Earth.[6]

The purpose of this example is to make these three points clear:

1. Everything which you endow on your creature will fall into one of the four causes.
2. If you leave any of the causes out, your creature cannot exist.
3. If the four causes have to be realised in the creature in your novel for it to exist, then the four causes also have to be realised in everything existing in the physical universe, in the real creatures, God's creatures.

I will leave you to ponder the first point and see if you can find aspects of your creature that do not fit into one of the four causes.

For now, let us consider the second point, that all four causes had to be present for your creature to exist, since '[e]ach of the four factors, taken by itself, is necessary, but none by itself is sufficient'.[7] One or two or even three of the four causes being present is not enough for a material being to exist, for all four are necessary to constitute such a being.

To return to the 'plasmata', if you wanted to make such a being in the visible universe, you would have to give it a body composed of matter (material cause). Moreover, it would have to be a type of being, having some form (formal cause), since to be formless is to be nothing: how can you exist if you don't exist in a certain way? The material and formal causes together would be the essence or nature of your creature, the seat of all of its powers, the things that it could do.

The 'plasmata' would also have to have something to produce it (efficient cause), as it was nothing before you came up with it, and what is nothing cannot bring itself into being! Finally, it would have to have a purpose. If you were to assign no task whatsoever to the 'plasmata', then it would not do anything, not even exist. Even if you made it just stand up like a lamp post, some purpose would be fulfilled. Because a thing exists, it performs some determinate function, and that function indicates its purpose. In other words, 'purpose' in the philosophical sense in which I am using it here, corresponds to any *determinate* action to which a being is directed. Because a thing does this rather than that—even if it does not do such things wilfully—it pursues a definite end in doing them.[8]

All four causes must be in place, then, for a physical thing to exist, and a thing must exist before it can be known. Looking at it this way, from the top-down perspective, as a creator of beings, we are able to understand what it takes to constitute a being. At the same time, we discover what can be known about a being, for according to the way that a being is put together, so also it is taken apart. It is the property of the human mind to know things in a composite fashion, by disassembling them as it were. We form a myriad of concepts that each fall into one of the categories of the four causes, and together provide us with a limited understanding of the being before us.

So, realism has us start with reality, taking its existence for granted. Reality reaches us through the senses, and they quickly reveal that their data needs explanation, because the data concerns effects. That explanation is provided by the intellect in the form of reasons or causes. There are four and only four different types of causes that can be ascribed to the effects that the senses observe. Those four causes encompass the entire scope of human knowledge.

Already, realism has provided some fantastic insights into reality. But there is more to come. We must keep our realist glasses on and penetrate even deeper into the mystery of 'what is.'

Two orders

In the remainder of this chapter, I will attempt to form a picture of the entire spectrum of reality as presented to the knowing mind, and not just the causes in isolation. It is the job of the branch of philosophy called 'metaphysics' to grasp the whole of reality[9] and that word makes some roll their eyes, while others tremble in fear. I will try to make the exploration as accessible as possible, but it will involve some deep philosophical concepts. Don't worry, though; this is as tough as it will get, and you are certain to pick up something from what follows. Meanwhile, if you don't grasp the whole of what you read, that will in no way impede you from understanding the rest of the book. If you would rather take a helicopter to the top, however, feel free to skip to the section entitled 'First cause or bust'. Before we start climbing, here is a bit of pep talk from Chesterton:

> There is nothing that really indicates a subtle and in the true sense a superior mind so much as this power of comparing a lower thing with a higher and yet that higher with a higher still; of thinking on three planes at once.[10]

Four Causes

Okay, so we have just identified what we are looking for: causes. But it turns out that there are echelons or series of causes in each of the four areas of causality, because most causes are also effects which themselves have causes. Thus, when I say that X is the cause of effect Y, we may ask: but is X itself caused in any way? Is X an effect of something else, just as Y is the effect of X? And if it is indeed the case that X is an effect as well as a cause, then X also has a cause which can be sought by the mind.

Say that I identify typing as being caused by fingers. That does not mean that my knowledge of typing is exhaustive, since I can continue pursuing causal knowledge. For instance, I can ask: Why is my finger typing? An answer is: in order to write a book. I ask further: Well, why are you writing a book? Answer: to inform readers about realism. Why do you want to inform readers about realism? Answer: to help them be reasonable in religion and science. And so on. What is happening here is that the mind is following *a causal chain*, that is, a series of causes in the line of *final* causality (purposes). The finger is typing in order to write a book in order to inform readers about realism in order to help them be reasonable in religion and science.

The mind can pursue such a causal chain in each of the four areas of causality, in order to seek the ultimate reason for an effect, the reason beyond which no further explanation can be given. We begin by finding the immediate or direct cause of an effect, one step up from sense data. Then we ascend higher up the mountain, seeking cause after cause until we come to the first link of the causal chain, the one that provides the explanation for the whole of the chain. Once we have reached that first cause, no further question can be asked, no further cause can be found, in that particular chain of causality. We have summitted Mount Reality.

Let us take another example to illustrate, in the area of material causality. We could ask of the typing finger: of what is it composed? Bone and tissues. But what is in bones? Marrow. And marrow is vascular tissue, which is composed of cells, which are made up of proteins, which are a series of amino acids, which are made of molecules, which are made of atoms, which are made of subatomic particles, and so on until we come to the ultimate substratum of all matter. Once we have reached a type of matter that cannot be broken into parts, that is a subject for other matter but which is not itself contained in matter below it, we know we have come to the end of the causal chain of material causality. In other words, we have attained the ultimate level of one of the aspects of reality.

(Note that pursuing a chain of material causes is more like drilling down into the mountain than ascending it. The reason is that matter is a receiver of change; it does not act, but is acted upon. Because of this passivity, it is represented as being on the bottom side of causality. Meanwhile, efficient, formal, and final causes are on the top side of causality, in that they act on matter. For them, finding a first cause is like ascending to the top of a mountain.)

We can broadly group all effects in reality into two different types: 'being' or the fact of a reality *being made* to *exist*, and 'becoming' or the fact of an existing thing *changing*. Aristotle speaks of these two different aspects of existing reality, or 'act', in the ninth book of his *Metaphysics*.[11] He calls 'being' *first act*, because it is required first for anything at all to exist. He refers to 'becoming' as *second act*.

It turns out that the type of causal chain that has to be in place to cause a thing *to be* (first act) is quite different from the causal chain that has to be in place to cause a thing *to change* (second act). The chain of causes making a thing be does not work at different times to cause the effect. Rather, all of the causes must be 'stacked' one upon another at a given moment and all be acting at the same time for the effect, the being, to be in place. Because of this 'stacking', the causal chain yielding being is sometimes referred to as the *vertical chain of causality*.[12] Travelling mentally on the vertical causal chain is equivalent to going up or down the mountain.

We need to look at an example, but before we do, we have to consider exactly what we mean by *being*. Effectively, we are

Four Causes

referring to all that exists outside the mind. This certainly includes things that exist on their own, substances such as rocks, trees, and kangaroos. However, it also includes existing *aspects* of substances. For instance, we can consider the kangaroo's colour (brown), its position (sitting), and its activity (eating) as beings. After all, the kangaroo's brownness really exists and so must qualify as a being in some sense. Even activity or becoming must be a being in some sense, since it exists outside the mind. When we think of activity as activity, in its relation to change, then we are thinking of it in terms of second act; when we think of activity in a static sense, as a state of the being to which it belongs, we are thinking of it in terms of first act.

Let us consider the hanging of a chandelier[13] in terms of being, that is, not as an activity (second act) but as a mode of being (first act), a state of existence which holds when supports sufficient to counteract the pull of gravity maintain an object above the floor. Considering 'hanging' in such a way, we are able to climb the vertical chain of causality to find the efficient causes of the being 'hanging'. We do not go back in time to investigate how the chandelier became hanging when previously it was not hanging—that's a horizontal inquiry. No, instead, we gaze up and ask ourselves: What causes are in place at each second such that the chandelier exists in the mode of being we call 'hanging'? We are freezing the chandelier in time to consider the state of 'hanging'. This is the vertical chain of causality. Let's start climbing.

The chandelier is hanging because it is attached to the ceiling by screws. But why is the ceiling in place over the chandelier? Because of the ceiling joists. Why are the ceiling joists in place over the ceiling? Because of the walls. Why are the walls standing? Because they are attached to the ground, which is held in place by the gravity of the Earth, a planet which is held in its orbit by the gravity of the sun. And so on... For the chandelier to hang *at any moment* (effect that is a state of being, 1st act), the Earth must hold up the walls must hold up the ceiling joists must hold up the ceiling must hold up the screws must hold up the hanging chandelier (chain of causes in 1st act). Remove any of these causes in the chain and the hanging does not exist. Our chain of causes provides us rational grounds for the existence of the being 'hanging'.

On the other hand, I can consider the chandelier by asking what made it start hanging, not what makes it hang at any given moment. This is to ask about the causes which changed the chandelier from non-hanging to hanging. My question is still the same: 'Why is the chandelier hanging?' but now I am not considering 'hanging' as a *being*, but as the result of a *change* that took place in the chandelier. What series of events preceded the current state of the chandelier to account for it hanging now? To answer that question, I must *go back in time* to look for the causes that led to the hanging of the chandelier. That causal chain is sometimes referred to as the *horizontal* causal line, because the effect is produced over a period of time and we imagine the passing of time as taking place in a horizontal time line. We see time as moving from left to right. Following the links of this chain is like going around the sides of a mountain rather than up or down it.

Say I explore in this way the 'efficient causes' or 'moving agents' for the current hanging of the chandelier. I might arrive at the following explanation: Workers at a factory assembled the parts of the chandelier, packed it away in a box, and put it on a shelf. Bob bought the chandelier, removed it from its box, and hung it from his ceiling. This explanation gives the series of *changes* that took place in the chandelier *over a period of time* that, in one way, account for it hanging now.

I must summarise the differences between the natures of the causes in these causal chains.[14] The primary difference is that causes in the vertical chain produce 'being', while the causes of the horizontal chain produce 'becoming'. Philosophical jargon refers to the causes of the vertical chain as being 'essentially ordered' because they are necessary for the existence of a being or state of being. The horizontal causes are referred to as 'accidentally ordered' because they only modify an already existing being.

From this primary difference flows a second: since 'being' cannot be constituted over a period of time (2a), the causes of the vertical chain must all act at the same time to produce their effect (2b), be stacked upon one another, whereas the causes of the horizontal chain act at different times (2b), as separate causal segments, to yield a certain change in a being.

Thus, *essentially ordered causes must be concurrent with their effect at every moment for the effect to exist* (3). Take away the screws or the ceiling or the walls and the chandelier does not hang at any moment. *Accidentally ordered causes, however, need not be concurrent with the effect at every moment for the effect to exist* (3). Those causes of the horizontal chain can perish—Bob dies, the chandelier box is destroyed, the chandelier factory shuts down—yet the chandelier still hangs. Those causes were only needed to bring the chandelier to a state of hanging, not to keep it in that state.

The third difference yields a fourth. Because the causes of the vertical chain are stacked one upon another, *those causes are hierarchical in their causal power*. The lower causes in the chain depend on the higher ones for their causal activity (4). The screws can act as causes to hold up the chandelier only if the ceiling is providing support; the ceiling can provide support only if the ceiling joists are supporting it, and so on. This dependence of lower causes on higher ones for causal power means that *there must be some ultimate source of that causal power*—a first cause of the vertical chain—for any of the causes to cause at all (5), and thus for the series of causes to exist. In the case of the chandelier, there must be some ultimate source of support for the walls, ceiling joists, ceiling, and screws to provide support themselves. Since they support in dependence on other supports, there must be some ultimate support not dependent on any other support, a first supporter which provides supporting power to the entire chain of supporting causes.

The causes of the horizontal chain, however, are not dependent upon one another to exercise their causal activity (4). In order to hang his chandelier, Bob does not need to have present in his house any of the previous causes in the chain of becoming, whether it be the factory workers, the store where he bought his fixture, or the car he used to drive it to his house. Thus, *the causes of the horizontal chain do not have an hierarchical relationship among themselves and so no first cause is as such required* (5).

The table below sets out the five differences between the two lines of causality. The flowchart that follows the table represents the choosing of the causal line to be investigated.

Table 2.1 Differences in two lines of causality

Types of differences	Horizontal line of causality	Vertical line of causality
1. Effect ↓	Becoming = change of being ↓	Being = state of existence ↓
2a. How long it takes ↓	Takes place in time ↓	Time not involved ↓
2b. When causes act ↓	Causes act at separate times ↓	Causes act at once ↓
3. Dependence of effects on causes ↓	Effect can remain after causes perish ↓	Effect does not exist if any of causes are ever missing ↓
4. Order of causes ↓	No intrinsic hierarchy to causes ↓	Higher causes have a greater causal power than lower ones ↓
5. Need of first cause	No need for a first cause	A first cause is needed for the causality of the entire chain

The Four Causes

What do you want to know about X?

| What is X composed of? | What is X? | What made X? | What is the meaning of X? |

- **Material Cause** (X's body)
- **Formal Cause** (X's nature)
- **Efficient Cause** (X's maker)
- **Final Cause** (X's purpose)

Do you want to know the cause at a given moment or over a period of time?

At a Given Moment → **Vertical Chain of Causality** (essentially ordered)

Over a Period of Time → **Horizontal Chain of Causality** (accidentally ordered)

The existence of God

Is there ever an end, we may ask, to the mind's journeying on the causal chains? This is the same thing as asking: is there some 'first cause', at the top of the chain, beyond which no further explanation can be sought, and which our minds can find? Is there actually a summit to Mount Reality? Or is there a plateau, with many causes at the top, instead of one? Or is there no summit at all, because the causes just go on forever, without there ever being a top?

Up to this point, we have assumed that reality is in the shape of a mountain. At the bottom, there are the many particular details revealed by sense data. Up higher are universal concepts that indicate the causes of those particular details. As we proceed upwards, the concepts become fewer and fewer until we come to the apex, where all causal explanations converge on a single first cause. Such is the shape of reality if it is in the form of a causal mountain.

When you reach the top of a mountain, there is nowhere else to go, because there is no higher point. A similar situation would obtain if our minds could reach a first cause. Upon finding such a cause, the mind could not continue past that point, for two reasons:

1. A first cause would provide a complete explanation for all of the effects below it, and so the mind is not left to look for other causes to explain those lower effects.
2. A first cause would not itself need any causal explanation, for it would not manifest any dependence in being or any of the properties of effects, such that the mind would need to seek a cause for it, outside of it.

If we want to find a first cause, we have to look at the vertical chain of causality. We want to go up the mountain, not around its sides. The accidental chain only tells us about changes in beings that already exist. Since it relies upon some realities already being in place, namely the reality of 'being', it cannot tell us about reality as such.

Four Causes

To find out about reality as such, we must find the causes of 'being' as such, and by that I mean that we must find the reason why anything exists at all. I am not referring any more to some aspect of a being, such as the hanging of a chandelier, but that anything is something rather than nothing. We expect being as such to tell us about all of reality, for 'being' is what is, what's real.

You might have noticed how important the notion of 'being' has been all throughout our discussion. In chapter 1, I mentioned that you have to know 'being' to apply the word 'is' to reality, an application that takes place whenever we speak.[15] I also mentioned that only someone holding the principles of epistemological realism can claim that humans actually grasp 'being' and so reality.

Here, in this chapter on causes, we must find the first cause of 'being', for whatever is responsible for being will be responsible for reality. Once a person adopts realism, admits that humans know 'being', that the word 'is' has meaning, then the path to the first cause is short and swift. It quickly becomes clear that reality is indeed in the shape of a mountain. The only thing the mind needs is contact with beings that testify to their own limitations and so demand a higher causal explanation for their being. And all of the beings we know testify to their own limitations.

Aquinas's famous five ways to prove God all point out some creaturely limitation that demands an uncreated source.[16] Each of these limitations is a limitation in being.[17] Each of them points to the need of a cause of being, a cause that can account for the very existence of limited beings that are not self-existing. *The things around us are effects in their very existence and thus their existence needs explanation.* Such an explanation can only be given by a *proper cause* of existence. A proper cause is one which directly accounts for the effect in question. For instance, shoemakers are the proper causes of shoes and dressmakers of dresses. And what is the proper cause of the limited existence of a creature? A creator. What does a creator do? A creator creates, that is, makes beings exist that do not exist of themselves. Once we understand the meaning of the word 'creature', we realise that unless there is a proper cause for that reality, a 'creator', then no creature would exist.[18] But creatures exist. Therefore, there must be a creator.

In the next section, I will spell out the italicised sentence of the last paragraph. First, though, I should note that some atheists, such as David Hume and Bertrand Russell, make a caricature of the proof I have just given. Here is what the latter has to say about it:

> I may say that when I was a young man ... I for a long time accepted the argument of the First Cause, until one day, at the age of eighteen, I read John Stuart Mill's Autobiography, and I there found this sentence: 'My father taught me that the question 'Who made me?' cannot be answered, since it immediately suggests the further question 'Who made God?'. That very simple sentence showed me, as I still think, the fallacy in the argument of the First Cause.[19]

What Mill's father was implying and Russell was accepting is the idea that 'everything must have a cause.' Thus, when you arrive at a so-called First Cause, you have not finished your causal search, but you still have to ask: 'Well, who caused the First Cause?' But this question is simply a red herring, for no theist believes that 'everything must have a cause' and our First Cause argument is not based on such a false principle. Precisely what the mind is seeking in climbing the vertical chain is a being who exists without relying on any other, who is not an effect, who requires no explanation, because he is his own explanation, one who causes without being caused himself, an *uncaused* cause. Thus, the answer to the question 'Who made God?' is simple: 'No one; God is uncaused.'[20]

First cause or bust

Let me illustrate in another way why there could not possibly be any reality whatsoever if there were no first cause of existence, if there were no God. Consider the table below:

Table 2.2

1. Impossible things	2. Possible, non-existing things	3. Existing things
A square circle	Bilbo Baggins	The planet Saturn
A rock heavier than God can lift	Winged horses	The land mass 'Australia'
Time travel	Velveeta cheese	Your mind
An infinite number	The spaghetti monster	Cockatoos

In the far left column are things the very notion of which implies a contradiction, like the phrase 'uncreated creatures.' Since the mode of being of a square, for instance, excludes the possibility of it being a circle at the same time, if, *per impossibile,* it did exist, then it would also not exist. It would be a square, in that it realised squareness, and it would not be a square, in that it did not realise squareness, as it was a circle. Even if we were to assign a name to square circle, such as 'squircle', we could not form a single concept matching up with that name, because the mind is something real, and just as no real being can exist and not exist at once and in the same respect, so also no mind can both think and unthink, attribute and not attribute, delimit and unlimit an idea at once. For such would be required to form a single idea 'square unsquare'. All of this offends the principle of non-contradiction, which, as I noted in the first chapter, must be held to rigorously if one wishes to use the intellect at all. As realists, we hold to the reliability of the intellect and so to its first principles.

In the middle column, we have beings which are the fruit of human imagination, but have not been endowed with extramental reality. What is lacking to them? An act of existence, an act to make them stand outside of nothing. What is privy to them? An image, an idea, something philosophers call 'logical being'.

The question that comes to our mind when considering the poor unfortunates in the middle column is: Why don't they exist? They could exist, but they have nothing of real being. Why didn't J. R. R. Tolkien and why doesn't Peter Jackson instantiate some real live hobbits for us, so that we can have a Shire on Earth?

Those asking such questions are illustrating Aquinas' proof for the real distinction between essence and existence propounded in chapter 4 of his *De Ente et Essentia.*[21] We all know that just because an idea or form or essence of some thing can be conceived, that does not mean that the thing actually exists. For it to do so, another component is required: the act of existence.

No literary author in the history of the world—Tolkien included—has ever provided his character with real existence, though Chesterton wrote a play, *The Surprise,* about a playwright with such power, and Pirandello a play about *Six Characters in Search of an Author.* The fact is that no human has power over existence *qua* existence, the ability to make real that which has nothing of being, that supreme omnipotence that has a power without limits because it is the very source of limits in the thing it creates.

And so, when we come to the third column, the column of things that are real, we see that there must be some reason why they are so, that is, why they are something rather than nothing, in Leibniz's words. If there wasn't a need for an extra cause to move from column 2 to column 3, then we would have to say that there is no difference between existing and not existing, which is surely not the case! Those in column 2 have essence without existence, while those in column 3 have both. And so the cause that bridges the appalling gap between the two is one that accounts for existence, that is, the very fabric of reality as such. This cause we commonly call God.

God, then, is the first cause of all existing things, and He provides a sufficient reason for there being a reality. His role is not of a single moment, but of every moment. He holds the universe 'between His index finger and thumb', such that, letting it go, it would fall into nothingness. Thus, even if the universe

> were entirely without end or beginning, there would still be exactly the same logical need of a Creator. Anybody who does not see that ... does not really understand what is meant by a Creator.[22]

It may be fashionable to deny God's existence, but to do so is to remove from reality its own basis of intelligibility. The reason is as follows:

- That which constitutes reality and makes it knowable is 'being.'
- 'Being' that does not exist of itself must have its source in some 'existence maker.'
- All beings within our common experience are beings that do not exist of themselves, and so must necessarily rely on an 'existence maker.'
- Therefore, one who denies that there is an 'existence maker' is unable to explain why there are beings at all.
- One who cannot explain why there are beings at all is not in a position to make coherent use of the word corresponding to 'being', the word 'is.' He will speak the word 'is' while refusing to acknowledge that its notion has a foundation for its reality and so its intelligibility.

Logically, then, to deny the existence of God is to take away the causal basis for the 'is' which we conceptualise from the world around us. How much safer it is for rational discourse and epistemological health to accept the data of sense telling us things are limited, and the intellect inferring from hence that they have their source in something unlimited.

Are you sure?

You make a nice argument and all that, someone may say, but can I be certain about your conclusion that God exists? Is your proposition 'God creates the beings in our world' a scientific one, in the sense that it provides a causal knowledge that is certain?

Recall that, for Aristotle, 'science' is the highest possible attainment of the mind, 'a type of perfect knowing that may be expressed in certain and necessary conclusions'.[23] Obviously, we cannot be certain of everything that we know. Thus, Aristotle identifies two lower grades of knowledge that provide less certainty:[24]

1. Opinion—'the type of knowing that is induced by reasoning that is logically probable'

2. Belief—'the type of knowing that results from persuasive argumentation'

The three grades of certainty derive from three ways of arguing. One who has scientific knowledge is able to provide a demonstrative proof of his proposition. This is a proof which establishes a necessary connection between a cause and effect, a proof which indicates a situation that cannot be otherwise than it is. Here is how Aristotle puts it:

> We suppose ourselves to possess unqualified scientific knowledge of a thing ... when we think that we know the cause on which the fact depends, as the cause of that fact and of no other, and, further, that the fact could not be other than it is.[25]

One possessing opinion, on the other hand, sets forth a dialectical argument. Such an argument sets forth evidence on opposite sides of a question, none of it conclusive, and then chooses one side as being the most probable explanation. This mode of argumentation is not able to establish a necessary connection between a given cause and a given effect, and so is only probabilistic.

The weakest certainty is provided by one arguing belief, because the weight of certainty rests more on the speaker's power of persuasion than rational argumentation. The demands of rhetorical flourish require a certain obscuring of an argument's logical structure, and rhetoric is directed more to compelling the will of the listener than his intellect. This weakens the intrinsic certainty of the orator's conclusions in the objective order.

Table 2.3 Aristotle's degrees of certainty

Type of knowledge	Degree of certainty	Mode of argument	Treated by Aristotle's book:
Science	Certain	Demonstration	*Posterior Analytics*
Opinion	Probable	Dialectics	*Topics*
Belief	Less than probable	Persuasion	*Rhetoric*

My claim is that I have provided demonstrative proof of a first cause for the existence of limited beings. An example will help illustrate why I make this claim. Consider the proposition 'Rain makes the ground wet'. Every realist would hold it to be absolutely certain. The reason for its certainty is the nature of water. Water, by definition, by its intrinsic constitution, by its essence, is wet. Because of this, water cannot—ever—be separated from wetness. Wherever there is water, there *must* be wetness, without a shadow of a doubt. Thus, when it rains, because there is contact between water and the ground, the ground *must* be wet. For ground in contact with water not to be wet, water has to be non-water. In other words, water has to be water and non-water at the same time, breaking the principle of non-contradiction.

The proposition 'rain makes the ground wet' reaches scientific certainty at the point that *we establish that there is a necessary connection between water as cause and wetness as effect, for we show that it is in the very nature of the cause to produce such an effect.*

I did something similar in our demonstration of God's existence, because I showed that, by their very nature, the denizens of the world around us are effects necessarily having a certain cause. They are all changing, limited beings, just by the fact that they are in the cosmos. By definition, by their very essence, they are creatures. Creatures, however, cannot exist without a creator. Thus, it is in the very nature of the things around us to be caused in their existence and so to have a cause for their existence. For this reason, the proposition 'God creates the beings in our world' is at least as scientific as the proposition 'Rain makes the ground wet'.

Primary and secondary causality

Before coming down from the summit of all reality, we have to pause and look closely at that specific 'activity' of God which is creation. It is a way of causing which has many profound differences from the way in which creatures exercise causality. God causes in making things exist and creatures cause by exercising their existence. God conferring causal powers on creatures makes it possible for those creatures to provide causal knowledge to a knowing mind.

These two levels of causal activity constitute a final distinction that I need to make in this chapter, and perhaps the most important distinction of this book. Stick with me as we head into the last leg of this difficult philosophical exploration.

Once we have understood that there must be a God who provides being to all limited creatures at each moment for them to exist, we must ask ourselves *how* He makes the universe function. The most important question is whether He endows creatures with the power to act on their own or not. We have already seen that creatures cannot have the power to *be* on their own (1st act), a reality that is appropriately implied in the very name 'creature'. They are *always* in need of God for existence, and it could not be otherwise. What about their activities (2nd act)? Does God confer on creatures a proper power, inherent in them, by which they can perform those activities? It depends on the way in which God creates: does He create things such that He endows them with proper causality, or does He create them in such a way that they *appear* to act on their own, but, in actuality, God alone acts in all of their activities?

Philosophers refer to God's creative activity as *primary* efficient causality (creating beings) and to the activity of creatures as *secondary* efficient causality (modifying beings), a terminology that naturally follows from the distinction between first act (being) and second act (becoming). Primary causality is a domain reserved to God alone. He is in the 'business of is-ness'; only He can communicate being, the act of existence, that is, 'create'. The question which I was asking above, then, is the following: do creatures really act? Is there any such thing as secondary causality? Or do creatures only appear to act?

A certain class of philosophers, called occasionalists, claim that God is the only agent operating in reality. This means that creatures do not act; their apparent action is only the *occasion* upon which God does this or that. For instance, we say that the fire causes burning because we feel the heat coming from it. This, however, assumes that fire has the ability to act as a cause, that it has an innate power. An occasionalist would hold that God is causing both the fire and the heat, and the fire is not exercising any causality whatsoever.

The occasionalist position destroys the entire edifice of our knowledge. We have seen that the mind gains knowledge by moving from effect to cause. Why do I feel heat? Because of the burning of the fire. But is it truly the fire that is producing heat? Yes, because God has endowed the fire with this power. Good! Then my inference from the heat (effect) to the fire (cause) is correct, and so I have true knowledge. If the fire cannot act on its own, however, *if it has not been given the power to exercise secondary causality*, then it is an illusion for me to call it a cause. In such a scenario, all knowledge is false except for the knowledge of God as First Cause. In all other areas, my intellect deceives me.

The occasionalist opinion illustrates that God does not have to endow creatures with their own proper activity when He creates them. He who can do the greater can do the less, and it is certainly a lesser feat to make creatures act than to create them from nothing, to take total charge of their becoming after having total charge of their being. Thus, it is possible that it is really God acting in all of the created effects which we see around us.

Realists reject occasionalism out of hand, however, for reasons that have become familiar to us by now:

- We have pledged ourselves to accept the immediate evidence of sense and intellect as being true.
- But the senses tell me that heat always follows standing next to a fire, and the intellect tells me the reason for that, namely that the fire is the cause of the heat.
- Thus, fire is an actual cause of heat. Indeed, it would seem ludicrous to say otherwise, which goes to show that a departure from realism is a departure from plain common sense.

On the opposite side of occasionalism is materialism, which holds that no primary causality is being exercised in reality. We have already seen why that opinion cannot be correct: it cannot provide any account for why reality exists at all and considers the universe as consisting of 'uncreated creatures'.

In the end, the materialist cannot explain why creatures have causal powers, and the occasionalist cannot explain why we have true knowledge. The realist explains both. The table below summarises the three opinions held on these two orders of causality:

Table 2.4 Views of causality in the universe

View of causality in the universe	Primary causality applies?	Secondary causality applies?	Explanation
Occasionalists	Yes	No	Only God acts in the universe. Creatures don't act.
Realists	Yes	Yes	Both God & creatures act in the universe.
Materialists	No	Yes	Only creatures act in the universe. There is no God.

The notion of creation, then, enables us to say that creatures are true causes and that therefore our causal knowledge drawn from creatures is correct. God endows creatures with existence and powers, and they make use of those powers. God creates and then creatures act.

But are primary and secondary causality compatible? Can both God and creatures act at the same time, such that they can both be truly said to be agents at every moment? Yes, they can, and to see this, we must look closely at the difference between 'creating' and 'creaturing', the former meaning the exercise of primary causality and the second the exercise of secondary causality.

Creating vs. creaturing

Creating is like no other activity, because it is not exercised on a pre-existing subject, on something already in being that is then modified.[26] When God creates *from nothing*, 'nothing' really

Four Causes

means nothing, that is, the absence of all reality. Thus, the 'from' does not refer to a substance that He modifies, but a state previous to His activity. There is nothing. God creates. There is something.

Following are seven characteristics that pertain only to God's creative primary efficient causality:

1. God's causation does not cause any change in the thing caused, properly speaking. Since there is no previous subject upon which His causality is being exercised, there is no modification of an already existing being. In the language of the philosophers, there is no transition 'from potency to act' in a subject. For there to be such a transition, a being must already exist, but this is precisely what is lacking in this special mode of causality.[27] Take Bob from the last chapter, for instance. We would not properly call his going from nothing to something a 'change' in him, because there was no 'him' to start with.

2. Because there is no transition from one state to another in the effect, the coming into being of the effect does not take place in time. For it to take place in time, there would have to be a movement, a process of succession where there would be a before and an after. Here, the before does not exist, and this removes the possibility of succession.[28] Bob does not ease away from nothing in a multi-stage process. At one moment he is not. At the next moment, in a *single* moment, he is.

3. This causality is not exercised by way of contact between cause and effect. The agent bringing things into existence has no means of acting on the effect-to-be by any intermediary, such as an arm or a hammer. Because the effect is brought into being from a state of non-existence, and there is no subject to be acted upon as such, the effect can only be brought into being by an immanent activity in the agent—an activity that remains within the agent—and not

a transient one, that is, one where the action of the agent would pass out of the agent into the effect. The only immanent activities are intellection and volition. Thus, this type of causality must be exercised by way of intellection and volition. And so, when we speak of creation 'from nothing', that does not mean that God takes a clump of nothing and forms it into a something. Rather, He makes some entity come into being merely by willing it. 'Let there be Bob.' And Bob exists.

4. The relation of effect to cause in this particular causation is one of essential, not accidental, subordination. What this means is that the effect is dependent on the cause for its existence at every moment, and not for a certain time. A son's life depends on his mother for the nine months preceding his birth, but afterwards he can live on, even if his mother dies. This is an accidental subordination of effect to cause (horizontal chain of causality). When the effect, however, is the very being of a thing, the cause cannot be taken away without the effect also disappearing.[29] This is the vertical chain, and again, time does not enter into its consideration. For instance, if God stopped existing, Bob would not have any means of his own to maintain himself in reality. He would immediately fade back into nothing.

5. An agent causing the very being of a thing must be able to communicate being. To do this, the agent cannot make use of some intermediary as an instrument for the coming-to-be of the effect.[30] Agents which act through some aspect of their being are using that aspect as an instrument to cause the effect. This is the way secondary causes act. They do not act through their being as being, but through some aspect of their being.[31] For instance, a hammer works to communicate force, not through its being, but through the hardness of its head. Similarly, Socrates generates a son through his human nature. The hardness is a form or aspect

of the totality of the hammer, just as human nature is an aspect or form of the totality of Socrates. One creating cannot act in this way, for creation requires the begetting of being, and only being, as being, can beget being. In creating Bob, then, God, by His being itself, causes Bob's being to exist outside of Himself.

6. This particular causality makes for no diminishing or change in the agent.[32] There is no diminishing because existence as such does not allow for diminution. Existence as such either is or is not. Degrees in existence are introduced only by limiting essences, certain created boundaries which restrict existence to a certain mode of being. Such essences are not in play here, however. Rather, we have an agent acting by his own being to give being to what was not. Such an agent could diminish in being only by losing being itself, that is, by self-annihilation, which is absurd. The diminishing of an efficient cause can take place only at the level of secondary causality, where a) one does not act through one's being, but through some aspect of one's being; b) one is causing some effect in a subject, and not giving existence itself. The arm swinging the hammer loses energy, as does the mother giving birth to the child. But God does not lose anything whatsoever (or gain either) by creating Bob. He neither grows nor diminishes. His action of creating is not a movement or change in Him.

7. An agent that brings something into being from nothing must possess infinite power, because there is no limit or boundary set by a *terminus a quo* or starting point for change. Thus, what comes into being only need fall within the range of what can be, that is, whatever can exist that does not of itself imply contradiction. In other words, the agent that brings a thing into being must have a power without limits, because it must be the very source of limits in the thing that it creates.[33] God thinks things into exist-

ence, such that things are for the sole reason that He wants them to be. He has absolute power over what is and what is not. For this reason, He can make *anything* exist; He has a power without limits.

From these seven characteristics of primary causality, we can draw up a chart giving the precise differences between the way that God acts and the way that creatures act, between creating and creaturing.

Table 2.5 Differences between creating and creaturing

Causation	First cause (God)	Second cause (Creatures)
Effect	Being itself	Some modality of being
Operates on	Nothing	A pre-existing subject[a]
Change in the affected subject	None, strictly speaking	Subject becomes in some way
Takes place	Outside of time	Over a period of time, by way of succession, by the realisation of an already existing possibility
Exercised	Only by immanent activity	By way of contact, for transient activity Also without contact, for immanent activity
Chain of causality	Essential	Accidental
Agent acts through	Its very being	Some aspect of its being
Effect on agent	Remains unchanged	Changes while causing
Power of agent	Infinite	Finite (cf. Aquinas, SCG, III, 102.4)
Extension	All beings	Some beings

a = 'No created being can cause anything, unless something is presupposed' (Aquinas, ST, I, q.45, a.5, ad 1).

Creatures cannot cooperate in any way in the action of the First Cause bringing things into being. Only God can create. No one can assist Him in that work. Bob is not able to do anything whatsoever before he exists.

However, when God gives things to exist in a stable way over a period of time, then they can make use of their being to act on their own and perform acts of secondary causality. God holding things in existence in a continuous fashion is thus what makes movement and time possible.[34] It is our common experience that the First Cause maintains creatures in being in a most consistent way, and with such a continuity that mathematical laws with great exactitude can be given for nature as a whole, natures or species

Four Causes

of animals and plants can be classified systematically, and humans can plan out their lives. This *conservation* of Creation not only enables creatures to act, but also enables human minds to know them, because our knowledge follows on the observation of the activities of other beings. Once we have sense data of what they are doing, we can reason to the causes of those doings.

This grand perspective of a beneficent Creator God conferring and conserving existence from a timeless eternity, in the exercise of primary causality, founds the entirety of the epistemological order. It makes the bridging of reality and mind possible. Because reality itself has an intelligible source, it is accessible to the rational mind in its entirety.

This elaborate philosophical viewpoint is also beneficial for the ontological order or reality itself, in that it allows for a Creator with a superior action that envelops but does not suppress the inferior action of His creatures. Distinguishing a separate activity for first and second causes means that both can operate at the same time, in complete concord, yet with second causes subordinated to the First Cause. In short, there exists between them a harmony, simultaneity, and ordination, as follows:

- **Harmony**—the First Cause acts only at the level of being and second causes act only at the level of aspects of being.[35] Thus, there is no interference of First Cause with the activity of second causes, whenever the First Cause maintains things continuous in being, that is, when He is not performing miracles (I will speak of them in the next chapter).[36]

- **Simultaneity**—the First Cause acts at every moment to sustain things in being, including the being of the powers by which they act. Second causes also act at every moment, to operate in using their God-given being and power.

- **Ordination**—Everything that secondary causes have or do comes firstly from the First Cause and is subordinated to that cause. The First Cause always retains absolute dominion over all causality, while giving rational creatures, for example, the power to exercise free will. All secondary causality is exercised within primary causality; all created effects depend more on the First Cause than on second causes.[37]

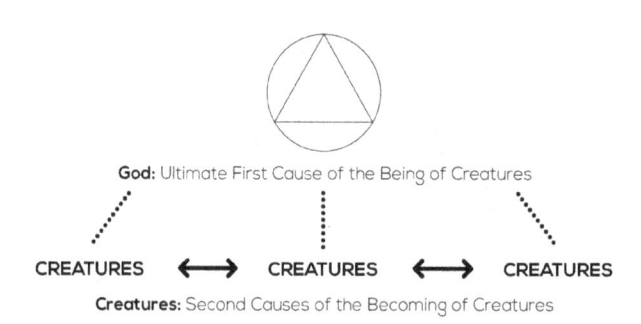

God: Ultimate First Cause of the Being of Creatures

CREATURES ⟷ CREATURES ⟷ CREATURES

Creatures: Second Causes of the Becoming of Creatures

God, in a single eternal act, outside of time, confers being on creatures and conserves them in being throughout time. Creatures, using the being conferred upon them by God, cause changes in one another throughout time.

Thus, the distinction between primary and secondary causality enables us both to make sense of there being a reality at all, and also to attribute to creatures their own proper activities. God endows them with existence and powers of being, and they make use of His endowments. Precisely because they act by their own proper activity, our knowledge of them as being causes is correct. Seen from this angle, the distinctions I have made in this chapter, based on epistemological realism, are necessary to justify both the reality of causation and our knowledge of it.

The entire argument might be summarised as follows:

- If creatures do not act by their own proper power, they are not causes.

- If creatures are not causes, then our knowledge of them as causes of the effects around us is false.
- If our knowledge concerning them is false, then nothing of what we know is true, because all of our knowledge comes from the senses.

⇨ Thus (going back the other direction), in order for true knowledge to be possible for a person, it is necessary that creatures be true causes.
- But they can only be true causes if they have the intrinsic power to exercise agency on others.
- But we cannot account for this power in creatures unless we say that there is a First Cause which founds the entire order of secondary causality whereby creatures are proper causes.

⇨ Thus, a First Cause is necessary both for creatures to be true causes and for us to have true knowledge.

By elaborating this metaphysical view, I am giving a gold standard for reality and reason. If they are to be justified and given their full rights, this epistemology and this metaphysics are necessary. It is in relation to this gold standard that I will be assessing the intellectual history of the human race in sections two and three.

Chapter summary

In chapter 1, we saw that the thinking subject
- takes in information from the senses, authority, and the intellect;
- judges with the mind on the truth of that information;
- and chooses what information and judgements to accept with the will.

We concluded that the person having the greatest scope for knowing will be one

- who accepts information from all three witnesses, that is, who is a realist;
- and who carefully and logically judges of the truth of the propositions he forms in his mind.

In this chapter 2, we saw that

- the proper object of the knowing mind, reality as such, ultimately presents itself under four aspects of explanation, four types of *reasons* which provide intelligible sense of that which a human being's limited knowing faculty cannot grasp in one fell swoop.
- these four types of reasons necessarily have two levels of explanation within themselves
    - one that accounts for their existence in reality, and
    - the other that accounts for their change while existing over a period of time.

The human mind can only explore reality under one of these aspects and no others, though there are many levels of reality within each.

This single view of the totality of reality is one that proceeds from

- epistemological realism, which makes use of the senses and intellect, believing them to provide true knowledge about reality;
- a series of distinctions that logically accounts for the facts of all reality, as they are presented to us by our knowing faculty and common human experience.

It is a view that was worked out with great toil and effort by an entire series of geniuses over the course of many centuries. It is a view that will be a benchmark for us in the rest of the book for evaluating intellectual endeavour in human history.

REALISM
Senses & Intellect

IDEALISM
Intellect Only

EMPIRICISM
Senses Only

The Well-Tempered Epistemology

Our remaining task in this first section of the book is to see where science and religion fit in human knowledge of reality. For a realist, where is religion on Mount Reality? And where is science?

Notes

[1] E. Gilson, *Methodical Realism* (San Francisco: Ignatius Press, 2011), pp. 29–30, emphasis added.
[2] See W. Clarke, *The One and the Many* (Notre Dame, Indiana: University of Notre Dame Press, 2001), p. 196.
[3] This paragraph is a summary of Aristotle's *Metaphysics*, 980a21–982b10.
[4] *Metaphysics*, 1013b16–1014a25. The explanations of the causes closely follows M. Adler, *Aristotle for Everybody* (New York: Simon & Schuster, 1978), p. 42.
[5] M. Adler, *Aristotle for Everybody* (New York: Simon & Schuster, 1978), p. 39.
[6] Note that if you decided that you wanted to execute an even more ambitious project and not only make entirely new creatures, but ones corresponding to concepts not taken from this cosmos, I would argue that your project would not be possible. You would not be able to form even one single concept. The reason is that all of our concepts are ultimately taken from sense, as we argued in the first chapter, and so there is no way

for the human mind to form an idea that cannot be traced in some way back to the material world, though it may have since been elevated to the transcendent level by the powers of our mind.

[7] Adler, *Aristotle for Everybody*, p. 41.
[8] See Aquinas, SCG, Book III, chapter 2, for a luminous proof.
[9] See Aristotle, *Metaphysics*, 982a5.
[10] G. K. Chesterton, *The Everlasting Man* (New York: Dodd, Mead & Company, 1930), p. 245.
[11] 1048a30–b9.
[12] For a defence of the existence of such simultaneous causal chains, see E. Feser, *Five Proofs of the Existence of God* (San Francisco: Ignatius Press, 2017), pp. 60–63.
[13] The hanging of a chandelier is a stock example for illustrating the vertical line of causality. Months after writing this chapter, I found the example in the newly released book *Who Designed the Designer?* (San Francisco: Ignatius Press, 2015), pp. 34–36.
[14] See also E. Feser, *Scholastic Metaphysics* (Heusenstamm, Germany: Editiones Scholasticae, 2014), section 2.4.2.
[15] See p. 23.
[16] Aquinas, ST, I, q.2, a.3; see E. Feser, *Neo-Scholastic Essays* (South Bend, Indiana: St. Augustine's Press, 2015), p. 87.
[17] J. Owens, *An Elementary Christian Metaphysics* (Houston: Center for Thomistic Studies, 1985), p. 350.
[18] See R. Garrigou-Lagrange, *God, His Existence, and His Nature* (St. Louis: B. Herder Book Co.), volume 1, paragraph 11.
[19] *Why I am not a Christian* (New York: Simon & Schuster, 1957), pp. 6–7.
[20] See W. Clarke's essay 'A Curious Blindspot in the Anglo-American Tradition of Antitheistic Argument', pp. 181-200, for a brilliant exposition of the long history of this sophism. The essay is reprinted in *The Creative Retrieval of St. Thomas Aquinas* (Fordham University Press, 2009), pp. 48–65. See also E. Feser, *Five Proofs of the Existence of God* (San Francisco: Ignatius Press, 2017), pp. 39–40, 83.
[21] For a full-blown defence of Aquinas's thesis, see Feser, *Scholastic Metaphysics*, section 4.2.1.
[22] G. K. Chesterton, *St. Thomas Aquinas* (London: Hodder & Stoughton Limited, 1933), p. 206.
[23] W. Wallace, *The Modeling of Nature* (Washington, DC: The Catholic University of America Press, 1996), p. 263.
[24] The quotations are taken from *Ibid.*
[25] *Posterior Analytics*, 71b8–b12; translation by R. McKeon, *The Basic Works of Aristotle* (New York: Random House, 1941), p. 111.

Four Causes

[26] See Aquinas, ST, III, q.75, a.8, ad 3.
[27] See Aquinas, SCG, Book II, chapter 17.
[28] See Aquinas, SCG, Book II, chapter 19.
[29] See Aquinas, ST, I, q.104, a.1.
[30] See Aquinas, ST, I, q.45, a.5; SCG, Book III, chapter 99, paragraph 4.
[31] See Aquinas, III, q.75, a.4.
[32] See Aquinas, *In Phys.*, paragraph 974; *In Met.*, paragraph 1661.
[33] 'To create a finite effect does not show an infinite power, yet to create it from nothing does show an infinite power' (Aquinas, ST, I, q.45, a.5, ad 3). See also SCG, Book I, chapter 43, paragraph 14; Book II, chapter 22.
[34] Dr Dennis Bonnette points out in an unpublished manuscript 'Insight to God Based on Motion' that this is the key point of St Thomas's 'first way', namely, that only a transcendent cause providing permanence in being from one moment to the next can account for the existence of movement.
[35] See Aquinas, SCG, Book II, chapter 21. God acts *through* secondary causes at the secondary level, but this is not His own proper activity, which is the subject of discussion here.
[36] See pp. 101–105.
[37] See Aquinas, ST, III, q.75, a.5, ad 1.

3 THREE KNOWLEDGES

*In physics numbers are everything,
in philosophy they are but little, and
in theology they are nothing.*

Robert Mayer

IN 1925, JOHN T. Scopes was put on trial in Tennessee for violating the state's Butler Act, which forbade teaching that humans descended from apes. It turns out that Scopes was not even sure that he had ever taught Darwinian evolution, but he was willing to be a scapegoat for a greater purpose: to give national attention to the ongoing conflict between science and religion in Protestant America.

The American Civil Liberties Union (ACLU) threw its tremendous resources into Scopes' cause, employing high flung rhetoric about academic freedom and the individual rights of teachers to convince the public that Darwinism should be taught to students. Later, on the advice of lawyer Clarence Darrow, the ACLU's strategy shifted to seeking to convince the grand jury that Darwinism posed no threat to religion. For the prosecution, however, evolution was detrimental to morality and an assault on Christianity.

Fast forward to 2004. A school board in Dover, Pennsylvania, made a policy requiring that a five minute statement be read to students about to undertake a week long study of Darwinism. The statement mentioned that evolution by natural selection is an unproven theory and that there are other competing explanations for the origin of life, such as intelligent design.

Enter the ACLU. It took the Dover School Board to court, claiming that intelligent design was religion and not science and so should not be taught at schools in a land where separation of

Church and State is sacrosanct. Judge Jones decided in the ACLU's favour by prohibiting the school district from 'requiring teachers to denigrate or disparage the scientific theory of evolution and from requiring them to mention Intelligent Design.'

And so, 'In 1925, the ACLU went to court to lift a prohibition against teaching Darwinism. Eighty years later, the ACLU persuaded a federal judge to prohibit teaching anything *but* Darwinism'.[1] In the first case, it was supposedly science usurping the rights of religion, and in the second, religion usurping the rights of science. But was either the case? What is the proper domain of religion and that of science? Are they mutually exclusive, in conflict, or in harmony?

Objects and methods

Having determined how reality is known and having summitted its heights, we are now ready to discover the respective domains of religion and modern science within reality. At first glance, it might seem that no discovery is needed. After all, isn't religion about God and supernatural things, and science about the laws of the physical world? Well, yes, they are. We must go deeper, however, using the tools that we have developed in the first two chapters.

We must first recognise that religion and science are bodies of knowledge. They investigate certain aspects of reality, collect evidence about those aspects, and then provide a rational account of them. Every body of knowledge possesses those three characteristics, namely, they each have an:

- **Object**—this is the aspect of reality studied by the discipline; for example, God in religion and physical laws in science

- **Method**—this is the way in which the discipline investigates reality; for example, studying the Bible in religion, or using a microscope in science

- **Doctrine**—this is the propositions which the discipline puts forward as having been discovered about its object by its method; for example, 'God is good' for religion, and 'Bodies fall to the Earth with an acceleration of 9.8 m/sec^2, for science.

In this chapter, we must find out the objects and methods of religion and science. We will leave their doctrines to sections two and three of the book.

First, however, we must make sure our epistedometer stays vertical by stating some fundamental realist principles about the objects and methods of all disciplines or bodies of knowledge.

As regards the *object* being considered by a discipline, a realist 'should always recognise that the object is what causes knowledge, and should treat it with the greatest respect'.[2] This is just another way of saying that we must let reality teach us and not legislate to reality what it must be.

A second principle concerns the *method* to be used when investigating the *object* of a body of knowledge. The principle runs this way: 'The realist must [] always insist, against the idealist, that for every order of reality there is a corresponding way of approaching and explaining it'.[3] This is as much as to say that different methods are to be used for investigating different aspects of reality.[4] (This realist principle—*'different methods of study for different objects of study'*—will come up often throughout this book.)

To illustrate this second principle, consider that if you want to cut something (object), you must choose a proper tool (method). Because cutting is a specific action with specific requirements for it to take place, you cannot use the same tool to accomplish it as you do for other activities. A hammer might be good for pounding nails, but it will not work for cutting. To pound nails (object), a flat, heavy, head is needed (method). To cut (object), on the other hand, you need a sharp instrument (method).

The same thing holds for investigating reality. We must use our faculties of knowing—senses, intellect, and authority—in the right combination to penetrate this or that aspect of reality.

Idealists and empiricists would have us always use the same human faculties to acquire knowledge. One demands that we only use the intellect, the other that we only use the senses. In chapter one, I compared this to climbing Mount Everest using only your favourite piece of equipment. I could also compare it to walking onto a worksite and demanding that only sharp tools be used, not blunt ones. The workers would be able to cut with their saws, but they would not have any hammers to pound in nails. The result would be a building with everything cut to size, but nothing holding together.

A similar result eventuates when idealists and empiricists present their all-encompassing view of reality. They have cut everything to the size of sense data or intellectual concepts, but the whole does not hold together.

The realist, on the other hand, recognises all human knowing faculties as being capable of grasping aspects of reality, and sees reality itself as having many different objects to investigate. Thus, the realist

- accepts material and efficient causes as being part of reality, when the senses reveal them
- accepts formal and final causes as being part of reality, when the intellect reveals them
- accepts evidence of reality presented by authorities, when those authorities are reliable
- chooses the right knowing tool when he wants to investigate this or that aspect of reality thoroughly and methodically.

As realists, then, we must carefully determine which knowing tools should be used by religion and science, instead of assuming that one tool will work. Let us start by considering science.

The domain of science

Whenever the word 'science' is used today, it is in desperate need of disambiguation. The reason is that the meaning applied to that term has changed several times over the course of its history, without the previous meanings ever having become obsolete. We have already seen Aristotle's use of the word in his *Posterior Analytics*.[5] For him, 'science' is a causal knowledge that is certain. The mind has science when it has found the one and only cause that can account for a given effect. It is with this sense of the word 'science' that we can speak of the various sciences or disciplines of thought: each of them provides certain knowledge of this or that aspect of reality.

The modern notion of science refers to a specific subset of those disciplines of thought that fall under the generic meaning of science. Today, it does not usually indicate knowledge that is certain, but rather 'the systematic study of the structure and behaviour of the physical and natural world through observation and experiment'.[6]

For the rest of the book, I will be using the word 'science' in this modern sense. The definition just given indicates both the *object* and the *method* of science as it is understood today. The object is the physical world, while the method—the 'scientific method'—is observation and experiment.

Within the physical world itself as object, there are various subordinate objects, that is, various aspects of nature, that can be considered by the scientist. Physicists consider physical bodies in general, chemists look at elemental bodies, while biologists study living bodies. Each of these scientists is considering natural bodies, but natural bodies at a different levels of unification.

There are two tasks immediately ahead of us, so that I can clarify science's epistemological territory. I must consider the objects that the various disciplines of science investigate—the aspect of the physical world they consider—and the degree to which the scientific method is an appropriate and effective method for investigating those objects.

Physical sciences

Let me start with what are called the physical sciences. They are the sciences that probe into inanimate bodies, bodies that are closest to matter as it is in itself, matter in its primitive form.

Because they are not complicated by the intricate arrangement of material parts found in living bodies, they provide a clearer read on what must pertain to all physical bodies.

There are three properties that belong directly and only to physical bodies, which help indicate the best method to investigate them:

1. **Physical bodies are material**, that is, they are composed of matter. This follows by definition from them being bodies, for bodies are made up of matter. Meanwhile, what does not have a body is not material.

2. **Physical bodies are quantified**, that is, they are extended over a certain area, such that they occupy space in the physical world. Material bodies have bulk, and this bulk is their quantity and so also what makes them quantifiable.[7] It is in this sense that Aquinas refers to quantity as flowing from matter.[8] Where you have a body, you also have dimensions of height, width, and depth; you have mass or weight, speed, acceleration; you have something that can be divided and measured. This does not mean that matter is *only* quantity or the only aspect of matter that science can investigate. Yet quantity is a primary aspect of matter, and so a primary object for those studying matter.

3. **Physical bodies are the subject of motion and change**. The reason why anything can change is because it is one thing and it *could* become something else. Matter is the source of this possibility, in that it is passive to every influence or determination and provides a substrate upon which changes can take place. Your carpet at home is inanimate matter, and as such is passive to your activity upon it, whether it be stepping upon it, burning it, rolling it up, vacuuming it, and so on. This passivity is the very nature of matter; as such, matter is constantly in a state of being influenced or moved by agents of change, both within it and outside of it.

From these three properties of physical bodies, we can easily see how appropriate the scientific method is for investigating them. With regard to the first property, materiality, recall that sensation provides immediate knowledge of what is material, intellect knowledge of what is immaterial. Those wanting to know material bodies as material, then, must make heavy use of the senses. This is one of the things that makes the scientific method a perfect fit for the physical sciences, for it accords a primal role to observation and experimentation, that is, the collection of sense data.

The second and third properties of bodies indicate that the quantification of movement will also be important in knowing them. Sciences, in the general sense of the term, are meant to provide causal knowledge of what happens always or for the most part. Thus, the physical sciences must provide general laws for the movement of bodies by somehow pinning down that movement. This is done by measurement, that is, by breaking continuous motion down into discrete mathematical units, and deriving quantitative formulas that accurately describe the motions observed and consistently predict future motions. Here, too, the scientific method is a perfect fit for the physical sciences, for measurement and quantification are key components of observation and experimentation.

Robin Waterfield describes the scientific method and its bond with the senses and quantity as follows:

> Scientific reasoning is a combination of forming testable hypotheses to account for observed phenomena, and of testing and re-testing these hypotheses by experimentation and logic ... *Throughout, everything should be quantifiable, measurable, and testable as far as is possible within the limitations of the technology currently available.*[9]

When a physical science is able to accomplish this quantification, it is called an 'exact' science. Jaki identifies modern science with exact science, which he defines as the 'quantitative study of the quantitative aspects of things in motion'.[10] We may say that this is at least the proper goal of the physical sciences, the term to which they should all tend, if they wish to be most effective in providing knowledge of physical bodies. They must seek to quantify physical motion, if they want to be exact.

Non-physical sciences

The natural or life sciences do not consider bodies as bodies, but rather bodies as living bodies. This object of study is not as quantifiable as the object of the physical sciences, rendering the scientific method less apt for the task of unlocking the secrets of living things, and making the life sciences much less exact.

What makes a given body more or less quantifiable is its level of materiality.[11] To the degree that a given being is more material, it is more subject to quantification. To the degree that it is less so, it is less subject to quantification. Inanimate beings such as atoms, crystals, and rocks, are simpler, being composed of fewer components. They are more material, closer to matter in itself, and so more easily quantifiable. Living beings like lions, lichen, and linseed, are complex, more immaterial than inanimate beings, and so much less quantifiable. In technical philosophical terms, they are more dominated by form, that immaterial principle that organises matter, giving it to be a certain type of being.

The geological sciences also have an object that is less tractable for the quantitative observation of the scientific method. The reason is that they study processes that took place in the past, and so processes which are not directly observable and quantifiable in the present. They do not consider physical bodies as such, but physical bodies in their history of activity. And history is hard to quantify.

From these considerations, we can draw a conclusion on the degree of exactitude that a given science will be able to attain. *The closer the object of a science's study is to physical bodies as such, the more it is able to be exact; the further a science's object of study is from physical bodies as such, the less it is able to be exact.* The physical sciences pertain more nearly to physical bodies as such and so are better able to be exact and realise science more perfectly. Life sciences and geological sciences, on the other hand, only consider certain types of physical bodies or consider them only under a certain aspect. Because their object is further away from physical bodies as such, their object is less subject to quantification.

The physical sciences, such as physics, chemistry, and astronomy, explicitly grasp quantities. Other sciences, such as geology, biology, and archaeology, do not explicitly grasp quantities, and so their work is more one of classification.[12] In the context of our analysis, the former realise exact science purely, while the latter mix science with philosophy of nature and other disciplines.

Being unable to achieve the same degree of formulaic exactitude in, say, biology as in physics does not mean that biology is not a science, but rather that it realises exact science to a lesser degree than physics. Since living bodies are not as subject to quantification as non-organic bodies, a sizeable portion of biology's study falls outside the realm of exact science and is inaccessible by the scientific method.

The chart below will help illustrate this gradation in the exactitude of sciences. The down arrow represents the *objects* of study becoming more specific: we start with the most universal study of physical bodies, physics. It deals with all bodies. Other sciences consider certain types of bodies. Chemistry considers elemental bodies, astronomy outer space bodies, biology living bodies, geology stony bodies, and archaeology relics of living bodies. Because the more specific sciences draw further away from matter as such, they are not as subject to the methods of inquiry that go with investigating matter. They belong more to other aspects of reality, which must be investigated using different methods from that of the scientific method, according to our realist rule 'different methods of study for different objects of study.'

Table 3.1 Objects of the sciences

More universal to more specific objects	Science	Object of study
↓	Physics	Matter and its interactions
	Chemistry	Composition, structure, and properties of elemental bodies and the changes they undergo
	Astronomy	Physical bodies beyond the earth's atmosphere
	Biology	Physical bodies which have life
	Geology	History of the earth, as recorded in rocks
	Archaeology	History of past human life, as revealed by relics left by ancient peoples

Science's causes

When science presents its findings, what sort of causal knowledge does it provide?

Here too, there is going to be a gradation among the sciences. Since each science has its own object and method, and so its own particular focus of study and its own particular way of pursuing that study, each science will find something different in reality. The physical sciences, by means of the scientific method, will be able to say much about material and formal causality, but not as much about efficient and final causality. The natural sciences, on the other hand, will not be able to discover as much about the formal causality of their objects as the physical sciences do, but will be able to probe more into the efficient and final causality of those objects.

Consider a person wanting to find precious metals. To do so, he designs a metal detector, a device directed solely to discovering metal objects.[13] Off he goes to the beach with his object (precious metals) and method (metal detector). He finds metal objects and only metal objects. He keeps the precious metals and discards the non-precious ones. There might be a rare piece of pottery or a plank from an old galleon buried in the sand, but our explorer will not find them, *because what he will and will not find has already been determined by his object and method.*

The same holds true for the sciences that we have considered. Each one of them will be limited by its object and method to what it will find in reality.

Physical sciences

The exact, physical sciences, for whose object the scientific method is specifically tailored, will almost exclusively discover the measurable aspects of bodies. Other bodily aspects fall outside that method's mode of investigation, just as non-metallic objects fall outside of the scanning ability of a metal detector.

The measurable aspects of bodies pertain directly to formal causality and indirectly to material causality. Those aspects, which are a matrix of quantities and qualities,[14] are forms inhering in matter, and are best analysed by the numbers resulting from measurement, which are then generalised into *formulas*. The measurements can often tell us something about the very nature of the bodies studied, that is, about what distinguishes them from all other beings, about their substantial principle. Scientists can thus use their measurements to say something about what physical bodies are in themselves. Through quantity, they discover 'the universal natures and inherent powers of things', facts that pertain to formal causality.[15]

Let us take an example from chemistry to illustrate. One major task of the first chemists was to figure out the most basic material components of the universe, what we now call the elements of the periodic table. These elements are the ultimate material bodies that can exist on their own and go into the making of compound material bodies.[16] To discover them, scientists had to painstakingly break down various compound bodies.

When the earliest chemists isolated a gas, they would then quantify it by *weighing* it. What they discovered when they did this for multiple gases is that elements, molecules, and compounds each have their own unique weight. This meant that the weight of a gas or a molecule could be used as a basis for making essential distinctions between them. Wallace explains this process of using quantities as a means for isolating different substances in nature as follows:

> One of the earliest procedures [of chemical experimentation and measurement] consisted in isolating various substances in the gaseous state, finding out ways they could be made to combine, and then measuring the precise weights and volumes that entered into combination. Repeated confirmation and analysis of such measurements led to the conclusions that *over ninety unit atomic weights are discoverable in nature, one for each chemical element.*[17]

Elements having weights that are discrete units apart indicated to chemists that there must be some material particle that gets added to lighter elements in order to make heavier elements. We now know that two particles of almost identical weight are involved in increasing the mass: protons and neutrons. The unique quantitative weights they give to the elements point to essential distinctions between those elements. Through the atomic masses of the periodic table, chemistry is supplying us, to a certain degree, with the formal and material causes of the elements.[18]

The efficient causality of inorganic bodies is more obscure than their formal causality. The reason is that they only act when acted upon, and so do not readily manifest their agency. They do not have self-movement, whereby they can exercise agency of themselves, only exercising agency when some body comes into contact with them. They do not act, they react. This is why '[r]eaction [] is more commonly used [] to describe the chemical phenomena associated with the elements'.[19]

Lions, for instance, both trod on earth and are supported by it, whereas atoms are just passive agents in a game of cosmic pinball. They have very little activity, which makes it difficult to speak about their causal powers. Physical forces such as gravity, even to this day, are not well understood.

This does not mean, however, that the scientific method is not able to provide valuable knowledge about the powers of elements as agents of efficient causality. When chemists of the 1800s began to compare the weights and properties of several elements, they discovered, to their amazement, that elements sharing a certain mathematical relationship in their quantitative weights also shared certain characteristic properties. Elements at intervals of eight would interact with other elements in the same ways. It was as if chemicals had octaves, like music! By making these discoveries, chemists were not just able to isolate the various elements—give formal and material causes—but they were also able to arrange the elements of the periodic table in columns according to their laws of interaction. Elements in one column have the same number of electrons in the outer orbits of their atoms, and interact well with atoms of other elements that will bring the number of electrons to a total of eight, which provides for the most stable bonds.[20] Explanations such as this concern the efficient causality of the elements, the way in which they exercise agency on one another.

What about final causality, we may ask? Does the scientific method provide knowledge of the final causes of inanimate bodies? Not directly. Final causes are not quantifiable, and so are not subject to measurement. For this reason, physical sciences such as chemistry will indicate purposes—the causal knowledge that final causes provide—only remotely, insofar as they are connected with other types of causality. When a chemist says, for instance, that water is a stable molecule binding together two atoms of hydrogen and one of oxygen, he is indicating an inherent tendency of water, and hence a purpose. Water inclines or is directed toward maintaining such a bond and no other, and so that is its purpose, in a certain sense. But there is not much useful information in such a statement. In the end, precious little knowledge can be gained of the final causes of the inorganic, for 'its intentions are not as discernible as they are in the plant and animal world'.[21]

Life sciences

We have just seen that the ease with which inanimate objects can be quantified makes their formal causes readily accessible to the human mind. Moreover, 'because of the preference for quantitative explanations, most demonstrations in science invoke formal causality of various types'.[22]

When we come to sciences that have animate beings as their object, however, we find that the formal and material causes are more elusive while the efficient and final causes are more apparent. Biological objects have a vast multiplicity of parts (material and formal cause) that all work together to perform a specific function (efficient and final cause), whereas chemical elements and molecules have a few parts that work together to perform an ambiguous function (efficient and final cause). For chemists, then, it is easy to examine the inorganic parts which are arranged in a certain form (material and formal cause), but difficult to say the nature and reason for their function (efficient and final cause). For biologists, on the other hand, it is easy to say the nature and purpose of a given biological function (efficient and final cause), but difficult to analyse the parts and their arrangement to know how they all work together to perform that function (material and formal cause).

Consider that if any one of us were asked the purpose of the parts of the eyeball, we could easily say what they do and why: eye parts are for sight (final cause), performing the activity of seeing (efficient cause). On the other hand, it would be quite difficult for us to say what each of those parts are (material cause) and how they all work together to serve that single purpose (formal cause).

This does not mean that life forms and their biological organs are completely impervious to quantification and analysis by the scientific method. On the contrary, that method has provided many amazing insights in our own day that have greatly enhanced our understanding of biological form, and I will consider some of its discoveries in chapters 10 and 11. The point here is the reinforcement of our realist principle 'different methods for different objects.' The scientific method, being one of observation and measurement, will be most successful with objects that lend themselves most readily to quantification, namely, inanimate objects. With objects less quantifiable, however, it will not be as successful, and a realist scientist will employ other methods more suited to those objects, in addition to the scientific method. Perhaps no greater epistemological sin can be committed than to use the same method to investigate all of reality, as if reality consists of an entirely homogeneous sameness that can be plumbed with a single methodology.

By way of summary of this analysis of the causal information that science provides, I must note the following:

- Science studies material bodies, which are best explored by heavy use of the senses.
- Science's particular method of observation and experimentation directly investigates the material and formal causality of bodies, and indirectly their efficient and final causality.
- The scientific method is successful in revealing material and formal causes to the degree that the bodies it studies are more material. Inorganic substances are more material than plants, which are more material than animals.
- The material and formal causes of inorganic substances are more evident than their efficient causality and final cause, while the efficient causality and final cause of organic substances are more evident than their material and formal causes. Thus, the scientific method has much more work to do exploring life forms and is less able to obtain complete results. For this reason, it has a greater need of being supplemented by other methods in the life sciences than it does in the physical sciences.

With regard to the certainty of science's conclusions, the same rules that I established in the last chapter apply. When science is able to discover a necessary fact in nature, one tied to the very nature of a thing, it is able to put forward a conclusion that is certain, and so scientific in the Aristotelian sense. For instance, 'water is a molecule composed of two hydrogen atoms and one oxygen atom' is a necessary proposition, because it is a statement of water's nature, something that cannot be otherwise, since water is water, wherever it exists.

When, however—and this is the case most of the time[23]—science is not able to demonstrate a necessary connection between cause and effect, but only provides a likely cause, then its conclusion has a probable certainty, and would be classed by Aristotle as *opinion*. An example would be the Big Bang Theory; generally, all of the conclusions of the historical sciences fall into this category.

Finally, when scientists use rhetoric to convince others of the truth of a proposition, their proposition has only the certainty of *belief*. When that is the only mode of argumentation they use to convince others, they are not really engaging in science, but pseudo-science. They are turning science into a political platform. Since the idea of the multiverse, by definition, cannot be supported by any empirical evidence (other universes being impossible to observe),[24] it would have this lowest grade of certainty.

In practice, scientists will need to employ all three modes of argumentation in order to communicate the truths they attain to others. They must, however, maintain each mode in its proper place, with rhetoric subordinate to dialectics, dialectics subordinate to demonstration, and demonstration resting on the self-evident propositions defended by realism. When this order is modified, communication becomes a tool for imposing one's views on another, not for leading another to objective truth.

Science's position on Mount Reality

Where, we may ask, is science's causal knowledge situated in reality's vertical causal hierarchy? Is it towards the lower part of Mount Reality, or is it located in its upper reaches?

One way of answering these questions is to see if science needs any other knowledge to be in place before it can go about its business of probing material bodies. If it relies on other knowledge, then that knowledge will be above it in reality's hierarchy.

Meanwhile, the knowledge that science establishes for other disciplines of thought will be below it in reality's hierarchy.

It turns out that science has to make several enormous assumptions before it can set out on the enterprise of quantifying matter:[25]

- The most basic assumption is that things exist.
- Another is that they can be accurately observed by the senses.
- A third is that they operate in such constant and consistent fashion that they may be said to obey laws.
- A fourth is that there is a universe, that is, a material world so unified and connected that laws which hold true for some material bodies will also hold true for the rest of them. Ultimately, it is such laws which scientists are after, rules or principles of nature which are operative always and everywhere in the universe.

We see from this that science needs realism, because it relies on concepts that only a realist epistemology can support, such as the concept of 'being'. 'Being' is not a quantity that can be measured and so will never be found by the scientific method. But if this concept, which derives from sense and intellect working together, does not correspond to reality, then nothing science says will correspond to reality, since every statement science makes relies on 'being'. For instance, the statement 'the acceleration at which bodies fall to the ground is 9.8 m/s^2' assumes that bodies and the ground are beings.

Science is also unable to establish that there is a universe, for it works by means of observation, and the universe—the totality of materially interacting things—cannot be observed. For one thing, it's way too big. For another, you would have to be able to step outside of it in order to observe it and while we say of some scientists that they live in their own universes, we are only speaking figuratively![26]

Because science must assume the truth of higher principles which are established by philosophy, its particular object is located on the lower end of Mount Reality. If it were in the higher reaches, it would provide fundamental principles to philosophy instead of receiving such principles from it. The truths of science depend on the truths of philosophy, in the same way that becoming (2nd act) depends upon being (1st act).

Before a human can walk (2nd act), he must first be a human (1st act). And so likewise, before reality can be measured (2nd act), it must first be real (1st act). Philosophy investigates reality as such, while science measures its physical aspects. If the philosophical truths about 'being' are not correct, then it is impossible for scientific truths about becoming to be so. In other words, there are certain metaphysical truths that must be in place before any scientific truth can exist.[27]

For instance, it is a law of physics that force equals mass multiplied by acceleration ($F = ma$). This is a quantitative mathematical description of the interaction of bodies, the impact that one body will make upon another. It is, however, a particular truth, holding true only for a specific class of beings, and expressing only a limited portion of the intelligibility of material bodies. It leaves room for a broader investigation and, more importantly, takes for granted higher truths which are outside of its scope. In other words, the formula takes as a given that bodies exist, leaving the establishment of that fact to a body of knowledge with greater scope. In this sense, the truths of science are contained within the truths of philosophy. Rizzi expresses this by referring to philosophical truths as the 'science before science'.[28]

Science has all the say in the realm of material bodies, while in all other realms, it has nothing to say, leaving the discourse to other disciplines of knowledge, such as philosophy and religion. Life far exceeds the mechanical, but science does not. A sign of this is that the quantities so favoured by science only find expression in reasoned discourse, that is, through words, and so quantities depend on them. 'The understanding of quantities rests on non-quantitative propositions', as Jaki says.[29] Quantity is the language of science, but words are the language of human beings, and it is human beings who do science.

Science, then, depends on philosophy—not on any philosophy, but specifically on a realist philosophy, for only realism can establish the assumptions which make science a logically viable enterprise. A realist can account for the existence of things outside the mind by the innate abilities of sense and intellect to connect with reality. A realist can account for the existence of a universe by the intrinsic nature of matter, which makes all matter the same—matter must be extended in space and quantifiable to exist at all. A realist can account for the existence of natural laws by the proof of a First Lawgiver able to mandate those laws for the whole of the cosmos. All of these conclusions flow from the realist's initial confidence in senses and the intellect, while other epistemologies, in their rejection or attenuation of one or the other of our faculties, cannot logically uphold the assumptions of science. Science, then, is beholden to realism, not to mention God.

Philosophy

Before speaking about religion, I must first turn to philosophy. When we speak of a person's philosophy, we mean the single view from which he interprets all of reality. It is the synthesis of all that he has achieved, or at least thinks that he has achieved, by the working of his reasoning faculty. It is his wisdom.

An interesting psychological fact which our common experience teaches us is that every human being likes to see reality from a single unified view, from what can be called a 'metaphysics'. Even those who refuse metaphysics and try to debunk it, such as Nietzsche, have to form a metaphysics in order to do so, as he did by uniting all reality under the viewpoint of a 'will to power'. Darwin's metaphysics was the struggle for survival, Marx's was material production, and Descartes's was critical doubt. Each of them in turn eschewed metaphysics, yet could not resist forming one, because of the very nature of human reason. This is why Jaki states that 'the only way to avoid philosophy is to say nothing'.[30]

Aristotle, in his turn, remarks in his *Protrepticus* that everyone should philosophise. For whether we wish to or not, we will seek to act from a unified set of principles, and it is much better if we do so after having reflected upon those principles and chosen them carefully by a process of reasoning, rather than having had them insinuate themselves into our lives willy-nilly. This is precisely what I have attempted to do in the first two chapters, by carefully choosing a philosophical mindset as being the best and then pursuing its principles to their logical conclusions.

Scientists look for the *immediate* causes of a given phenomenon, ones that can be inferred directly from sense data. Philosophers, on the other hand, look for reality's ultimate causes: material, formal, efficient, and final causes—all of them. For instance, with respect to the reality 'life', the philosopher wants to know:

- what the ultimate components of life are (material cause)
- what the essence or nature of life is (formal cause)
- what ultimately makes life (efficient cause)
- what the ultimate purpose of life is (final cause)

Think of a teacher writing on a chalkboard in the act of teaching. The scientist needs to explain to us how chalk interacts with slate. The chalk is the immediate cause of the white trace appearing on the chalkboard. Soft calcium silicate (chalk's chemical composition) embeds itself into hard blackboard slate when pressure is applied. That is how those two bodies interact.

The philosopher, on the other hand, seeks the ultimate causes of teaching. What is its nature? Why does it take place? What does it produce? The answers to these questions cannot be provided by observation and experiment, but rather are found at the level of abstract ideas.

The philosopher obviously must trust and make use of his senses, for 'philosophical questions are certainly concerned with the everyday things that are before our very eyes'.[31] However, he quickly leaves sense data behind, as they only take him one step up the causal mountain, and there are many more to be mounted. From there, he uses careful reasoning processes within the confines of his intellect, such as those we pursued in the last chapter. As we saw then, philosophy relies much more on the intellect than the senses.

Philosophy, in this book, is being used to judge the relationship between religion and science. The reason is that 'both science and religion are governed by philosophy'.[32] I said in chapter 1 that our judgement is the ultimate determinant for our decision as to what is true and false.[33] Since our philosophy determines the way we see reality as such, it affects each judgement that we make about reality. Thus, our philosophy has a say in everything in our life.

The way in which a person's philosophy is formed varies greatly. Sometimes, his religion dictates his perception of the whole of reality (religion → philosophy). At other times, he forms a philosophy by means of reason alone, and then goes on to construct a religion based on that philosophy (reason → philosophy → religion). Most often, a person's upbringing and the spirit of his age have the greatest influence on his worldview.[34] Regardless, a person's worldview is his philosophy, and his philosophy determines his relationship to reality, when all is said and done.

We have already seen how a philosophy that is realist promotes religion. From the limitation of created effects, human reason, without supernatural assistance, infers necessarily the existence of God, for the existence of the things around us would be incomprehensible if there were no source of their existence at each moment, because they are clearly not self-existing. That being who has the infinite power required to make things be that have nothing of existence, we commonly call God.

All of this is strictly within the bounds of human reason and the domain of its highest natural pursuit, philosophy. In that realm, there is no need for authority, the mind alone sufficing to attain sure notions about God, when it adheres strictly to the laws of its own operation, that is, to logic. By a chain of powerful inferences that start with sense observation but then quickly retire into exclusively intellective reflection, the philosopher reaches the domain of primary efficient causality, there forming a coherent notion of reality as a whole. In achieving that causal climb, he is even referred to as a natural theologian, because he is at the intersection of reason and religion.

A person's philosophy or worldview determines his relationship to reality, his epistemological attitude, his method of discovery. We have embraced realism, being compelled to do so by reality itself, which, once properly understood, forced us into its arms. We have also seen the broad outlines of realism's metaphysics or view of the whole of reality, as well as its fruitfulness for the mind. In the next section of the book, we will consider how embracing or rejecting realism, likewise, determined the ability of past civilisations to attain knowledge of reality.

The domain of religion

Turning now to religion, we find that it occupies an entirely different realm of human thought than that of science, in all of the aspects which we considered. While science applies human reason to the witness of sense, religion applies human reason to the witness of authority; as science primarily investigates immediate material and efficient causes, religion primarily pursues ultimate final ones.

The reason for this differences lies in religion's specific object, which is remote from the physical bodies science considers. Religion seeks to provide an account of the ultimate meaning of the world in general and human beings in particular. For monotheistic religions, God is that ultimate meaning and so, for them, God is their object.

It is common today to perceive reason and religious belief as belonging to entirely different regions. Science is seen as establishing its viewpoint by means of empirical evidence and reason, while religion is regarded as requiring blind faith in its dogmas. In this scenario, science has reason as its tool, while religion has emotion. In other words, science is reasonable, while religion is irrational.

It is true that some religions appeal to personal feelings or religious experience to establish their value. They are generally referred to as *fideistic* religions, or ones where the intellect has no role to play in the act of faith. In terms of the Aristotelian categories of certitude, the 'dogmas' of such religions have only the certainty of belief, since the tools of rhetoric are the only ones used to argue their 'truth'. These religions are likely to come conflict with science, because their beliefs are held regardless of any empirical evidence to the contrary, reason not being accepted as having any say in the religious equation.

A realist judges the claims of this or that religion by the degree that it accords with reason. Recall that a person's attainment of any truth depends on the judgement of his intellect. Therefore, just as the scientist must use his judgement to interpret the reams of empirical data that his devices provide him, so too each individual must judge the claims of this or that religion whether they are reasonable.

To the degree that a religion demands blind faith, that is, unreasoning faith, to that degree it deserves the name of a cult. It would be unreasonable of God to provide us with reason as our highest faculty and then not appeal to that faculty in the communication of ultimate truths. An important test of every religion's reasonableness, then, is whether or not it holds that human reason plays a role in religious belief. A religion is credible to the degree that it can bridge reason and faith, without reducing any of reason's powers on the one hand or emptying faith of mystery on the other.

We have already seen that the powers of natural reason, unaided by God, can investigate God—to a degree. That particular area of realist philosophy which considers God—natural theology—provides rationally deduced truths that double as religious truths. These truths can be demonstrated scientifically and so have the highest degree of certitude.

A first key test of a religion's reasonableness is whether it accepts metaphysical proofs for the existence of God, such as those set forth in chapter 2, as having validity and providing certainty. There are several reasons why reasonable religion needs to uphold natural theology:

1. Only the metaphysical path to God's existence has an absolute objectivity. Other paths rely on one's trust in human authority speaking in the name of God or a personal religious experience or probabilistic proofs deriving from science.
2. A religion denying the validity of those proofs—and the reasoning that led to them—must maintain an idea of God that is different from the God that reality manifests and so an idea of God that is necessarily false.
3. A religion denying the existence of a point where reason and faith meet will necessarily separate them into mutually exclusive areas. The result is that reason will be seen to stand in one camp and faith in another camp, the camp of unreason.
4. Realist philosophy not only provides science with fundamental truths, but also religion, yet with this difference, that those fundamental truths for science are outside science's proper domain, at a higher level of Mount Reality, while the same truths are within the proper domain of religion, though located in religion's lowest region.

Religion's exclusive truths

Philosophy cannot provide all of religion's truths. If it could, the object of religion would fall completely within the domain of human reason. Humans would be able to know God completely, without there being any mysteries. In other words, humans would be God, since God would not be above them, but at their same level.

It should be clear that our discussion of God in the last chapter, difficult though it was, did not remove all possible questions about God. In a sense, it led to more questions: How does God create? How is it possible to encompass past, present, and future all at once? How is it possible to exist always without being created? These, and many more questions, we cannot possibly hope to answer.

Religions seek precisely to clear away some of the mist on the top of Mount Reality that still remains there even after philosophy has summitted it. They do so by means of the supernatural dogmas, which they claim God has communicated to certain members of the human race. These are mysteries which, by definition, can never be attained by mere reasoning from created effects. An example of such a dogma is the Christian belief that God created humans for a supernatural purpose, a purpose beyond our condition as human beings, namely, Heaven. This dogma is not included in the natural order and so humans need information from beyond that order to know that aspect of reality. Since we cannot obtain such information by our natural reasoning, we can only know about it through a revelation from a supernatural agent, and we cannot provide for it a philosophical proof, such as the one laid out in chapter 2 for God's existence.[35]

Though the supernatural truths cannot be established by arguments taken from the world around us, that does not mean that they are to be held on blind faith. On the contrary, reason has an important role to play. It must provide evidence, not that the religious dogma itself is true, but that the authority claiming to have a message from God is trustworthy. If the messenger is reliable, then so are the truths.

Allow me to use the religion most familiar to me, Catholicism, as an example. Books of Catholic apologetics try to convince their readers that the truths they propose are revealed by God. They do so by rational argumentation. Specifically, they set forth 'motives of credibility' or reasons to believe. Those reasons are calculated to convince prospective converts that the Church has its dogmas from God. They are meant to employ probabilistic argumentation in order to lead to a conclusion that, in Aristotle's certitude ranking, would be a well-founded opinion.

To show an instance of this religious way of appealing to reason, consider the dogma that Jesus Christ is God. The dogma cannot be proven directly by reason, as that would require some natural means to determine that a human soul was united with the divinity. Such a hypostatic union (the union of two natures in one person) is accomplished by a power and operation that is wholly mysterious for us, being beyond all of our experience, and escaping our powers of investigation.[36] As a result, only indirect indications may be offered for Christ's divinity. For the rational Christian, those credibilities, taken as a cumulative whole, lead one to conclude that Jesus Christ is God. Examples of these motives of credibility are the following:

- The innumerable miracles Christ worked during His public life, which
    - were of all different classes
    - were supernatural
    - were worked to establish His divinity, and
    - are historically certain
- the sublimity of His life and teaching
- His Resurrection from the dead
- the many prophecies of the two millennia preceding His birth which He fulfilled, and the many prophecies of His own which came true both in His own lifetime and afterwards
- the propagation, holiness, fruitfulness, unity, and stability of the Church which He founded.

The collective body of these evidences, which are within the scope of human reason as historical facts, point overwhelmingly to something beyond the human. Since no direct proof is possible, reason as such is not forced but is only 'motivated' to believe and so room is left for an act of faith. Because the evidence is so striking, however, an untoward will must intervene for assent of judgement to that evidence to be refused.

Needless to say, apologetics is outside the scope of this discussion, but the example is meant to illustrate the epistemological territory of reliable religion. Religions must be realist, in the sense that they must provide to the human intellect all of the resources necessary to arrive at the conclusion—beyond a reasonable doubt—that a certain authority claiming to be God or speaking in the name of God is perfectly trustworthy. Here we have a second key to test the reasonableness of a religion, namely whether it provides motives of credibility in support of its supernatural dogmas.

To sum up, religion, by definition, concerns the ultimate meaning of all things. The fundamental truth of the existence of God can be attained by reason alone. Purely supernatural truths, however, can only come to us from powers beyond this earth, and thus they are believed on the authority of one communicating them. Realist religions will firstly support realist metaphysical proofs for God's existence and secondly will argue rationally that their supernatural dogmas have truly come from God. Idealist religions, on the other hand, will demand blind faith when reason presents solid empirical or philosophical evidence that is contrary to their dogmas.

Distinguishing religion and science

By distinguishing carefully the domains of religion and science, I have attempted to show that, by definition, there is no conflict between the two. Religion primarily communicates ultimate final causes while science treats of immediate material, formal and efficient causes. Their causal territory being at two different levels of Mount Reality does not just mean that they do not come into conflict. It also means that they are—or at least should be—in harmony, for the simple reason that nothing that actually exists in reality can come into logical contradiction with anything else that actually exists. If there is such a contradiction in our minds, it is not because reality is at fault, but because our knowledge of it is deficient.

How is it that religion and science have come into such conflict in our day and age? The reason is that, having rejected realism for centuries now, the Western world no longer recognises the careful distinctions I have made as holding any validity.

Many modern day scientists, for example, only accept two of the causes—material and efficient causes—as providing any real knowledge. The reason is that those causes are manifest to the senses, upon which the scientific method relies so heavily. Formal and final causes, on the other hand, are inaccessible to the senses and can be known by the intellect alone. Making a metaphysics out of their method, empiricists conclude that such causes—along with anything else their method does not reveal—do not exist. In this universe, they say, there are no immaterial forms nor any purpose above matter. By this denial of the immaterial, they deprive religion of its own proper domain of knowledge. In the third section of this book, we will see how scientists began their attack on the immaterial in the seventeenth century (chapter 8), an attack which has developed up to the present day, when many scientists claim that the universe (chapter 9), life (chapter 10), and the human species (chapter 11) are all without form and purpose.

On the other side, there are some idealist religious believers who undermine the validity of scientific inquiry, saying that creatures do not have any causal power proper to themselves. They reject the evidence of material and efficient causation that comes to our senses on a constant basis, trumping that evidence with faith propositions. In the second section of this book, we will see religious pagans (chapter 4), Muslims and Catholics (chapter 6), as well as Protestants (chapter 7) falling into greater or lesser degrees of this occasionalism.

We can thus reduce the conflict between religion and science to this: *science destroys religion when it says that there is no such*

Three Knowledges

thing as formal and final causes, making all causality exclusively matter's domain; religion rules out science when it denies to creatures the material and efficient causality that they evince, making all causality exclusively God's domain. This is a conflict between domains of knowledge, a teleological tiff, a wrangle of reason, a metaphysical melee, a philosophical fracas. One side or the other reduces reality, denying the existence of the other side's domain of knowledge. A false epistemology is adopted and used as a cudgel to beat out of existence the opposing study's domain. Believers become idealists, denying the senses, while scientists become empiricists, denying the intellect. Above the two stands the realist, the one who starts by respecting reality and refusing to reduce it, even when the going gets tough, when difficult thinking is needed to maintain all of the causes and keep them in their proper positions. Neither material nor final causes are to be shouted out of existence, due to the simple fact that reality proclaims them so loudly.

REALISTS
God causes being.
Creatures cause becoming.

IDEALIST BELIEVERS
Only God causes.

Simple Epistedometer

EMPIRICIST SCIENTISTS
Only creatures cause.

The overall scuffle can be represented by a simple epistedometer, which focuses on one's conception of primary and secondary causality. Religionists destroying science will assign both causalities to God, while scientists destroying religion will assign both to creatures.

Better yet, however, is for us to fit out an epistedometer in greater detail, anticipating the attacks of religion on science and science on religion. Anti-religion scientists will adopt an empiricism which, by overemphasising the senses and material causes, will necessarily reduce the intellect along with formal and final causes. Anti-science religionists will adopt an idealism which, by overemphasising intellect along with formal and final causes, will necessarily reduce the senses and the material and efficient causes they reveal. The mildest form of either type of reductionist ignores the causes in question; worse than this is positively doubting the existence of those causes; and worst of all is denying them.

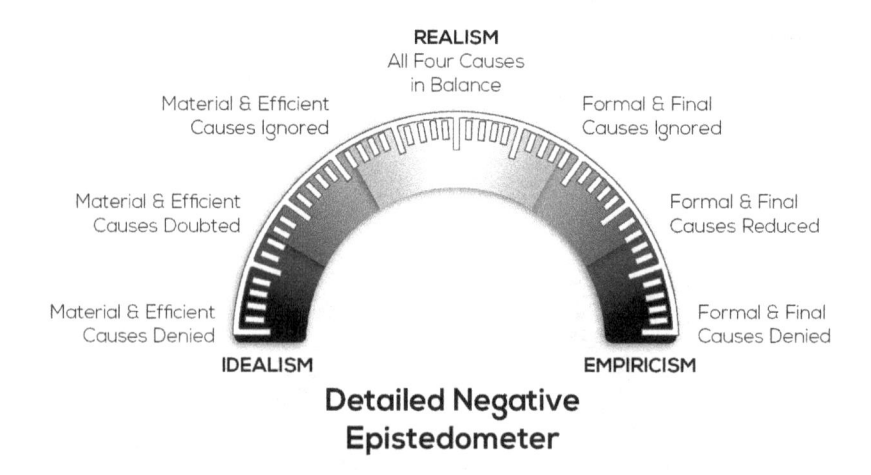

REALISM
All Four Causes in Balance

Material & Efficient Causes Ignored

Formal & Final Causes Ignored

Material & Efficient Causes Doubted

Formal & Final Causes Reduced

Material & Efficient Causes Denied

Formal & Final Causes Denied

IDEALISM

EMPIRICISM

Detailed Negative Epistedometer

This detailed epistedometer focuses on the *negative* aspects of idealism and empiricism, the way in which they *deny* aspects of reality and our knowledge. An epistedometer can also be constructed that focuses on the *positive* aspects of those false epistemologies, or the *affirmations* that they make about their favourite causes. At the mildest stage, they will be only methodological empiricists or idealists, wherein they exclusively look for and consider in reality the two causes that they favour. More dedicated empiricists and idealists will state that their two favourite causes alone provide true knowledge, while the most ardent adherents will state that only those two causes exist.

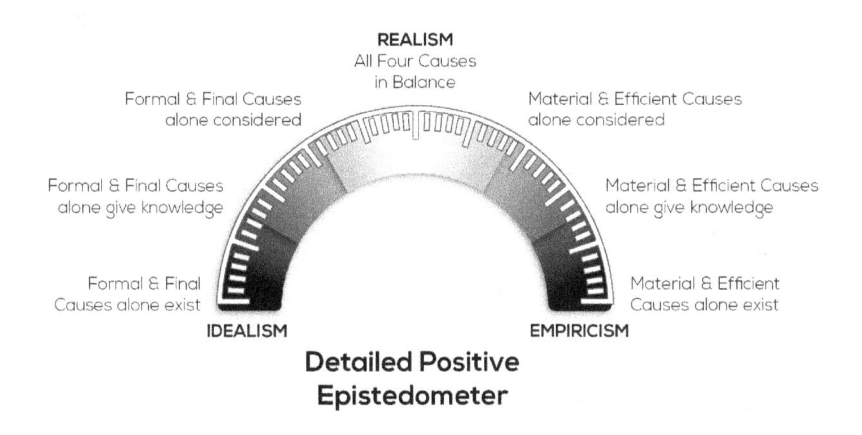

REALISM
All Four Causes in Balance

Formal & Final Causes alone considered

Material & Efficient Causes alone considered

Formal & Final Causes alone give knowledge

Material & Efficient Causes alone give knowledge

Formal & Final Causes alone exist

Material & Efficient Causes alone exist

IDEALISM　　　　**EMPIRICISM**

Detailed Positive Epistedometer

What about miracles?

No discussion of the relationship between religion and science is complete unless it includes the topic of miracles, that is, the 'wonders performed by supernatural power as signs of some special mission or gift and explicitly ascribed to God'.[37] It is clear that, if there be a First Cause of the universe, existing outside of it and giving it to exist, then that First Cause has the power to work miracles, for working a miracle demands less power than sustaining the universe. Jaki cites the unlikely figures of John Stuart Mill and Somerset Maugham as stating it to be merely logical to admit the possibility of miracles if you admit the existence of God.[38]

A miracle by definition is outside of the scope of science. The reason is that science is only able to discover secondary causes of given effects. In the case of a miracle, however, the First Cause is altering His typical causation of the universe, and therefore it is impossible and wrong to say that some natural cause is responsible.

Thus, it must be granted up front that miracles stymie science. The latter restricts itself to finding the immediate causes of given effects. It seeks only secondary causes, and the activity of the First Cause is beyond its scope. When God works a miracle, then, the causes accessible to the scientific method are not in play and science is unable to assign a cause to the activity.

This does not mean, however, that God changes or breaks the laws of nature when He works a miracle.[39] From a realist's perspective, it is even impossible for God to do so. Recall from the last chapter that God, as First Cause of all beings, must provide existence for them in all four areas of causality—material, formal, efficient, and final. Of those four, the formal cause is the equivalent of the 'law of nature', God making things to exist with a certain fixed nature that *goes with* their very being. Furthermore, because a thing's nature is an aspect of the very being of a thing, there is only one way to change that nature: annihilation. If the nature of a thing changes, it is a different being. Thus, the only way for God to change the laws of a given nature would be to annihilate it and re-create it with a different nature. Since this is not a real changing of the laws of nature, realists would claim that, technically, God cannot change nature's laws.

Would God annihilate anything that He has created? Aquinas, for one, answers in the negative, saying that God works no miracles by annihilation.[40] The whole purpose of a miracle is to manifest God's power and goodness, he argues. Annihilation, however, would be a manifestation of weakness, not of power. It takes strength to preserve a creature in existence, but letting it fade back into nothing would seem to indicate a loss of power.

It is more correct, then, to say that God *suspends* the laws of nature when He works a miracle,[41] in that the normal workings of nature do not manifest themselves—not because they have been changed, but because they have been prevented from acting. At the same time God suspends natural laws, He produces an extraordinary effect by means of direct creation or by using a creature already existing as an instrument of His power. Thus, when Jesus cries out, 'Lazarus, come forth', the normal corruptive processes eating away at Lazarus's body are suspended and God communicates to the voice of the God-man the power to restore life to that same body. The course of nature has been changed, but the laws of nature have not been changed. Lazarus's body would have rotted away as normal, if a divine agent had not prevented it from doing so. Similarly, a bullet will kill me when I am shot, unless I am being protected by a bullet-proof vest. The difference is that I understand when and how a bullet-proof vest protects from a gunshot wound, but I do not understand when or how God raises a dead body to life.

What can the human mind do when faced with a suspension of the laws of nature? It certainly does not have to stop thinking, for miracles, while eliminating scientific knowledge, do not eliminate knowledge as such. On the contrary, miracles rely upon the consistency of nature and make an appeal to knowledge. An article in *The Catholic Encyclopedia* explains this as follows:

> A miracle is a fact in material creation, and falls under the observation of the senses or comes to us through testimony, like any natural fact. Its miraculous character is known:
>
> from positive knowledge of natural forces, for example, the law of gravity
>
> from our positive knowledge of the limits of natural forces. Thus, we may not know the strength of a man, but we do know that he cannot by himself move a mountain ... As soon as we have reason to suspect that any event, however uncommon or rare it appear, may arise from natural causes

or be conformable to the usual course of nature, we immediately lose the conviction of its being a miracle. A miracle is a manifestation of God's power; so long as this is not clear, we should reject it as such.[42]

On the one hand, if God only worked miracles, then there would be no consistent laws of nature and so no science. On the other hand, if God never worked miracles, men would easily lose sight of God and fall into unbelief. The *occasionalist* subscribes to the first scenario, holding God to be the only agent in the universe; the *empiricist* subscribes to the second, holding there to be no God and hence no miracles.

As realists, we must again hold a middle ground: miracles are certainly possible and therefore are to be subject to our reasoning judgement, just as the rest of reality. When reliable evidence from outside of us, provided by the senses, the intellect, or authority, testifies to the existence of a miracle, then that evidence must be accepted. When, on the other hand, the evidence is insufficient, the effect is not to be ascribed to God's direct power, but to merely natural causes.

Table 3.2 *Three views on miracles*

Miracles in the universe	Miracles occur?	Natural events occur?	Explanation
Occasionalists	Yes	No	Everything is a miracle.
Realists	Yes	Yes	Great consistency in nature, but miracles sometimes occur.
Materialists	No	Yes	There is only consistency in nature; miracles never occur.

The Catholic Church is known to be extremely cautious in declaring claimed miracles authentic. Fr Jaki, in his introduction to a Nobel Prize winning surgeon's account of a miracle the surgeon witnessed at Lourdes, indicates how few of those miracles have been approved by the Church:

> It is a well known fact that out of the hundreds of startling cures, documented in impressive dossiers, the International Medical Commission judged only about a hundred to be

medically unexplainable. Of these only about a half have so far been declared by Church authorities to be miracles.[43]

The reason for the hesitation is twofold:

- when believers are too credulous and assign false causes to what can be explained by merely natural effects, they expose their belief to ridicule
- when God is portrayed as working miracles constantly and arbitrarily, He is easily seen as acting without wisdom and as preventing men from understanding His own creation.

Before closing, I must reiterate that belief in the existence of God is the only logical support that can be given to a nature acting consistently, and a reality in which all natural bodies obey the same set of laws. Thus, those wishing to exclude the possibility of miracles by rejecting God must also reject the intellectual foundations of science.

Section summary (chapters 1–3)

In this first section, three major questions have been addressed:

1. How do we know?
2. What do we know in general?
3. What do we know through religion and science?

The answer to the first question is clear: we know as realists. This means primarily that our knowledge is dependent on reality, and we learn from it by means of both our knowing faculties, the senses of our body and the intellect of our soul. The most immediate evidence for realism is the way we live our lives. We constantly interact with reality by a symbiotic use of our senses and intellect, and we find that we could not live otherwise, even if we tried.

When we investigate our knowing closely, we find that we cannot account for our most basic notion, that of 'being', unless we use the principles of realism. The concept of 'being' cannot be taught and so must be formed by the intellect acting on sense data.

Nor can we account for our human communication unless we embrace realism. All rational speech assumes that sense really detects spoken sounds and intellect thinks of concepts about reality from those spoken sounds.

Only realism, then, can provide a coherent view of human knowledge and communication. These considerations lead reasonable persons to choose 'realism' as their epistemology. Those opting for another epistemology must necessarily disconnect themselves from their own humanity and put on an artificial and restrictive relationship to reality.

When a realist takes a good look at reality in order to find the answer to the second question, what we know, he finds that reality presents itself to his human mode of knowing as being ultimately comprised of four aspects, which must all be assigned to beings of the cosmos to account for their very existence: a body (material cause), an essence (formal cause), a maker (efficient cause), and a purpose (final cause). Thus, a table (formal cause) is made by a carpenter (efficient cause) out of wood (material cause) to provide a flat surface for dining (final cause).

These four causes can be approached from two different angles, namely, insofar as they are realised in a being or beings changing from one moment to the next (accidentally ordered causality), or insofar as they are realised in a single being to constitute it at each moment (essentially ordered causality). If a person fixes his intellectual gaze on the latter aspect and tries to discover what is ultimately needed to constitute a being, by ascending higher in the chain of causality, he realises that there must be some self-existing source of existence providing existence for everything in the contingent universe at every moment for things to exist at all. This First Cause of existence has a domain of causality exclusively His own, that of creating. His causality founds the causality of creatures, secondary causality, 'creaturing', a causality that enables humans to learn from the universe and do science.

Moving on to the third question, the respective domains of religion and science, we found that realism divides disciplines of knowledge according to the different objects which are presented to the mind by reality, and determines the methods appropriate to the disciplines based on those objects.

Scientists are those people who specialise in investigating the material composition of bodies and the laws of their interaction. Meanwhile, religionists are those who accept the testimony of some authority as providing an accurate account of the ultimate meaning of the universe and human existence. Science relies on realism, because it must assume the existence of reality and a consistent universe in order to pursue its object. These assumptions are provided coherent rational support by the natural theology which directly follows from realism. Religion also needs realism, because religion needs to be reasonable. Religion can only be reasonable if it accepts the truths of natural theology which realism argues, and seeks to convince the intellectual judgement of prospective believers of its supernatural dogmas by rational arguments.

Religion and science come into conflict only when their practitioners step away from realism. They can do this by refusing to acknowledge causes outside those specific to their domain of knowledge. Religion-reducing scientist empiricists can tend to the denial of the causes closest to the immaterial and the intellect, formal and final causes. Science-slamming religionists, on the other hand, can tend to the denial of the causes closest to matter and the senses, material and efficient causes.

By embracing realism, we obtain a worldview that is immediately and indubitably evident in the lived experience we all share. We possess a most satisfactory vision of the universe, one that harmonises the natural and supernatural orders, and so also science and religion as bodies of knowledge. We relate to reality's richness without reducing it by an arbitrary epistemological fiat.

The claim that realism alone is reasonable and able to maintain peace between science and religion, however, needs to be supported by something more than abstract arguments. We must have concrete examples as well. For these, we must turn to human history. We now have the tools necessary to evaluate the annals of human thought from a particular perspective: did the presence or absence of realism in the mentality of past peoples factor into their ability to be reasonable, to know reality, to keep religion without impeding science or science without impeding religion? Yes, of course it did. Let us turn first to religions of the world in section two to see that such was the case, and then to modern science in section three to see the same.

Notes

[1] J. Wells, *The Politically Incorrect Guide to Darwinism and Intelligent Design* (Washington DC: Regnery Publishing, 2006), p. 156.
[2] E. Gilson, *Methodical Realism* (San Francisco: Ignatius Press, 2011), p. 104. The realist doctrine on the perception of the object as the first step of all knowing, as expressed by Gilson, was wholly embraced by Fr Jaki. See H. Relja, *Il Realismo di S. L. Jaki* (Rome: Ateneo Pontificio Regina Apostolorum, 2008), chapter 3.
[3] *Ibid.*
[4] See Aristotle, *Metaphysics*, 995a10–20.
[5] 71b10–15.
[6] Definition taken from the New Oxford American Dictionary (Oxford University Press, Inc., 2005). The word 'scientist' did not appear until 1833. See J. Hannam, *The Genesis of Science* (Washington, DC: Regnery Publishing, 2011), p. 346.
[7] See S. Jaki, *Means to Message* (Grand Rapids, Michigan: William Eerdmans Publishing Company, 1999), p. 146.
[8] *In Met.*, paragraph 892; see also ST, III, q.77, a.2.
[9] *The First Philosophers* (Oxford University Press, 2000), p. xvii, emphasis added.
[10] *Questions on Science and Religion* (Pinckney, Michigan: Real View Books, 2004), p. 12. H. Relja notes Jaki's departure from realism in his reduction of science to the study of quantities. See *Il Realismo di S. L. Jaki*, pp. 87–91.
[11] A. Rizzi, *The Science before Science* (Baton Rouge: IAP Press, 2004), pp. 193–194.
[12] W. Wallace, *The Modeling of Nature* (Washington, DC: The Catholic University of America Press, 1996), p. 226.
[13] This example is adapted from E. Feser, *Neo-Scholastic Essays* (South Bend,

Indiana: St. Augustine's Press, 2015), p. 22.
14 On the fact that measurements are the quantification of the qualities of bodies, see H. Relja, *Il Realismo*, pp. 52–57.
15 E. Feser, *Neo-Scholastic Essays*, p. 82.
16 See Aristotle, *Metaphysics*, 1014a26.
17 *The Modeling of Nature*, p. 38, emphasis added.
18 For a defence of the formal distinction between molecules, see D. Oderberg, *Real Essentialism* (New York: Routledge, 2007), pp.89–90. See also W. Wallace, *The Modeling of Nature*, pp. 45–49.
19 W. Wallace, *The Modeling of Nature*, p. 52.
20 See B. Wiker and J. Witt, *A Meaningful World* (Downers Grove, Illinois: IVP Academic, 2006), pp. 136–144.
21 W. Wallace, *The Modeling of Nature*, p. 53.
22 *Ibid.*, p. 296.
23 See *Ibid.*, p. 282.
24 M. Heller notes in his *Ultimate Explanations of the Universe* (Heidelberg: Springer-Verlag, 2009), p. 121, '[W]e can hardly call a concept "strictly scientific" which conjures up so many existences (universes) beyond the possibility of any experimental verification whatsoever.'
25 For a technical treatment of science's suppositions, see W. Wallace, The Modeling of Nature, pp. 298–299.
26 See S. Jaki, *Means to Message*, pp. 143–148.
27 'Intricate patterns, the business of science, must, in order to exist, inhere in beings or things that exist', says S. Jaki in *The Savior of Science* (Port Huron, Michigan: Real View Books, 2006), p. 87.
28 A. Rizzi, *The Science before Science*, pp. 27–30 and passim.
29 Cited in S. Trasancos, *Science Was Born of Christianity* (The Habitation of Chimham Publishing Co., 2014), p. 34.
30 *Questions on Science and Religion* (Pinckney, Michigan: Real View Books, 2004), p. 7.
31 J. Pieper, *Leisure, the Basis of Culture* (Indianapolis: Liberty Fund, 1952), p. 99.
32 S. Jaki, *A Mind's Matter* (Grand Rapids, Michigan: William Eerdmans Publishing Company, 2002), p. 209.
33 See p. 9.
34 James Hannam correctly remarks in his *The Genesis of Science* (Washington, DC: Regnery Publishing, 2011), p. 26: '[Our worldview] is often deep-seated, almost unconcious, and we rarely think about it. We find it hard to imagine that the world could function in any other way and feel that the ideas we have learned to believe are, in some sense, self-evident.'

[35] See pp. 50–52.
[36] See Aquinas, *De rationibus fidei*, chapter 6; Gregory the Great, *Forty Gospel Homilies* (Kalamazoo, Michigan: Cistercian Publications, 1990), p. 25; John Chrysostom, *Homilies on First Corinthians*, Homily XXXIV, 2.
[37] J. Driscoll, 'Miracle' in *Catholic Encyclopedia* (New York: The Encyclopedia Press, Inc., 1913), vol. X, p. 338.
[38] S. Jaki, *Means to Message*, pp. 181, 193.
[39] See Aquinas, ST, I, q.105, a.6.
[40] ST, I, q.104, a.4.
[41] See D. Oderberg, *Real Essentialism*, p. 149.
[42] J. Driscoll, 'Miracle' in *Catholic Encyclopedia* (New York: The Encyclopedia Press, Inc., 1913), vol. X, pp. 339–340.
[43] *The Voyage to Lourdes* (Sterling Heights, Michigan: Real View Books, 2007), p. 18. See also S. Jaki, *Means to Message*, p. 188.

II Religion

4 PAGAN PANTHEISM

All great cultures that witnessed a stillbirth of science ... have one major feature in common. They were all dominated by a pantheistic concept of the universe going through eternal cycles.

Fr Stanley Jaki

PERHAPS THE MOST famed physician of ancient times, aside from Hippocrates, was Galen of Pergamon. Born in the second century AD, he travelled widely throughout the Roman Empire to amass ideas and techniques with respect to medical practice. His careful dissection of monkeys and pigs led him to formulate many theories about the workings of physiological systems. For instance, his idea that the brain controls the motions of the muscles via the nervous system is still accepted to this day.

At least one of his ideas, however, was dead wrong. It concerned the circulatory system, which effectively he did not believe was circulatory. For him, the heart produced a bright, arterial blood, while the liver produced a dark, venous blood, after which both types took a one-way trip to the organs of the body, where the blood was consumed. Thus, for Galen, the heart and the liver were continually generating anew all of the blood needed for the body. By and large, this idea was accepted in the West... for the next 1500 years.

It was not until the Englishman William Harvey published a 72 page work at an annual book fair in Frankfurt in 1628 that Galen's theory was overturned. Harvey's argument was a quantitative one. He estimated certain key measurements of the heart's processes to see how much blood passes through the heart and thus how much blood the body would have to produce in one day if it were making blood anew. He kept his estimates purposely low, knowing that far too much blood would still be required with lower numbers.

Harvey put his low estimate of the human heart's capacity at 1.5 imperial ounces of blood [43ml], with 1/8 of the blood being expelled with each of its beats, or 1/6 ounce [4.7ml]. Then, given a low estimate of 1000 heart beats every half hour, a total of 10 pounds, 6 ounces of blood passes through the heart every thirty minutes.

The problem this analysis presents for Galen's theory is that 'more blood passes through the heart in consequence of its action, than can be supplied by the whole of the ingesta [our food intake]'.[1] Clearly, the great quantity of blood passing through the heart cannot be new blood continually produced by the body.

Harvey's simple calculation led him to confirm by experimentation his own theory, namely that blood both flows from the heart and back to it. Blood is not continually generated anew, but rather is recycled by moving throughout the body in a circle.[2]

After the fact, Harvey's observations seem obvious. Yet, the historical record testifies that it took a millennium and a half for Galen's theory to be overthrown by quantitative analysis. Why such a long time, we may ask? Why didn't others before Harvey include experimental measurement in their investigation of the body's processes?

The answer lies in the long-term acceptance of Aristotle's physical science, a science of which today 'hardly a page can be salvaged'.[3] That science held, on principle, that the properties of bodies are best known and explained by final causes, not material ones. As a result, physicists who followed Aristotle—and they were many throughout history—did not look to quantify physical bodies in order to learn their properties.

This second section of the book will consider historical examples of idealist philosophies and religions which impeded scientific progress, and of realist philosophies and religions which aided that progress. We begin in this chapter by considering pre-Christian cultures.

Science requirements

The further we go back in the past, the more the paper trail of human history thins out, and so the more difficult it becomes to assess the thinking of this or that people. Thankfully, however, the writings left by ancient civilisations are quite sufficient to motivate an Everest-like paper mountain of scholarly discussion, and so also to keep said scholars gainfully employed.

What concerns us most here is what information can be drawn from ancient documents that will enable us to discern the *worldview* that governed each of the ancient cultures. Ultimately, that worldview dictated what past peoples would produce in their civilisation and specifically what intellectual achievements they would attain.

What we know for certain is that ancient worldviews were not driven by empirical science, as is the case with the overall modern worldview. Rather, religion almost always dictated the way reality was seen. When it wasn't religion, it was philosophy, not science.

Jaki considers several ancient civilisations with great thoroughness in his *Science and Creation*.[4] His purpose is to discover what effect ancient religions had on scientific pursuits. In his assessment of the scientific achievements of past cultures, he makes a tally of their individual inventions. At the same time, he indicates that discoveries of natural secrets do not qualify for science, at least in the sense in which he takes science. For him, science proper is physical science, the quantitative study of objects in motion, and thus to evaluate a culture's science is the same as to evaluate its ability to quantify motion, that is, the ability to find natural *laws*, not natural *secrets*.

This is the approach that I are taking here. I want to see to what degree the worldview of ancient cultures led to establishing scientific methodology on a firm theoretical basis or led away from it. By doing so, I will easily be able to note what epistemology was involved and the role it played.

When considering the documents left by the Indians, the Chinese, the Mayans, the Incans, the Egyptians, the Babylonians, and so on, Jaki kept running across two common characteristics of pre-Christian religions, besides Judaism. One was a belief in pantheism, and the other was a belief in eternal cycles. These two ideas may be explained as follows:

- **Pantheism**—the universe is the ultimate reality. The universe is not a caused fact, an effect, but an uncaused entity. It is not to be explained, but taken for granted. I note with Maritain:

   > For a system to be pantheistic, it need not explicitly identify God and creatures (very few pantheists fulfil this condition). It is sufficient that its teachings are logically irreconcilable with an absolute distinction between God and creatures.[5]

- **Cycles**—the universe has a natural rhythm that repeats itself over extreme periods of time, and the cycle goes on forever. Humans themselves are part of the cycle. They die and are reborn forever in various forms, being bound to live the same events over and over again.

Among those ancient pantheists, there were general two intellectual types: the 'crass' and the 'elaborate' pantheists. The crass pantheist was not able to reason to an ultimate first principle of the universe; the elaborate was, but still associated that first principle with the universe itself. The crass doubted senses and intellect, slipped into various degrees of idealism and materialism, and was unable to embark on the search for causal knowledge; the elaborate was able to adopt some form of epistemological realism, and used it to attain some causal knowledge. Neither did exact science.

Let us consider these two religious worldviews and their respective impact on intellectual endeavour.

Crass pantheism

We saw back in chapter two the full panorama of human pursuit of knowledge, starting with the data of sense, seeking causes for change over time in the horizontal line of accidental causality, then rising higher to consider the essential causes of beings, and finally ascending to a first transcendent cause of existence. If these are as three stages in the progress of human thought, then the crass pantheists only reached the first stage.

It is very difficult to abstract from life in the twenty-first century, making our habitual notions recede, setting to the side our technological way of life, and projecting our imagination and ourselves into the far distant past. Above all here, we must try to consider what it would be like not to have ready-made answers to the ultimate questions about life and ponder what manner of metaphysics we ourselves would construct if we had to do everything 'from scratch'.

Judging by the historical record, it seems that reality's most imposing fact for one starting at a sort of intellectual ground zero is that of change. All ancient cultures were struck by the kaleidoscope of variation in real time presented by the senses. Considering sense evidence alone, everything seems to be inconstant and fleeting. No matter what we look at in one moment, it will not be completely the same the next moment. The mind, however, wants knowledge that is constant, knowledge whose truth remains true not for a few seconds or a few days, but for as long as possible, and even forever.

The senses make prominent display of reality's passing aspect, revealing motion, while leaving the intellect to grasp the unchanging essences underlying that motion. Thus, if a mind focuses solely on the data of sense, reality takes on an ephemeral and illusory cast. Resting there, a person will start to doubt both reality's reliability and the intellect's ability to know it.

At the same time, there is one aspect of nature's spectacle that seems to have imposed itself on ancient peoples as being more than mere chaos, and this is its patterns of cycles. As Dauvillier notes: 'All the phenomena that we observe are cyclical, from the meteorological, biological, geochemical cycles to the geological cycles'.[6] The recurrence of the seasons, the rising and the setting of the sun, the waxing and waning of the moon, the rotations of the heavens, the births and deaths of organic life, are all so many evidences that circular patterns are built into the very fabric of reality. Here we have something constant which the intellect can latch onto.

If the mind makes this observation and goes no further, then cyclical change does not present itself as an *aspect* of reality, but as the *whole* of reality. A key characteristic of circles is that they participate in the infinite. They have no edges, no beginning and no end. To illustrate this, imagine someone driving around a perfectly circular track at a constant speed, the wheels always turned to the same angle. Under these conditions, the driver can go around the track forever without a single change (ignoring friction and fuel consumption). And so, if the heavens are turning around in circles, and Earth processes are going around in circles, then perhaps the heavens and the Earth are eternal. Such was the inference of the pantheists.

There is a true premise behind this false conclusion, namely the idea that *nothing comes from nothing*. If at any point nothing whatsoever existed, then nothing would exist today. Thus, there must be something that has always existed if we are to account for anything existing at this moment. What is that thing that has always existed? The simplest and most straightforward answer is to say that, since natural processes seem to go in cycles, and cyclic things can go on forever, it is the universe itself that is eternal. This is a process of reasoning in the horizontal chain of causality, reaching back in time to find some explanation for the series of events that has led to the present moment.

It seems that this notion of an eternal cyclic history to the universe was adopted by all non-Jewish, pre-Christian societies, whereas the idea of a linear history of the universe, with beginning, middle, and end, was unknown in the ancient world among those not following Moses' religion.

When this crass pantheism becomes the master thought of a civilisation, and that culture is unable to make further progress in causal reasoning, then it is only natural that some mythology will start to encrust itself around that metaphysical kernel which is still

Pagan Pantheism

in a stage of philosophical infancy. Once mythological barnacles have become firmly established, it is most difficult for a nation to shake them off so as to re-evaluate and re-found the worldview upon which its culture rests. Reason has great difficulty detaching itself from an entrenched mythology, so as to breathe independently and question the rationality of that mythology.

I will consider the impact of crass pantheism on two of the ancient civilisations treated by Jaki: India and China.

India

In India, the mythologies of Hinduism and Buddhism that wrapped themselves around crass pantheism were decidedly pessimistic. We are all just caught up in an endlessly turning wheel, that is mindlessly churning away throughout the ages, carrying us along in its fatalistic and repetitive motion. '[T]he wheel of Buddha always moves round and never moves on.'[7] Two things must be accomplished by that wheel for it to repeat forever: it must both erase the events of the past and repeat them. They must be erased before they can be repeated, and they must be repeated in order to maintain the natural cycle.

We can easily see how this metaphysical paradigm leads to a belief in reincarnation, and also how it is a doctrine of despair. Humanity is simply a cog in the nature machine. The machine's consistency does not mean that it has a rational source, but rather that it cannot be escaped; it will kill us and bring us back to life forever. The only solution is to detach oneself from one's surroundings, to try to remove oneself somehow from the world of sense, to be totally indifferent to the world. Jaki remarks:

> The best that man could do in the midst of an illusory and depraving reality was to keep himself aloof, and view everything with compassion ... in its essence this was not so much an active programme as a meek attitude of non-involvement. It frowned on activity as the source of the world's troubles, it aimed at leaving them untouched lest they hurt more by being treated through intervention.[8]

The impact that this notion has on one's epistemological relationship to reality is devastating. An eternally cyclic universe with no first principle is radically irrational, a series of blind forces, completely oblivious to the hopes and aspirations of rational humans. Nature is like a capricious animal; it just does what it does, without there being a reason for it. It is incompatible with human beings, not presenting anything comprehensible to the mind, such that some sort of understanding can be reached, a basis for building a working relationship and living in harmony. There is no going from effect to cause, no reason to expect that there is some intricate order to be discovered, a way for the mind to proceed from nature to its author by definitive, conclusive steps. The ultimate culprit for this impasse is the ever-changing data of sense. 'The fearful prospect of never-ending cycles filled one with distrust and hostility toward the world of senses', says Jaki.[9]

This notion of fatalistic cycles seems to have caused the ancient Hindus to neglect history, such that they did not give authors and dates to their works and continually and indiscriminately modified them over time. There was no point of leaving an exact record for posterity, as the turning of the wheel on the one hand would wipe out the deeds of the present, and on the other bring them back once again.

Nor would such a pantheist see any need to investigate the past, for the doctrine of eternal cycles eliminates any linear view of history. Such a view is necessary to believe in the possibility of mankind making lasting progress. To achieve such progress, the future must continually build on the past in a stepwise fashion. In a system of cycles, however, the advancements of today are destined to be erased tomorrow. Nature always wins; it cannot be fought. The best one can hope for is to reach a supreme state of insensitivity within oneself, seemingly through a supreme neglect of everything else. Or, if you are fortunate enough to be born at a better stage of the cycle, enjoy it while it lasts, for things will be getting worse soon.

Pagan Pantheism

REALISM
All Four Causes in Balance

Material & Efficient Causes Ignored

Formal & Final Causes Ignored

Material & Efficient Causes Doubted

Formal & Final Causes Reduced

Material & Efficient Causes Denied

Formal & Final Causes Denied

IDEALISM

EMPIRICISM

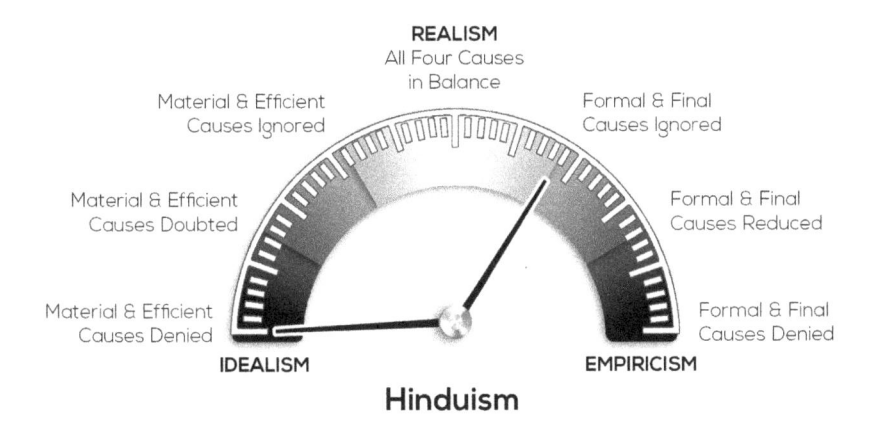

Hinduism

If I were to try to evaluate the Hindu mentality anachronistically according to our modern philosophical categories, I would have to call it mainly *idealist*, because of its mistrust of sense, but also in some sense *empiricist*, because of its trust in an ideology built wholly on the data of sense. There is a true basis for conjecturing that nature is eternal and cyclical, but that conclusion is far too hasty, given many other pieces of information which contradict it. The human mind easily takes the part for the whole, stopping short in its intellectual investigations, weary of pursuing truth, and so jumping straight to a conclusion instead of waiting and reflecting longer. Early civilisations tended to ignore much of the causal information that reality provides. This is what led the ancient Indian mind to become entrenched in a simplistic ideology, which rendered it unable to adopt an optimistic, realist perspective, set out on the pursuit of causes, and conquer the causal chains.

China

While the ancient Chinese packaged their crass pantheism in a more optimistic mythology, the same underlying metaphysics produced like effects. Jaki points out that the Chinese once believed in a personal, supreme Lawgiver, but that the idea faded away well before the time of Confucius, to give way to 'universism', 'the consideration of the universe as the ultimate entity'.[10] Even Joseph Needham, a great Sinologist but also a Marxist, had to admit candidly that the Chinese abandonment of monotheism was a disaster for their intellectual history. Afterwards, according to him, the Chinese

> had an intellectual failure of nerve. They no longer felt confident that their limited mind could grasp and control the laws of Nature because Nature itself was not subject to a Mind and Lawgiver who transcended it.[11]

The systems of thought which replaced theism were Confucianism and Taoism, originating in the sixth century BC. Though there were stark differences between the two systems, yet both were pantheistic, both believed in eternal cycles, and both, as a result, shared an important epistemological starting point: reality is to be fathomed by intuition, not by reasoning.[12]

To take Taoism as an example, nature for it was 'an all-encompassing living entity animated by impersonal volitions ... As a result Nature could not be expected to yield her secrets to analytical reasoning or to systematic research activity'.[13] Yet the Taoists were able to recognise a certain goodness in the heavens and so, for them, the rhythm of nature was a model of imitation and conformity. Instead of seeking to escape the cycle, they tried to cooperate with it, by conforming their garb and customs to the movements of the heavens.

At the same time, the Tao or all-embracing order is not the product of a loving, personal God, but of the blind interaction of two opposing forces, the Yin and the Yang. The former is a principle of stability and the latter of change. Everything is in a

Pagan Pantheism

state of eternal emergence from them and dissolution into them, in a cyclic aeon of 31920 years, the Great Period, at the consummation of which every process returns 'to its original form and condition'.[14]

While Taoism did not generate despair on the social level, it did on the epistemological level. No cause for the operations of the Yin and Yang could be located, no particular significance ascribed to sequences of events, no rational order found in the nature with which one communes. Such was the attitude toward reality that pervaded Chinese culture for centuries, and which was prevailing at the time the Western world gained access to that culture.

When Jesuit missionary Fr Mateo Ricci travelled to China in the sixteenth century and lived there in the midst of the Chinese intellectual elite, he made the following assessment of the state of Chinese knowledge as he found it:

> The Chinese have no [physical] science at all; one may say that only mathematics is cultivated, and the little they know of it is without foundation; they stole it from the Saracens ... Physics and metaphysics, including logic, is unknown among them.[15]

Worse still, he found the Chinese denying the first principles of intellectual thought: 'the second chapter of [Ricci's] catechism was devoted to the refutation of the Taoist claim that the "nothing" can for ever give rise to "everything"'.[16] Though the principle that *nothing comes from nothing* is implicit in crass pantheism, yet it can also be denied in a civilisation where the first principles of the intellect have not been defined and laid down as inviolable. Furthermore, unless one holds that 'a thing cannot be and not be at the same time', 'effects cannot be greater than their causes', and like fundamental axioms upon which all reasoning rests, one cannot logically proceed from cause to cause in a process of discursive thought. *The denial of the first principles of the mind is a key characteristic of empiricists,* though the Chinese also had some characteristics of *idealism.*

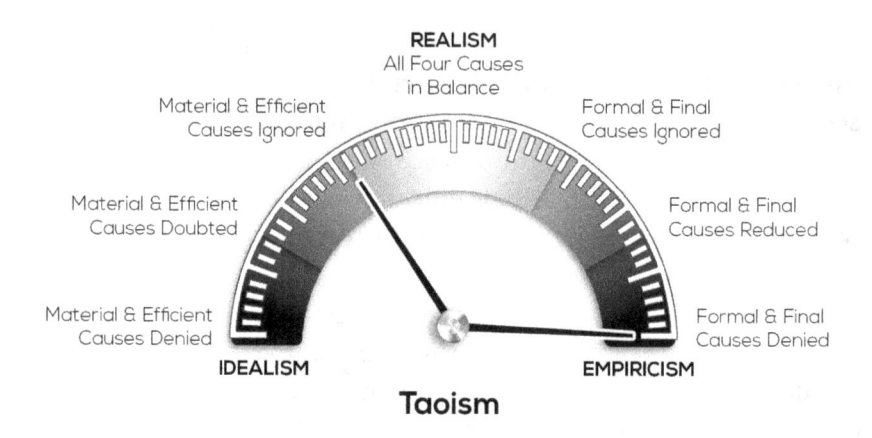

```
                        REALISM
                     All Four Causes
                       in Balance
   Material & Efficient                Formal & Final
     Causes Ignored                    Causes Ignored

  Material & Efficient                      Formal & Final
    Causes Doubted                          Causes Reduced

 Material & Efficient                        Formal & Final
    Causes Denied                            Causes Denied
       IDEALISM                               EMPIRICISM
                         Taoism
```

Thus, the Chinese initially held to a theology which realism supports—monotheism—but then turned to a pantheistic ideology which undermined the intellect's ability to know causes. While the Hindu philosophy and religion turned Indians away from science because of too much confidence in the intellect to know the whole, Taoism turned the Chinese away from it because of too little confidence, so little that the most primitive principles of the intellect were denied. In both cases, the mind did not yet have the strict fences of logic and causal definitions to keep it on the path of truth and so it struck out aimlessly on paths of incoherence.

This is not, of course, to say that either India or China were not home to amazing practical inventions and feats of engineering during the course of their long histories. Stacy Trasancos goes out of her way to note them,[17] but only so as to contrast them with Jaki's main object of scrutiny, the ability of cultures to formulate physical laws, which is science proper. Discovery must be accompanied by mathematical justification to qualify. The technology of the ancient civilisations shows that sufficient intelligence was on hand for science, but also that some obstacle was in the way, because they failed to give birth to it.

Why was science stillborn in cultures that had the three standard ingredients given by 'all-knowing sociologies of science': talents, social organisation, and long periods of peace?[18] Jaki's contention is that the death in the womb was delivered by an epistemology deriving from a pantheistic theology. He considers other such cultures in his *Science and Creation* and *The Savior of Science*, buttressing the argument with his remarkable research, but let these examples suffice to provide a pattern for the reduction and even destruction worked on both philosophy and science by a religion of crass pantheism.[19] When one conceives the ultimate reality as being a universe going through eternal cycles, one is necessarily deterred from seeking causal knowledge from the universe.

Elaborate pantheism

Of all the ancient peoples, those who seemed most confident in the powers of the mind were the Greeks, the 'chosen people of reason'. They alone, it seems, were able to discover the laws of the mind—logic—and apply those laws to reason philosophically to a first principle of reality, rather than assigning that principle blindly to an amorphous and inscrutable universe. By establishing fundamental principles for inquiring into reality, they provided for their minds so many guardrails that would prevent aimless wandering in the realms of contradiction.

For instance, Democritus (460–370 BC), an early Greek philosopher, stated, 'Nothing can come into being from that which is not, nor pass away into that which is not'.[20] Thus, he formulated the rule for reality that Ricci was trying to teach the Chinese 2000 years later.

Thales

The first known true philosopher in Western history, Thales (624–546 BC), set the Greeks on the path of hunting for ultimate causes. By proposing this metaphysical task to human reason, he was inviting it to find a rational principle for all reality *within* the universe, instead of identifying the ultimate *with* the universe. Thales believed that there is a hierarchy in reality, such that some things come from others which come from others until we arrive at the ultimate source of the whole. Perhaps more surprisingly, he believed that reason is able to discover that first principle. The most important aspect of his project, in terms of the history of human thought, is that he directed the mind to finding reality's causal hierarchy. This was the track that would first lead to finding ultimate causes within the universe, and then finally to reasoning to a single First Cause outside the universe, a reasoning that sets the human mind free from the shackles of pantheism.

After some deep pondering on his self-assigned intellectual goal, Thales came to the conclusion that water was the ultimate source of all bodies, and he set forth rational evidence to support his thesis.[21] This was a crude metaphysics indeed, radically empirical, yet it gave reason its own territory apart from religion proper. Thales was looking for answers about the world around him different from those provided by mythology, or even complementary to them. He was making the transition from *mythos* or the use of traditional stories to explain reality, to *logos*, the use of reasoning to explain reality. Theological poets wrote about mythology, while Thales wrote about the causes of reality, as Aquinas explains:

> Thales is said to have been the originator of speculative philosophy because he was the only one of the seven wise men, who came after the theological poets, to make an investigation into the causes of things, the other sages being concerned with moral matters.[22]

Thales' emancipation of reason from religion was crucial, because all of the pantheistic religions taught certain *a priori* principles about reality that were not true, and which ended up dictating whatever other conclusions would be drawn about reality. By setting the mythology to the side (while still not giving it up), Thales was able to go to reality itself for his answers.

Pre-Socratics

From Thales' reduction of the universe to a primitive material cause, later thinkers, called the Pre-Socratics, went progressively deeper into reality, introducing distinctions and divisions, identifying multiple causes and their respective explanatory roles. The Ionians—Diogenes and Anaximenes, Hippasus and Heraclitus, among others—developed the line of Thales, proposing their own *material* candidates as the ultimate source of reality. Empedocles and Anaxagoras went further, recognising that material bodies of themselves are inert, needing some cause to bring them into interaction, and so they introduced *efficient causes* to account for movement. For Empedocles, it was love and hate which made the world go 'round, while Anaxagoras ascribed it to an intellect, thus meriting from Aristotle the praise of being like a sober man among many drunkards, delirious in their opinions. Meanwhile, the famous 'pi man' Pythagoras thought that numbers gave being to things, his numbers resembling the role of *formal causes*. Moreover, while many of these philosophers referred indirectly to *final causality*, in speaking of the good, none of them ascribed to it actual causal powers. Overall, each school was holding a *single cause* as accounting for the whole of reality without incorporating all four causes into their metaphysical systems.[23]

All of this intellectual ferment had the quite positive effect of pushing the sluggish and fallen human mind to exercise the whole of its natural powers in seeking to understand reality. Thus, while the Greeks were by and large committed to eternal cycles in a pantheistic universe, like the Indians and Chinese, yet they were able to detach themselves sufficiently from mythology to allow reason some freedom to philosophise. Robin Waterfield says that 'they were the first to make and explore the consequences of the assumption which is absolutely crucial to the development of science, that the human rational mind is the correct tool for understanding the world',[24] using the term 'science' in its Aristotelian sense. It was this positive epistemological attitude which enabled the Greeks to invent philosophy and intensively pursue causal knowledge for two centuries.

Sophists

In the fifth century BC, however, an odour of epistemological despair wafted into the burgeoning intellectual enterprise, threatening to turn it sour. For while the Greeks were amazed at the many new ideas and positions being spouted by the various philosophical schools, at the same time they were scandalised that no one agreed. The masters of the schools all seemed to be brilliant, but they contradicted one another. Both empiricists and idealists were in the plenty, but they seemed to be both right and wrong, without there being any way to reconcile the two. Meanwhile, the number of new and weightier problems to be solved appeared momentous compared to the few simple questions that had been answered.

From this double scandal were born history's primeval reductionists, the Sophists. They were radically sceptical, saying that since there are two contradictory arguments about everything, it is not possible to attain truth by philosophical disputation. What then is the point of discussion? To persuade, to bring the other around to your position. The Sophists set about to perfect the art of rhetoric, where the goal was to convince your opponent—of what, it did not matter. Aquinas pithily summarises the difference between the Sophists and the philosophers who preceded them:

> The philosopher and the sophist direct their life and actions to different things. The philosopher directs his to knowing the truth, whereas the sophist directs his so as to appear to know what he does not.[25]

Pagan Pantheism

One of the immediate results of sophistic scepticism is immorality. If there is no truth, then each person is a law unto himself or, as the Sophist Protagoras famously put it:

> Man is the measure of all things—of the things that are, that they are; of the things that are not, that they are not ... Each and every event is for me as it appears to me, and is for you as it appears to you.'[26]

From such a perspective, everyone is master of his own reality and cannot be imposed upon by any norm external to himself. There is no truth or real knowledge, and so no moral standards. Freedom from objective truth is freedom from moral obligation. This 'freedom', however, is bought at the cost of denying one's knowing powers and breaking one's epistedometer.

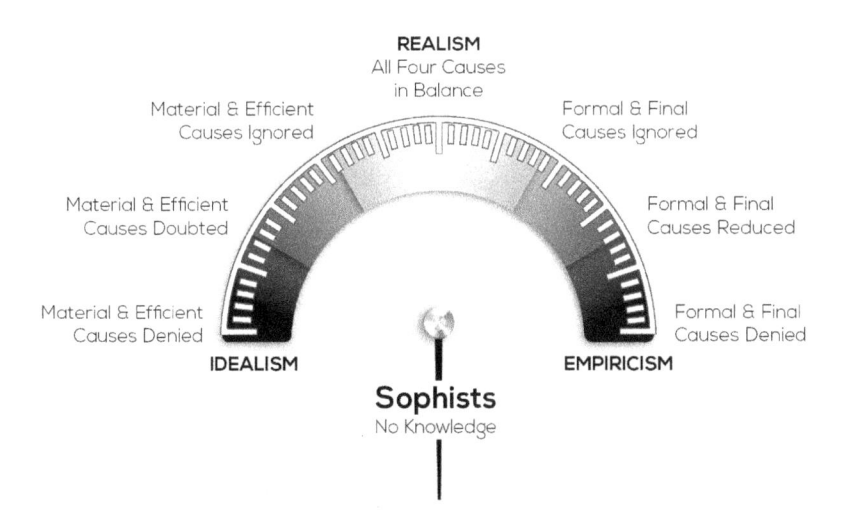

REALISM
All Four Causes in Balance

Material & Efficient Causes Ignored

Formal & Final Causes Ignored

Material & Efficient Causes Doubted

Formal & Final Causes Reduced

Material & Efficient Causes Denied

Formal & Final Causes Denied

IDEALISM

EMPIRICISM

Sophists
No Knowledge

Socrates

At the height of the Sophists' popularity and power, there entered on the scene the mysterious figure of Socrates (469–399 BC). He made it his life's work to contradict their entire program both on the intellectual and moral levels. While the Sophists said that it was impossible to attain truth, Socrates would draw the truth from any passer-by through a series of carefully phrased questions. While the Sophists preached a life of pursuing selfish success, Socrates claimed virtue as a human's supreme good and meaning.

In addition to taking on the Sophists, Socrates also set out to refute the Ionians. They, like Thales, reduced all reality to some primal element, a material cause, and so reduced all knowledge to sense or body knowledge. For them, everything is just the random product of the mechanical interaction and combination of material bodies. There is no reason or meaning to life and the universe, no *telos* or purpose. By this line of positive argumentation, they arrived at the same conclusions that the Sophists reached by their path of negative doubt, and so were with them helping to destroy both reason and morality.

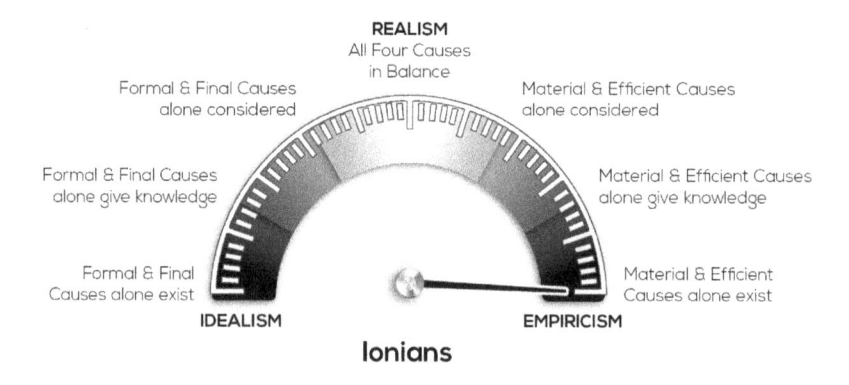

REALISM
All Four Causes in Balance

Formal & Final Causes alone considered — Material & Efficient Causes alone considered

Formal & Final Causes alone give knowledge — Material & Efficient Causes alone give knowledge

Formal & Final Causes alone exist — Material & Efficient Causes alone exist

IDEALISM — **EMPIRICISM**

Ionians

Plato's dialogue *Phaedo* is quite representative of Socrates' counter-argumentation and philosophical system.[27] In it, Socrates has been condemned to death for corrupting the Athenian youth, when he has actually been teaching them virtue. His friends are assembled around him on the day of his execution and are astonished that Socrates is so calm when his life is just about to be ended. This launches them into an extended discussion on the immortality of the soul. Socrates explains in detail his reasons for believing that he will live on after his death. For instance, he states that the cyclic patterns of nature must be mirrored in human life, and thus life must follow death, just as death follows life. This shows that Socrates also believed in reincarnation and eternal cycles.[28]

But his friends are not completely satisfied with this, and bring forward difficult objections, so difficult that some are led to believe that even the great Socrates will not be able to refute them. This motivates Socrates to provide a weightier argument, but not before lending the youth some preliminary advice: never become a *misologist* or hater of argument, because of conflicting opinions in a discussion. The conflicting opinions are not a sign of the inability of human reason to find the truth, but rather of the need of reasoners to improve their reasoning skill. There is no worse evil that can come to a person than to lose trust in reason.[29]

David's 'The Death of Socrates' depicting a scene from Plato's Phaedo. (Image courtesy of Wikimedia Commons)

Then, Socrates sets forth his deeper argument for the soul's immortality. In his youth, he explains, he was attracted by the explanations which the materialists assigned as causes of phenomena. Later on, however, he came to the conclusion that matter is only a condition for causation, and not an actual cause.[30] The *real* causes are forms. By these, he means abstract concepts like 'beauty', 'goodness', 'greatness', and so on,[31] which somehow exist outside the mind in a state of absolute perfection. According to Socrates, forms provide the true knowledge of what is real.

For example, why is this flower beautiful? 'If anyone tells me', he says, 'that what makes a thing beautiful is its lovely colour, or its shape or anything else of the sort, I let all that go, for all those things confuse me.' Rather, 'I believe it is safe for me or anyone else to give this answer, that beautiful things are beautiful through beauty'.[32] If colour made things beautiful, then everything that had colour would be beautiful. Such, however, is not the case. It is much more fitting to say beauty makes things beautiful, that is, they are beautiful because they participate in the form of beauty.

Moreover, it seems evident to Socrates that these forms, in which natural things participate, are ordered according to intelligence. Furthermore, because intelligence orders things according to what is good and best, then the reason why anything in nature acts is because it is pursuing what is best for it.[33] Thus, in the mind of Socrates, all of nature is animated and striving for its perfection or natural purpose. For this reason, natural motion is to be explained in terms of final causes, not material ones, purposeful strivings rather than natural forces.

Lastly, Socrates believes that knowledge is not something that is acquired from the outside, but rather something we are born with.[34] It is there somehow from a past life, but we have forgotten it. The best means to remember what we know is the dialogue, a careful process of argumentation in which two parties seek the truth by questioning one another. The mind, stimulated by such discussions, is able to find what it already knows. In this view, knowledge does not start with the senses—one of the golden rules of realism—but is pre-loaded from birth. We do not know reality by looking at reality, but by looking within ourselves.

To summarise, Socrates' philosophy of nature and knowledge contains the following key points:

1. All true causation is in formal causes and final causes, that is, the form in which the things around us participate, and the perfection for which they strive.
2. As such, only formal and final causes give true knowledge. Forms pre-exist in our minds when we are born, but in a forgotten state. There is no gaining of knowledge, but only a remembering of knowledge that has fallen into disuse. Material and efficient causes explain nothing. Material phenomena themselves are mere appearance.
3. Reason is to be trusted, but to an extreme degree, in that Socrates believes that the way that the mind conceives things, in universal concepts or forms, is the way that they actually exist outside the mind.
4. The data of the senses is illusory and does not provide true knowledge. Knowledge is not gained in realist fashion, by starting with sense data and then abstracting a universal concept from that sense data by our intellective power.

Socrates, in short, has all the hallmarks of an *idealist.*

Socrates' contributions

The drama of Socrates' noble effort to save the soul of Greek thought had an enormous impact on the future of the West, and his influence is felt even to this day. Without naming them as such,[35] Socrates rightly established the importance of formal and final causes. The human mind is capable of knowing the essences of things (formal cause) and everything has a purpose (final cause). Moreover, the perfection of each form is in the attainment of its end. Therefore, purpose is the most important of the causes. Many centuries later, Aquinas would agree in saying that the final cause is 'the cause of the causality of all causes'.[36]

Socrates ultimately defeated the Sophists through his dialectical reasoning. He restored meaning to human life (the pursuit of virtue) and to human intellectual endeavours (the pursuit of essences and their definitions). He established *telos*, purpose, as the key to both the ontological and logical orders. But, as so often happens in fierce opponents of error, Socrates went too far. The Sophists removed purpose from reality, so Socrates would restore it... by making it the whole of reality. Everything that exists is pursuing a goal, that which is best for it, which means that all of nature is animated in some way, a notion that is otherwise well supported by Hellenistic mythology. Heavenly bodies strive in their circular paths to achieve a regularity like unto that of God, and even rocks are somehow self-motivated, for they fall to the Earth after being thrown upwards in an effort to return to their natural place.

Thus, when Socrates looks out upon reality and seeks an explanation, he believes that the final cause provides the complete reason for what we see, while the formal cause provides the complete reason for what we cannot see. Final causes explain becoming and formal causes being. Those two causes alone, then, are the domain of true reality and hence of scientific knowledge; material and efficient causes are the domain of the passing and illusory. Qualities, not quantities, are the proper arena of knowledge.

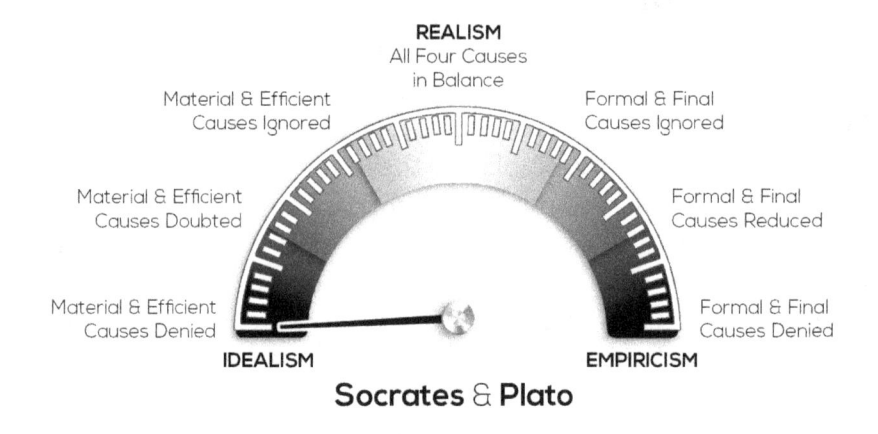

Socrates & Plato

Plato

Following on this perspective, Socrates' foremost disciple Plato (428–347 BC) constructed a notion of the universe wherein the data of sense are considered to be misleading, and if they provide any assistance at all, it is as a representation of the Forms, those pure essences like 'goodness' which exist outside of the material world. Plato kept everyone's necks continually craned upwards, beyond the world of sense, in order to contemplate the perfect world above. Strangely, he does not even attribute any efficient causality to his pure Forms (they don't do anything), a lacuna for which Aristotle frequently reproaches him.[37]

Socrates' and Plato's problem was that their worldview did not allow any reconciliation of mechanism with animism, of material and efficient causes with formal and final ones. Either bodies moved of their own volitions (animism) or they moved by blind forces (mechanism). With the former, purpose was saved and with the latter it was eliminated[38]. There seemed to be no third possibility, no way for the one reality to contain all four causes. Mechanist materialists were selfish corruptors, emptying life of meaning, and ruining the morals of the youth. Thus, mechanism had to be defeated and, with it, secondary material and efficient causality. That, however, is the precise area of physical knowledge. Thus, Socrates' over-emphasis on purpose, while having a positive effect on human morals, at the same time sealed off the path to scientific endeavour, at least as we know it today.

Socrates and Plato also failed to find a way to reason to a first principle of the universe. Gilson points out that Plato piously paid homage to the pantheon of Greek gods, but he could not connect them with his philosophy.[39] Plato's forms were not gods and his gods were not forms. Thus, says Taylor, 'there was a really unsolved conflict between the Platonic metaphysics and the Platonic religion'.[40]

Reason had been detached from poetic, mythological theology, but it could not yet construct a natural, rational theology, in which reason and religion could be wed. For this to happen, all four causes—material, formal, efficient, final—had to co-exist in a single metaphysics. Such a *tour de force* was left to Aristotle's realism.

Aristotle's realism

Greek philosophy needed systematisation, and it received all that and more from Aristotle of Stagira (384–322 BC), also known as 'the Stagirite' because of his birthplace, and 'the Philosopher' because of his overwhelming contributions to philosophical thought. Son of a physician, feet firmly planted on the ground, a close observer of nature, extremely cautious in drawing conclusions, Aristotle applied his immense genius to the penetration of reality with a scope that astonishes.

Aristotle of Stagira, nicknamed 'The Philosopher' and 'The Stagirite'. (Image courtesy of Wikimedia Commons)

Though he was educated in the school of thought begun by Socrates and filled out by Plato, Aristotle disagreed with their philosophy on several key points:

1. We are not born with knowledge that we must strive to remember, but rather we are born knowing nothing, and gain knowledge by contact with reality, observing it with our senses and making inferences from it with our mind.[41]

2. The data of the senses is not illusory, but the starting point for knowledge, providing particulars. Sense knowledge is the lowest way of knowing, higher knowledge being the grasping of causes. This latter knowledge is greater to the degree that the causes known are higher in the causal chain, that is, they are more universal.[42] The greatest knowledge possible is wisdom, and is possessed by one who knows the first causes and principles of all reality.[43]

3. There are four causes—material, formal, efficient, and final—and they all provide true knowledge of reality.

These three points are nothing more than the foundational principles of epistemological realism. Aristotle, after all, was its originator. Having laid this most solid rational foundation for the penetration of reality, he put it to most effective use, setting out to climb to the top of the causal chain in order to reach the prize of wisdom, a goal which he attained. Let us see how he did it.

Proof of the First Unmoved Mover

Following his realist principles, Aristotle started with sense data. Gazing at the world around him with keen insight, he recognised that all motion consists of two aspects, one active (mover) and the other passive (moved). *'Whatever is moved is moved by another'* is his famous dictum.[44] What he means by this is that, whenever physical motion takes place, two parts are required: an active part, a mover; and a passive part, a moved.

This principle holds true for both living and non-living things. When living things move themselves, there is still a mover and moved, since one of their parts is necessarily moving another, such as nerve impulses (mover) moving my index finger (moved). Non-living things only move when some external mover exercises causality on them. For example, a non-living ball moves only when an outside force (mover) is applied to the ball (moved). Therefore, no matter what motion is in question, both a mover and a moved are always necessary. Movement cannot take place without both.[45] Considering Aristotle's discovery of this principle, Gilson cannot withhold his praise: 'No one has ever better discerned the mystery that the very familiarity of movement hides from our eyes.'[46]

Taking this principle, which he learned by observing moving bodies on Earth, Aristotle boldly applied it to the motions of the entire universe, thus inaugurating that fundamental metaphysical exercise of analogical thought, whereby ideas taken from common experience are applied to the whole of reality. If everything in motion, he reasoned, has a certain dependence on a mover, then all of the motions that I see around me must have their source in something independent of movement, in something unmoved.

To see why this is so, let us take an example of a series of movers. For instance, at this moment, impulses from my brain (A) move the neurons in my fingers (B) move the keys on my keyboard (C) move electrical charges on the motherboard (D) move characters to appear on my screen (E). Clearly, in this series, the movement of E depends on that of D depends on that of C and so on until we get to A. In E, we have the case of a thing that is moved, but does not move anything else. In D to B, we have the case of things that are moved by a previous agent, but also themselves move another thing; they are called 'moved movers'. D, for instance, is *moved by* C **and** *moves* E.

So, let us say that you observe effect E appearing on the screen and you ask what causes it to be there. If you are given the answer of 'electrical impulses from the motherboard' (D), you immediately realise that the answer is incomplete, since you know that the movement of the impulses must in turn depend on something else in order to move. The impulses are moved movers. Because they are so, their movement in turn needs an explanation. If D moves E, what moves D? And if C moves D, what moves C? Questioning in this way, you realise that you will have to keep asking about the source of movement as long as you are given a moved mover as the answer. *Thus, the only type of mover that can break the chain of questioning and give a final explanation for the entire series of questions is an unmoved, first mover, a 'thing that moves others without itself being moved.'* Unless we come to such a mover, we cannot explain the series of movers, we cannot account for the very existence of the motion in it. But there is motion!

Aristotle looked around him and asked why anything moves at all. He noted that all of the things falling under his observation—whether it was things on earth or in the heavens—manifested themselves to be moved movers. By his principle 'everything that is moved is moved by another', however, those moved movers have to have a cause of their movement. The only way to account for their movement, then—that is, for *all* movement—is that there is some unseen Unmoved First Mover that is the ultimate cause of all motion. Notice that Aristotle is reasoning in the line of essential causality. He is not considering movement over a period of time, but the movement of the universe at any given moment.

As far as it goes, the reasoning is perfectly correct. As Aristotelians would say, 'A series of moved movers cannot proceed to infinity in the line of essential causality.' Thus, there must be a First Unmoved Mover for there to be any motion at all. By this syllogism, the inventor of syllogisms became the first to join reason and theology, nature and supernature, intellect and Intellect.

This astonishing intellectual feat was made possible by realism. Aristotle had discovered the way in which the mind is made to know reality (epistemology), along with the laws of its operation (logic), and he then proceeded to apply the mind in its fullest capacity. The result was success, the discovery of the real first principle of the universe, established indubitably by rational argumentation.

Let us go back quickly over the entire process. Aristotle starts with reality, as brought to him by the data of the senses. Observing that data very closely, his intellect formulates a principle about reality *a posteriori*, moving from effect to cause. That principle must necessarily be true—'everything that is moved is moved by another.' If the principle were false at any time or place, then a contradiction would exist: a thing would be both moved and unmoved at the same time in the same respect. Furthermore, if contradictions can exist in reality, then the mind can know nothing whatsoever. Thus, the principle of motion must be held as a principle for all of reality. If it holds for all reality, then reality must have at its apex some entity which is the very source of all motion, a first unmoved principle of motion.

Such was the very first path blazed for natural theology, a trail of metaphysical reasoning moving from effects to a first cause of the whole of reality, without any aid from divine revelation. Solely by the power of his senses and intellect, Aristotle was able to construct a coherent metaphysics that was also a natural theology.

Missing Creation

The only problem was that it was deficient in one of its key aspects. Aristotle was absolutely correct in reasoning that there must be a Unmoved First Mover if any movement at all is to exist, but at the same time he conceived God's moving activity incompletely. He did not see God as giving existence to all reality, as exercising primary causality, as creating and conserving being[47]. For him, the Unmoved Mover is the ultimate source of local motion, of movement in place, for example, of a body moving from point A to point B. The Unmoved Mover does not cause things to exist; rather he enables them to move from one place to another. He accounts for there being movement, not for being itself. He makes the world turn, but he does not make the world.

Pagan Pantheism

Why did Aristotle so limit God's activity? Because he had no notion of creation. *He realised an extrinsic cause was needed to explain all becoming, but did not realise one was needed to explain all being.*

One unfortunate result of his oversight was that Aristotle thought he could prove that the universe is eternal and uncreated, like God. He comes to the conclusion by starting with a question: Did the Unmoved First Mover start things in motion at a given time or has he been moving things eternally?[48] Well, he answers, starting things in motion requires two activities on the part of the Unmoved Mover: he has to start things in motion *and* keep them in motion. Furthermore, as we will see, you can be an Unmoved Mover if you perform one activity, but not if you do two. If God were responsible for both the starting and continuing of motion, then he would have to keep the universe at rest at one moment, then get it started moving another moment. This means that he would have to change/move. But he is the Unmoved Mover! It becomes necessary, then, to reject the idea of motion starting in time and embrace in its place the idea of eternal motion. The universe is co-eternal with the Unmoved Mover, whose single eternal job is to provide the motion component of the ever-existing whole.

Thus, while the Philosopher succeeded in climbing the entire vertical chain of secondary causality (becoming), reaching a primary source of motion at each moment, he did not attain primary efficient causality itself (being). Reason had attained full emancipation from mythology, but the natural theology it constructed was too primitive. Without the distinction between essence and existence, Aristotle was not able to separate his Unmoved First Mover from the universe and conceive him as causing its existence. Thus, his God is different from the Christian God in three key respects:

- the Unmoved First Mover does not exercise any efficient causality on the universe, that is, he does not create

- the Unmoved First Mover has no knowledge of the universe, because thinking about things below him is a taint on his perfection[49]
- the Unmoved First Mover is immaterial, but still within the universe, not separate from it. He is the 'first among equals' of the most perfect beings in the heavens.[50]

Since this Unmoved Mover does not design the universe or even know about it, he is hardly a figure to be worshipped.[51] As Gilson remarks, 'with Aristotle, the Greeks had gained an indisputably rational theology, but they had lost their religion'.[52]

Bad consequences

Aristotle's inability to find creation had a devastating effect on many of his conclusions. A whirling universe kept in motion by an unmoving, utterly passive God became the master idea which he went on to apply to every corner of reality. He switched from being a realist, moving *a posteriori* from effects to causes, to being an idealist, starting with this primal idea—partially, but not wholly warranted by reality—and then drawing from that idea *a priori* many false conclusions about reality.

The entire problem, as we just saw, was that Aristotle did not see God as moving things from non-being to being, from nothing to something, but from something unmoving to something moving. For God to do this while remaining Himself unmoved was quite difficult. How is it possible, Aristotle asked himself, to exercise causality on another without moving? After pondering for surely a long while, he comes up with a beautifully realist response: by being a final cause, through the force of attraction.[53] Consider that you are driving along, hours separating you from your last meal, hunger gnawing at your stomach, thirst gripping your throat, and suddenly there comes into view a billboard with a monumental hamburger stationed next to a tall glass of a thirst quenching drink. Immediately, your mouth begins to water and you desire to drive quickly to the place where these objects can be obtained. In other words, the billboard has exercised causality upon you without performing any activity other than existing, without changing in any way. It has acted as an unmoved mover. And this is the way, says Aristotle, that God moves the universe—He is an irresistible cosmic advertisement that sets the denizens of the universe moving towards a more God-like state.

How so? Well, you see, it goes like this. There exists in the heavens an intelligent, animate series of bodies called the *Primum Mobile* or First Moved. They somehow know about the eternal, perfect, unchanging, immaterial being of the universe, the Unmoved First Mover. Knowing his perfect mode of life, they are drawn to live like him to the best of their ability: *they are set in motion by their desire to imitate the Unmoved Mover*, as our salivary glands are moved by the unmoving billboard.[54] How do the heavenly animate bodies imitate him? Firstly, with their minds by always contemplating what he is thinking about—himself—and then with their incorruptible bodies by changing as little as possible, eternally moving in perfect circles. They undergo a minimum of movement, while forever contemplating and imitating God. Such is the single and eternal effect exercised by the Unmoved First Mover.

Does this single effect suffice for the movement of the entire universe? Yes, for it is the movement of the First Moved that sets off a chain reaction of movement throughout the universe. Aristotle sees the universe as consisting of 'a series of concentric spheres',[55] that are more or less close to the Unmoved First Mover. The First Moved heavenly bodies are the very closest and, as we have seen, they are set into motion by their attraction to the First Mover. Next come the Fixed Stars, which are moved by their attraction to the First Moved. Thus it goes, as we get farther from the First Mover, and closer to the centre—and bottom—of the universe, Earth. The First Mover moves the First Moved move the Fixed Stars move Saturn, and so on. The bodies in each sphere of the universe move because of their attraction to the sphere higher to them, until we come to the First Mover, who does not move at all.

The Unmoved First Mover, then, is at the origin of a succession of movements, with the heavenly bodies both being moved by the bodies higher than them and moving the ones lower than them. With this notion, Aristotle can satisfactorily explain why there is motion at all, at any given moment. His reasoning leading to the existence of an Unmoved First Mover, as cause of the motion of the universe, was perfectly correct. Everything else, however, was incorrect, all because of his fatal error about God, namely, that his Unmoved Mover moves only by final causality, and not also by efficient causality. All of the other conclusions *would have been correct*, if indeed God only moved by final causality. But Aristotle did not see how God could move by efficient causality while remaining unmoved—he did not think of creation—and so he believed there was only one possible agency for the Unmoved Mover. Latching on to that one possibility, and implicitly discarding the other, he put on an idealist epistemology and proceeded to derive an entire series of false conclusions about the universe.

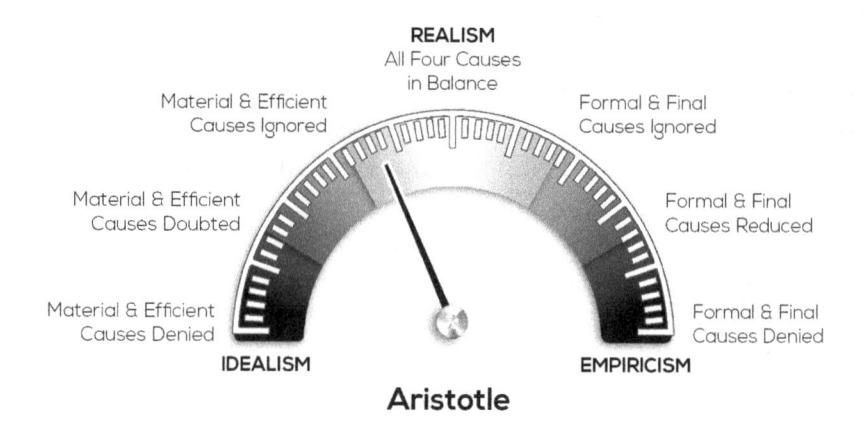

REALISM
All Four Causes in Balance

Material & Efficient Causes Ignored

Formal & Final Causes Ignored

Material & Efficient Causes Doubted

Formal & Final Causes Reduced

Material & Efficient Causes Denied

Formal & Final Causes Denied

IDEALISM

EMPIRICISM

Aristotle

Errors in physics

Aristotle's false notions about the physical universe, based on his incomplete natural theology, were to maintain hegemony in the Western mind for the next millennium and a half. Under such a framework, an important section of reality in the area of material causes was ignored, exact science was kept from being born, and certain irrational notions triumphed.

All this was mainly due to three false ideas firmly embedded in Aristotle's vision of the universe:

- the universe runs on eternal cycles
- the universe is uncreated and necessary
- the whole of the universe's motion is explained almost entirely by means of final causality.

'The universe runs on eternal cycles.' We have already seen the deleterious effects of this first point in other ancient cultures and so we should not be surprised to find similar ones here. Aristotle, in fact, held that 'every art and every philosophy has often been discovered and lost again'.[56] St Thomas explains that the Philosopher necessarily held this position to 'save the eternity of the world. For ... it would seem absurd that the human race should be without these [every art and every philosophy] for an infinite period of time'.[57] Such a viewpoint cannot fail to diminish hope in the progress of the sciences.

'The universe is uncreated and necessary.' If the universe is uncreated, it also has to be necessary, that is, it can only exist as it does. The reason is that it has not been brought into being by some cause that configures it. Rather, it is self-existing and so must necessarily be what it is. No other universe is possible. Moreover, being uncreated means it does not have an efficient cause. Causes, however, are precisely what give knowledge to the mind. The universe being uncaused, then, Aristotle does not look for an explanation for the being of anything. He takes the existence of everything for granted. In this system, it would seem futile to investigate the universe *as a whole* in order to find in it physical laws, laws which could only come from a lawgiver. Being uncreated, the universe is a law unto itself.

Lastly, 'the whole of the universe's motion is explained almost entirely by means of final causality.' In Aristotle's concept, if there is any order in the universe to be found, any 'oneness' that justifies using the word 'universe', it is because each thing, in moving, strives towards a perfection tied to the perfection of the Unmoved Mover. Each body in the universe seeks to imitate the bodies higher than it, which ultimately seek to imitate the Unmoved Mover.

To see what scientific explanations derive from this concept of movement arising from final causality alone, consider Aristotle's explanation of the movement of rocks. He notices that rocks, when thrown upward, always move back down to the ground. Today, we explain this phenomenon by the material force of gravity. Aristotle, however, accounted for it by an intrinsic inclination built into rocks. Rocks are heavy bodies, and heavy bodies tend by their very nature to be on the ground.[58] The reason is that the ground is their 'natural place', which serves as a sort of 'home base' for them. It is the place where they best achieve their purpose, the place most suited and so most beneficial for their nature. Why is the ground the best location for rocks? Because it is the closest to the centre of the Earth, which is at the bottom centre of the universe, and is where heavy bodies tend. It is there that the rock 'experiences in the most favourable manner the influence of the celestial motions and astral light, the sources of all generation and of all corruption within sublunary bodies'.[59] In other words, the closer a rock is to the centre of the Earth, the more benefits it receives from the superior bodies in the heavens, and so the more it is able to be like them.

Because the rock, by its nature, necessarily tends towards the ground, the only possible reason a rock could be moving upwards is if some violence is being exercised upon it *from the outside*, working against its natural inclination. There is no question of some force being imparted to a rock, which inheres in the rock and moves it upwards after it has left the hand of a thrower. In

Aristotle's view, the rock would not receive such a force within itself, because forces pushing it upwards are against its nature.[60]

Thus, when I throw a rock up in the air, I am exercising violence upon it, forcing it away from its natural tendencies. After being thrown, the rock strives to get back to the ground. Another *outside* force, air, pushes on it from behind, exercising a similar violence on it to that of my hand. When my hand performs the action of throwing, it displaces the air around the stone, causing the air to circle around it, such that it moves the stone forward to the next portion of air, which is then disturbed by the stone and acts on it in the same way, and so on for the rest of the stone's movement. In short, my hand moves the stone and the air surrounding the stone keeps it in movement. Finally, the intrinsic inclination of the rock overcomes the force of the air and it is able to return to the ground, its natural place.[61]

Aristotle's explanation stops there, content, without ever having spoken of any of the material cause concepts so familiar to us, concepts such as 'gravity', 'kinetic energy', 'mass', 'velocity', 'acceleration', and so on. The final cause is considered as having done all the causal explanation work that these concepts do for us; all motion is tied back to an attraction for and corresponding striving for a higher being. In this view, the

> investigation of any realm, living or not, [is] not considered satisfactory without attributing, rightly or wrongly, purposes to processes and phenomena of every kind.[62]

Aristotle starts by assigning to bodies a purpose they do not have, namely, that of being in the place where they can best receive the influences of the universe. He then gives them a power they do not have—that of striving to reach a place—so that they can fulfil their natural purpose. This leads him to the fallacy of panteologism or the seeing of wilful purpose everywhere.

Another infamous scientific conclusion that Aristotle draws from his model is found in his *On the Heavens*.[63] There he states that of two bodies falling to the ground, one weighing twice as much will fall twice as fast. After all, its heavier weight makes for a stronger inclination towards the centre of the Earth.[64] Jaki groans at the ready acceptance of this statement for 1700 years, and wonders why no one tried to drop differently weighted objects from a worksite as an experimental test of Aristotle's dictum.[65] It did not happen because the final cause had a preponderant share of the realm of knowledge, and so the only law of motion admitted in physics was the striving of bodies, with the result that no one thought of measuring and quantifying motion. In the end, 'there is hardly a page that can be salvaged from Aristotle's physical, astronomical, and chemical science, apart from what is purely geometrical there'.[66]

Aristotle was not following the principles of his own realism. We saw in the last chapter that, for the realist, a different method must be used for the investigation of each aspect of reality.[67] Thus, for example, since biology studies living things (aspect A) and inorganic chemistry non-living things (aspect B), then two different methods (method A & method B) must be used to study those two objects, if they are to reveal their intelligible content. Aristotle, however, was applying the methods of biology to the whole of reality. He was treating rocks as if they were living things, having an immanent activity whereby they could resist outside forces in order to pursue their own purposes. 'Aristotle [] exaggerated the scope of a particular science ... [by] biologizing inorganic nature'.[68] Why did he do this? Because, as we have seen, the incomplete aspects of his natural theology turned him into an idealist and drove him to impose *a priori* conclusions on reality that were not supported by his own realism. This prevented him from developing today's scientific method as the proper way to investigate the motion of inanimate bodies.

The failure of the Stagirite in physical science, despite his momentous triumphs in fathering philosophical disciplines, only goes to illustrate that even a little deviation from realist principles spells intellectual catastrophe. As Aristotle himself says, 'A small error in principles leads to great errors in conclusions.'

In a sense, the Philosopher both undervalued and overvalued matter. He undervalued it in failing to see that it has been endowed with ordered forces by a Creator. He overvalued it by conceiving inorganic matter as striving for certain ends.

We take it for granted today that forces such as gravity and the interactions of chemicals cause inert bodies to move. It all seems so simple and obvious when the explanations appear in a high school textbook. The historical record, on the other hand, makes it seem far from obvious. Aristotle's physical science would not be definitively overturned until the fourteenth century, over 1700 years after his death. The full rights of reality were asserted by a realism assisted by the doctrine of creation in time.

Chapter summary

In this chapter, I have:

- given a broad overview of the intellectual history of the ancient world
- assessed certain cultures according to their epistemology
- assessed how each culture's epistemology affected its ability to attain causal knowledge.

An idea more or less common to all ancient cultures was that the universe is a self-existing entity going through eternally repeating cycles.

The Indians and Chinese spun mythologies around their pantheism, which mesmerised their minds and prevented the pursuit of both philosophy and science. The senses were mistrusted and the first principles of reason denied. Lacking confidence in the reliability of reality and human ability to know it, these cultures were not able to put solidly into place any of the links of the causal chain. They did not philosophise, in the strict sense.

The Greeks managed to detach mind from mythology and launched an optimistic reason in a search for the secrets of the universe. From the efforts of various philosophical schools, they were able to distinguish the ultimate aspects of reality—the four causes—though each school placed too much emphasis on one or two of them, without being able to construct a coherent metaphysics of the whole. Socrates and Plato, in particular, placed their entire emphasis of knowledge on formal and final causes, while relegating material causes to the realm of illusion.

Aristotle was the first to work all four causes into a coherent metaphysics. He started by laying down the principles of epistemological realism, the way in which humans know reality; and the principles of logic, the laws by which reason may arrive at true conclusions. To this day, his realism and logic must be adhered to if one desires to obtain true causal knowledge about reality.

With these rational tools in place, the Philosopher started with the data of the senses and reasoned *a posteriori* in the vertical line of causality to an Unmoved First Mover of the entire universe. In doing so, he became the first to attain a metaphysics that provided a coherent, logical view of the whole of reality, the first to unite philosophy with religion.

While Aristotle's system was coherent, it was yet not the only possible explanation for reality. Aristotle did not realise this, however. He thought that his system was necessarily true, that the Unmoved First Mover could only exist as he conceived him. Not seeing the key distinction between essence and existence, Aristotle thought that a First Mover could be unmoved if he caused movement, but not if he caused things to come into existence, if he effected the transition from non-being to being.

Because he thought his view of God was the only one that could be logical, the Philosopher boldly drew far-reaching and erroneous conclusions from his system. Among these postulates was the over-emphasis of of the work of final causality in physical motion, a viewpoint that prevented the quantitative analysis of moving bodies that makes for exact science.

Thus, while Aristotle advanced the true understanding of reality more than any other in the ancient world, he was still missing a whole order of causality (primary causality) and leading his successors to neglect material and efficient secondary causality. It was the theology that he had constructed from reason that led him to so reduce reality, and its influence put 'physics into a straitjacket for two thousand years',[69] thus stalling the birth of science. Philosophy had practically reached its apex with Aristotle, but exact science did not even get started. That start could only come by completing Aristotle's metaphysics and contradicting his physics. This did not happen until the scholastic age, to which we now turn.

Table 4.1 Pagan views on the universe

Pagan Pantheists	Doubted	Causal knowledge	First principle of the universe
Crass Pantheists	Sense & intellect	Accidental chain only	Unknowable
Pre-Socratics	Either sense or intellect	Essential chain in one of the four causes	One of the four causes
Socrates & Plato	Senses	Essential chain in formal and final causes	Undefined
Aristotle	Neither	Essential chain in all four causes	The Unmoved First Mover

Notes

[1] Chapter 9 of Harvey's *De Motu Cordis et Sanguinis*.
[2] See W. Wallace, *The Modeling of Nature* (Washington, DC: The Catholic University of America Press, 1996), pp. 350–355, for Harvey's method of argumentation. For another account of Harvey's story, see J. Hannam, *The Genesis of Science* (Washington, DC: Regnery Publishing, 2011), pp. 261–266.
[3] S. Jaki, *A Mind's Matter* (Grand Rapids, Michigan: William Eerdmans Publishing Company, 2002), p. 169.
[4] New York: Science History Publications, 1974.
[5] *An Introduction to Philosophy* (London: Sheed and Ward, 1930), p. 22.
[6] Cited in S. Jaki, *Science and Creation* (New York: Science History Publications, 1974), p. 352.
[7] G. K. Chesterton, *St. Thomas Aquinas* (London: Hodder & Stoughton Limited, 1933), p. 95.
[8] *Science and Creation*, p. 12.
[9] *Ibid.*, p. 11.
[10] *Ibid.*, p. 40.

[11] This is S. Jaki's paraphrase of Needham in Jaki, *The Savior of Science* (Port Huron, Michigan: Real View Books, 2006), pp. 34–35.
[12] S. Jaki, *Science and Creation*, p. 27.
[13] *Ibid.*, p. 29.
[14] *Ibid.*, p. 33.
[15] *Ibid.*, p. 36.
[16] *Ibid.*, p. 38.
[17] *Science Was Born of Christianity* (The Habitation of Chimham Publishing Co., 2014), pp. 57–71.
[18] *The Savior of Science*, pp. 36–37.
[19] J. Maritain's summary of the history of philosophy in the pagan world is also highly recommended. See *An Introduction to Philosophy*, pp. 17–33.
[20] Cited in E. Gilson, *God and Philosophy* (New Haven: Yale University Press, 2002), p. 17.
[21] Aristotle, *Metaphysics*, 983b20–27.
[22] *In Met.*, paragraph 77; translation R. Blackwell, *Commentary on Aristotle's Metaphysics* (Notre Dame, Indiana: Dumb Ox Books, 1995), p. 28.
[23] See Aristotle, *Metaphysics*, 983a24–988b21 for this history.
[24] *The First Philosophers* (Oxford University Press, 2000), p. xix.
[25] *In Met.*, paragraph 575; translation Blackwell, *Commentary on Aristotle's Metaphysics*, p. 212.
[26] Translation R. Waterfield *The First Philosophers* (Oxford University Press, 2000), p. 213.
[27] For Jaki on the *Phaedo*, see *Questions on Science and Religion* (Pinckney, Michigan: Real View Books, 2004), pp. 33–34; *Impassible Divide* (New Hope, Kentucky: Real View Books, 2008), pp. 22–23; *The Mirage of Conflict* (New Hope, Kentucky: Real View Books, 2009), pp. 54–55; *Means to Message* (Grand Rapids, Michigan: William Eerdmans Publishing Company, 1999), p. 205; *The Road of Science and the Ways to God* (Port Huron, Michigan: Real View Books, 2005), pp. 20–21; *God and the Cosmologists* (Fraser, Michigan: Real View Books, 1998), p. 182; 'Socrates or the Baby and the Bathwater' in *Faith and Reason*, Spring, 1990. See also A. Taylor, *Plato* (London: University Paperbacks, 1960), pp. 183–208.
[28] *Phaedo*, 70c–72e.
[29] *Ibid.*, 89a–91c.
[30] *Ibid.*, 99b.
[31] *Ibid.*, 100b.
[32] *Ibid.*, 100d; translation H. Fowler, *Plato's Euthyphro, Apology, Crito, Phaedo, Phaedrus* (Cambridge, Massachusetts: Harvard University Press, 1914), p. 345.

Pagan Pantheism

[33] *Ibid.*, 97c–98a.
[34] *Ibid.*, 72e–77d.
[35] See A. Taylor, *Plato*, p. 202.
[36] *In Met.*, paragraph 782; translation Blackwell, *Commentary on Aristotle's Metaphysics*, p. 288. See also Aquinas, ST, I, q.105, a.5.
[37] See, for example, *Metaphysics*, 991a11.
[38] The medievals called this the fallacy of *opus naturae = opus intelligentiae*, wherein everything in nature is seen as being under the immediate direction of intelligence. It errs in not seeing that purpose can be implanted in natural things, which then pursue that purpose mindlessly. See W. Wallace, *The Modeling of Nature*, p. 17.
[39] *God and Philosophy* (New Haven: Yale University Press, 2002), pp. 30–31.
[40] *Plato*, p. 232.
[41] *Posterior Analytics*, 99b30.
[42] See *Metaphysics*, 980a21–982a3.
[43] See *Metaphysics*, 982a4–982b10.
[44] *Physics*, Book 8, chapter 4, 256a1.
[45] See W. Craig, *The Cosmological Argument from Plato to Leibniz* (Eugene, Oregon: Wipf and Stock Publishers, 1980), pp. 28–29.
[46] *The Spirit of Medieval Philosophy* (New York: Charles Scribner's Sons, 1940), p. 66.
[47] Such is the majority opinion of modern scholars, though it is contested by some. Aquinas, for one, believed that Aristotle understood the distinction between essence and existence (*In Met.*, paragraph 295), and so saw God as being an efficient cause (*In Met.*, paragraph 1174, *In Phys.*, paragraph 974). But it was customary in the scholastic age to interpret Aristotle benignly. See E. Grant, *The Foundations of Modern Science in the Middle Ages* (Cambridge: Cambridge University Press, 1996), pp. 164–165.
[48] *Physics*, 250b11.
[49] *Metaphysics*, 1074b15–36.
[50] E. Grant, *The Foundations of Modern Science in the Middle Ages* (Cambridge: Cambridge University Press, 1996), p. 67.
[51] Hannam goes so far as to say that Aristotle's First Mover 'was nothing like the God of the Bible' in *The Genesis of Science* (Washington, DC: Regnery Publishing, 2011), p. 72.
[52] *God and Philosophy* (New Haven: Yale University Press, 2002), p. 35.
[53] *Metaphysics*, 1072a26–b14.
[54] See Grant, *The Foundations of Modern Science*, p. 67.
[55] D. Ross, *Aristotle* (London: Methuen, 1964), p. 96.

[56] Metaphysics, 1074b11.
[57] *In Met.*, paragraph 2598; trans. Rowan, p. 823.
[58] Grant, *The Foundations of Modern Science*, p. 60.
[59] P. Duhem in S. Jaki, *Scientist and Catholic: Pierre Duhem* (Front Royal, Virginia: Christendom Press, 1991), p. 199.
[60] See R. Dales, *the Scientific Achievement of the Middle Ages* (Philadelphia: University of Pennsylvania Press, 1973), p. 102.
[61] Grant, *The Foundations of Modern Science*, pp. 61–63.
[62] Jaki, *Science and Creation*, p. 104.
[63] 274a1.
[64] For other false Aristotelian scientific conclusions, see S. Jaki, *The Road of Science and the Ways to God* (Scottish Academic Press, 1978), p. 22.
[65] *The Savior of Science*, p. 40. See also *Means to Message*, p. 205.
[66] *A Mind's Matter*, p. 170. See also Jaki, *The Mirage of Conflict*, p. 49; *Impassible Divide*, p. 20.
[67] See p. 73.
[68] E. Gilson, *Methodical Realism* (San Francisco: Ignatius Press, 2011), p. 72.
[69] Jaki, *The Road of Science*, p. 21.

5 CATHOLIC CREATIVITY

The timidity, the hushed voice [of Aristotle], is characteristic of the best Paganism.
Adopted into Christianity, the doctrine speaks loud and jubilant.

C. S. Lewis

IN THE ANNALS of science history, it would be hard to find a more dedicated physicist than Frenchman Pierre Duhem (1861–1916). During his preparatory education at Collège Stanislas in Paris, his life's vocation was awakened by his professors of science. Seeing his precocious aptitude for mathematics and 'his enormous esteem for the beauty of physics', they considered him as 'destined for making discoveries'.[1]

After a series of intellectual triumphs at Stanislas, Duhem was one of 40 students chosen from around France to enter the elite École Normale, at which he became the head of his class. His fellow students were astonished at his single-minded dedication to a vision that had already become a life-goal that he set for himself, namely, working out a perfect form of physics,[2] one in which every mathematical detail would relate to aspects of physical reality.[3]

When he graduated and took up a professorship at Bordeaux, his mother and sister were dismayed at the bachelor bent his life was taking. To their urgings that he should be thinking about marriage, he would only reply that all was to be kept for science, that there would be nothing—and no one—between him and science. These turned out to be famous last words, however, for even such a dedicated man, for an arranged visit of a family with five daughters led to Pierre's marriage with the youngest of them six months later, when he was 29.[4]

Everything seemed to be set for Duhem the accomplished scientist to establish his family. But tragedy soon struck. Less than two years after his wedding, Pierre was laying to rest the remains of his stillborn son and his wife Marie-Adèle, who had not survived the childbirth. Left with his infant daughter Hélène and a deep personal sorrow, Duhem tried to pick up the pieces of his life and soldier on.[5]

Naturally enough, he buried himself once more in the study of science. Still pursuing his goal of a perfect form of physics, he embarked on an odyssey of historical research, begging texts from libraries, poring over medieval manuscripts, filling notebook after notebook with excerpts. Pierre wanted to establish a pattern for the fruitful methodology that would lead him to his goal, but his researches ended up bearing another fruit: a ten volume work on the history of science entitled *Système du Monde*.[6] His explorations in putting together this monument led to the serendipitous discovery that modern science owes its origin, in a large degree, to medieval Christianity, a thesis diametrically opposed to the standard narrative of his time and ours. The purpose of this chapter is to support it.

Fixing Aristotle

Aristotle had performed an immeasurable service to the human race by defining the epistemology of the human mind—realism—and systematising the laws by which it attains truth—logic. The scope of his contribution, the penetration of his discourse, and the completeness of his synthesis of reality would assure him a foundational role in the intellectual progress that came after him. The medievals testified to this by calling him 'The Philosopher'. But, as we saw in the last chapter, the Aristotelian corpus could not be adopted wholesale. It contained many irreplaceable insights and concepts in natural philosophy and metaphysics, but was terribly off track in the realms of natural science. The precise point where Aristotle went wrong was in his conception of God and divine activity.

Thus, Aristotle left a double task for future generations who wished to continue his pursuit of a rational grasp of all aspects of reality:

- the adoption of the vast majority of his philosophy, especially his realism and logic
- the correction of his notion of God, and the use of the corrected notion to re-found the natural sciences.

This was no easy task. It is somewhat like finding the manual for an inoperable Saturn 7, then being required to find its fundamental flaw, fix that flaw, and redesign the entire rocket accordingly. Some would take the manual and say there was nothing wrong. Others would change the plan in places that did not require change, while leaving the flaw unfixed. Still others would improve the plan here or there, but would not realise that more basic changes needed to be made.

Thankfully, Aristotle's amazing synthesis of reality was finally fixed, and what we know as modern science was born from that repair. Surprisingly, the fixture occurred in the world of the Middle Ages, a world with an intellectual climate driven by religion, but a religion that was realist.

I must track this story, as it provides another example of how an epistemology driven by religion has an immense effect on a culture's ability to know reality. There are three main aspects to this tale:

- the way in which the Christian doctrine of creation naturally engenders a realist epistemology
- how the medieval Church created a society of free intellectual inquiry, one in which neither theology nor the Bible impeded the progress of science
- how medieval Christian thinkers perfected Aristotle's philosophical realism and replaced his physics.

Let us consider these points in turn.

Christian realism

In medieval Christendom, the prevailing worldview was not determined by philosophy, but by religion. The Church influenced both the religious beliefs of the populace, and the way in which society was organised. I must first consider the type of worldview that Catholic beliefs engendered, and then consider the medieval society it produced.

Recall the view of reality that we worked out in chapter 2, by the use of reason alone. It was a tough climb up to the top, but we did it. In the end, it would have been easier if we had just been provided the conclusions up front and did not have to work them out on our own. We could have become professional realists and taken on a complete realist worldview without having done all of the philosophical hard work.

In a sense, the Christian faith has just such an influence on the human mind, by providing up front a worldview that matches exactly with the worldview worked out by a professional realist using his natural reason at full capacity. That Christian worldview flows ultimately from the doctrine—believed on faith—of creation in time by a transcendent God.

Let us make the connection between creation and realism by using a Biblical example. The very first words of Genesis say, 'In the beginning, God created heaven and earth.' The very first words of John's Gospel say, 'In the beginning was the Word ... all things were made through Him and without Him was made nothing that has been made.' By the opening sentence of Genesis, Catholics understand that the universe came into being in time from no pre-existing substance by the creative action of God; by the opening sentence of the Evangelist, Catholics understand that creation proceeded from God's Wisdom and so the mark of rationality pervades all of Creation.

Catholic Creativity

These two ideas make instant metaphysicians out of the least of the believers, providing a clarity beyond anything Aristotle was able to work out with his careful reasoning. Consider just six corollaries that a philosopher reflecting deeply on the creation doctrine can draw from it and how those corollaries are in perfect agreement with realism as an epistemology and the conclusions that realism necessarily draws about reality. Since this will involve technical philosophical considerations like those of chapter 2, I invite the less philosophically inclined to skip to the 'Summing up' section below.

1. God is able to be unmoved and cause innumerable effects.

God is a Creator. Before Creation, there is only God. At Creation, God brings into existence 'from' nothing the entire cosmos in some form. Thus, God stands completely outside of the universe and sets it in motion, not by a final causality, not by attracting an already existing universe to imitate Him, but by making the universe exist when previously nothing of it existed.

The only way to accomplish this, as we saw in chapter 2, is by means of a power, whereby a thing exists simply by God wanting it to exist.[7] When God wants things to happen, He does not stretch out His arm and pull a lever. Rather, He simply wills it to be and it is.

But God does not just will that the universe exist. He also wills for it to continue in existence and its history to unfold in a way that matches His plans for it. At the same time, God does not change, as otherwise He could not be the first principle of the universe. Thus, *God must be able to want and cause everything that happens in the entire universe for all time, by a <u>single</u> act of His will.*

To illustrate what this means, consider that you want your super-smart robot to go to the grocery store for you to get some milk. In desiring this, it is clear that you desire many other things at the same time, in the same act of your will. You also want him to leave your house, get into the car, start it, drive to the store, go to the aisle where the milk is kept, pay the cashier, and so on.

Similarly, God is able to desire many things at once. The difference is that God does not have to act after willing, in order to execute all that He wills. What He wills is accomplished *by the mere fact of Him wanting them and that alone*. Thus, with a single, eternal act of will, God is able to cause the being of the universe, its conservation in being, and all that has happened and will happen in it for all time.[8] Having only *one* eternal act, which is the same as His being, God is completely unchanging in Himself.

Because God's eternal act of will includes innumerable aspects, that act causes innumerable effects in the universe. Thus, He is an Unmoved Mover, as rightly demanded by Aristotle's realism, but He moves the universe as efficient cause, not just as final cause. While remaining unchanged in Himself, God is at the same time the source of the universe at every moment, always sustaining it in being and looking after it with His eternal Providence. As First Cause, He creates a universe investigable by science, and as Creator He deserves the religious homage of His creatures.

This nuanced metaphysics flows from the Scriptural interpretations given above. John speaks of the universe being created through a Word, and Genesis has God create by speaking. Both perspectives serve to indicate an eternal concept in the mind of God which includes the entire created order. As the Psalmist says, 'Our God is in heaven: he hath done all things whatsoever he would' (Ps 113:11). And: 'Let all the earth fear the Lord, and let all the inhabitants of the world be in awe of him. For he spoke and they were made: he commanded and they were created' (Ps 32:8–9). These verses could serve as descriptions of the exercise of primary causality.

2. There is a 'universe.'

Accompanying the notion of creation in time is that of the unity of the entire created order. The whole cosmos comes from a single, transcendent source, and so has a top-down unity wherein each thing has some relation to every other thing. Thus, it truly deserves to be called a 'universe' or 'a strict totality of consistently interacting things'.[9] By saying that God created the 'heaven and the earth', Genesis is wanting to indicate His causation of the *whole* of the cosmos, in its two main parts, as Jaki is fond of pointing out.[10]

Now, realism also supports the existence of a universe. Each of our minds forms a notion of matter from contact with the outside world, and the realist trusts in the intellect's ability to form true notions about that world. But for the notion 'matter' to be true, it must apply in a unified way to all that is material, since the properties of matter must pertain to all material things. Thus, all material things have a unity and this unity is given the name of 'universe.'[11] Our idea of matter, then, indicates a unified universe, unified in the sense that the properties of matter pervade the whole of it.

3. The universe is caused.

Instead of the universe being a self-existent, eternal being, under the Christian perspective it is something brought into being. The universe being created means that it is not necessary, but contingent, that is, caused and thoroughly dependent upon another. It is not its own reason, but rather has a meaning and purpose outside of itself.

How is it dependent? In its very being. It is a creature, and so must be established in all four realms of causality at the level of being for it to exist. God, in bringing the created order into existence from nothing, must provide:

- material for bodies (material cause)
- stable natures or essences (formal cause)
- powers inherent in creatures (efficient causality)
- purposes implanted in nature (final cause).

The Creator God communicates to each individual substance a nature with its mode of operation. This enables creatures to act by their own proper operation in the order of secondary causality. For Aristotle, both God and creation were determined to certain necessary operations; for the Christian realist, God acts with supreme independence and creatures act with limited independence. That realist perspective is consistent with Aristotle's doctrine on the four causes, and even enriches it, by providing a sufficient reason for the four causes' existence in creatures.

4. There is a rational order to the whole of the universe.

Everything that God creates is good and He creates through His intellectual Word, according to Genesis 1 and John 1. Thus, all that He does is ordered. God does not act haphazardly, in acts of raw power, but rather with an ordained power, a power that executes what His intellect and wisdom indicate, and His will commands.[12] If some created effects escape our comprehension, that is not due to them lacking intelligibility, but to the weakness of our rational power. For the Christian, the natural order presents an inexhaustible field for discovery; it is made reasonably and we are made with reason. This theology confirms the realist's optimistic trust in the powers of sense and intellect to know reality.

Jaki points out,

> It is nowhere hinted in the Bible that when God wills, He does so capriciously, that is, independently of the consistency of His intellect. Will and intellect are never separated in the God of the Bible. On the contrary, Yahweh is always a reasonable God, indeed the supreme meaning and reason in every aspect.[13]

5. There is one truth.

If there is a single source for all of creation and hence a universe, then there is necessarily also one reality and so one truth. What universal principles hold for one aspect of reality must be true for the whole of reality. Contradiction is impossible. Since everything proceeds from one eminently consistent Being, then the whole must be consistent. There cannot be two sets of truths belonging to two different orders, such as faith and reason, natural and supernatural, religion and science.

No discovery or true proposition, then, is to be feared. Whatever the human mind is able to discover will be in harmony with the wisdom of its Source, the good God. Nature is not an unintelligible mass of blind forces, but the exhibition of a supreme order. It was for this reason that the medieval mind considered God as revealing Himself in two books: one was the Bible, and the other was the 'book' of nature.[14]

The realist likewise must hold to the doctrine of a unified truth, because of his trust in the powers of the intellect. The working of the mind is valid only if its first principle, that of non-contradiction, is valid for all reality. But that principle is not valid if there are double truths, such that a proposition can be both true and not true at the same time, and in the same respect.

6. The heavens are not more exalted than the Earth.

Most ancient civilisations paid divine honours in some fashion to heavenly bodies, while Aristotle and especially Plato considered them to be superior at least to the degree that their behaviour was not comparable to what happens here below. The stars were seen as being divine and eminently ordered, while the Earth was mortal and chaotic.

Meanwhile, Genesis presents humans as being higher than the whole of material creation, placing the heavenly bodies in a subordinate position. God exists before the heavenly bodies, creates them only on the fourth day, and creates them for the service of humans, in that they provide humans light and establish for them the cycle of days, nights and seasons (Gen 1:14–18). Those cycles are not an indication of a blind fatalism in the universe, but rather of God's fidelity. The regularity of heavenly motions is consistently used in Scripture to indicate that nothing 'could conceivably undercut the efficacy of God's decrees'.[15] They have a validity that is eternal.

With regard to the effects that heavenly motion exercises on us and the rest of the things on Earth, Aristotle held that these effects were necessary, meaning regular and unstoppable. The higher spheres determine the lower spheres, including the Earth. But if the stars determine our behaviour, how is it that we have free will? Aristotle struggled with this question.[16] But Genesis, after having run through the entire cosmos, comes to the creation of man and indicates that he is accorded special privileges beyond the rest of the material order. Man alone is created to God's image (Gen 1:27), that is, with an immaterial and immortal soul, and man is commanded to rule over the Earth (Gen 1:28). Man's powers of intellect and will, then, place him above all other creatures brought into being during God's *hexameron* or six day work. Thus, it is a quite straightforward work for Aquinas to hold that the movement of the celestial bodies does not influence either our intellects or wills.[17] The reason that he gives is that human 'understanding surpasses all bodies in the order of nature.' This perspective could not fail to support the realist's trust in the ability of sense and intellect to establish a bridge between mind and reality.

In short, Genesis presents humans as being over the entire material order, including the heavenly bodies. And God is over everything, the supreme source of the created order. Primary and secondary causality are situated precisely in their specific orders, rendering the universe both intelligible in itself and for the human mind. It is a universe where religion and science co-exist without conflict and in perfect harmony.

Summing up

In these six points of philosophical development from a Catholic interpretation of Scripture, we have a theological perspective that leads directly to an epistemological realism. The Indians and Chinese were pointed away from realism by their pantheistic theology. Aristotle found realism, but he had to ignore Greek theology to do so. Christians, however, had realism dropped in their laps by the revelation of the doctrine of creation in time.

Having seen how realism is the epistemology which naturally flows from Christian faith, I now must consider what type of intellectual culture a fully Christian world produces. Was the Christendom of the Middle Ages repressive, an enemy to all free thinking, an obscurantist, darkly world, where ignorance and illiteracy reigned? Or was it a society of immense intellectual ferment, a golden age of rational progress, an age wherein secular learning advanced by giant strides, plumbing depths of reality never previously penetrated in human history? Let us consider the answers to these questions.

The Church and secular learning

Christianity began its conquest of minds and hearts in the midst of a pagan Roman Empire at the height of its power. From the start, Christian thinkers could have looked upon all secular learning as rubbish and given a cultish cast to Christianity, wherein faith would be blind, totally divorced from reason.

Though there were a few impulses in that direction among the early Fathers, that is not what happened. Rather, Greek philosophy and science were seen as a means of supporting faith. They were assigned the picturesque role of being 'handmaidens of theology'.[18]

Grant believes that Christianity's peaceful co-existence with secular learning, from its beginnings, might be due to its slow spread throughout the Roman Empire.[19] The slow development would force Christians to assimilate the influences of their milieu, to a certain degree, rather than impose their views unilaterally upon others, as Islam would do when it arose and spread like wildfire.

While that is a partial explanation, Jaki provides a deeper reason in his *The Savior of Science*.[20] The new Christian faith held that a transcendent God created the universe *and* took on a human nature at a certain point in human history. Believing this, Christians also had to believe there was an intimate connection between the natural and supernatural orders, between creation and Creator, earth and heaven, reason and faith. Christians could not feel threatened by the natural order or knowledge of that order, because God Himself was at the source of that order, and God Himself had entered that order in Jesus Christ.

If a person believes that there is one God, that He is good, and that He is the source of all that is, then he cannot attack anything in the natural order without implicitly attacking his own belief that it comes from God. Nothing could incarnate this principle in Christian minds like the Incarnation of Jesus Christ, which they believe occurred by the union of a human nature and a divine nature in a single divine person.

Thus, when we come to the Middle Ages, we find Church and State working closely together to create an intellectual context 'with the conditions that made it feasible to pursue science and natural philosophy on a permanent basis'.[21] Grant reduces those conditions for the flourishing of science in a religious society to three:[22]

1. Science is recognised as independent.
2. Science is protected by the secular state.
3. Science is favourably regarded by religious authorities.

All of these conditions, he says, obtained in the medieval Christian state:

> In late medieval Latin Christendom the third condition was clearly in effect. Because the Church looked with favour on science, secular authorities also adopted a beneficent approach toward it—they had no reason to oppose science and natural philosophy. Indeed, they found many occasions to favour the disciplines. Because the second and third conditions were fulfilled, the first was almost met as well during the late Middle Ages.[23]

In Grant's eyes, then, the Church's favourable regard toward science enabled it to be protected by the State and be pursued in independence from theology. One reason churchmen were happy for science to be studied alongside theology is that they themselves were often both theologians and natural philosophers. Most of them

> believed that natural philosophy was essential for a proper elucidation of theology ... Indeed, some of the most noteworthy accomplishments in science and mathematics during the Middle Ages came from theologians.[24]

Because reason and faith dwelt in such harmony, medieval scientists had a great freedom of inquiry in pursuing knowledge of the natural world:

> Although theology was always a potential obstacle to the study of natural philosophy, theologians themselves offered little opposition to the discipline, largely because they were too heavily involved in it.[25]

This statement may seem startling to those who know something of the conflicts between religion and science in the past 500 years. Certain literal interpretations of the Bible have often been used to contradict the legitimate findings of empirical science. In medieval Christendom, however, the Bible did not pose any obstacle to scientific pursuits. The reason lies in Catholicism's relationship to its sacred text.

Catholicism and the Bible

For Catholics, the Church comes first and the Bible comes second. Catholic apologists do not begin by trying to convince this or that prospective convert that the Bible is from God. Rather, they present motives of credibility in order lead a person to a moral certainty that the Church is a divine institution and thus worthy of belief when speaking on behalf of God. Once a person believes that the Church is from God, then that person will believe that the dogmas which the Church binds her members to believe are also from God. One of those dogmas is that the Bible is inspired by God.

Catholics, then, believe that the Bible is inspired, not because they think that the Bible (or any other book) is able to attest to its own inspiration, but because the Church says it is inspired. St Augustine famously expresses this sentiment in saying, 'I would not believe the Gospel, unless the authority of the Catholic Church commanded me'.[26]

The relationship of Catholicism to its sacred text is a key determinant of its relation to secular learning. It stands in contrast with Islam and Protestantism, religions I will consider in chapters 6 and 7, respectively. In Catholicism:

1. The Biblical text is not seen as interpreting itself, for authentic interpretation belongs solely to the Catholic Church.[27]
2. The Biblical text is subordinate to an authoritative body. That body is a religious body which proposes truths of faith from the text, not truths of physical science.

Those who believe that a sacred text speaks on its own authority will tend to interpret it in a strictly literal sense, with an interpretation that does not pass through a careful discernment on the part of reason, one which is accepted on faith alone and which is not likely to be compared carefully with real data from reality. Those, however, who believe that God willed the meaning of the sacred text to be conveyed by divinely sanctioned human authorities will think that human reason will need to be applied in the interpretation of the text.

Likewise, when a sacred text is subject to a religious body, as in Catholicism, it is seen as being directed primarily to proposing religious truths, not secular truths. The Church, throughout its history, has used the Bible on countless occasions to support a dogma of faith, on behalf of religion. The Church does not use it to propose secular truths to its adherents, though there are certainly many secular truths in the Bible. By this practice of the Church, Catholics understand the Bible's proper role as a religious text. That is why, in the Middle Ages, 'Biblical texts were not employed to 'demonstrate' scientific truths by appeal to divine authority'.[28] In another place, the same author provides an example:

> When [Bishop] Nicole Oresme inserted some fifty citations to twenty-three different books of the Bible in his *On the Configurations of Qualities and Motions*, a major scientific treatise of the Middle Ages, he did so only as examples, or for additional support, but in no sense to demonstrate an argument.[29]

When a sacred text stands on its own, however, and precedes religion, it is naturally seen as being directed to communicating all knowledge, instead of having as its primary purpose the communication of revealed, supernatural truths. Thus, text-based religions will tend to see their sacred text as meant to teach things like natural science. When this happens, they will hold to the interpretation of nature intimated by their text, even when that interpretation contradicts natural facts. In other words, they will tend to be idealists, imposing ideas supposedly revealed by God on God's natural world, despite evidence to the contrary. Institution-based religions, on the other hand, will tend to be realist, in that they will have 'different methods for pursuing different intelligible objects': they will have recourse to authority when seeking supernatural truths, and have recourse to reason when seeking natural truths. The chart below provides a comparison of the relationship of major religions to their sacred texts.

Table 5.1 Relation of religions to their sacred text

Religion	Sacred Text	Sacred Text receives its authority from:	Interpretation is:	Resulting epistemology
Catholicism	Bible with 73 books	The Catholic Church	Mediated by human reason	Realism
Fundamentalist Protestantism	Bible with 66 books	Itself	Not mediated by reason	Idealism
Islam	Koran	Itself	Not mediated by reason	Idealism

Catholic realism

Having seen the general intellectual ambiance of the Middle Ages, I now turn to consider how scholars of that period fixed up Aristotle's synthesis of reality. By that time, the Church had possessed a positive attitude towards natural philosophy for over a millennium, 'an attitude that was developed and nurtured during the first four or five centuries of Christianity'.[30] We may well ask, then, why Catholics had not worked out their own metaphysics and natural science after such a long time. The answer lies in the particular aims of the Christian world during its first millennium, as well as the persecutions and political difficulties it faced before it could properly establish its own society.

The fact is that, when Jesus Christ appeared among men, He did not provide a philosophy or even a theology for His followers. 'Taken in itself, Christianity was not a philosophy. It was the essentially religious doctrine of the salvation of men through Christ.'[31] Thus, after the Ascension of Christ into Heaven, it remained for Christians:

- to work out the harmony of the dogmas of Christian faith with reason (theology), and
- to work out a metaphysics or rational view of all reality that coupled seamlessly with those dogmas (philosophy).

Intellectual efforts in the first five centuries of the Church were mainly directed to apologetics and theology, to drawing in new believers and fighting off heresy. The synthesis of supernatural truths with natural knowledge begun at that time was far from complete by the time the barbarian invasions began. Saint Augustine had made the bravest effort, but he only had available to him 'methods borrowed from Plato and Plotinos'.[32] Those methods gave an incorrect view of human nature's makeup and way of attaining truth. Thus, while Saint Augustine was equipped with a vast genius, the concepts in his metaphysical toolbox were but crude tools for constructing a philosophical synthesis for all

Catholic Creativity

reality; in several respects, he was an idealist. Because of this, he was not able to join the Christian God with the Platonic universe. In the words of Gilson, 'he never had the philosophy of his theology'.[33] For the synthesis to take place, the realism of 'The Philosopher', Aristotle, was needed.

But the Christian world did not have ready access to the Stagirite until the beginning of the thirteenth century. The reason for the delay is that he had been lost to the West for centuries. When Christianity began, Greek science was accessible to everyone, since Greek-speaking East and Latin-speaking West were contained in a single Roman Empire. When that Empire was divided into East and West in the late third century, however, the Greek language and hence Greek learning began to decline in the West. This was disastrous for Latin intellectual history, because 'Greek had been the language of science'.[34] Thus, if there were no Greek speakers, by and large there was no science.

The isolation of the Greeks in the East, combined with the crumbling of the Roman Empire, caused the ushering in of the so-called 'Dark Ages', as Grant notes:

> For various reasons—including civil strife over the imperial succession that resulted in an empire split into western and eastern halves, economic deterioration because of waning trade and crushing taxes, and the massive migrations and invasions of Germanic and Celtic peoples into areas formerly dominated by Rome—most urban centres in Western Europe were in serious decline from approximately the fourth to the ninth centuries.[35]

During this time of the re-building of Europe, not much more could be done by scholars than preserve the knowledge of the past. The political atmosphere did not provide the stability and infrastructure needed for an intellectual golden age. That would have to wait until the High Middle Ages, a period of time that 'transformed Western Europe from an intellectual embarrassment to an intellectual powerhouse'.[36]

Christian conquests in Spain during the twelfth century provided both 'settled conditions' and 'direct contact with the large body of Arabic literature'.[37] Latin-speaking scholars of the West were all too aware of their 'intellectual deprivation' and their corresponding need to acquire science from other cultures if they were to have it at all. This humility in ignorance sparked 'the great age of translation', wherein 'scholars of the Western world acted to acquire the scientific heritage of the past', an effort which constituted 'one of the true turning points in the history of Western science and natural philosophy'.[38]

The most important author to translate was the 'master of those that know',[39] Aristotle. His natural philosophy was to become the core of the legacy of the Middle Ages.[40] It was Ramon of Sauvetat, the bishop of Toledo from 1126–1151, who had the works of Aristotle and his Arab commentators translated into Latin,[41] and these translations soon spread throughout the academic world of Christendom. Their impact was sudden and overwhelming:

> The physics of Aristotle and Avicenna provided the Parisian masters with principles so vastly superior to anything they had ever known that their discovery amounted to a revelation ... For the first time and at one fell swoop the men of the Middle Ages found themselves face to face with a purely philosophical explanation of nature.[42]

As we have already seen, Aristotle was the only thinker in the ancient world who was able to attain a metaphysics that was a natural theology at the same time, that is, he was the only one to construct a rational synthesis of all reality. Because Aristotle 'imposed a strong sense of order and coherence on an otherwise bewildering world',[43] all of the scholars in Christendom, practically to a man, became Aristotelians. This was true to such a degree that 'medieval natural philosophy was almost wholly based on Aristotle's natural books'.[44]

By the the very fact that medieval philosophers, who were called 'scholastics', embraced Aristotelianism, they also embraced realism. Aristotle's successes in metaphysics, after all, came from his identification of the way in which the human mind knows reality and his employment of a method of philosophising tailored to that human mode of knowing.

While I am claiming that the Christian faith naturally matches up with a realist philosophy, I are not claiming that it automatically produces philosophical geniuses like Aristotle, able to construct that philosophy. Medieval Catholics relied on Aristotle to show them the natural knowledge that would match up with their supernatural knowledge, because they had not found it themselves.

At the same time, once their philosophic knowledge was provided its Stagirian jump start, when they assimilated Aristotle's thought into a culture of an intellectual intensity similar to that of The Philosopher's Greek world, the scholastics were able to make momentous advances on his thought. To do so, they had to understand him properly (something the greatest Islamic philosophers failed to achieve), adopt what was true of his thought, leave behind or correct what was erroneous, and create a new synthetic body of human knowledge. They did all of this.

An important part of the process was not adopting Aristotle lock, stock, and barrel, blindly kowtowing to the Stagirite no matter what he had to say. The scholastics needed to know where to draw the line between adoption and rejection of Aristotelian doctrine. The line that they used was their religious faith, for Catholicism came into direct conflict with some of Aristotle's pet theses, and the scholastics were Christians first and philosophers second.

The Catholic scholastic mix of acceptance and rejection of Aristotle turned out to be the perfect formula for intellectual success. It is an interesting and even astonishing fact of intellectual history that the scholastics were led by religious doctrines of faith to contradict some conclusions of their favourite philosopher, and that doing so led them to perfect his realist philosophy and found modern science by overturning his false natural science. I will first consider how Aristotle's philosophy was perfected by scholastics, and then how his science was overturned.

Faith fixing reason

In 1267, St Bonaventure indicated the primary conflicts that existed between the teachings of Catholicism, and the teachings of Aristotle and some of his Muslim commentators. The latter thought that they could prove by rational argumentation three propositions which were contrary to the Catholic Faith, says Bonaventure:

- the eternity of the world, founded upon the circular nature of movement and time
- the fatal necessity of events, founded upon the revolutions of the spheres
- the oneness of the intellect, founded upon the oneness of the separate Intelligence.

All this is false. The first error is against Scripture; the second error is destructive of free choice; the third error eliminates the distinction of personal merits, since the soul of Judas becomes one with that of Christ.[45]

The first problem, Aristotle's contradiction of the Catholic dogma of creation in time, posed the greatest difficulties.[46] The second and third problems, championed by Aristotle's Muslim commentators, contradicted both faith and reason. In face of these major conflicts, there were three choices available to medieval society:

1. Forbid the works of Aristotle outright, because of their errors
2. Take from Aristotle what was true and reject what was false
3. Hold the principle of 'double truth', namely that something can 'be true for faith and false for philosophy, and vice versa',[47] and thus both Aristotle and faith can be held as true, though they contradict one another.

All three of these solutions were tried. The first reaction was to forbid the teaching of Aristotle. This was done initially in Paris in 1210, shortly after The Philosopher appeared there for the first time in Latin dress. 'The provincial synod of Sens decreed that the books of Aristotle on natural philosophy and all commentaries thereon were not to be read at Paris in public or secret, under penalty of excommunication.'[48] This ban for Paris was confirmed by Pope Gregory IX in 1231, and Innocent IV extended it to Toulouse in 1245.

But, in the end, the ascendancy of the Stagirite over the medieval mind could not be arrested. The Paris ban was lifted after 40 years, driving most scholars to pursue the second solution, the sifting of Aristotle.[49] It is this relationship to Aristotle's works that concerns us most here; the proponents of the 'double truth' solution will be considered in the next chapter.

Scholastics sifting The Philosopher succeeded in taking from the Aristotelian corpus an immense weight of valuable and true thinking, while filtering out what was false. One thinker especially was able to construct a new metaphysics upon which the entire body of Catholic belief could rest without any offense to reason. Let us see how he did it.

Aquinas's Christian philosophy

Thomas Aquinas's (1225–1274) *Summa Theologiae* stands as the greatest harmonising of faith and reason ever achieved, where the two walk hand in hand without the least disagreement. Its backdrop is what Gilson terms a 'Christian philosophy', that is, a rational account of the ultimate principles of reality attained via insights from supernatural truths. This does not mean that Aquinas uses his faith to prove philosophical truths, for he proves them on the basis of reason alone. Rather, it means that his faith assisted his reason to make philosophical discoveries. In this sense, Aquinas's philosophy was Christian at the moment of discovery, but not at the moment of proof.[50]

The most important discovery that Aquinas made was in the realm of metaphysics. By means of that discovery, he was able to formulate a notion of 'being' superior to the philosophers that went before him. The Christian thinkers Augustine, Damascene, and Anselm conceived 'being' respectively as eternal immutability, an 'infinite ocean of entity', and 'that whose very nature it is to be'.[51] Aquinas, on the other hand, emphasised existence in his notion of 'being'. For him, 'to be is to exist'.[52]

Taking this notion of 'being', Aquinas then applied it to all reality. For him, creatures are beings that are brought into existence. Existence, for them, is something received, something caused, something donated. God, however, whose Biblical name is 'I am Who am' (Ex. 3:14) is a being who exists without being brought into existence. 'He Who is' has being of Himself. His being is unreceived and uncaused, a being that is co-extensive with His very identity, a being that is being itself rather than a being that is this or that type of being.

God, then, is pure Existence. The things in the world, however, are received existences, that is, creatures. Each of them, as such, must have at least two metaphysical parts, an act of existence and an essence or receiver of existence. If they did not have the second part, then they would be pure existence, like God. They would have existence without limitation. But, on the contrary, creatures have strict limits to their existence. Horses can only do horsey things because they have a horse essence, dogs can only do doggy things because they have a dog essence, and humans can only do human things because they have a human essence. In these examples, the horse or dog or human existence is limited to the boundaries of the horse or dog or human essence into which it is received. God's existence, on the other hand, is not limited, for it is not received into anything. He just is, that's all. With Him, it's 'He is', not 'He is as horse' or 'He is as human', as it is with all creatures.[53]

Muslim philosophers had already spoken of a distinction between existence and essence, but they spoke of existence as an accident, as something added to being. Aquinas, on the other hand, understood that this could not be.[54] Rather, existence must be 'the act by which substance has being'.[55] Existence does not come after being, but rather is a principle that establishes a being.

Aquinas used the correct distinction between existence and essence, which he attained by insight from faith, but which he argued from purely rational principles (in his *De Ente et Essentia*), and made it the cornerstone of a new metaphysics. It was a metaphysics which used a great many components of Aristotle's Saturn 7, but which had fixed its fundamental flaw—Aristotle's notions of 'being' and 'God'—and had re-drawn the plans on the basis of the fixture. 'Thus,' says Chesterton, 'began what is commonly called the appeal to Aquinas and Aristotle. It might be called the appeal to Reason and the Authority of the Senses'.[56]

In the end, it was Aquinas's faith that had enabled him to go further with reason than Aristotle, because that faith indicated to reason that there must be a real distinction between existence and essence in every creature, as Gilson points out:

> In an eternal and uncreated world, such as that of Greek philosophy, an essence is eternally realized and is inconceivable save as realized. It is of some moment, then, to understand that the real distinction of essence and existence, although clearly formulated only at the beginning of the thirteenth century, was always virtually present after the first verse of Genesis.[57]

In another place, Gilson says the following about Thomas's 'Christian philosophy':

> Thomism was not the upshot of a better understanding of Aristotle. It did not come out of Aristotelianism by way of evolution, but of revolution. Thomas uses the language of Aristotle everywhere to make the Philosopher say that there is only one God, the pure Act of Being, Creator of the world, infinite and omnipotent, a providence for all that which is, intimately present to every one of his creatures, especially to men, every one of whom is endowed with a personally immortal soul naturally able to survive the death of its body. The best way to make

> Aristotle say so many things he never said was not to show that, had he understood himself better than he did, he could have said them. For indeed Aristotle seems to have understood himself pretty well ... The true reason why [Thomas's] conclusions were different from those of Aristotle was that his own principles themselves were different ... [I]n order to metamorphose the doctrine of Aristotle, Thomas has ascribed a new meaning to the principles of Aristotle ... We are living in times so different from those of Thomas Aquinas that it is difficult for us to understand how philosophy can become theology and yet gain in rationality. This, however, is exactly what happened to philosophy in the *Summa theologiae*, when Thomas changed the water of philosophy to the wine of theology.[58]

Aquinas was able to attach himself to the Stagirite while remaining more attached to Catholicism. The fruit was a perennial philosophy. With the Chinese and Indians, *mythos* destroyed *logos*; with Aristotle, *logos* destroyed *mythos*; with Aquinas, *mythos* perfected *logos*. This is no small reason to believe that Aquinas's *mythos* was not mythology.

St Thomas Aquinas. (Image courtesy of Wikimedia Commons)

Aquinas's contribution to science

Aquinas's primary and even sole focus was the elucidation of a wholly rational basis for the Catholic faith. He was not a scientist and it seems that science did not interest him. Yet his work as a philosopher had an important impact on the future of science, in two respects.

The first aid that Saint Thomas provided future scientists was his perfection of metaphysics. The synthesis of reality that we worked out in chapter 2, which is essentially that of Aquinas, is the *only* worldview that prevents religion and science from coming into any conflict whatsoever. The reason is that it alone

- maintains separate orders of causality for God and creatures
- maintains the proper relationship between those orders, wherein secondary causality is subordinate to primary causality, in harmony with it, and acting at the same time as it
- allows all four classes of causality—material, formal, efficient, and final—their full scope.

The doctrine of creation in time led Aquinas to conceive of a universe that was contingently created by God to have necessary laws. He and other scholastics convinced the Western world that such was the universe we live in, and exact science can only have a coherent basis in such a universe. The reason is that exact science must assume that the universe has rigorously consistent natural laws that can be discovered by rational minds. We should not be surprised, then, that scholastics coming after Aquinas directly prepared the way for the launching of modern science that was to take place in the seventeenth century.

Jaki points out that Aquinas's realism anticipated the same mentality with which the great names of modern science would approach reality. Saint Thomas's proofs for the existence of God, which relied upon realist assumptions, 'embodied a stance in epistemology which, as further events were to show, contained a directive instinctively obeyed by the scientific movement.' This stance included a full-blooded conviction of the contingency of the universe and the ability of the human mind to understand it. The Newtonian and Einsteinian phases of science, which later postulated laws for the universe as a whole, were steeped in that same epistemology.[59]

Aquinas did not just postulate his balanced worldview, he lived it. His writings modelled a mentality of healthy non-discrimination in regard to the proper rights of religion and science, of faith and reason. Because his books were to carry so much weight after his death (to this day, there are schools of Thomism), he became a standard for realist rectitude for future generations, as Chesterton points out:

> [Aquinas] gave, by his view of Scripture and Science, and other questions, a sort of charter for pioneers more purely practical than himself. He practically said that if they could really prove their practical discoveries, the traditional interpretation of Scripture must give way before those discoveries. He could hardly, as the common phrase goes, say fairer than that. If the matter had been left to him, and men like him, there never would have been any quarrel between Science and Religion. He did his very best to map out two provinces for them, and to trace a just frontier between them.[60]

The second aid that Aquinas gave to future scientists was his rehabilitation of matter. Socrates and Plato had de-reified matter, emptying it of intelligible content and relegating it to the category of illusion. Aristotle partially restored matter by classifying it among his four causes and considering sense data taken from matter as true knowledge. Yet, as we have seen, he made both the heavens and movement too spiritual, attributing too much to final causality. This led to the quantitative aspects of material causes being ignored.

But Saint Thomas, being a follower of Christ, could not neglect matter. Christ was both God and man. He was the divine come down from Heaven, taking up a material body, a body which was

Catholic Creativity

crucified, died, buried, and rose again. This doctrine of the Incarnation engendered a new perspective towards reality in the Christian world, a perspective unknown to the pagans, what Chesterton refers to as 'a new Christian *motive* for the study of facts, as distinct from truths.' He explains further:

> There really was a new reason for regarding the senses, and the sensations of the body, and the experiences of the common man, with a reverence at which great Aristotle would have stared, and no man in the ancient world could have begun to understand. The Body was no longer what it was when Plato and Porphyry and the old mystics had left it for dead. It had risen from a tomb. It was no longer possible for the soul to despise the senses, which had been the organs of something that was more than man ... When once Christ had risen, it was inevitable that Aristotle should rise again.[61]

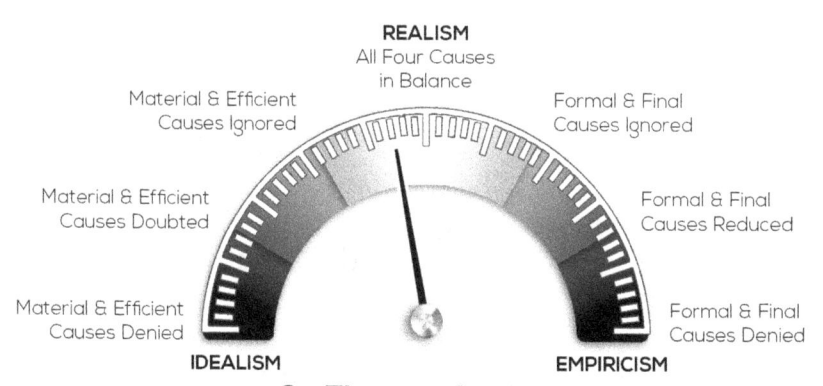

REALISM
All Four Causes in Balance

Material & Efficient Causes Ignored

Formal & Final Causes Ignored

Material & Efficient Causes Doubted

Formal & Final Causes Reduced

Material & Efficient Causes Denied

Formal & Final Causes Denied

IDEALISM

EMPIRICISM

St. Thomas Aquinas

Now, Saint Thomas embodied this new Christian attitude towards reality, this desire not to neglect the least of the aspects of God's intelligible Creation, not to deny the humblest creature its ontological rights so as not to slight the Creator. Thus,

> the Thomist philosophy began with the lowest roots of thought, the senses and the truisms of the reason; and a Pagan sage might have scorned such things, as he scorned the servile arts. But the materialism, which is merely cynicism in a Pagan, can be Christian humility in a Christian. St. Thomas was willing to begin by recording the facts and sensations of the material world, just as he would have been willing to begin by washing up the plates and dishes in the monastery.[62]

While Saint Thomas practically adopted wholesale Aristotle's science,[63] of which hardly a proposition was correct,[64] he yet promoted a realism that would soon give birth to modern science. He successfully completed the reformation of Aristotle's philosophy, but left the task of reforming Aristotle's science to others. Let us see how they did it.

New method in science

We saw in the third chapter that science today concerns itself with motion and its quantification.[65] Then, in the fourth chapter, we noted that Aristotle, following Socrates, explained all motion by means of qualities.[66] Things move because of some native desire in them for their natural place; they are internally impelled to seek what is best for them. Such was the perspective which dominated going into the Middle Ages. Science had to be released from the grip of this over-emphasis of final causes to find its proper home in the world of quantities.

To defeat Aristotle's explanation of natural motion, one which 'seems to have been admitted almost unanimously by the physicists of Antiquity',[67] a wholly different conception of the universe was needed, the Christian conception. If you believe that the universe was created in time by a transcendent God, then you can easily posit that God conferred unchanging properties or *forces* on matter, and that these unchanging properties or forces can in turn be communicated between material beings. Not only can individual things be secondary causes, but also matter as such. Under this view, matter's impersonal forces can act automatically or mechanistically in cosmological beings, and those forces can drive motion forward, in addition to intrinsic desire or raw external force, the only two options foreseen by Aristotle.

Grant remarks on how the medievals' conception of nature as capable of secondary causality flowed from their perception of God as primary cause:

> [T]he idea that God was the direct and immediate cause of everything yielded to an interpretation of the world that assumed that natural objects were capable of acting upon each other directly. God had conferred on nature the power and ability to cause things. He had made of it a self-operating entity. Nature, or the cosmos, was thus objectified and conceived as a harmonious, lawful, well-ordered, self-sufficient whole, which could be investigated by the human intellect.[68]

With this Christian realism taking hold, a new breed of scientists began to emerge in the twelfth century:

> The striking thing about this century [the twelfth] is the attitude of its scientists ... [T]he conviction of these scientists that nature operated in a uniform manner, according to rational laws which man had the power to discover, their intense interest in the natural world for its own sake, their habits of precise observation of natural phenomena, and the high value they placed on man as a rational being, portend a new age in the history of scientific thought.[69]

Because the medieval scientists had a different conception of the universe from Aristotle, it was, as it were, a different object of investigation from the universe that Aristotle studied, at least in its physical aspects. Just as Aristotle had developed a method for investigating physical bodies in an uncreated universe, so too the medievals had to develop their own method for investigating such bodies in a created universe.

They did indeed develop their own method, but first they had to isolate scientific considerations from the considerations of theology, treating science as its own discipline with its own methods. This is similar to what we today call 'methodological empiricism', wherein scientists purposely ignore all non-scientific considerations when studying physical bodies, in order to isolate more effectively their quantitative aspects. Such an isolation can be acceptable, as long as such scientists do not turn into radical empiricists, claiming that their method can only discover material and efficient causes.[70]

As Grant explains, the scholastics developed a certain 'methodological natural philosophy':

> [M]edieval natural philosophers sought to investigate the 'common course of nature,' not its uncommon, or miraculous, path. They characterized this approach admirably by the phrase 'speaking naturally'—that is, speaking in terms of natural science, and not in terms of faith or theology. That such an expression should have emerged and come into common usage in medieval natural philosophy is a tribute to the scholars who took as their primary mission the explanation of the structure and operation of the world in purely rational and secular terms.[71]

This willingness to focus on nature alone helped medieval scholars develop a scientific method, a proper procedure for discovering natural laws, a way by which nature was to be approached so as to be known. It was mainly by their method, similar in many respects to the scientific method as we know it today, that medieval scientists 'were able eventually to outstrip their ancient European and Muslim teachers'.[72]

One of the principal exponents of this new scientific method was Robert Grosseteste (~1168–1253), bishop of Lincoln, England. Dales summarises the key aspects of his method:

- Any complex phenomenon of nature must first be analysed into its simplest components.
- Then, the investigator ... must frame a hypothesis which would show how these elements are combined so that they actually produce the phenomenon under investigation.
- In addition to this framework, Grosseteste employed experiments ... as an integral part of his investigation:
    - as aids in accomplishing his analysis,
    - as suggestions in framing his explanatory hypothesis,
    - and as tests of the truth or falsity of a hypothesis.
- He also insisted that no accurate knowledge could be had of nature without mathematics ...
- When one controls his observations by eliminating any other possible cause of the effect, he may arrive at an experimental universal of provisional truth.[73]

Today's scientists would recognise this 'highly developed experimental method'[74] as essentially the same as their own, though they would not recognise it as being motivated by a Christian worldview. This is not to say that medieval science was the same as modern science, for the scholastics 'were much less rigorous in their method—especially its experimental side—than any modern scientists'.[75] But this is to be expected of a method that was in its infancy. The fact remains that the method differs little from that which scientists use today.

And though the method was just starting to be employed for the first time, it was still used to make many advancements in the explanation of nature. The most important of these was a new theory of physical motion to replace Aristotle's false notion of the same.

New ideas on physical motion

The only solid critique of Aristotle's theory of motion in pre-medieval times was put forward by John Philoponus, an Egyptian Christian who flourished in Alexandria from AD 490–570.[76] Way back then, he maintained three items that have quite a modern ring to them, that

- 'the arrow continues moving without being in contact with any moving force, because ... [of an] *energy* that plays the role of moving force'[77]
- God, being almighty, could impart a *kinetic force* to heavenly bodies whereby they could move automatically without angelic assistance
- the stars are composed of fire, not a type of matter fundamentally different from anything we find here on Earth.[78]

But Philoponus's insights did not give birth to quantitative empirical science. With the crumbling of the Roman Empire, the Christian intellectual train of thought was lost. For several centuries afterwards, by and large only Muslims read Aristotle and his commentators. Avicenna developed to a certain degree Philoponus's theory on forces being impressed upon bodies,[79] but he stayed close to Aristotle, still tying his notion of physical motion to that of natural place.[80] The work of correcting Aristotle's notion of local motion was left to the Christian Middle Ages and it was there that 'medieval scientists did some of their most impressive and fruitful work'.[81]

The new explanation for physical motion developed by the medievals is referred to as 'impetus theory', with the impetus being a force that is imparted to bodies that fall towards the Earth or are thrown as projectiles. It was a commonplace in the Middle Ages to inquire about the role that this impetus or impressed force plays in physical motion.[82] The primary figure to develop this theory was Father Jean Buridan, a French scholastic philosopher born at the end of the thirteenth century.

Like so many others of his time, Buridan wrote commentaries on the works of Aristotle. In his *Physics*, Aristotle says that a rock thrown from one's hand moves upward because 'the air that has been pushed pushes [what is thrown] with a movement quicker than the natural locomotion of the projectile wherewith it moves to its proper place'.[83] In other words, there are two forces fighting against one another, the internal force of the rock 'wanting' to return to the ground, and the air outside the rock pushing the rock upwards, away from where it wants to go. The quicker movement of the air overcomes the rock's striving for the ground, at least at first, and this explains why the rock moves upwards, in a direction contrary to its natural inclination.

Buridan did not think that this made sense.[84] After all, from our common experience, doesn't air resist movement instead of aid it? Take the case when we want to throw ourselves forward, instead of a rock. When we run as fast as we can to make a long jump, we feel the wind opposing our forward movement, not aiding it. Thus, it is surely not air that moves rocks forward, but rather a certain *impetus* that is imparted to the rock, that is, a certain force that is communicated to the rock by the hand. This impetus does not proceed from the essence of the rock as such, as if the rock was wanting to move, but rather is an accident that comes to the rock for a time and then fades away.[85]

According to Buridan, there are two factors that make for a greater or smaller impetus. One is the *speed* with which the projectile is launched and the other is the projectile's *density*. Bodies are more susceptible of receiving an impetus insofar as they have a more concentrated mass and are thrown with more force.

Moreover, the reason why bodies falling towards the Earth move faster and faster, with an *accelerated motion*, is that gravity builds up a greater and greater impetus in the body during the time of the flight. At first, gravity alone acts on the stone dropped from the top of the building. But since it communicates an impetus to the stone, that impetus also acts on the stone, continually accumulating and so continually increasing the stone's velocity until the stone hits the ground.

So far, Buridan is sounding very modern, and not very medieval. The movement of thrown rocks, he says, can be accounted for by a force that is imparted to them, and which is greater in proportion to their speed and density. Furthermore, when bodies are dropped from a certain height, this same force builds up exponentially in them by means of gravity.

But, if we are able to explain the movement of bodies on Earth in this way, why not also those in the sky? Many scholastics thought that heavenly bodies were moved by the angels. This was a compromise between Aristotelianism and Christianity, in that the heavenly bodies were demoted from being eternal intelligent gods, but they were still held as being moved by 'intelligences', that is, by the angels. Buridan, however, boldly applies impetus theory, formulated for bodies on Earth, to bodies in heaven, noting that there is no need for the angels to move the stars. God could just provide the stars an initial impetus at the beginning of creation, and that impetus could suffice for the stars to move on their own from that point forward, since there is no resistance to their movement in space. It would be good for us to hear Buridan's own words on this:

> If you make a large and very heavy mill wheel rotate swiftly, and then you cease to move it, it will still keep on moving for some time because of its acquired impetus. Indeed, you cannot make it stop right away. But because of the resistance which results from the gravity of the mill, the impetus would continually diminish until the mill ceased to turn. And perhaps, if the mill should last forever without any diminution or change, and there were no other resistance to corrupt the impetus, the mill would move forever because of its perpetual impetus.
>
> And thus someone might imagine that it would not be necessary to posit intelligences to move the heavenly

bodies, because Scripture does not say anywhere that they ought to be posited. For it could be said that when God created the celestial spheres, He began to move each one of them as He wished. And they are still moved by the impetus He gave them, because this impetus is neither corrupted nor diminished, since it has no resistance.[86]

There are several points to note about Buridan's impetus theory and his application of it to movements on Earth and in the heavens:

1. Buridan speaks of motion in terms of forces instead of desires, in terms of material and efficient causes instead of final ones. Forces can be measured and quantified, while desires cannot.

2. While Buridan does not make use of mathematical formulas in elaborating his theories, yet those formulas are just one step away. Gilson remarks:

   The expressions [Buridan] uses are sometimes so precise that it is difficult to resist mentally substituting for them the equivalent algebraic formulas: 'If he who hurls projectiles moves with an equal speed a light piece of wood and a heavy piece of iron, these two pieces being otherwise the same in volume and shape, the piece of iron will go farther because the impetus imparted to it is more intense'.[87]

3. Buridan's statements about the ability of heavenly bodies to remain always in motion without additional impetus, because they receive no resistance to their movement, are an anticipation of Newton's first law of motion, the law of *inertia*.[88] That law states that a body at rest tends to stay at rest, while a body in motion tends to stay in motion. Because it is at the basis of Newton's second and third laws, and because the three laws were the first construction of exact science on a grand scale, Jaki says that 'in a sense, [] the whole edifice of physics and of exact science rests on the first law'.[89]

4. Buridan also anticipates Galileo's law of falling bodies, which states that the distance travelled by a body in downward flight increases exponentially with time. To be precise, it is proportionate to the square of the time elapsed. If, as Buridan states, gravity imparts ever more impetus to a naturally falling heavy body, then it is clear that the velocity of its fall must have an exponential growth.

5. Buridan does not have recourse to an *a priori* theory (idealist principles) to explain movement, but rather to common experience. Besides the examples of the long jump, stone throw and mill's wheel that I have mentioned, he also speaks of a spinning top, a sharp arrow, and a ship moving through water.[90] His mode of arguing *a posteriori* (from sense data) suggests a fundamental disposition of empirical science: the need to verify scientific hypotheses with sense observations and experimentation.

6. In bringing forth his theories, Buridan explicitly makes mention of their epistemological backdrop. It is his belief in a) the creation of the universe b) in time c) by a transcendent God that leads him to see the possibility of matter itself possessing motive properties. At the beginning of time, God could have imparted to matter an initial impetus sufficient to keep it in motion without any further pushes.

No wonder Gilson exults in saying that 'the clarity with which Buridan describes the data defining the movement of a body is remarkable'.[91] No wonder Jaki calls Buridan's essay on *impetus* the 'most important passage ever penned in Western intellectual history as far as science is concerned'.[92] No wonder that Duhem, constantly hearing around him the mantra that the Church suppressed science and the Enlightenment birthed it, while unearthing Buridan's manuscripts from the library in Bordeaux, enthusiastically shared his discoveries each night with his daughter Hélène.[93]

As Aquinas's *theology* begot a new and more realist metaphysics than that of Aristotle, so Buridan's *theology* begot a superior and more realist physics. In the words of Jaki,

> Just as in the case of Aristotle, where a theology (pagan, pantheist, and non-creationist) determines the physics of motion on earth, in Buridan's case theology (Christian or strictly creationist) determines physics; but with a result as different as the two theologies are different. In the case of Aristotle theology stifled physics; in the case of Buridan theology laid the possibility for physics by inspiring the formulation of the physics of impetus.[94]

Buridan's comprehensive, precise, and clear formulation of impetus theory, along with other scholastic theories and corollaries, became part of an extensive database of scientific concepts that would be passed down the generations until the so-called Scientific Revolution burst forth in the Europe of the seventeenth century. What had to be done then was not to come up with a new idea of nature or a new method to investigate it; all of that was already in place. It was more a question of taking old ideas and arranging them and applying them in different ways. The work of Galileo, for instance, was that

> [h]e brought together all the significant concepts, definitions, theorems, and corollaries on motion and arranged them into a logical and ordered whole, which he then applied to the motion of real bodies.[95]

Aristotle's pagan vision of the universe had been corrected and replaced by a Christian vision. It was from that vision that modern science was born.

Realism weakening
As a sort of epilogue to this chapter, I cannot fail to note the sad fact that the perfect realist balance of the Middle Ages was but a passing phenomenon. The seeds of its destruction were already being sown in the fourteenth century. The medievals had loosened

the overweening grip which final causality had held on science, thus making accessible to human minds secrets of reality that had as yet never been fathomed. They had done it by formulating a worldview which held all of four causes in perfect equilibrium.

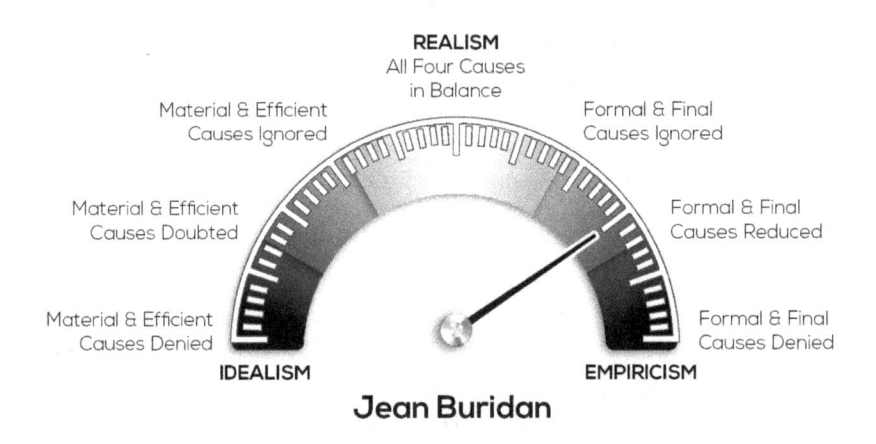

REALISM
All Four Causes in Balance

Material & Efficient Causes Ignored

Formal & Final Causes Ignored

Material & Efficient Causes Doubted

Formal & Final Causes Reduced

Material & Efficient Causes Denied

Formal & Final Causes Denied

IDEALISM

EMPIRICISM

Jean Buridan

There was a temptation, however, to go too far in correcting Aristotle by rejecting the very reality of final causality in physical bodies. Buridan himself fell into this temptation. He, for example, denied that final causality played any role in irrational agents,[96] and partially rejected formal causes,[97] though he still accepted the metaphysical proofs for the existence of God.[98] In this sense, he was halfway to the empiricist nominalism already being called 'the modern way' in his day.[99]

A battle between nominalist empiricism and realism for the position of the prevailing epistemology of the European worldview would continue for several centuries, until 'the modern way' finally triumphed in the eighteenth century. After having seen the triumph of realism, I now must turn to consider the genesis of its formidable opponent.

Chapter summary

In this chapter, we have seen how Catholic Christians embraced the full implications of the doctrine they believed on faith, namely that of creation in time, the belief that the universe at one point did not exist and at another was brought into existence by a transcendent, almighty Creator, and to this day is continually sustained in existence by Him. Their worldview engendered a rich and precise realist epistemology, one which held to the fact of a universe, its contingency, its rationality, and the ability of the human mind to know it.

When the Catholic states of the Middle Ages formed into the multi-national entity known as 'Christendom', they created an environment ideal for intellectual progress, one which included:

- a positive attitude toward secular knowledge
- a clear distinction between the domains of religion and science
- a great freedom of inquiry when pursuing natural philosophy.

The great minds of Christianity, however, were not able to effect on their own a complete marriage between the dogmas of their faith and truths attained by natural reason. They needed the assistance of Greek thought, and specifically that of the realist Aristotle. When his works became available in medieval universities at the beginning of the thirteenth century, they were immediately recognised as works of genius and assimilated.

At the same time, Aristotle's works sought to prove by natural reason propositions contrary to the Catholic Faith. In reaction, some scholastics chose reason over faith, while others chose faith over reason. Most chose both, with yet the faith remaining uppermost. Foremost among them was St Thomas Aquinas, who managed to embrace key philosophical concepts in Aristotle's writings, enrich them, and form a new metaphysics and natural theology, such that Aristotle compared to St Thomas is as 'the difference which exists between a city seen by the flare of a torchlight procession and the same city bathed in the light of the morning sun'.[100] St Thomas both perfected epistemological realism and rejuvenated respect for material causes and the data of the senses.

Yet the realm of quantitative exact science was still yet to be discovered. In this area, Aristotle was a hindrance, not a help. Based on their Christian worldview, medieval scientists developed their own methods for investigating nature, used them to recognise some major errors of their favourite philosopher, and established a new paradigm of physical science. Jean Buridan of the University of Paris, for instance, was able to propose an entirely different system of explanation for physical motion, one which focused on material/formal causes and which lent itself to quantification, experimentation, and formulation in mathematical terms.

Ultimately, the Christian scholastics, doubling as theologians and natural philosophers, provided to the scientific age its own foundations. In the eyes of Grant, they had:

- 'created an extensive and sophisticated body of terms that formed the basis of scientific discourse'
- 'posed hundreds of specific questions about nature', with proposed answers 'that included a massive amount of scientific information', such that 'the revolution in physics and cosmology was not the result of new questions put to nature in place of medieval questions', but 'more a matter of finding new answers to old questions'
- passed on 'a remarkable legacy of relatively free rational inquiry.'[101]

The great scientists of the Renaissance all knew about the work of 'Parisian masters' like Buridan. Copernicus, Galileo, Leonardo da Vinci, and Descartes built on that work in their own discoveries. Duhem proved as much in his voluminous works on medieval science, bringing to bear his original research into documents that had long been buried under the sands of time. Though his conclusion contradicts the standard narrative of his time and ours, it seems difficult to see how it can be refuted. Modern science came from medieval science. And medieval science came from a Catholic worldview.

Insofar as Catholicism fostered realism, it also fostered intellectual progress. For realism and intellectual progress are well-nigh inseparable. This is the only chapter where we see theology aiding science, and science harmonising with theology, where religion, reason, and science co-exist not only without any altercations, but also in a sweet, synthetic harmony. In the next two chapters, we will see other religious worldviews bringing them into conflict.

Notes

1. S. Jaki, *Scientist and Catholic: Pierre Duhem* (Front Royal, Virginia: Christendom Press, 1991), pp. 34–35.
2. *Ibid.*, pp. 38–40.
3. *Ibid.*, p. 71.
4. *Ibid.*, p. 48.
5. *Ibid.*, p. 49. See also S. Jaki, *Reluctant Heroine: The Life and Work of Hélène Duhem* (Edinburgh: Scottish Academic Press, 1992), pp. 5–9.
6. Jaki, *Scientist and Catholic*, p. 89.
7. See pp. 59–60.
8. Cf. Aristotle, *In Phys.*, §§988–989.
9. This is Jaki's definition in several of his books.
10. See *Bible and Science* (Grand Rapids, Michigan: William Eerdmans Publishing, 1996), p. 46; *Genesis 1 Through the Ages* (Edinburgh: Scottish Academic Press, 1998), pp. 266–279; *A Mind's Matter* (Grand Rapids, Michigan: William Eerdmans Publishing, 2002), p. 149; *Impassible Divide* (New Hope, Kentucky: Real View Books, 2008), p. 65.
11. See S. Jaki, *Means to Message* (Grand Rapids, Michigan: William Eerdmans Publishing Company, 1999), p. 148.
12. See Aquinas, ST, I, q.25, a.5, ad 1.
13. *The Road of Science and the Ways to God* (Port Huron, Michigan: Real View Books, 2005), p. 42.
14. E. Gilson, *History of Christian Philosophy in the Middle Ages* (New York: Random House, 1955), p. 120.
15. Jaki, *Bible and Science*, p. 33.
16. See H. Relja, *Il Realismo di S. L. Jaki* (Rome: Ateneo Pontificio Regina

Apostolorum, 2008), p. 133.
17. SCG, Book III, chapters 84–85.
18. E. Grant, *The Foundations of Modern Science in the Middle Ages* (Cambridge: Cambridge University Press, 1996), p. 4.
19. *Ibid.*, p. 5.
20. Port Huron, Michigan: Real View Books, 2006.
21. Grant, *The Foundations of Modern Science*, p. 171.
22. *Ibid.*, p. 183.
23. *Ibid.*
24. *Ibid.*, p. 175.
25. *Ibid.*, p. 200.
26. *Contra Manicheos*, Book 4, chapter 5.
27. Denzinger-Hünermann, *Compendium of Creeds, Definitions, and Declarations on Matters of Faith and Morals* (San Francisco: Ignatius Press, 2012), paragraph 1507.
28. E. Grant, *The Foundations of Modern Science*, p. 175.
29. *Ibid.*, p. 84.
30. *Ibid.*
31. E. Gilson, *God and Philosophy* (New Haven: Yale University Press, 1941), p. 43.
32. *Ibid.*, p. 57.
33. *Ibid.*, p. 60.
34. E. Grant, *The Foundations of Modern Science*, p. 18.
35. *Ibid.*
36. *Ibid.*, p. 171.
37. *Ibid.*, p. 27.
38. *Ibid.*, p. 23.
39. Dante, *Inferno* canto 4, line 131.
40. E. Grant, *The Foundations of Modern Science*, p. 53. See also R. Dales, *The Scientific Achievement of the Middle Ages* (Philadelphia: University of Pennsylvania Press, 1973), p. 61.
41. Gilson, *History of Christian Philosophy*, p. 235.
42. *Ibid.*, p. 244.
43. Grant, *The Foundations of Modern Science*, p. 54.
44. *Ibid.*, p. 161.
45. Cited in Gilson, *History of Christian Philosophy*, p. 403.
46. Grant, *The Foundations of Modern Science*, p. 117.
47. Gilson, *History of Christian Philosophy*, p. 398.
48. Grant, *The Foundations of Modern Science*, p. 70.
49. *Ibid.*, p. 71.

Catholic Creativity

50 For this important distinction, see J. Wippel, *The Metaphysical Thought of Thomas Aquinas* (Washington, D.C.: The Catholic University of America Press, 2000), p. xviii, footnote 13.
51 Gilson, *History of Christian Philosophy*, p. 368.
52 *Ibid.*
53 *Ibid.*, pp. 368–369.
54 See Aquinas, *In Met.*, paragraph 558.
55 F. Copleston, *Aquinas* (Harmondsworth, Middlesex: Penguin Books, Ltd., 1955), p. 103.
56 *St. Thomas Aquinas* (London: Hodder & Stoughton Limited, 1933), p. 28.
57 *The Spirit of Medieval Philosophy* (New York: Charles Scribner's Sons, 1940), p. 436.
58 *History of Christian Philosophy*, p. 365.
59 Jaki, *The Road of Science*, pp. 37–39.
60 *St. Thomas Aquinas* (London: Hodder & Stoughton Limited, 1933), p. 102.
61 *Ibid.*, pp. 138–139.
62 *Ibid.*
63 See Grant, *The Foundations of Modern Science*, p. 88, for an exception.
64 S. Jaki, *The Mirage of Conflict* (New Hope, Kentucky: Real View Books, 2009), p. 49.
65 See p. 77.
66 See p. 146.
67 P. Duhem cited in Jaki, *Scientist and Catholic*, p. 225.
68 Grant, *The Foundations of Modern Science*, p. 21.
69 Dales, *The Scientific Achievement*, p. 37.
70 Some theists appear to be naive in their acceptance of a certain brand of methodological empiricism that even refuses to allow the scientific method itself to reveal reality's causal richness, when that richness includes final causes. See T. Bethell, *Darwin's House of Cards* (Seattle: Discovery Institute Press, 2017), pp. 171–173.
71 Grant, *The Foundations of Modern Science*, p. 195.
72 Dales, *The Scientific Achievement*, p. 62.
73 *Ibid.*, p. 64. The bullet points are my own addition to the text.
74 *Ibid.*, p. 174.
75 *Ibid.*, p. 175.
76 See Grant, *The Foundations of Modern Science*, pp. 28–29.
77 P. Duhem cited in Jaki, *Scientist and Catholic*, p. 225, emphasis in original.
78 Jaki, *Science and Creation*, pp. 186–187.
79 Grant, *The Foundations of Modern Science*, pp. 94–95; Dales, *The Scientific Achievement*, p. 110.

[80] Gilson, *History of Christian Philosophy*, p. 194.
[81] Dales, *The Scientific Achievement*, p. 102.
[82] Grant, *The Foundations of Modern Science*, p. 141.
[83] *Physics*, Book IV, chapter 8, 215a16–19, translation R. McKeon, *The Basic Works of Aristotle* (New York: Random House,1941), p. 284.
[84] Gilson, *History of Christian Philosophy*, p. 515.
[85] In the language of the philosophers, the impetus is not a proper accident, but a mere accident, not one that is attached to the rock as such, but one that comes and goes in the rock. See A. Rizzi, *The Science Before Science* (Baton Rouge: IAP Press, 2004), p. 200.
[86] Cited in Dales, *The Scientific Achievement*, pp. 116–117.
[87] Gilson, *History of Christian Philosophy*, p. 516.
[88] Hannam notes a difference between impetus and inertia in *The Genesis of Science* (Washington, DC: Regnery Publishing, 2011), p. 181
[89] "The Physics of Impetus and the Impetus of the Koran" in *Modern Age*, Spring, 1990, p. 153. Jaki details the trail from Buridan to Newton in his *Questions on Science and Religion* (Pinckney, Michigan: Real View Books, 2004, p. 134): 'The greatest breakthrough represented by Newton's three laws is tied to the first, the law of inertial motion. That law was not Newton's invention. He inherited it from Descartes, who owed it to his Jesuit teachers at La Flèche, who in turn got it from the Collegio Romano, where it had been received from the Dominicans in Salamanca, who took it from the Sorbonne. It was there that Buridan formulated the law of inertial motion.'
[90] S. Trasancos, *Science Was Born of Christianity* (The Habitation of Chimham Publishing Co., 2014), p. 153.
[91] Gilson, *History of Christian Philosophy*, p. 516.
[92] Cited in Trasancos, *Science Was Born*, p. 159.
[93] Jaki, *Scientist and Catholic*, p. 61. See also Jaki, *Reluctant Heroine*, p. 25.
[94] "The Physics of Impetus and the Impetus of the Koran" in *Modern Age*, Spring, 1990, p. 155. For Jaki elsewhere on Buridan, see *God and the Cosmologists* (Fraser, Michigan: Real View Books, 1998), pp. 205–209; *Scientist and Catholic*, pp. 85–88, 226–229; *Bible and Science*, pp. 102–109; *Impassible Divide*, p. 43; *The Mirage of Conflict*, p. 37.
[95] Grant, *The Foundations of Modern Science*, p. 104.
[96] E. Feser, *Neo-Scholastic Essays* (South Bend, Indiana: St. Augustine's Press, 2015), p. 160; Grant, *The Foundations*, p. 195.
[97] Gilson, *History of Christian Philosophy*, p. 512.
[98] Jaki, *The Road of Science*, p. 43. For other aspects of Buridan's realism, see W. Wallace, *Causality and Scientific Explanation* (Ann Arbor, Michigan: University of Michigan Press, 1972), vol. 1, pp. 104–109.
[99] Grant, *The Foundations of Modern Science*, p. 160.

6 MUSLIM MONOTHEISM

Science flies us to the moon ...
Religion flies us into buildings.

Atheist physicist Victor Stenger

ON 12 SEPTEMBER 2006, Pope Benedict XVI travelled to the University of Regensburg in Germany, where he had once been professor of theology. During his visit, he delivered a lecture on the relationship between faith and reason. The primary point which he sought to establish was that God should be conceived of as acting reasonably in all that He does. But the way in which he supported this thesis sparked enormous controversy.

The Pontiff had recently been reading a medieval dialogue between a Byzantine Christian emperor, Manuel II Paleologus, and an erudite Persian Muslim on the subject of Christianity and Islam, that took place in the year 1391. One of the objections that Paleologus had towards Islamism was its inability to reconcile faith and reason, nature and supernature. In the Koran, Allah contradicts himself. For instance, near the beginning, surah 2.256 says that people must not be forced to convert. But, later in the work, there is an extensive section encouraging holy war against the infidel, that is, conversion by the sword. The Emperor's point was that, with Allah's actions and words being presented as irreconcilable with human reason, Muslims doing Allah's work do not see an obligation to respect the reason of their fellow human beings. They spread their faith through violence, and this is unreasonable, since faith is an act of the intellect.

Pope Benedict quoted the Emperor as saying,

> [N]ot acting reasonably is contrary to God's nature. Faith is born of the soul, not the body. Whoever would lead someone to faith needs the ability to speak well and to reason properly, without violence and threats ... To convince a reasonable soul, one does not need a strong arm, or weapons of any kind, or any other means of threatening a person with death ...[1]

This statement the Pontiff wholeheartedly endorsed. But he also quoted another sentence of the Emperor, which he did not endorse, but rather noted as being unacceptably brusque. It read as follows:

> Show me just what Muhammad brought that was new and there you will find things only evil and inhuman, such as his command to spread by the sword the faith he preached.[2]

After the speech, Muslims around the world were outraged. *Wikipedia* recounts the aftermath as follows:

> Demonstrations in the Muslim world took place as if the comment, the 'offending' judgement on Islam, was from the Pope himself ... Some protests reflected a level of hysteria quite out of proportion to the text of the Pope's lecture. Security was discreetly stepped up around and inside the Vatican City, because of concerns about the possibility of acts of violence. Thousands of people took part in many protests. At least five churches were attacked by Palestinians in the West Bank and Gaza. In the West Bank city of Nablus, firebombings left black scorch marks on the walls and windows of the city's Anglican and Greek Orthodox churches. At least five firebombs hit the Anglican church and its door was later set ablaze ... Later that day, four masked gunmen doused the main doors of Nablus' Roman and Greek Catholic churches with lighter fluid, then set them afire. They also opened fire on the buildings, striking both with bullets. In Gaza City, terrorists opened fire from a car at a Greek Orthodox church, striking the facade. Explosive devices were set off at the same Gaza church on Friday, causing minor damage ...

> Several organisations, such as Al-Qaeda and the Mujahideen Shura Council threatened in a joint statement: 'you and the West are doomed as you can see from the defeat in Iraq, Afghanistan, Chechnya, and elsewhere ... We will break up the cross, spill the liquor and impose the jizya tax, then the only thing acceptable is a conversion (to Islam) or (being killed by) the sword ... God enable us to slit their throats, and make their money and descendants the bounty of the Mujahideen.'[3]

In this chapter, I will consider the effect that the theology of a wholly wilful and transcendent God has generally on the pursuit of human knowledge and specifically on pursuing exact science.

Muslim culture

It is one of the strange twists of human history that sixth-century Christians lost Greek philosophy in the West, eighth-century Christians gave it to the Muslims in the East, and thirteenth-century Christians had it restored to them by Muslims in the West. Thus, while Church thinkers were bereft of most Platonic and Aristotelian works from the 500s to the 1200s, the Muslim world started benefiting from their presence in the 700s. This was one of the reasons why Christian medieval philosophy was 'at least two centuries behind that of Arab speculation'.[4]

The early Muslims had a great love of learning and set about on the same task that Catholics were to tackle in earnest several centuries later: they had to reconcile their religion with their reason.[5] Based on our epistemological analyses of the past chapters, it would seem that Islam had everything going its way for making this synthesis and great intellectual advances to boot, including belief in the creation of all by a supreme God and the establishment of the Islamic equivalent of Christendom. In the words of Jaki,

> For the first time in world history a giant and vigorous empire was steeped in a conviction that everything in life

and in the cosmos depended on the sovereign will of a personal God, the Creator and lord of all.[6]

There is no question that the early medieval Muslims had a more advanced culture than the Christians of the same period, and this is attested by the intellectual ferment among them. Jaki, with his accustomed thoroughness, lists many of its fruits: assimilation of paper making from the Chinese, meticulous translations of Greek philosophical and scientific works, medical skill in optometry and the treatment of diseases, new developments in algebra and trigonometry.[7] But technological inventions and advances in purely abstract disciplines are not the object of our inquiry. In this section of the book, I am seeking to investigate the answers to two questions about various historical cultures:

- What philosophy and specifically what epistemology did the theology of the culture yield?
- What in that epistemology led to, or prevented, intellectual advance?

While we can rightly admire the brilliance of Islamic scholars in certain practical sciences and we can recall that they kept Greek philosophy alive in the early medieval period when the Christian West was seeking to stabilise its own culture, our real focus here is the consideration of how the Muslim religion influenced Islamic thinking. Because Islam is a text-based religion, unlike Catholicism, which is an institution-based religion, I must zero specifically in on Islam's religious text, the Koran, to see the picture it forms of God/Allah and the corresponding worldview it produces.

The Koranic worldview

The Bible and the Koran present God in strikingly different ways. Jaki sums this up pithily by saying, 'Yahweh is not Allah'.[8] While the Bible presents God as being reasonable, the Koran presents Allah as being wilful. The difference is enormous.

If God is reasonable, then everything He does must conform to right reason. He must adhere to the principles of:

- contradiction—'a thing cannot be and not be at the same time, in the same respect'
- identity—'a thing is what it is'
- causality—'every effect has a cause.'

These principles (and a few others) are at the foundation of the structure of logic by which reason operates. To deny that they hold true for all reality is to render reason incapable of drawing conclusions from premises, for the simple fact that those principles are assumed in all premises.

A believer holding that God acts reasonably maintains that God's power is only exercised within certain limits: God cannot do anything that would imply a contradiction. He cannot make a rock heavier than He can lift, create an uncreated creature, or legislate something that is inherently evil, like murder, to be good. It is for this reason that Aquinas holds that God cannot change the past, saying the following:

> *Nothing that implies a contradiction is within God's power.* For the past not to have happened, however, implies a contradiction. For just as it is a contradiction to say that Socrates is sitting and he is not sitting, so also it is a contradiction to say that he sat and he did not sit. The reason is that saying that he sat is to say that it took place in the past, while saying that he did not sit is to say that it did not take place in the past. Thus, it is not within God's power to make that which is past not to have happened.[9]

We are here at the very crossroads of faith and reason. Can they be harmonised or will they forever be irreconcilable? The answer depends wholly on whether God acts within reason's scope or not.

- If He does not, then the universe He created is unintelligible to reason and so also the truths that He reveals to His chosen messengers.
- If He does, then nothing of what He creates or reveals can be in opposition to the necessary conclusions of ratiocination, of logical thinking.

In Christendom, while some held faith and reason to be dichotomous, the majority of theologians yet maintained 'that [reason's] necessary conclusions were necessarily true and they denied that what was necessary for reason could be false for faith'.[10] As we will see in the next chapter, reason was even held to take precedence over the Bible, when the latter seemed to be in contradiction with it.[11] But for now, I note once more with Jaki: 'It is nowhere hinted in the Bible that when God wills, He does so capriciously, that is, independently of the consistency of His intellect'.[12] 'If there is any epistemology in the Bible, it is the epistemology of moderate, and therefore, metaphysical realism.'[13]

The Allah of the Koran, however, is presented to the believer as an absolutely transcendent, almighty being, not bound to any law whatsoever. Those who think to find causal patterns in nature are implying that the acts of Allah are constrained to a framework consonant with human reason. But Allah is not tied down to any norms. 'The Creator-God (Allah) of the Koran was to remain free of any consistency which a world created freely by Him might "impose" on Him.'[14] In places, the Koran even denies free will to men, for men acting on their own volition would loosen Allah's control of his own creation, which must be absolute.

A theological system which conceives of God as having a will that is absolutely supreme is called 'voluntarist'. Here is Maldamé's explanation of such a system:

> According to some, the term 'all-powerful' must be understood in its literal sense: all-powerful means powerful without limits, without reservations of any kind. Will is limitless and independent of all logical constraint. God is confessed as being the almighty, capable of all, without any reservation or the possibility of any kind of demand on our part. This conception is called 'voluntarist'.[15]

In his book *The Mystery of Reason*, Haffner points out some passages of the Koran which lead to such a conception of Allah:

> Islam [] contains many elements which militate against a rational approach to faith ... [S]ome passages of the Koran smack of voluntarism, or the tendency to stress strongly the divine Will at the expense of divine Rationality. This is expressed by the very frequent use in the Koran of the phrase 'Allah does what He pleases.' For example 'He chastises whom He pleases; and forgives whom He pleases' (5.40). Furthermore, the following verse of the Koran also carries a voluntarist touch: 'Allah makes whom He pleases err and He guides whom He pleases' (14.4).[16]

Jaki likewise remarks:

> In the Koran no conspicuous effort is made to tie the sovereign decisions of God to His nature, that is, to His rationality. In other words, the will of God seems to be above any norm, however sound and intrinsically just may a norm appear to human reasoning.[17]

At the same time, there are other Koranic verses indicating that there is an order to creation and implying that the human mind can come to the knowledge of God by a process of reasoning that starts with God's created effects. Thus, by no means does the Koran systematically and consistently present Allah's activity as being beyond reason's scope. Why, then, we may ask, have the majority of Muslim thinkers throughout the ages read the Koran in a voluntarist sense?

Perhaps the very status which the Koran holds for members of Sunni Islam leads to the answer. In their eyes, their sacred text is co-eternal with Allah and partakes of his very divinity.[18] While existing from all eternity, it was yet revealed in time, through Allah's messenger, Mohammed, who uttered 'letters and sounds ... that signify the meaning of God's eternal speech insofar as it has entered time'.[19] In a sense, the Koran plays the same role for Muslims that Jesus Christ does for Christians, in that in both cases, an eternal entity proceeding from God becomes incarnate in time as a revelation to the human race. The Koran, then, is like unto an incarnation of God Himself. But the fact is that the Koran contradicts itself in many places, and it has no systematic order. Thus, one moving from the Koran to Allah would naturally infer that Allah is able to contradict himself and does not follow any specific intelligible order in his actions.

Moreover, Muslims hold that Allah has a language and that that language is Arabic. Thus, language is not a merely human construct, but also belongs to God, at least in the sense of an 'inner speech'.[20] From this perspective, the text of the Koran is not so much the ideas of God expressed in the language of men as the precise thought and speech of God as God.[21] The very letters and words are sacred. Thus, when one seeks to discover the meaning of those words, it would seem disrespectful to find multiple senses in them by a process of reasoning, and reject one while choosing another. Adhering to a literal interpretation for one passage and a figurative one to another becomes akin to superimposing human reason over the divine mind. In short, holding the text of the Koran to be so numinous that it is the words of God in the language of God makes all non-literal interpretations seem unorthodox.

Such is the theological starting point which the Islamic sacred text provides to adherents from which their rational synthesis of reality or philosophy is to be constructed. The first Muslims to get cracking on the project were called the *mutazilites*. They believed that reason was to be employed in attaining a correct understanding of revelation, and were willing to weaken the sacredness of the Koran. Thus, when they came across passages which offended reason in some way, they interpreted them figuratively. For instance, when the Koran represented Allah in anthropomorphic fashion, that is, in a way that applied human characteristics to him, they said that he did not literally exist in that way. They maintained the same perspective for passages that denied free will, and held that Allah was bound to act reasonably. Good and evil were not whimsical decrees of God, part and parcel with the very nature of reality.[22]

But this way of treating the Koran was not pleasing to the Islamic traditionalists, for the reasons just given. They wanted the sacred text to be read according to its immediate sense and accordingly 'adhered to literalism and determinism'.[23] It turns out that mutazilite philosophy was already headed for determinism—the idea that God alone has freedom—but regardless, the traditionalists gained political power in the ninth century and 'severely repressed' the mutazilites.[24] One of the latter, Al-Ash'ari, defected from the school and constructed another which championed the absolute freedom of Allah.[25]

With such views on God and His causality, so different from those of medieval Christendom, it was impossible for Islamic states to create an environment that favoured secular learning. Recall from last chapter that Grant identified three conditions needed for intellectual life to be fostered in a religious society: the pursuit of secular learning has to be independent, be recognised by the state, and be sanctioned by religious authorities. According to Grant, 'In medieval Islam, none of these conditions was met'.[26]

Since neither state nor religious Islamic authorities favoured secular learning, such learning was generally unknown to theologians and, when studied, was studied privately. Grant explains:

> In Islam ... natural philosophers were usually distinct from theologians. Scholars were either one or the other, rarely both. Moreover, natural philosophy was always on the defensive; it was viewed as a subject to be taught privately and quietly, rather than in public, and it was taught most safely under royal patronage, as seen in the careers of some of Islam's greatest natural philosophers.[27]

In the end, the religious worldview in Islam, predicated on a voluntarist notion of Allah, radically divided faith and reason, religious knowledge and secular knowledge. In Christianity, revelation aided realism, but in Islam, it hindered it, by compartmentalising truth and making reality inscrutable. As such, Islamic thinkers could only choose faith or reason as providing truth, not both.

Two options

With faith and reason being divided, only two possible paths were left to Muslim scholars.

- One is *theologism*, which sets up religious revelation as the sole path to truth. Everything that happens in the universe is ascribed to the causality of God alone. Human reason can learn nothing from creatures.
- The other is *philosophism*, which sets up human reason as the sole path to truth. Reality is divided into two realms whose truths contradict one another, the realm of faith and the one of reason. Reason is seen to provide real truth, while faith provides a certain pseudo-truth.

The first option clings to the unicity of truth while jettisoning intellect and sense; the second option saves reason, but makes faith unreasonable. Both cast off philosophical realism.

Muslims scholars pursued both paths in the course of the multi-century Islamic cultural heyday. The philosophists were able to derive new and important distinctions for philosophy, but were not able to construct a perfect metaphysics or begin looking for quantitative laws of motion, the two great successes of the last chapter. The road to such successes was blocked by the enormous obstacles put in their way by theologism and philosophism. These abstract systems, taking flesh in various figures in the Muslim world, had the following results:

1. **Theologists**—these found the use of reason in interpreting the Koran to be unorthodox. Whatever it said has to be literally true, no matter what reason says. The theologists used theology to destroy all other, non-fideistic forms of human knowing. The greatest names of this school were Al-Ash'ari and Al-Ghazali.

2. **Philosophists**—these wanted to remain orthodox Muslims and be free to engage in non-theological intellectual pursuits. To achieve this, they paid verbal respect to the Koran,

while pursuing philosophical studies in total independence from it. Philosophy in this context was a mere intellectual exercise, to be pursued for its own sake, without having the right to apply its conclusions to reality, whose whole domain was already occupied by religion. The greatest names of this school were Alfarabi, Avicenna, and Averroes. They tended to find it difficult to remain orthodox Muslims in the midst of their philosophical endeavours. This is why Chesterton says, '[W]e may say broadly of the Moslem philosophers, that those who became good philosophers became bad Moslems'.[28]

Let us consider these two paths separately.

Muslim theologism

Al-Ash'ari, who died in 936, founded a school of Muslim thought which became the benchmark for Muslim orthodoxy.[29] He and his fellow theologians were able to achieve 'a true "Moslem philosophy," in this sense at least that their conception of the universe was in deep agreement with the Koranic conception of God', namely, that of a voluntarist Allah.[30] Gilson describes their system as follows:

> [E]verything is created by the sole *fiat* of God, nothing is independent of his power, and good as well as evil only exist in virtue of his all-powerful will ... According to the Ash'arites, the world was made up of moments of time and points of space, connected together by the sole will of God, and whose combinations were therefore always liable to be altered by free interventions of the divine power.[31]

In other words, the universe is wholly digital. It is not a continuous river of events and things, flowing beneath the primary causality of God. Rather it is a universe of dots, where each dot is a moment and each moment is a new creation on the part of Allah. He makes everything again at each discrete point of time, such that there is no real sameness from one second to another.

Such a view is the equivalent of the occasionalism mentioned in chapter 3.[32]

The advantage of this perspective to the traditionalist Muslim is that it does not require any consistency from Allah whatsoever. Since he creates the whole of reality 'from scratch' at any given time, then reality at each second is wholly within his determination. There is no connection between one moment and the next at the level of the universe. There is no thread or fabric to created reality.

The way old televisions worked can provide us an image to help us understand this notion of the universe. When the television does not have power, its screen is totally black, like the nothing of the universe without the creation of God. Then, with the power on, the cathode ray tube at the back fires colours on the screen 40 times a second. Each of those 40 times, the colour rendered can be completely different from the colour that was just fired. In between the firings, there is nothing; we are back to the original blackness. But the person watching does not see that blackness because the firings are so rapid, and for the same reason, he does not realise that there is a discontinuity in the firings. For all he knows, the colour is coming out as a continuous stream.

So it is with the Ash'arite world. Allah brings reality into being anew at each moment, without there being any inherent continuity between one moment and another.

One important consequence of this notion for the pursuit of human knowledge is that creatures have no causal power, and so humans cannot gain causal knowledge from them. This is why Al-Ghazali (1058–1111), a spiritual successor of Al-Ash'ari, 'argued fervently against the notion of secondary causality, contending that all we perceive is the succession of events, not any causal connection between them'.[33] Just as the colour on the TV screen at one moment is not the cause of the one that appears next, so too my application of pen to paper in the composition of a letter is not what causes the marks to appear. Rather, Allah creates me and the paper and the pen anew in each of their states throughout the letter's writing. I am not causing the pen to write and the pen is not causing the marks of ink on the paper. Allah alone is doing all.

Moses Maimonides, a medieval Jewish thinker (1135–1204), uses this pen and paper image to explain Ash'arite thought. Gilson begs leave for an extended quotation from Maimonides speaking about their perspective, and I do the same:

> They [the Ash'arites] assert that when man is perceived to move a pen, it is not he who has really moved it; the motion produced in the pen is an accident which God has created in the pen; the apparent motion of the hand which moves the pen is likewise an accident which God has created in the moving hand; but the creative act of God is performed in such a manner that the motion of the hand and the motion of the pen follow each other closely; but the hand does not act and is not the cause of the pen's motion; for, as they say, an accident cannot pass from one thing to another ... There does not exist anything to which an action could be ascribed; the real *agens* is God ... In short, most of the Muslim theologians believe that it must never be said that one thing is the cause of another; some of them who assumed causality were blamed for doing so ... They believe that when a man has the will to do a thing and, as he believes, does it, the will has been created for him, then the power to conform to the will, and lastly the act itself. ... Such is, according to their opinion, the right interpretation of the creed that God is efficient cause.[34]

On the side of human knowledge, the consequences of this position are obvious. If creatures are not causes, then there is no connection between them and the effects that I see around me. As such, there is nothing to learn from the created world. It is not the fire that is causing the heat, water that is causing the wetness, air that is causing the coldness. Every movement of the mind from created effect to created cause is false in itself. *Both sense data and intellectual conclusions from them are deceitful.* Such a position breaks epistedometers, because it does not allow any causal knowledge.

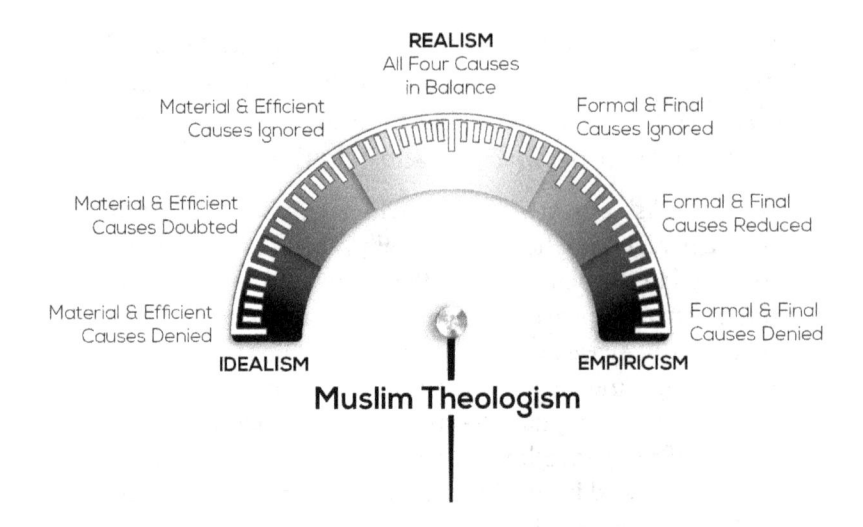

```
                    REALISM
                 All Four Causes
                   in Balance
Material & Efficient              Formal & Final
  Causes Ignored                  Causes Ignored

Material & Efficient              Formal & Final
 Causes Doubted                   Causes Reduced

Material & Efficient              Formal & Final
  Causes Denied                   Causes Denied
      IDEALISM                      EMPIRICISM
              Muslim Theologism
```

The Ash'arite conclusions, including the denial of free will,[35] flowed from the effort to account for Allah's absolute freedom. To do so, it was necessary to deprive Allah's creatures of the powers he confers upon them. This is why Gilson reflects:

> When and where piety is permitted to inundate the philosophical field, the usual outcome is that, the better to extol the Glory of God, pious minded theologians proceed joyfully to annihilate God's own creation.[36]

Clearly, there is no room for either philosophy or science in a world where God alone acts. Philosophy's job is to begin with created effects and climb the causal chain to reach the ultimate causes of those effects. But there is no chain here, only a single jump: effect → Allah. The job of science is to describe the laws of matter and motion by making inferences from observed data, but Allah's universe does not have laws. 'Orthodox Muslim scholars did their utmost to undermine the notion of a universe operating

Muslim Monotheism 213

along consistent laws, calling it a taint on Allah's absolute freedom to do whatever He wanted.'[37]

Throughout Islamic history, the orthodox view of Muslim theologians did not just see secular learning as a waste of time, but also a threat to society, as Grant points out:

> Most Muslim theologians opposed [secondary causation], fearing that the study of Greek philosophy and science would make their students hostile to religion. Because of this perceived incompatibility, Greek natural philosophy was usually regarded with suspicion and was therefore rarely taught publicly. Philosophy and natural philosophy were often outcast subjects within Muslim thought.[38]

Sometimes, the suspicion of the theologians turned to violence. The aforementioned Al-Ghazali, for instance, encouraged such violence against philosophers in his *The Incoherence of the Philosophers*. After seeking to undermine various philosophical views, he posed himself the following question:

> Now that you have analysed the theories of the philosophers, will you conclude by saying that one who believes in them ought to be branded with infidelity and punished with death?[39]

He answers that, with regard to three philosophical opinions, 'to brand the philosophers with infidelity is inevitable.'

With Muslim theologism in the driver's seat, the validity of non-Koranic knowledge was wiped out, religion was used to destroy science, and sometimes as well to destroy people pursuing science.

Muslim philosophism

Though a strictly logical adherence to the voluntarism of the Koran shuts off the path to the pursuit of knowledge, Muslim scholars were not by any means all voluntarists. Many were motivated by the saying of Mohammed that 'the first thing which God created was knowledge or Reason' to conclude that philosophising was one of their religious duties.[40] By means of this attitude, Muslim savants made important contributions to philosophy, which were invaluable for the Christian West. They preserved their freedom to philosophise, however, only by maintaining the truth of the Koran, even when it contradicted their philosophical conclusions. This was accomplished by barring reason from the domain of faith; the latter was to be accepted as true not because it was reasonable, but because it was orthodox. Faith was unreasonable and true; philosophy was reasonable and true.

Alfarabi

The first of these figures was Alfarabi, a pious Muslim in the tenth century (died 950). Though the Koran does not indicate that the universe had a beginning in time, yet it does speak of Allah as Creator. This idea gave Alfarabi greater insights into the notion of being than those attained by Aristotle, and enabled him to originate three monumental metaphysical concepts:

1. the 'epoch-making distinction of essence and existence in created beings'[41]
2. the notion of the contingency of created beings, that is, their dependence at the level of being
3. the distinction between *necessary* and *possible* being,[42] wherein necessary beings cannot not exist, for example, it is impossible for God not to exist; while possible beings can exist or not exist, for example, horses and centaurs.

Did these realist metaphysical distinctions serve as a key for Alfarabi to correct Aristotle's metaphysics and initiate a new view of the physical universe? No, for his ideas of 'God' and 'being' were still quite flawed. He had added features to Aristotle's Saturn 7, but could not manage to redesign it.

One major problem with Alfarabi's universe was that the heavens were eternal and uncreated. Allah did not bring them into being and thus there was no question of the heavens being endowed with motion by a superior cause, Buridan's insight that led to his non-Aristotelian explanation of all physical motion.

Jaki explains how Alfarabi's different notion of creation prevented him from seeing what Buridan saw:

> [Alfarabi was] the one who first formulated the notion of the contingency of any being other than the Creator with respect to existence. Furthermore, he did so with an explicit view to the Koran's doctrine of creation, that is, with a view to Allah's absolute power and sovereignty over all beings. Yet, that doctrine was not such as to prevent Alfarabi from saying that the starry heavens were divine and existed necessarily, which is the very opposite to being contingent with respect to existence. If, however, the heavens existed necessarily, they had to be eternal and their motion, together with all motion anywhere else in the universe, had to be eternal. In such an outlook it was impossible to do what Buridan did. Buridan, who found in the Christian dogma of creation in time and out of nothing a crucial insight for a concept of cosmic motion with an absolute beginning, could also consider any lesser motion, such as the flight of a javelin, as a motion in which the mover was so superior to the moved thing that it did not have to remain in actual contact with the moved thing. Was it impossible to do the same for an Alfarabi or an Avicenna, or in general for Muslim thinkers, because perhaps of an ambiguity or a lack of sufficient explicitness in the Koran about creation in time and out of nothing?[43]

Avicenna

Later, perhaps the greatest name in Arab philosophy, Avicenna (980–1037), initiated the notion of the primary cause, that is, a cause whose 'proper effect is the very being of the thing caused'.[44] He also was the first to distinguish between essentially and accidentally ordered chains of causality.[45]

What are all of these distinctions, we may ask, but the necessary metaphysical tools by which human reason is able to climb to the top of the vertical causal chain, as we saw in chapter 2? And this is exactly what Alfarabi and Avicenna did, each of them formulating surefire proofs for the existence of God. Working on the wisdom of Aristotle and the doctrine of creation, they were able to construct complete syntheses of reality, in that they included all of reality in a single entire causal order.

While being complete, however, their metaphysics was yet imperfect. There were still more distinctions to be made. Avicenna, for instance, held that existence was an accident of essence, something, as we saw in the last chapter, that Thomas Aquinas would later refute.[46] He also believed in emanationism, a form of pantheism which holds that the universe flows from the being of God instead of being created distinct from Him. Thus, God is somehow part of the universe which He creates. Avicenna's God is not that of the Koran, nor that of the Bible.

From this we can see that, setting himself free from theology, Avicenna largely fell back on Aristotelian philosophy as his default working model, with its pluses and minuses. Here is how Jaki describes Avicenna's God and universe:

> In Avicenna's world, which is eternal and necessary, everything is neatly placed along a chain of emanation from the First Cause ... God is said to generate the First Intelligence, out of which proceeded the Second. It is with the Second Intelligence that the purest materialization, the formation of the outermost sphere, took place. The Third Intelligence was embodied in the sphere of fixed stars. Intelligences of lower order generated in turn the spheres of the five planets, of the sun and of the moon. While this last Intelligence was too weak to generate another Intelligence, it produced both the world of terrestrial matter and acted as an 'intellectus agens' for all men.[47]

This is an Aristotelian universe with efficient causality added. The Unmoved Mover actually generates something, the First Intelligence, which goes on to produce a Second, which goes on to produce a third, and so on, until the whole process runs out of steam with the last Intelligence generated. Not being able itself to produce spirit, it produced matter, the Earth and us poor earthlings stuck at the cosmic drain hole, who are left to eke out our existence sharing that last intellect.

While Avicenna makes God an efficient cause—an improvement on Aristotle's universe—he yet conceives the divine activity falsely.

- God does not create but rather generates. He does not make things to be that previously had nothing of being, but rather makes other beings flow from or be generated from his own being.
- God acts necessarily or deterministically, not freely. He does not choose to produce other beings or to do anything at all. Rather, whatever he does just happens automatically, because of what he is, not because of what he decides.

This metaphysics does not leave any place for the exact sciences, which occupy such a sensitive epistemological corner of human intellectual endeavour. Avicenna's physics, like that of Aristotle, was 'dominated by the notion of quality, not, like our own modern physics, by that of quantity. Accordingly, it is less interested in measurements than in classifications'.[48]

To find exact science, one must have in mind a universe that works both according to determined laws and is freely created. It must be a universe that combines the necessary and the contingent. God must choose freely to create and how He creates. This enables Him to design creatures, mandate laws by which they operate, and bestow upon them proper causal powers. Such a universe from a freely creating God presents real causal information to knowing human minds. It is a universe where science can exist. It is a universe that has reason and design behind it—God's reason and design.

A necessary universe, however—one that flows automatically from God's being, and is not produced by His intellect—does not have any reason or design behind it. It is a universe inaccessible to science.

Averroes

The last of the great Muslim philosophers was Averroes (1126–1198). He had the most influence on Christian philosophers and is the clearest example of philosophism. He completely separated faith from reason, held them both to be true, and held them both to be in conflict.

Averroes (Image courtesy of Wikimedia Commons)

- **Faith**—For Averroes, the Koran is 'truth itself.' Since it was put down for the entire world, it must be directed to everyone. Now, there are three types of human minds: men of demonstration, men of dialectic, and men of exhortation. What is miraculous about the Koran is that each type of mind is able to find in its pages what will satisfy and convince him.[49] In this sense, the Koran was the source of a certain subjective truth adapted to individual believers.

- **Reason**—In philosophy, Averroes adhered religiously to Aristotle. He even went so far as to criticise Alfarabi and Avicenna for thinking that they could improve on the Stagirite and had the following to say about his master: 'The doctrine of Aristotle is supreme truth, because his intellect was the limit of the human intellect. It is therefore rightly said that he was created and given to us by divine providence, so that we might know all that can be known'.[50]

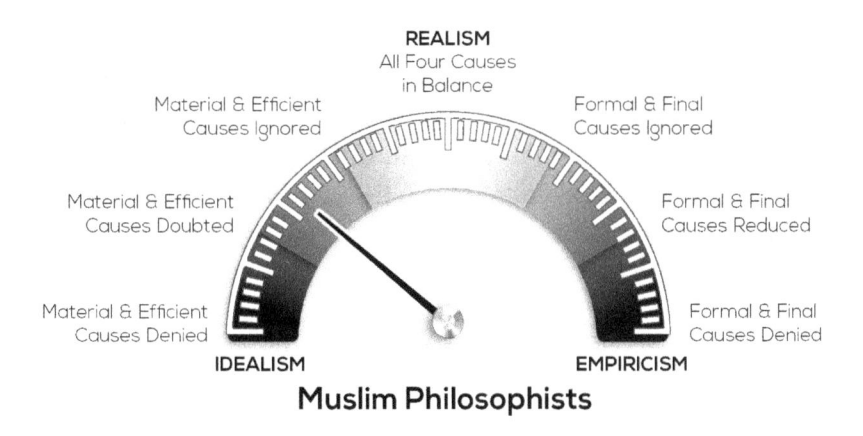

Muslim Philosophists

Averroes was able to attach himself to the Koran and Aristotle at the same time, by effectively holding that faith is irrational and philosophy is the realm of real knowledge. Gilson remarks, 'In the doctrine of Averroes, there is absolutely nothing that philosophy does not know better than simple faith',[51] and that Averroes 'considered [theology] a mixture of reason and faith, fatal to both'.[52] Thus, for him, philosophy was the realm of thinking and knowing, while faith was the realm of believing. But there could be no meeting between the reason and religion.

After Averroes, Islamic culture declined and was unable to sustain high scholarly speculation. The theologism of Al-Ash'ari triumphed as Muslim orthodoxy and, for the most part, reigns to the present day. The theology of the Koran made available only the avenues of God destroying man (theologism) or man destroying God (philosophism). Islamists made the pious choice of theologism, to the detriment of rational thinking and behaviour.

The Muslim world had been unable to give birth to exact science, but yet had made important advancements in philosophy, thanks to Aristotle and the doctrine of creation in the Koran. These developments were not to be lost, for '[t]he Arabic theologians and philosophers bequeathed their developments of the cosmological argument along with the legacy of Aristotle to the Latin West, with whom they rubbed shoulders in Muslim Spain'.[53]

We have already seen how Aquinas profited from both bequests in his construction of a Christian philosophy. But he 'was saying things so obviously true that from his time down to our own day, very few people have been sufficiently self-forgetful to accept them'.[54] I will now consider how other Catholics, ignoring St Thomas's work, travelled with the Muslim thinkers on the same paths of theologism and philosophism.

Catholic theologism and philosophism

As human reason in the Islamic world sometimes wielded theology as a club to beat down philosophy and at other times seized on philosophy as a sword for slaying theology, so too in medieval Catholic Europe.[55] The two extremes of theologism and philosophism came to blows time and time again, without either of them fully perishing down to the present day.

Catholic philosophism

The first tendency to manifest itself after the coming of Greek and Arabic wisdom to Christendom was decidedly philosophism. Many scholars appreciated the writings of Averroes—he even earned from them the moniker of 'The Commentator' for his interpretations of Aristotle. But, as we have seen, one of the positions of Averroes was that philosophy was to be kept strictly separate from theology. Thus, when Averroes (and Aristotle) contradicted the teachings of the Catholic faith, some were tempted to say that his conclusions were 'philosophically correct', even though they did not agree with theology. Reason proved Averroes correct, while the Church proved faith correct.

Gilson gives an important example of such a conflict:

> For instance, if the eternity of the world is a necessary rational conclusion in philosophy, then to believe that the world has had a beginning is to accept as true, on the strength of revelation, something that contradicts one of the necessary conclusions of natural reason.[56]

Those who held this position were called 'Averroists.' Not only were they willing to accept the eternity of the world as a necessary conclusion of reason, they also embraced the other theological positions of Aristotle, which both prevented the birth of exact science and contradicted Catholic dogma, positions such as:

- God can only produce one effect
- God is not free
- the world runs in a deterministic fashion.

As we saw with the Muslim philosophers, the problem with strictly segregating philosophy and theology, and having someone believe by faith something that he denies with reason, is that faith becomes irrational. When a person's faith is irrational, his philosophy (and behaviour) suffer. When his philosophy suffers, the door is closed to science. In the end, there is only one road to granting full rights to reality, the same full-throttle realism that trusts the ability of senses and intellect, holds to the intelligibility of all four causes, and uses them to prove the existence of the first cause. To be all a realist can be, faith, reason, and science must co-exist peacefully in a human's mind.

Medieval ecclesiastics recognised the danger that the Averroists presented to the faith and did not allow them to continue blithely on the philosophist path. The Bishop of Paris condemned 13 propositions of Averroist origin in 1270 and seven years later lambasted 219 others that were mostly Averroist. Meanwhile, the Lateran Council bound all Catholics to believe in creation in time in 1274.[57] As we have seen, a necessary condition for Catholics correcting Aristotle's physics and metaphysics was that they hold to the Church's doctrine of creation in time over his doctrine of an eternal, uncreated world.

Catholic theologism

The backlash against the Christian philosophists on the part of the Church ignited the opposite extreme, that of theologism. Seeking to save the Church from Aristotle and Averroes, some thinkers did not reconcile faith with reason, but had faith overtake reason's territory. Many of them were Franciscans. One of them, Bonaventure, was a saint.

To vindicate God's prerogatives, St Bonaventure (1221–1274) thought it safer to attribute effects more to God than to creatures, when there was a philosophical doubt. Thus, he said:

- it is better to attribute more to grace than free will when speaking of a person's good works, even if such an attribution turns out to be false, as piety and humility profit thereby[58]
- it is better to say that creatures do not produce new effects, but only unfold effects set in place by God from the beginning of the world[59]
- since God is truth, He must illuminate us in some way when we know any truth whatsoever.[60]

Muslim Monotheism 223

While St Bonaventure was not an extremist and did not want to destroy natural reason, the fact was that he started the Franciscans on the path of theologism. Later thinkers, travelling much further on that path, would draw the following conclusions from the three starting points above:

- humans are completely depraved and their good actions come entirely from God
- creatures do not act at all; there is no secondary causality, but only God's primary causality
- the only truth is theological, revealed truth.

Since I am especially interested in the destruction of causality and therefore of the ability of humans to have true knowledge, I must consider the Franciscan William of Occam (1280–1349; also spelled 'Ockham'). His name frequently echoes even in our own day, often being pronounced with approval by atheists[61] and dismay by believers. Like so many, he set out with good intentions: he wanted to save God from Aristotle. Just as commonly, he pursued those intentions in the wrong way. Gilson describes his purpose and that of fellow Franciscan Duns Scotus (1270–1308) as follows:

> Scotism and Ockhamism are dominated by the desire to ensure the freedom of the Christian God with respect to the world of things. Greek necessitarianism is the Carthage they are eager to destroy. Their theologies are wholly dominated by the desire to eliminate the naturalism of the Greeks and the Greco-Arabian notion of a God who, precisely because his is a self thinking thought, *allows the world to flow from his intelligible perfection as necessary consequences follow from their principles.*[62]

It was this last idea, that of emanationism, that especially irked Occam. Recall that such was the position held by Avicenna. For him, God has an eternal being and essence. The essence is like a blueprint of the universe, which God eternally and automatically executes. All beings flow from the being of God according to the ideas and order of those beings in His mind, without God making any free choices about creation. God can neither stop nor change this process, any more than He can stop being God. He is eternally tied to executing what is found in the ideas or essences in His mind.[63]

How would Occam destroy this system? Well, if Avicenna holds that all flows automatically from the universal ideas of God, it seems that the easiest route would be to declare that God has no such ideas. This is exactly what Occam does. He does not want God's will to be obliged to obey anything, not even His own mind. Thus, he claims that when God creates, God does not follow any plan in His mind, or create creatures according to certain forms or types. God does not make dogs according to the type of 'dogginess', nor cats to that of 'felinity.' There is no form or essence in reality that is shared by all dogs. Rather, they and everything else in the universe are just a series of individuals. We can group them into categories as much as we like, and form universal ideas about those groups, such as 'dogs' and 'cats'. But, in reality, each dog is completely different from every other dog. In other words, there is no such thing as formal causes.

By making this his position, William delivers God from all necessity, from acting according to a regular pattern, as Gilson indicates:

> The God in whom Occam believes is Yahweh, who obeys nothing, not even Ideas. Duns Scotus had submitted to the free will of God the choice of the essences to be created; instead of letting God be free to choose between essences, Occam suppresses them.[64]

William achieved his goal, but destroyed human knowledge in doing so. The reason is that all of our ideas are certain forms of the things outside of us. As we saw back in chapter 1, the senses provide us with the individual and the intellect with the universal.[65] But Occam is saying that God does not create according to universal Ideas. Moreover, if there are no universals in the Creator, then there are no universals in creation. All of our ideas,

Muslim Monotheism 225

then, like 'dog' and 'cat', are simply descriptive names that we apply to various individuals outside of our mind: they do not correspond to anything in reality as such. For Occam, the only thing that God creates are individuals, and so the only thing that exists are individuals. Thus, universal ideas have no value; they do not give us knowledge of reality.

Another consequence of this radical epistemological individualism is the destruction of the principle of causality. Occam accurately notes that while our senses give us the sensation of wood being lit on fire at one moment and heat coming out at the next, they do not tell us that the one comes from the other. This connection is made by the mind, and in doing so, it is going beyond mere individual events to make a generalisation about them, that 'burning produces heat.' In that statement of cause and effect, I have used multiple universal concepts: 'burning', 'production', 'heat'. Because I used universal concepts, William tells me that my statement has no certainty. I can give the name of 'cause' to fire and 'effect' to heat, but because of the universal concepts involved, I cannot know that they are more than just names or that heat is *really* coming from the fire outside my mind.[66]

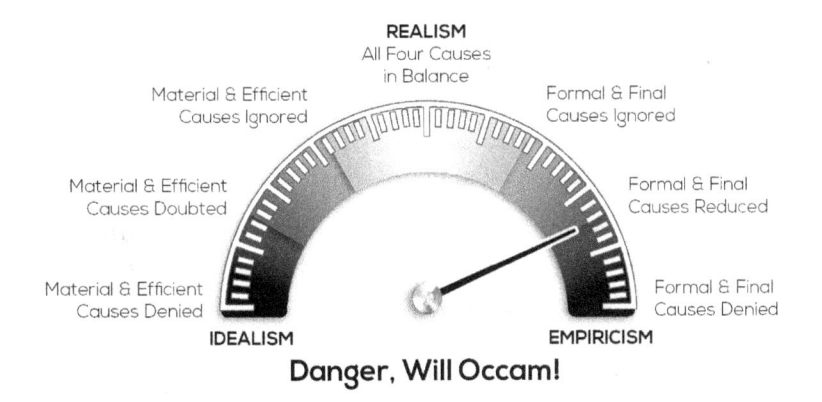

REALISM
All Four Causes in Balance

Material & Efficient Causes Ignored

Formal & Final Causes Ignored

Material & Efficient Causes Doubted

Formal & Final Causes Reduced

Material & Efficient Causes Denied

Formal & Final Causes Denied

IDEALISM

EMPIRICISM

Danger, Will Occam!

By his system, Occam was looking to overthrow—in the Catholic world at least—over a millennium of epistemological realism. For the longest time, it had been taken for granted, as flowing immediately from common sense, that we were safe in trusting *both* our senses and our intellects. But William denied there was any validity to the principle of causality, one of the principles at the basis of all reasoning done by the intellect. By doing so, he was opening the door to radical empiricism, wherein truth only comes from experience, and scepticism, wherein all reasoning about reality is held in doubt. Since these attitudes eventually took over the Western world, Gilson says that Occam is the 'initiator of the modern way',[67] by which he means the modern reality mentality, our default epistemological worldview.

It is not a little ironic that a man looking to save the prerogatives of God initiated a system of philosophy which led to the destruction of religion. For when Occam 'destroyed' the credibility of the principle of causality, he made it impossible for the human mind to reason from created effects to the First Cause. Under his system, there can be no natural theology; only realism, combining sense and intellect, can reason to God, and indeed reason at all.

Gilson accuses Occam of breaking down medieval thought[68] by making faith incomprehensible:

> The dissolving influence exercised by his doctrine in the history of medieval scholasticism is due to the fact that, professing as he did a radical empiricism in philosophy, he had to reduce the understanding of faith to a bare minimum.[69]

When a person believes on a blind faith that is completely incomprehensible to reason, he does not believe for very long.

While Occam's system helped science to some degree in that it focused some scholastics on the data of sense and led to a more active experimentation with nature, yet it was no foundation on which to build science. For science also wants to form universal notions about reality. It wants to discover quantitative laws of motion that hold true for real, moving bodies. But, if universal ideas say nothing about reality, then the findings of science have no value for real life. It is for this reason that some medieval scientist followers of Occam held that scientific arguments can only at best be probable, and so cannot provide 'science' in the sense of certain knowledge.[70]

The Church censured the system of Occam, the faculty at Paris condemning some of his propositions in 1339 and 1340.[71] Occamism even became such a political problem a century later that his followers were banished from France by Louis XI in 1474.[72] But these measures did not stop the spread of his ideas, as testified by the modern world and as we will see in the next chapter.

Chapter summary

In this chapter, we have looked at various failed attempts to reconcile religion with faith. In the Muslim world, the words of the Koran are held to be so sacred as to be the actual speech of Allah. This leads some Muslims to see the Koran as a certain incarnation of Allah and consider all that it says to be literally true regardless of any considerations that human reason might bring to bear upon them. This relationship of a set of believers with their sacred text demands that they accept certain propositions as being true on the basis of authority alone.

Because the Koran contains contradictory propositions and hence propositions that violate the laws of reason, its believers cannot hope to keep faith and reason in harmony. Thus:

- reason can be used to support faith against reason,
- reason can work independently of faith,
- but reason cannot work in unison with faith.

The first option is theologism and the second is philosophism.

With theologism, faith seeks to destroy reason in the interests of what are held to be divinely revealed truths. For example, Muslim thinkers Al-Ash'ari and Al-Ghazali started with the supremely free will of Allah to reason that absolutely all effects proceed from him. Thus, there is no such thing as secondary causality, wherein creatures produce their own proper effects. As such, reality does not present any causal information for human minds to know other than that everything comes from Allah.

This system became the standard for Muslim orthodoxy, and has led to many Muslims acting unreasonably on behalf of Allah, in the belief that their actions do not have to conform to reason to be holy. To this day, many Islamists believe that spreading their faith by violence is pleasing to the Almighty.[73]

In Christendom, St Bonaventure started to exaggerate the proper causality of God in difficult theological areas in order to be on the safe side. This initiated a way of thinking, particularly for his fellow Franciscans, which reached its full philosophical term in the system of William of Occam. Like the Muslim theologians, Occam would not countenance any constrictions on God's free will. He delivered God from His own intellect, by holding that God did not have any universal ideas or patterns to which He created the universe. This meant in turn that the universal ideas of human beings have no correspondence to reality, ideas like the principle of causality, one of the first principles on which all human knowledge depends.

Those coming after Occam and following his line of thought concluded that it was impossible to know God by natural reason. No religious truth can be known objectively and by all. Thus, faith should have nothing to do with reason or with the public life of society. God should play no part in the running of states and the ruling of men. God, today, has been exiled from modern secular states by the descendants of theologians.

The other extreme is philosophism, wherein reason ignores the truths of faith, in order to draw its own conclusions in complete independence. The foremost representatives of this mindset among Muslims were Alfarabi, Avicenna and Averroes. Divorcing their minds from the theology of the Koran, they were able to enrich the metaphysics of Aristotle with invaluable new distinctions. They attached themselves to Aristotle to their utmost, even holding to the Stagirite's pantheism by making Allah part of the universe. At the same time, their hearts were still attached to Islam, which led them to hold to a certain degree the idea of double truth, the idea that contradictory propositions can both be true, one in the realm of faith and the other in the realm of reason.

Some Catholic philosophers, finding Aristotle and his Muslim admirers most convincing, held them to be true, even when they contradicted truths of the Catholic faith. Those philosophers became philosophists, ascribing different and conflicting truth territories to faith and reason. Their stance led ecclesiastical authorities to condemn various false philosophical propositions, and the Pope to define 'from the chair' that Catholics must believe in the doctrine of creation in time. This was the doctrine that assisted medieval thinkers such as Aquinas and Buridan to peer more deeply into reality with their reasoning faculties than Aristotle and the Muslims had.

In the next chapter, we will look at the theologism of Protestantism, its handling of reason and faith, and the corresponding consequences for exact science.

Notes

[1] Pope Benedict XVI, *Discourse to the University of Regensburg* (12 September 2006).
[2] *Ibid.*
[3] Article 'Regensburg Lecture', accessed 21 April 2015.
[4] E. Gilson, *History of Christian Philosophy in the Middle Ages* (New York: Random House, 1955), p. 179.
[5] *Ibid.*, p. 182.
[6] *Science and Creation* (New York: Science History Publications, 1974), p. 193.
[7] *Ibid.*, pp. 194–198.
[8] *The Road of Science and the Ways to God* (Port Huron, Michigan: Real View Books, 2005), p. 42.
[9] ST, I, q.25, a.4; my translation, emphasis added.
[10] Gilson, *History of Christian Philosophy*, p. 388.
[11] See p. 250.

12. *The Road of Science*, p. 42.
13. S. Jaki, *A Mind's Matter* (Grand Rapids, Michigan: William Eerdmans Publishing, 2002), p. 155.
14. S. Jaki, *The Savior of Science* (Port Huron, Michigan: Real View Books, 2006), pp. 77–78.
15. 'Evolution and Creation: How to Terminate with a False Opposition Between Chance and Creation an Epistemological Note' in Arber, Cabbibo, and Soronado (editors), *Scientific Insights into the Evolution of the Universe and of Life* (Vatican City: Pontifical Academy of Sciences, 2009), p. 424.
16. *The Mystery of Reason* (Leominster, Herefordshire: Gracewing, 2001), p. 31.
17. *Science and Creation*, p. 202.
18. D. Burrell, 'Creation' in T. Winter, ed., *The Cambridge Companion to Classical Islamic Theology* (Cambridge: Cambridge University Press, 2008), p. 145.
19. P-A. Hardy, 'Epistemology and divine discourse' in T. Winter, ed., *The Cambridge Companion to Classical Islamic Theology* (Cambridge: Cambridge University Press, 2008), p. 290.
20. *Ibid.*, p. 293.
21. Al-Ghazali and Ibn Taymiyya had a different view on how Allah makes use of words, but 'the picture of divine discourse in both ... portrays the Qur'an as a static container of meaning ... both [Ghazali] and Ibn Taymiyya find in the Qur'an a repository of unambiguous knowledge in which each sentence has the possibility of a clear and literal meaning' (*Ibid.*, p. 303).
22. Gilson, *History of Christian Philosophy*, p. 182.
23. W. Craig, *The Cosmological Argument from Plato to Leibniz* (Eugene, Oregon: Wipf and Stock Publishers, 1980), p. 49.
24. *Ibid.*, p. 51.
25. Gilson, *History of Christian Philosophy*, p. 183. See also Jaki, *Science and Creation*, pp. 203–205.
26. *The Foundations of Modern Science in the Middle Ages* (Cambridge: Cambridge University Press, 1996), p. 183.
27. *Ibid.*, p. 182.
28. *St. Thomas Aquinas* (London: Hodder & Stoughton Limited, 1933), p. 97.
29. Craig, *The Cosmological Argument*, p. 51.
30. Gilson, *History of Christian Philosophy*, p. 185.
31. *Ibid.*
32. For a treatment of the Muslim identification of all agency with creation, see David Burrell's article 'Creation' in T. Winter, ed., *The Cambridge*

Muslim Monotheism

[33] *Companion to Classical Islamic Theology* (Cambridge: Cambridge University Press, 2008). See also p. 104 above.
[33] Craig, *The Cosmological Argument*, p. 50.
[34] Cited in E. Gilson, *The Unity of Philosophical Experience* (London: Sheed and Ward, 1938), pp. 46–47.
[35] Craig, *The Cosmological Argument*, p. 50.
[36] Gilson, *The Unity of Philosophical Experience*, p. 37.
[37] Jaki, *The Savior of Science*, p. 78.
[38] *The Foundations of Modern Science*, p. 178.
[39] Cited in *Ibid.*, p. 180.
[40] Gilson, *The Unity of Philosophical Experience*, p. 34.
[41] Gilson, *History of Christian Philosophy*, p. 185.
[42] Craig, *The Cosmological Argument*, p. 81.
[43] 'The Physics of Impetus and the Impetus of the Koran' in *Modern Age*, Spring, 1985, pp. 157–158.
[44] Gilson, *History of Christian Philosophy*, p. 210.
[45] Craig, *The Cosmological Argument*, p. 96.
[46] See p. 176.
[47] *Science and Creation*, p. 211.
[48] Gilson, *History of Christian Philosophy*, p. 194.
[49] *Ibid.*, p. 218.
[50] Cited in *Ibid.*, p. 220.
[51] *Ibid.*, p. 219.
[52] *Ibid.*, p. 389.
[53] Craig, *The Cosmological Argument*, p. 110.
[54] Gilson, *The Unity of Philosophical Experience*, p. 61.
[55] See *Ibid.*, p. 33.
[56] *History of Christian Philosophy*, p. 388.
[57] Aquinas holds that it is impossible for human reason to prove either that the world is eternal or had a beginning in time (ST, I, q.46, a.1), and so creation in time is believed on faith. The reason is that the existence of the world depends on God's free choice, and, given that He wills to create, He has two choices as to *when* to do so: to create the universe from all eternity, or to have the universe come into being when previously there was nothing besides Himself. If reason showed us that He had to choose one of these options, it could prove that option to us. But since it is not able to do so, we are not able to know which He chose unless He tells us.
[58] Gilson, *The Unity of Philosophical Experience*, p. 52.
[59] *Ibid.*, p. 54.
[60] *Ibid.*, p. 56.

[61] See G. Smith, *Why Atheism?* (Prometheus Books, 2000); P. Atkins, *On Being* (Oxford: Oxford University Press, 2011), p. 33.
[62] *History of Christian Philosophy*, p. 410, emphasis added.
[63] *Ibid.*, p. 213.
[64] *Ibid.*, p. 498.
[65] See p. 7.
[66] See Gilson, *The Unity of Philosophical Experience*, pp. 82–83.
[67] *History of Christian Philosophy*, p. 487.
[68] Gilson, *The Unity of Philosophical Experience*, p. 91.
[69] *History of Christian Philosophy*, p. 489.
[70] Grant, *The Foundations of Modern Science*, p. 143.
[71] Gilson, *History of Christian Philosophy*, pp. 499–500. See also J. Hannam, *The Genesis of Science* (Washington, DC: Regnery Publishing, 2011), pp. 163–164.
[72] *Ibid.*, p. 793.
[73] Even Jaki received backlash for his writing on Islam, as he states in his autobiography *A Mind's Matter*, p. 257, that copies of his *Science and Creation* 'were on occasion burned by zealous Muslims', and his Farmington Institute Lectures were interrupted by Islamists.

7 PROTESTANT BIBLICISM

Reason is the devil's greatest whore.

Martin Luther

On 4 February 2014, there was held in my home state of Kentucky a debate that attracted three million online viewers. It pitted Bill Nye 'The Science Guy' against arch-creationist Ken Ham at the latter's Creation Museum.

Nye became famous as a 'science communicator' through his PBS children's television series which aired from 1993 to 1998. In each episode, he introduced his pre-teen audience to a topic of science in such an engaging and entertaining fashion, that the show won nineteen Emmy awards during its six year run.

But, as Casey Luskin of the Discovery Institute remarks, there is a dark side to Nye that has only come out in the past few years. That dark side, in the words of Luskin, is that Nye 'advocates a hardline, intolerant, and divisive atheistic worldview.'[1] This became readily apparent in 2010 when Nye was named 'Humanist of the Year' and, in his acceptance speech, expressed his view on his own significance, and ostensibly that of the rest of the human race:

> I'm insignificant ... I am just another speck of sand. And the earth really in the cosmic scheme of things is another speck. And the sun an unremarkable star ... And the galaxy is a speck. I'm a speck on a speck orbiting a speck among other specks among still other specks in the middle of specklessness. I suck.[2]

His opposite in the debate was Ken Ham, founder of the organisation Answers in Genesis (AiG), which has for its goal the promotion of what is known as young-earth creationism. This ambiguous term 'creationism' refers not so much to the belief of creation in time, but rather to a belief in the *way* in which creation in time was accomplished. Many fundamentalist Protestants hold that God created the universe six thousand years ago, in a period of six days of twenty-four hours each, according to the strict literal sense of the first chapter of Genesis, and for this belief, they are accorded the label 'creationist'.

During the debate, Nye the Science Guy presented a barrage of scientific arguments supporting the Big Bang model of the universe, which postulates that the universe began in time 13.7 billion years ago, with our solar system coming along 4.6 billion years ago. Meanwhile, Ham, who is not a scientist, appealed to the authority of the Bible as the Word of God. If the Bible says that the universe and Earth are six thousand years old, then that is the way that it must be, regardless of what science has to say.

Nye used science to preach atheism, while Ham used the Bible to preach science. The former was treating natural science as revelation and the latter revelation as natural science. Neither seemed to think that the two pertain to separate areas of knowledge, which are distinct but compatible. Nor was there any one there that night in Kentucky to indicate how the findings of modern science are at the least reconcilable with the Christian faith and, better yet, supportive of it.

While *Wikipedia* reports that most thought Nye won the debate, many scientists criticised The Science Guy for giving Ham media time by accepting the latter's invitation. Others thought that Nye was seeking to rejuvenate his public persona, which had faded with the passing of his PBS program, and shortly after the debate, he capitalised on his renewed publicity to issue a book against creationists, *Undeniable: Evolution and the Science of Creation*. Meanwhile, Ham reported that, thanks to money coming in after the debate, AiG was now able to commence the first phase of its $73 million project to build a replica of Noah's ark, a project that had stalled up to that point due to lack of funds.

Nye stuck to his science; Ham stuck to his faith. Where, we may ask, was the truth in all of this? Is the Bible meant to trump science? Are created facts able to trump the Creator? In this chapter, I must address the first question, before moving on to section three to answer the second question.

Luther's irrationalism

Faith divorced from reason makes humans act irrationally, and worse, it has them do so in the name of God. Occam set Christianity on the path of derationalising reality. Aquinas set it on the path of harmonising all realities—those of faith and of reason, of heaven and of earth. The Catholic Church embraced Aquinas as her Common Doctor and excommunicated Occam[3], but she could not halt the latter's influence. His thought infected many Catholic minds and it slowly eroded their faith and morals. Eventually, an entire body of Catholics threw off reason and, with it, faith in the Catholic Church. Today, we call them Protestants. Because their theological path originated with William of Occam, the latter is sometimes referred to as 'the first Protestant'.[4]

We saw in chapter 5 that medieval Christendom was able to craft and embody a supremely realist worldview, one that was aided rather than obstructed by religion.[5] We also saw that the delicate realist balance was too fragile to be maintained for long. Thomism, or the school of those who follow Aquinas in philosophy and theology, by no means gained the ascendancy throughout the Catholic world in the centuries following his death.[6] In the 1500s, the Dominicans followed the Angelic Doctor more or less to a man, but other monastic orders looked to less balanced and hence less realist minds to frame their synthesis of reality. One such order, the Augustinians, followed the thought of William of Occam,[7] and one of their monks at the dawn of the sixteenth century bore the name of Martin Luther (1483–1546).

In his biography of Luther, Fr Hartmann Grisar, SJ, notes the negative and positive effects exercised on the mind of Luther by

Occam, who served as a springboard for Luther's development of his own system.

Occam's negative effect

One negative effect was to give Luther an extreme distaste for philosophical argumentation and, by extension, for the very use of reason.[8] The great intellectual jousts generated in the universities by scholastic philosophy had similar results to those of humanity's first period of intense philosophising in the ancient Greek world. On the one hand, they led to many new insights and distinctions, a sharpening of the reasoning faculty, and the classification and clarification of many subjects which before had only been treated ambiguously. On the other hand, they led to scepticism. Disputes became more detailed and prolonged, conclusions seemed to be less and less certain, and the difference between important, unshakable truths and trivial, disputed ones faded into obscurity.

The latter situation obtained in the works of Occam, who wrote voluminously, turning questions around and around with the acuteness of his mind, but often leaving that of his reader unsatisfied by saying that nothing could be proved with certainty. Luther's passionate and impatient nature found such abstract mental work tedious, as he did not have a philosophical mind. This, combined with the intrinsic distastefulness of theological hair-splitting, led him to reach for the solution that served him well throughout most of his life, the nuclear one. He would not engage scholasticism, but shout it down. He would not reason his way to a conclusion, but be done with reason.

Thomas Neill sums up Luther's attitude towards philosophy and intellect as follows:

> There have been many persons–many, like Luther, with doctor's degrees–who were happily nonrational. But there are few, indeed, who have made as vicious an attack on reason as [Luther]. All philosophers were anathema to him. He calls Aristotle an 'urchin who must be put in the

pig-sty or donkey's stable'; the Sorbonne is 'that mother of all errors'; the theologians of Louvain are 'coarse donkeys, cursed sows, bellies of blasphemers, epicurean swine, heretics and idolators, putrid puddles, the cursed broth of hell.' Not only philosophers, but philosophy itself is viciously attacked by Luther. In 1536 he wrote: 'I shall have to chop off the head of philosophy.' Again: 'One should learn philosophy only as one learns witchcraft, that is to destroy it.' Luther carries his assault to reason itself by attacking man's very mind. 'Reason,' he wrote, 'is contrary to faith ... In believers it should be killed and buried.' It 'is the devil's handmaid and does nothing but blaspheme and dishonor all that God says or does.'[9]

Meanwhile, Grisar points out that Luther had similar things to say about Thomism:

> Luther pours out his ire on the 'asinine coarseness of the Thomists', on the 'Thomist hogs and donkeys,' on the 'stupid audacity and thickheadedness of the Thomists,' who 'have neither judgment, nor insight, nor industry in their whole body.' ... 'The opinions of the Thomists, even though approved by Pope or Council, remain opinions and do not become articles of faith, though an angel from heaven should say the contrary.'[10]

Occam drove a wedge between natural and supernatural, between reason and faith; Luther cuts them off completely. For Occam, it is impossible to make faith and reason agree, but that's no reason to throw out one or the other. No, we will keep both, and be uncertain about both. Luther will not have any of this. For him, there is only one truth, that of faith. For him, like Occam, faith and reason cannot get along. Instead of trying to give them their own territories, however, so as to allow them both to exist, he tosses reason overboard. 'The Sorbonne, that mother of all errors,' Luther fulminates, 'has defined, as badly as could be, that if a thing is true, it is true for philosophy and theology; it is godless in it to have condemned those who hold the contrary',[11] because such a decision makes the articles of faith 'prisoners to the judgement of reason'.[12] In the speculative realm, only faith has a claim to truth. At the end of the day, Luther could not be bothered with reason, because Occamist philosophising had bothered him so much.

Occam's positive effects

Such was a negative effect of Occam on Luther, negative in that it led Luther to push aside the intellectual faculty. Occam's positive influence concerns the ways in which the Occamist spirit contributed to Luther's own system of thought.[13] For Luther had a certain rational system at the heart of his worldview, even while proclaiming irrationality to the world with his entertaining and zoological vituperation. Occamism lent quite a contribution to the formation of this worldview.

Firstly, Luther imbibed the Occamist questioning and critical attitude, by which one subjects everything to one's own judgement. Even his *Commentary on Romans*, written before his break with the Catholic Church,

> manifests that spirit of criticism and arbitrariness, bold to overstep the barriers of the traditional teaching of the Church, which he had [] received from his Occamist masters ... We shall not be mistaken in assuming that [Luther's] doctrinal arbitrariness was, to a certain extent at least, a result of the atmosphere of decadent theology in which his lot had been cast.[14]

Thus, Luther did not see dogmas in terms of degrees of certitude, where one Church decision is infallible, another holds great weight, while another is mere opinion. For him, everything was in the realm of opinion; there were no fixed truths.

> In consequence of his training, which consisted exclusively in the discussion of speculative controversies, he had come to see in the theological doctrines merely opinions of the schools, on which it was permissible to sit in judgment. He

had forgotten that there existed a positive body of unassailable doctrine.[15]

When a monk is schooled in hyper-criticism, is placed in positions of authority at a young age, is extremely confident in his self-sufficiency, and is led to think that there is no fixed truth, he quite easily believes himself empowered to construct a new faith. Such a monk was Dr Luther.[16]

Martin Luther (Image courtesy of Wikimedia Commons)

For this construction, Occam also provided a starting point. For he had proposed a theory on the imputation of righteousness which Luther would develop to the nth degree.[17] Occam thought that the necessity of supernatural habits for salvation—that is, the need of God-like virtues in a person's soul to make him worthy of heaven—could not be established by faith or reason. This led him to doubt the existence of such virtues, and propose, *as a possibility*, that God held a person slated for heaven merely by a certain imputation, without any actual change taking place in the person. Salvation could be a completely external thing, such that there is no working together of first and secondary causes to accomplish it, but rather is solely the work of God.

Occam, who seemed averse to drawing any sure conclusions, proposes the system as a possibility; Luther elevates it to a certainty, even quoting Occam 'in such a way as to represent him as teaching as a fact what he merely held to be possible'.[18] This system of a merely external salvation leads directly to the key beliefs of Luther regarding justification by faith alone, and the inability of grace to render a person able to perform supernatural acts worthy of Heaven. That system applies theologism to each person's salvation. God does all; we do nothing. It is a work of primary causation, without any input from secondary causes.

As far as God Himself goes, Occam helped Luther conceive of God in voluntarist terms, similar to the way Muslims think of Allah. For Occam, God's spiritual attributes, such as His wisdom, cannot be proved by natural reason.[19] We cannot even know that God is our final end and happiness, or that there is a final cause of all things. This ignorance on our part makes it impossible for us to assign any reason for God's activity. The only option is to consider God as an entirely wilful being, where 'God's outward action knows no law, but is purely arbitrary'.[20] The thing for a person of faith to do is blindly submit himself to God's will, which is utterly beyond the ken of human reason.

As we saw in the last chapter, when one makes the divine will stand isolated from the divine intellect, one turns God from a loving father into an autocratic dictator, deciding what is and what is not according to *ad hoc* fiats rather than wise order.[21] Luther adopted the voluntarist view of God, with its theological consequences, the most important of which was seeing human salvation as being entirely God's decision, such that humans have no say whether they go to heaven or hell. Already in his pre-break commentary on Romans, Luther 'teaches the absolute predestination to hell of those who are to be damned, a doctrine which no Occamist had yet ventured to put forward'.[22]

Luther did not maintain rational consistency in holding this dogma, as in the same Commentary, he speaks both of a person's inability to contribute to his own salvation and the need for him to do so. Nor did he realise that he was contradicting himself. Grisar explains:

> In [Luther's] mind are combined two widely divergent ideas, viz. that God does everything in man who is devoid of freedom—and that man must draw nigh to God by prayer and works of faith. It is a strange psychological phenomenon to see how, instead of endeavoring to solve the contradiction and examine the question in the light of calm reason, he gives free play to feeling and imagination, now passionately proving to the infamous Observants [a certain target of Luther's polemic] that man is absolutely unable to do anything, now insisting on the need of preparation for grace.[23]

Luther's system

In summary, Luther was schooled in a decadent Scholasticism in the line of William of Occam, which contributed to his passionate character taking up the following positions:

1. **no reason**–an extreme dislike for philosophical and theological reasoning, leading him to condemn speculative reasoning altogether

2. **inscrutable God**–metaphysics being unable to prove anything certain about God, God's activities are to be considered impermeable to reason and so arbitrary

3. **faith alone**–reasoning and religious authority having been set aside as paths to truth, the individual faith of the believer emerges as the sole avenue to knowledge.

The first step is the firm and even violent setting aside of reason as a path to knowledge. With reason cast aside, the believer—second step—has no cause to look into an objective reality, an objective God, an objective Church. He does not begin with sense data to move from there to metaphysical truths, proven by natural reason, and then on to revealed truths, supported by natural reason. The worldview of that realist path has the intellect as its guiding leader, the faculty that Luther considers to be the devil's greatest whore.

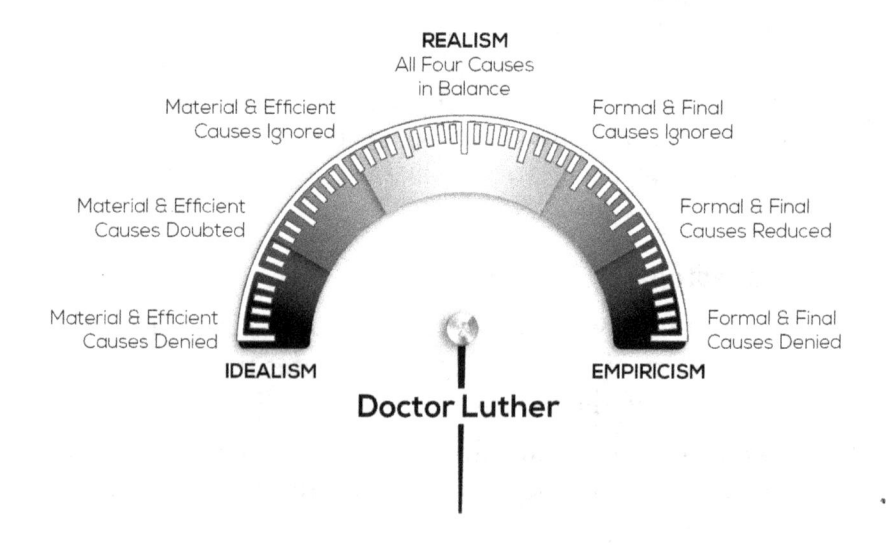

REALISM
All Four Causes in Balance

Material & Efficient Causes Ignored

Formal & Final Causes Ignored

Material & Efficient Causes Doubted

Formal & Final Causes Reduced

Material & Efficient Causes Denied

Formal & Final Causes Denied

IDEALISM

EMPIRICISM

Doctor Luther

The third step is to find a new path to truth. That path is faith, not faith in the sense of propositions supported by rational motives of credibility, but a faith without reason. The faith of 'faith alone' is one built on the will, for 'as reason is banished to the foulest place in the house, if not killed and buried, the other spiritual faculty, the will, must be correspondingly exalted'.[24] Free and arbitrary choice must rule the believer, instead of a choice indicated by rational judgement. Believers in an arbitrary God are godlike in being arbitrary themselves. When religion was reasonable, every person could find the truth in the same God, in the same set of dogmas, in the same Church. Religion being made wilful, however, each person must choose his beliefs on his own, without any rational direction being given from the outside.

In this light, it was logical for Luther to propose

> unrestrained freedom for everyone to believe what he wanted ... Each man was to be his own priest and prophet ... Luther could insist: 'Neither the pope nor the bishop nor any other man has the right to dictate even so much as one syllable to a Christian believer, except with the latter's consent.' The whole rule of faith was to be found in the Bible, he asserted, and the Bible was to be interpreted by everyone for himself, even by a 'humble miller's maid, nay, by a child of nine if it has the faith.'[25]

The new 'reformed' Christians were not to look for a rational synthesis of all reality with their intellect, nor to adhere to the words of an external authority. Rather, they were to open the book of the Bible and find there, by means of private inspiration, the whole of what they needed to know about life and the universe. It would produce in them a personal faith, which need only correspond to the believer's feeling about what is right, and need not match up with reason or reality. That faith, and that faith alone, was to be the guide for each individual's life.

Luther thus constructed a worldview on two columns: Scripture alone and faith alone. Since those columns were established to support individual feeling in opposition to reason, they inevitably drove reason from religion, as McNamara points out:

> The principle of "sola scriptura," or the use of scripture alone rather than tradition and reason to guide behavior, could be seen by some as an antirational trend in religion. The overemphasis on personal faith as the primary route to salvation had the side effect of valuing a stance (trust, faith) over rational deliberation about moral choices and so forth. The sola scriptura doctrine shifted the accent away from rational interpretative traditions and argument onto the individual with his idiosyncratic interpretative tendencies and his haunted, lonely conscience. That move alone would not have been fatal to the reason-religion relationship had it not been for the second idea—that faith alone saves. If faith was all that really counted, then you did not need established and rationally justified doctrines, traditions, priests, rituals, or institutions. Indeed, these things were even considered harmful.[26]

Calvin and other Protestants

I have focused on Luther, but I could look at and analyse other reformers to reach the same general results as with the ex-Augustinian monk. For instance, these two paragraphs from Neill show that John Calvin conceives of God in the same way as Luther:

> Calvin posits an almighty, unlimited God like that of the Catholics before him; but whereas the Catholics had stressed God's intelligence and necessary justice, Calvin stressed His will, a will which he made as arbitrary, as erratic as the earthly despot's whim. 'The will of God,' he wrote, 'is the highest rule of justice. What He wills must be considered just, for this very reason that He wills it. Therefore when it is asked why the Lord did so, the answer must be, because He would.'
>
> This sovereign God rules the world exactly as He pleases—and it is not for man to inquire into the nature of God's rule or into its justice. Christians had till Calvin's day

insisted that God could, of His very nature, do no injustice or no evil, for such action would be self-contradictory—like a circle being a square. Calvin's God, however, does not seem to be limited to doing what is reasonable, just, and good. He does whatever He wants, and there seems no way of knowing what He will want.[27]

The Reformers, despite their many differences and variegated personalities, generally bore certain common stances in their notion of godly religion. They all denied the ability of natural reason to prove the existence of God and had recourse to other, non-intellectual means to connect with Him, primarily religious sentiment, a certain non-rational feeling in the believer for which God is thought to be responsible. They all saw God's will as being inscrutable to the human mind and so upheld a faith that was blind and a natural order that was arbitrary. They all refused the Church as being the possessor of divine authority and held up the Bible as the sole authority.[28]

We have already seen the difficulties created for Muslims by their inability to reconcile religion with faith, because of the Koran's inconsistencies: it made the religious unreasonable and the reasonable faithless. Here, we see the same difficulties entering the Christian world, from outside of its sacred text, but also by means of it. Before the rise of the Reformers, the Bible was given an authoritative interpretation by a living body, the Church, an interpretation that was sometimes literal, at other times allegorical, but always logical. Under the Reformers, however, there is no authoritative body outside the individual believer and there is no natural theology or body of immutable revealed dogmas to guard the Bible from contradictory interpretations by the 'unstable and unlearned' (II Pet 3:16). The Bible was printed in the thousands and tossed into the laps of miller's maids and nine-year-olds with the injunction to find their God in it. Find one they did, a god proceeding from blind, wilful impulses that was more a manifestation of their creativity than of God the Creator.

The Protestant system has a single human faculty—religious sentiment—obtain all knowledge of reality by means of a single method—reading the Bible. Because faith and Bible were expanded far beyond their proper epistemological domains so as to occupy the totality of reality's geography, they were certain to come into conflict with every discipline of natural knowledge. This was especially true, however, in regard to science. In the 1500s, the groundwork laid for modern science by medieval scholastics was about to bear fruit in an explosion of scientific development. Protestantism would use the Bible to contradict the science, while Catholicism would use the science to change its interpretation of the Bible.

To track this history, I must first consider in general the relationship between the Bible and science. Then, I must consider how the Biblical epistemologies of Catholicism and Protestantism either turned believers against the findings of science or left them free to embrace them.

The Bible and science

Those who believe that Scripture is inspired generally hold that it has two authors, God and the individual composer of each book. To understand the Bible's meaning, it is crucial, then, to understand the purpose of those authors in their writing. What truths did they intend to convey in the Bible? How did they intend to convey those truths?

The same sorts of questions pertain to every book, for the simple reason that words are limited and cannot say everything at once. For instance, I cannot use scientific language and non-scientific language at the same time. I cannot write fiction and non-fiction at the same time. I cannot teach embroidery at the same time that I teach organic chemistry. No, whenever I write or communicate, because I am making use of words, which are determined to a specific sense, I must limit myself to a specific aspect of reality—a single topic—and a specific way of communicating that reality—a single writing or speaking style. To the degree that I depart from that unity of communication, to the same degree does my communication break down and my reader or listener become befuddled by my words.

To take an example of the difference, let's say that I am writing a popular biography of a girl named Sally and I want to describe an early morning scene. I could say something like, 'As Earth's luminous, life-giving sun began to poke its head above the cover of the distant hills, Sally saw the sky purpled and pinked with a magnificent display of pastel colours.' I cannot use words speaking with scientific exactitude, for then I would lose my intended communication, which is to portray a beautiful sunrise by means of metaphor. Even to use the word 'sunrise' is to err scientifically. For technical exactitude, I would have to say something like 'The 29.78 kilometre per second counter-clockwise rotation of the Earth in relation to the sun at latitude 34.96 S, longitude 149.67 E caused Sally to see the Earth's terminator pass away on the west horizon at 21:37 Greenwich Mean Time on 22 July 1987.'

Now, if I were writing the biography and my reader understood that it was a popular work, it would be unreasonable for him to read the Sally sunrise sentence and say: 'The author errs! The sun does not move in relation to the Earth, and therefore is improperly described as poking its head above the covers!' It would even be wrong for the reader to say that the sentence was false or untrue, for this would imply that the statement that the sun rises does not have any corresponding true sense, no matter how it is understood. But it is our commonsense experience to see the sun moving in the sky in relation to us, and so the word 'sunrise' does relate to something real outside the mind.

This illustration of the relationship between the meaning that an author intends to convey and the words that must be chosen to convey that meaning enables us to pose a more specific question: Does the Bible want us to read it like a science textbook using scientific language? Or is it meant to be read in another way?

248   *The Realist Guide to Religion & Science*

The answer is obvious from the very beginning of the Bible, which presents serious challenges for anyone seeking to find properly scientific information about the formation of the world, at least anyone possessing today's extensive knowledge of the universe's true architecture. In the first chapter of Genesis, God is described as creating a roof over the Earth (the 'firmament'), with there being water above that roof, as well as water surrounding the sides of the Earth (1:6ff.). The Earth brings forth plants on the third day (1:11–13), which sprouted without the sun, which was not created until the following day (1:14–19). That same chapter describes God as speaking to Himself and the animals (1:22), and as moving over the waters that He later separates (1:2).

A graphic of the Hebraic conception of the world, which is followed by the Bible. The Earth rests on columns, is surrounded by water at its sides, and has a roof above it.
  (Image © Michael Paukner; reproduced with permission)

This incompatibility between a literal, scientific reading of Biblical passages like Genesis 1, and the actual facts of the created world presents an apparent dilemma for believers. It seems to force them to either accept the Bible and reject the facts, or reject the Bible and accept the facts. In reality, however, one can easily both accept the facts and accept the Bible, by reading such passages in a non-scientific sense.

We will first see how Catholics have met this difficulty, and then how Protestants have met it.

Catholic interpretation of the Bible

Principles of interpretation

Catholics do not start with the Bible, moving from it to build a body of doctrines. Rather, they start with a body of doctrines which they claim to have come from Jesus Christ and interpret the Bible in line with those doctrines. This is a first limitation on the reading of Scripture: its meaning must match with the teachings of the Catholic faith. If a given interpretation of the Bible contradicts a Catholic dogma, then that interpretation must be rejected, not the Catholic dogma.

Implicit in this limitation is a restriction on the Bible's scope. The Bible is at the service of Catholic teaching; it is ordained to manifest what is necessary for salvation. Everything else falls outside of the Bible's scope. This is not to say that the Bible does not teach natural truths; it is to say that the Bible teaches natural truths only insofar as they are needed to support supernatural truths. Of such natural truths, the only one that might, in theory, come into conflict with science, is the teaching that the human race derived from a single set of parents created directly by God.[29] We will see in chapter 11 that there is not, in practice, any conflict with science in this Biblical teaching.[30] As for the rest of Catholic teachings, there is no need to have recourse to facts of physics or astronomy to support them, and so no need to hold that the Bible wishes to teach such facts.

The second limitation Catholics place on the Bible's meaning comes from the side of reason, and is expressed in the fundamental exegetical principle of the Fathers of the Church: 'it is not lawful to depart from the obvious literal sense, unless reason prohibits it or some necessity forces us to leave it'.[31] This principle indicates a balanced flexibility in the reading of the Bible. God is presumed to have intended the direct sense of the text as being the Bible's meaning. If that direct sense, however, is shown to be erroneous by information outside the Bible, that sense cannot be God's meaning, since God is truth. In this way, natural knowledge can play a negative role in the reading of Scripture, by excluding certain readings from being God's intended meaning. In the words of Fr Chaberek,

> In the Catholic tradition, if a truth of natural knowledge is duly proven, it has to be accepted as a criterion of interpretation of Holy Scripture ... a well-established scientific theory [can be] a criterion by which the Bible is to be interpreted.[32]

Aquinas provides further clarification of this principle with his summary of Augustine's division of the principle into two parts:

> Two things must be observed in questions of this sort, as Augustine teaches. First, one must hold unshakably that Scripture is true. Second, since Sacred Scripture can be interpreted in many ways, one must not hold to a given interpretation so firmly that, once that interpretation is clearly shown to be false, he presume to assert that the false interpretation is Scripture's meaning, lest, by doing so, he expose Scripture to ridicule by non-believers, and close off for them the path to belief.[33]

These two rules strike a middle ground between faith and reason, preserving on the one hand the doctrine that Scripture cannot err, and on the other the doctrine that there cannot be two truths, one for faith and one for reason. If Scripture, according to its literal sense, says that there is a roof above the Earth, and meanwhile our senses tell us that there is no such roof, then our conclusion is clear: 'If a literal interpretation is really and flatly contradicted by an obvious fact, why then we can only say that the literal interpretation must be a false interpretation'.[34] Once we have flown to space—and have not crashed through a roof on the way—we are to reject the strictly literal reading for a more allegorical one.

Application of principles to Genesis 1

It would be helpful for us to take a quick look at Catholic understandings of Genesis 1, in order to illustrate these principles of interpretation more clearly. Catholics, as we have seen, are required to believe that God created the entire universe, bringing it into existence at a specific time some moment in the distant past. They are not, however, required to hold any particular dogma regarding aspects of the way God brought things into existence, in relation to:

- time: whether God created everything in an instant, in six days, or in intervals over billions of years
- periods: the number of stages in which God created the universe, whether it be a single stage, the six stages described in Genesis 1, or more stages
- order: what God chose to create in each stage, such as plants first, then animals, or vice-versa

Up to the eighteenth century, there was not overwhelming evidence against a literal understanding of Genesis 1, and so that literal understanding was the majority opinion among Catholics for 1700 years, that 'God created the world successively in six natural days, namely, each of twenty-four hours, just as the first and direct sense of the sacred text sets forth'.[35]

St Augustine was a famous exception to this view. He taxed his mind to the utmost on the subject, ultimately writing three commentaries on the first chapters of Genesis by the end of his life. Something that particularly puzzled him was how the light created on the first day could exist without there being light-bearing bodies, which were created on the fourth day. Furthermore, how could this light mark the days and nights of creation, when it is the movement of the sun which indicates day and night? Augustine turned these questions over and over in his mind, looking for a solution. His ultimate conclusions about Genesis 1 were as follows:

> According to Scripture (Ecclus. 18:1), God has created all things at once. *The six days of creation are a metaphor intended to help our imagination.* By a single instantaneous act, God has created out of nothing all the beings which then were, and, in them, all those that have come to be ever since the first instant of creation, as well as all those that still are to come up to the end of the world.[36]

Thus, Augustine began by trying to take the six-day description literally, then found it to conflict with sense observation, as well as a literal reading of another passage of the Bible, and so decided to interpret it figuratively. His motive was to keep the Bible from conflicting with reason. Out of respect for the Bible, he would not attribute to it a meaning that jarred with common sense. The idea that there is light independent of a light-bearing body does exactly that. Thus, when the Bible speaks of that light, it is not speaking literally.[37]

In between the strictly literal interpretation and the allegorical one, there is a middle ground, which we can call 'progressive creationism'. It holds that Genesis 1 is not an exact, historical account of the unfolding of creation, yet at the same time, it does contain historical elements. God did not create everything at once, but rather created some material beings in an initial instant and then progressively added material beings to the universe at later times. This did not happen in six periods of twenty-four hours, nor did it happen in the exact order indicated by Genesis 1. Nonetheless, the general framework of Genesis 1, which portrays God as adding to His Creation over time, is correct.

With the advent of the scientific discoveries of the eighteenth century, Catholics almost universally abandoned the strictly literal reading of Genesis 1 that had held sway for so many centuries. Some exegetes opted for the allegorical interpretation with Augustine, while others chose some permutation of a progressive creation model. Just as the Fathers had the freedom to choose anything from a strictly literal reading to an allegorical one, so did they. The rules remain the same: neither reason nor Catholic teaching are to be contradicted.

As science progresses, it seems best to read Genesis 1 according to a model of progressive creationism. We now know, for instance, that there are sudden explosive appearances of plant and animal life in the geological record that cannot be accounted for by purely natural processes (more on this topic in chapters 10 and 11), and so must be accounted for by God's intervention.

Today, it is clear that Genesis 1 is not meant to provide a strict history of the universe. In the words of Ruffini,

> God could very well reveal (and who doubts it?) in what order and in what time He made the various things appear in the world; but in His inscrutable wisdom He preferred to leave such questions to human research.[38]

The positive sense of Genesis 1

What is Genesis 1 saying then, for the standard Catholic exegete? Primarily, it is conveying certain important religious truths to the popular mind, and especially to that of the ancient Hebrews. What are those truths?

- that God is outside of the universe and the single source of its totality.
- that humans are the highest of His creations in the material order and have lordship over the Earth.
- that the Sabbath day rest must be religiously observed.

How does it convey these truths? By a grandiose description of Creation, whereby God is first described as creating everything (the heavens and the earth) in verse 2, and then creating each of the parts of the world that make up its whole in the succeeding verses. The parts are described in such a way that the popular mind can easily see that the entire world is included. The Fathers and the Scholastics saw Genesis 1 as describing God making three sections of the world in days 1 to 3, and then adorning those three sections in days 4, 5, and 6 (see the chart below). Jaki reads the chapter as describing the world as a tent, the most common dwelling place in those days, which God constructs in its totality, which is first described in its main parts, then in its main particulars.[39]

Table 7.1 Scholastic division of the six days of creation

Day	Work of distinction	Creation	Day	Work of adornment	Creation	Area
1	Light separated from darkness	Light	4	Sun, moon, stars placed in the heavens	Heavenly bodies	TOP
2	Upper waters separated from lower waters	Firmament	5	Waters adorned with fish, air with birds	Fishes, birds	MIDDLE
3	Sea separated from dry land	Dry land, plants	6	Earth adorned with other animals and men	Other animals, men	BOTTOM

As we have previously seen, the religious truths of Genesis 1 are of enormous significance for the mind of the believer, and they even have profound consequences for his epistemological outlook and scientific endeavour. What we find in that chapter, when we analyse it according to realist exegetical principles that make room for reason and faith, is a device to make those truths accessible to every mind, something that would have been frustrated if the creation of the world had been narrated in the language of a scientific article. As Jaki says, the Hebrews 'did not take Genesis 1 for a physics textbook, for the very simple reason that they had no physics'.[40] Thus, it would have been *unwise* on the part of God to provide supernatural revelation to His people, only to hide it under a scientific language completely incomprehensible to them. In other words, communicating those natural,

Protestant Biblicism 255

cosmological facts in the Bible would have been an obstacle to its purpose of communicating revealed truths.

What would happen today if we tried to read that first chapter in a literal sense? What if we postulated that God wanted the Bible to teach physics to the Hebrews and so He revealed to Moses *how* He created the world, not just *that* He created the world? People would begin laughing straight off when hearing talk of Earth's roof and its super-terrestrial waters. Scriptural faith would be exposed to ridicule as being a set of fanciful beliefs, proper to children, but not rational adults. This eventuality must be avoided at all costs. We must not try to turn Moses into an inspired precursor of Newton, says Renié.[41] For if we do, reflective minds will easily conclude that the Bible cannot be the Word of God and therefore Christianity is false.

Jaki makes mention of a priest working in the slums of Paris who claimed that 'the apparent conflict between science and the six-day-creation story was much more effective in promoting atheism among the poor and the relatively uneducated than were the social injustices that cut into their flesh and blood'.[42] More later about the disastrous effects on souls of turning the Bible into a work of science.

For now, we must state that if, for believers, Scripture is inerrant, its proper meaning can never be something conflicting with reason, that is, something erroneous. Thus, whenever a believer encounters a fact in nature that contradicts the literal sense of the Bible, he must say that the Bible, in that instance, is not to be taken literally, at least, if he wants to save his reason. In the words of St Augustine: 'Whatever they can really demonstrate to be true of physical nature, we must show to be capable of reconciliation with our Scriptures'.[43] In many cases, this means that the Bible must be understood as conveying a religious truth in popular language, not a scientific truth in technical language.

All of this is explained with perfect clarity and magisterial precision in Leo XIII's encyclical on Scripture entitled *Providen-*

tissimus Deus, a passage that lays out the Catholic Biblical science interpretative model:

> [T]he sacred writers, or to speak more accurately, the Holy Spirit 'who spoke by them, did not intend to teach men these things (that is to say, the essential nature of the things of the visible universe), things in no way profitable unto salvation.' [St. Augustine, De Gen. ad litt., i., 9, 20] Hence they did not seek to penetrate the secrets of nature, but rather described and dealt with things in more or less figurative language, or in terms which were commonly used at the time and which in many instances are in daily use at this day, even by the most eminent men of science. Ordinary speech primarily and properly describes what comes under the senses; and somewhat in the same way the sacred writers—as the Angelic Doctor also reminds us—'went by what sensibly appeared,'[I, q.70, a.1, ad 3] or put down what God, speaking to men, signified, in the way men could understand and were accustomed to.[44]

Thus, whenever the Bible speaks in terms that offend scientific exactitude, it is simply using a popular language which follows the immediate data of sense, and not the more sophisticated sense knowledge which is obtained by careful observation and the use of measuring devices. Meanwhile, for Catholics, none of these matters touch upon dogmatic truths. They are required to believe that:

- God created the universe and sustains it
- faith and reason can never come into conflict.

They are not required to believe that:

- the universe is a certain age
- God created that universe in a period of six twenty-four hour days
- the sun goes around the Earth or vice versa, and so on.

Of themselves, these last issues do not have any direct bearing on the domain of faith. They are natural issues, not supernatural ones. No matter what science discovers about the physical universe, it cannot in any way impinge on Catholic beliefs. If the Bible, however, is presented as teaching a physical science revealed by God, that is, if physical truths are presented as supernatural truths, then they can and will come into conflict. This does not happen in a religion, such as Catholicism, which does not have recourse to its sacred text as the ultimate source of all truth, but rather uses the sacred text as a secondary support for supernatural truths already believed.

In the end, the Catholic Church only binds her members to believe a select number of supernatural truths, along with the natural truths closely connected to them. In all other questions, she leaves her children to hold their own opinions. Pope Leo clarifies this matter as well:

> The unshrinking defense of the Holy Scripture [] does not require that we should equally uphold all the opinions which each of the Fathers or the more recent interpreters have put forth in explaining it; for it may be that, in commenting on passages where physical matters occur, they have sometimes expressed the ideas of their own times, and thus made statements which in these days have been abandoned as incorrect.
>
> Hence, in their interpretations, we must carefully note what they lay down as belonging to faith, or as intimately connected with faith—what they are unanimous in. For *'in those things which do not come under the obligation of faith, the Saints were at liberty to hold divergent opinions, just as we ourselves are,'*[In Sent. ii., Dist. q. i., a. 3] according to the saying of St. Thomas. And in another place he says most admirably: 'When philosophers are agreed upon a point, and it is not contrary to our faith, it is safer, in my opinion, neither to lay down such a point as a dogma of faith, even though it is perhaps so presented by the philosophers, nor to reject it as against faith, lest we thus give to the wise of this world an occasion of despising our faith.'[Opusc. X][45]

Thus, while Catholics are free to hold their own opinions on questions of physical science, they are advised not to hold up those opinions as dogmas of faith. If they do, one who disagrees with them will believe that he must change his opinion if he wants to become a Catholic, a belief that might place a stumbling block in the way of his acceptance of Christ.

Protestant biblicism

The liberty granted to Catholics in scientific opinion could not easily be granted to adherents of the new faith of Luther or Protestants of any stripe. For the Reformers rejected every mediating authority between the believer and the Bible. This elevated the Bible to the status of the sole rule of faith, the beginning and the end of all truth, a position Jaki refers to as 'biblicism'.[46] With the removal of a definitive, living interpreter for the Bible, Protestants isolated the sacred text in a way similar to the Muslims with their Koran, and so restricted themselves to the same two possibilities: reason or faith, but not both.

If the Bible is read as the sole means which God provided to connect with Him, then it must be interpreted literally, for its meaning must be directly accessible to all. The literal sense, however, conflicts with reason in many places. What is the believer to do in such cases? Follow Luther's advice and cast reason overboard. In Luther's mind, Genesis 1 was written to humiliate the believer's mind.[47] In other words, it was a means for God to show the believer that human reason is not to be trusted, for it conflicts with God's own word. Thus, the thing to be done for the glory of God was to abandon reason; at this point, we will not be surprised to learn that Luther uses Genesis 1 as an opportunity to call reason 'altogether leprous and unclean'.[48]

When reason is abandoned, the metaphysical proofs for the existence of God that we worked out in chapter 2 fall to the ground. By them, we established that God must be sustaining all creation in existence *at every moment*, if reality is to make any sense. This is the proper, direct activity of the First Cause which underpins all of the activity of secondary causes. For this reason, no matter what scientists discover about the activity of secondary causes, it can never remove the need for a First Cause. It is ridiculous to suppose that the natural activities of God's creatures could show that there is no need for a Creator.

But, once we reject realism and throw out philosophical reasoning, then we only see God as manifesting Himself by some sort of extraordinary, miraculous activity *within* His own Creation. We think of God as having basically the same type of causal activity that creatures enjoy, only with more power. Under this perspective, human reason is only able to discover God when God does something in nature that is greater than what we can do.

This is why Protestants who decide that the arguments of philosophical realism have no value are left to make use of what is called a 'God of the gaps' argument to establish God's existence. What this means is that they look around in creation, seeking phenomena that cannot be explained by scientific reasoning. 'Aha!' they say once they have found a gap in scientific knowledge, 'God must be operating there, in that area that you cannot explain'. They see all causality in reality as *secondary causality*, with that causality being *divided* between God and creatures. What creatures can do in the natural world is explained by science and what creatures cannot do is explained by religion.

This view ends up pitting science against religion in a competition for causal explanation. Because God and creatures are assigned the same causal territory, so also are religion and science. As a result, the more science advances, the more religion retreats. Moreover, when someone with such a notion of God comes to believe that science has explained everything, it is only logical for him to become an atheist. Science has, for him, shown that the 'God hypothesis' is unnecessary. God has nothing to do in His own universe.

Such a metaphysically impoverished notion of God is behind the absurd 2010 BBC Horizon show 'The End of God'. In it, historian of science Dr Thomas Dixon looks high and low for God: in the ravings of women claiming to have visions, in claimed cures at Lourdes, in the religious experiences of Franciscan nuns and Buddhist monks, and in any apparent gap of natural knowledge. His conclusion? That it is a cinch to explain all these things by natural causes, and thus there is no role for God in the universe. For the only business that Dixon's God can engage in is difficult secondary causation. Because of this, Dixon never gets close to addressing the most fundamental question: why does anything exist at all? This is the metaphysical query that leads to Aquinas's foolproof First Cause arguments, but it never gets a hearing when the God being searched for is a mere secondary cause.

For the philosophical realist, nothing that the scientist finds can affect the rational arguments God's existence, but for the biblicist, those findings are encroachment on God's territory. Here, we are at the heart of the conflict between faith and science introduced by the Protestant rejection of reason. Once realism is gone, the universe is perceived as being capable of existing and acting independently of God. Thus, when scientists attempt to explain everything in the universe without having recourse to God, believers fear that scientists have shown that there is no reason for God to exist.

Such is the origin of the modern phenomenon of scientific data turning believers into atheists. It is Gilson's opinion that this is what occurred in the case of Charles Darwin. The latter was raised as a Protestant and had started down the path of becoming an Anglican clergyman before deciding to pursue natural science. Darwin believed that Genesis 1, when frequently speaking of God creating plants and animals 'according to their kinds' (1:12, 21, 24–25), teaches that God created each species directly. This teaching appeared to conflict with the scientific conclusions he was developing from his investigations in the Galapagos Islands (in chapter 11, I will examine closely the worth of the claims of his theory). And so, he was left with the choice of which I have been speaking, faith in the Bible or adherence to (apparent)

Protestant Biblicism

scientific evidence. 'The Bible or the transformation of species: such was [] the basic option for Darwin from which he must proceed'.[49] It is clear which choice Darwin made.

According to Gilson, Darwin hesitated 20 years before publishing his *On the Origin of Species* because he anticipated that his theory would destroy the faith of others, as it had destroyed his own. Eventually, he not only overcame his hesitations, but he even prided himself as being the one who removed the notion of creation from biology, in the sense of the direct creation of each individual species.[50]

Gilson notes that the word 'evolution' was not Darwin's own and did not appear in the *Origin of Species* until its 6th and last edition.[51] For Darwin, the word connoted the development of something already latent in an organism, whereas his theory held that organisms were *transformed* into new ones. Thus, Darwin made use of the word 'transformism'. By the time the 6th edition came around, however, he was willing to embrace the verbal ambiguity of the word 'evolution' because it was the popular term being used by the anti-creationists of his day in opposition to the direct creation of each species by God. By taking up the word, Darwin wanted to associate himself with their platform.

This case study is a perfect template for a pattern that has repeated itself time and time again in the past five centuries in Protestant circles. It involves three steps, transforming the believer into an anti-religious secularist:

1. The believer holds to a false exegesis or interpretation of the Bible.

2. When that interpretation is shown to conflict with reason, the believer loses faith in God.

3. In order to save reason, the new atheist initiates a campaign to eliminate the Bible's supposed encroachment on reason and science.

Ironically, the Protestants, by elevating the Bible to a self-interpreting source of all truths natural and supernatural, end up destroying in many the belief that it contains any truth at all.

The creationists

This brings us to modern day biblicists, the 'creationists' of this chapter's introductory story. They are not so much ones who believe in a Creator God—which I have argued is a logical conclusion of realist argumentation—as ones who choose faith over reason in having the Bible dictate science. For them, the Bible wishes to teach science and does so without error, as indicated in the chart below.

The chart also indicates the position of liberal Protestants and modernist Catholics. They do not believe that God is the author of the Bible, considering the Bible to be a merely human document, and so one containing errors just like any other human document. Like the Reformers, they interpret the Bible with a strict literalism, but, instead of following the Reformers' track of theologism—contradicting reason with Scripture's literal sense—they prefer a philosophism that 'saves' reason, contradicting faith with Scripture's literal sense. Since, in this second section of the book, we are focusing primarily on theologism, reserving philosophism for the third section, we will here consider only the fundamentalist Protestants, who are most faithful to their religious roots.

Table 7.2 Views on science in the Bible

Positions	Bible teaches science?	Bible errs in science?
Protestant Fundamentalism	YES	NO
Liberal Protestantism Modernist Catholicism	YES	YES
Orthodox Catholicism	NO	NO

While Jaki notes that the biblicism of all of the Reformers is to be blamed for today's fundamentalist Protestant creationists, yet he lays a particular onus on the shoulders of Calvin: 'Latter-day creationism owes much to the biblical literalism advocated by Calvin with sweeping diction and apparent rationality'.[52]

Calvin insists on Creation in six, twenty-four hour days. The waters above the firmament are not figurative. Plants grew without sun and moon so that we might learn to refer all things to God. Calvin had a 'resolve to hold as high as possible the dependence of nature on God. He took each and every verse of that chapter as a literal divine revelation about God's total absolute power which can bypass nature at any time.' He 'presents Moses as one who reported God's creative acts to be such as to confound nature's laws.'[53]

But a God Who confounds nature's laws at the same time that He establishes nature's laws poses immense theological problems. He is not a God acting with consistency or wisdom, two qualities which the Bible attributes to Yahweh incessantly. The stability of the physical world is used by the Old Testament as a proof by way of sign of the stability of God's covenant with His people and His salvific will.[54] The Bible even employs the notion of 'natural laws' to this end.[55] And, as we saw in chapter 3, for a philosophical realist, God does not change the laws of nature; He only suspends them in extremely rare circumstances.[56]

Not only would a God Who intervened in His own nature to reconfigure it be acting inconsistently, He would also, by doing so, be preventing His rational creatures from using their reason to understand what He had created. Humans are able to do science only because of the stability of secondary causes, a stability which can only come from a transcendent Creator Who, being outside the universe, can configure it with hardfast laws.[57] If the Creator intervenes periodically in nature to upset its consistency and so prevent our understanding nature's past, then it is clear that the Creator does not want us to make sense of what He has created. Why, then, we may ask, did He bestow upon us the faculty of knowing? For the Reformers, God gives us reason only to humble it, to crush it by the omnipotence of His absolute power. The human mind hopefully looks for knowledge in nature, only to be disappointed and so forced to admit the incompetency of its rational faculty.

This Reformist notion of God is much closer to Allah than the God found in the Bible which Protestants claim to tout so highly. One of the devices that the Bible uses to portray God as acting in a wholly consistent and rational way is to make reference to the stability of the Earth. Psalm 92 starts by stating that the Lord 'has made the world firm, not to be moved.' Verse 10 of psalm 95 uses the same language, and many more passages from the Bible could be cited wherein Scripture supports geocentrism when read in a literal, scientific sense, and supports God's consistency when read in a spiritual sense.

These two possible interpretations were available to all and sundry when the Polish cleric Nicholas Copernicus arrived on the European scene. He was attracted to the heliocentric model of the universe because of its ability to account for the movement of the planets in terms of much greater mathematical simplicity than the Ptolemaic geocentric model in vogue at the time. He did not have scientific proof for heliocentrism, and its main problem was that it seemed to contradict the evidence of the senses that the Earth is not moving. For him, the heliocentric model, far from being an attack on religion, was a support for it, and thus in the preface and first book of his *De Revolutionibus*, he proposed it as adding weight to proofs for the existence of God.[58]

The highest figures in the Church at the time seemed to see it the same way, for the Pope and his entourage received Copernicus in the Vatican Gardens and listened with interest to his lectures on heliocentrism.[59] There was no reason for Catholics to feel threatened by it, since it had been discussed extensively in medieval Christendom by figures such as Father Jean Buridan and Bishop Nicolas Oresme.[60] The latter proposed a new interpretation of the halting of the sun in Josue 10:12–14, compatible with heliocentrism, and Copernicus used the non-Biblical arguments of the medievals to defend the Earth's daily rotation.[61]

The Reformers were less tolerant of Copernicus. Luther called him a fool four years before he had even published his work, when rumours about it were just starting to spread.[62] Calvin, showing that his vitriol could match that of his German kindred spirit, denounced those people who are

> frenetic, not only in religion, but in order to show that they have a monstrous nature in every respect, say that the sun does not move, and that it is the Earth which moves and turns. When we look upon such souls, we must truly say that the devil has possessed them and that God presents them to us as mirrors in order to make us live in His fear.[63]

Jaki quotes the famous historian of science Alexandre Koyré summing up the situation:

> While Copernicus found encouragement on the part of high dignitaries of the Catholic Church ... even from Pope Paul III who accepted the dedication [of Copernicus' work], Luther and Melanchthon went on the attack already before its publication.[64]

This first real crossing of swords between the Bible and science was begun by a set of men who had set the Bible above reason, something the Church had never done. This paved the way for a constant conflict between religion and science that endures to this day and is personified by the 'creation science' movement.

Three positions of creation scientists

Modern-day biblicists are not opposed to science in itself; they are just opposed to science finding anything that conflicts with their interpretation of the Bible. As we have already seen, the Bible read both literally and scientifically advocates a picture of the Earth that is manifestly wrong. Thus, we should expect the creationists to hold that the Earth is flat[65], with a roof above it, and a massive abyss of water surrounding its sides. They are not, however, consistent in their literalism, and so do not embrace all of the science that the Bible supposedly teaches. I will consider here three positions which creationists believe are revealed truths taught by the Bible, but which conflict with legitimate scientific findings. I will begin by explaining the views of the creationists and then give the scientific reasons as to why those views are almost universally rejected today. A key characteristic of their imposition of a scientific sense on the Bible is that it commits them to a scientific postulate as being divine. Once this happens, nothing in heaven or on earth, no sense data or intellectual reasoning, can affect the foregone conclusion.

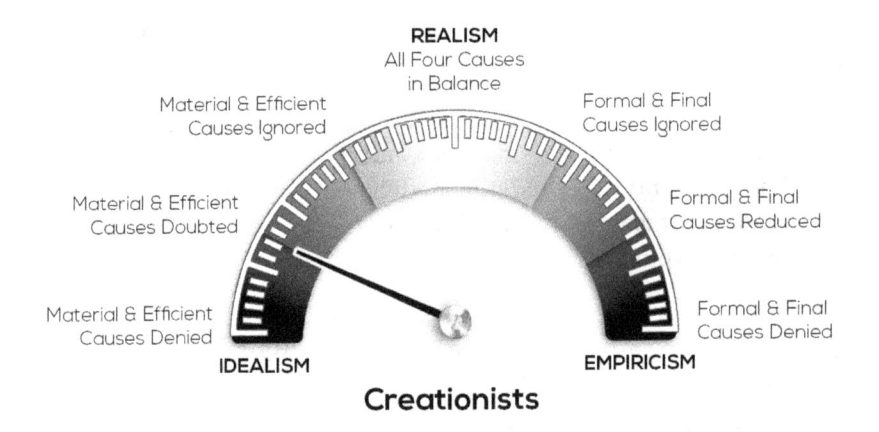

Creationists

REALISM — All Four Causes in Balance
Material & Efficient Causes Ignored
Formal & Final Causes Ignored
Material & Efficient Causes Doubted
Formal & Final Causes Reduced
Material & Efficient Causes Denied
Formal & Final Causes Denied
IDEALISM
EMPIRICISM

Geocentrism

First comes geocentrism. In point of fact, there are very few fundamentalist Protestants who hold that the Earth is motionless and the centre of the universe. There is, however, a Protestant convert to Catholicism, Robert Sungenis, who has dedicated himself to promote the theory, and his primary motivation is his belief that geocentrism is taught infallibly by the Bible. He wrote a 1000 page work, *Galileo Was Wrong: The Church Was Right*,

Protestant Biblicism 267

in order to convince readers to 'give Scripture its due place, and show that science is not all it's cracked up to be'.[66]

There is another theological reason for his campaign: certain scientists have drawn *philosophical* conclusions from the heliocentric theory that are injurious to religion. For them, the Earth not being the centre of the universe shows that humans are insignificant and without purpose. If humans are off-centre in their own solar system and on the margins of their own Milky Way galaxy, then how could they possibly be of any significance? Heliocentrism proves that humans cannot be the creation of a loving God, but rather must be the chance result of blind, random processes.

Sungenis seems to agree with their inference. 'If you see the Earth as just a humdrum planet among stars circling in a vast universe,' he says, 'then we're not significant, we're just part of a crowd.' 'But if you believe everything revolves around Earth, it gives another picture–of purpose, a meaning of life.' In my mind, it would have been much simpler to answer the scientists by saying that much more goes into an individual's significance than his geographical or, if you wish, universal location. For instance, should we hold that people who live on the equator have a greater intrinsic worth than those who inhabit the antipodes, because of their centrality?[67]

As usual, Chesterton says all that needs to be said in one sentence:

> I do not believe in dwelling upon the distances that are supposed to dwarf the world; I think there is even something a trifle vulgar about this idea of trying to rebuke spirit by size.[68]

Instead of opting for this tack, Sungenis latches onto geocentrism as a means to restore purpose to the human race, offering $1000 on his website to anyone able to refute his arguments. To this day, no one has yet been able to ... in *his* mind.[69] Sungenis rests his case on science being unable to prove anything with metaphysical certainty. Since science can never collect all of the data in the universe, there is still a remote possibility that there exists some hidden force or some unknown cause which, if we knew about it, would show that the Earth is the centre of the universe. Thus, Sungenis's procedure is to cast doubt on legitimate scientific inferences, then claim that there is a gaping void of knowledge that needs to be filled, and finally hold up the Bible as filling the void by providing the certain answers that are beyond the reach of science.

The Young Earth

A more properly creationist position is the Young Earth hypothesis. According to it, God created the universe in exactly the time indicated by Genesis, six days, and it is only as old as the number of years that can be counted in the Bible by summing up the genealogical tables that start with Adam. This makes for 6,000 years.

This belief acts like a benchmark for Biblical orthodoxy in Protestant Fundamentalist circles, as one of their own testifies:

> Many Christians are raised to believe that they are faced with a stark choice: Either they accept the most literal Young earth account of Creation or they abandon their faith.[70]

In his attractive book *In the Beginning*, Dr Walt Brown pursues the same strategy on behalf of a young Earth that Sungenis employs for a central Earth. The literature commonly refers to the strategy as the 'God of the gaps' argument explained above. Natural processes and modern science interpreting those processes are not able to explain adequately what we see: there is the gap. Thus, the only way we can explain what we see is by having recourse to the power of God: God must have caused this or that inexplicable natural phenomenon by a special intervention into His own creation, outside of natural processes.

To advance his case, Brown must attack evidence for an old universe on the one hand, and that for an old Earth on the other. Two characteristics of his strategy are that

- he seeks to poke holes in scientific theories that make sense of the totality of empirical data without proposing his own scientific theory to account for that data
- he is forced to reject the idea that the universe has acted according to a consistent set of laws and pattern of behaviour since its inception, an idea that naturally follows from belief in an all-wise Creator.

As an example of the first characteristic, he consistently argues that it is impossible to explain the differences of composition and behaviour in the moon and the planets by natural processes. We observe that the planets are of different colours, rotations, orientations, magnetic fields, surface composition, etc., and science is unable to explain those differences. The same holds true for the moon. In Brown's mind, none of the scientific theories for its formation are plausible: it could not have been the result of a collision of a body with the Earth, nor a body captured by the Earth, nor a body built up from small particles.[71] The implication, therefore, is that *the solar system does not have a history of formation*; rather, it was created as is, with all of its variety, by a direct act of God's omnipotence.[72] Thus, scientists should throw up their hands when observing all of that variety in their telescopes, say that it is impossible to explain, stop theorising about the developments of the past, and abandon their research. Brown, in other words, is seeking to induce a certain intellectual despair in the ability of the mind to go from effect to cause, from observation to explanation, so that all can be attributed to God and nothing to creatures. This is the very hallmark of theologism.

As I write this, much prominence is being given in the news to the activity of the New Horizons probe. It was launched by NASA back in January 2006 and reached Pluto on 14 July 2015. During its flyby of the dwarf planet, it provided the first photos by which the human race could see the actual topographical features of Pluto. Various of its features were described as a whale, a heart, and a doughnut. People naturally wonder how those features got there, that is, the natural causes that formed them. The presence of such features implies that there is such a natural history to Pluto.

A photo of Pluto taken by the New Horizons probe.
(Image courtesy of Wikimedia Commons)

But Brown and the creationists would have us believe that Pluto was created by God 'as is', such that there is no history and hence no trail of causes to be investigated. It is this idea that eliminates the need to do science.

The second characteristic of Brown's attack on scientific arguments for an old Earth and an old universe is his rejection of the consistency of natural laws. Scientists today look at the laws of the universe as we are able to observe them, and apply those same laws to the past. If natural laws have constantly changed in the past, science cannot be done, for current natural processes would then teach us nothing about the past. Consequently, scientists assume nature to be consistent, an assumption that is called *uniformitarianism*, and that was systematised by Charles Lyell, a contemporary of Darwin. Uniformitarianism is the friend of realists, because it:

- makes historical science possible
- is consistent only with belief in an all-wise Lawgiver, for the only way to give a coherent account for a uniform universe is that its laws have been determined by God
- is consistent with our common experience of the consistency of nature
- has enabled scientists to make incredible discoveries and attain a much deeper knowledge of the grandiose architecture of the universe.

At the same time, some scientists take natural laws to be so consistent that miracles are absolutely impossible. For them, there is no God, and the natural universe is the only reality. This is a thesis with which the realist must obviously disagree, and on two counts:

- natural reason can prove the existence of God with absolute certainty
- many miracles have been observed with great scientific precision that are so clearly beyond the powers of natural processes that it would be superstitious to ascribe them to any power other than that of God.

As we saw in chapter 3, God's miracles are neither a changing of the laws of nature, nor an intervention in His own Creation, properly speaking.[73] They are still an exercise of His primary causality, the only causality He employs, and so are extraordinary only from our perspective, and based upon our knowledge of the consistency of natural processes. Moreover, God only works miracles as a manifestation of His goodness and power, *not arbitrarily* or without reason. Thus, miracles are extremely rare. In the end, the principle of uniformitarianism should not be seen as a threat to believers, but rather as a support, as long as it does not exceed its proper boundaries.

Table 7.3 Views on nature and miracles

Views on nature and miracles	Laws of nature can change?	Miracles are possible?
Creationists	YES	YES
Realists	NO	YES
Atheistic scientists	NO	NO

The greatest opponents of uniformitarianism are the creationists. They are forced to opt for an inconsistent universe, since a consistent one testifies to an old Earth and universe. In their mind, God periodically intervenes in His own Creation, not just to perform miracles, but to change natural laws. This idea they call 'Biblical catastrophism', defined as 'the doctrine that, at least on the occasions mentioned in Scripture, God has directly intervened in the normal physical processes *of the universe*, causing significant changes for a time'.[74] Whenever science draws conclusions against their interpretation of the Bible, conclusions that assume a consistency in natural laws, the creationists answer by saying that nature did not always act according to those laws.

For instance, Brown opines that radioactive decay might have been much quicker in the past than it is today.[75] If such was the case, then the radioactive dating of certain Earth rocks and asteroids to 4.55 billion years is inaccurate. Thus, we must look to something more reliable for the age of the Earth, that is, we must look to the Bible according to its literal interpreters.

What about the light of stars and galaxies? Measurements of the light wavelength of certain stars and galaxies indicate that it has taken their light millions and billions of years to arrive at Earth. To avoid this problem, Brown has recourse to the same strategy of nature law changes: he believes that the speed of light has slowed over time. It used to be much quicker and so the light from those distant stars has actually reached us in a shorter period than our measurements have indicated.[76]

Sometimes, you hear creationists proposing the idea that God just created the trail of starlight at the same time that He created the star. They do not realise that they are repeating a proposal of William of Occam with such a theory. For Occam once stated that 'the light of stars and the stars themselves could be conceived as existing independently of one another'.[77] If that is the case, we are not even able to say that stars are the cause of starlight. Having detached one effect from its cause, we will naturally move on to affirm that we can never safely infer that this or that creature is the cause of a given effect. It is at this point that all of our causal knowledge becomes false.

Happily, Brown shrinks from this extreme theologism, telling his readers that there is so much specific information in each star beam, that it would seem difficult to hold that it is coming directly from God and not the star.[78] Unfortunately, such problems do not stop other creationists from stating that God created the stars and their light beams to Earth at the same time.[79] I will turn to their book now. First, however, we must ask ourselves: is God's honour really served by destroying the very foundations of human reasoning in order to uphold a strictly literal interpretation of the Bible?

The Universal Flood

The last and most important position which creationists commonly adopt and which openly conflicts with the findings of science regards the Flood narrative of Genesis 7 and 8. The language used in those chapters, if taken in a strictly literal sense, would seem to indicate that the Flood covered the entire Earth, and this is the way that the fundamentalists read it. In the words of John Whitcomb and Henry Morris,

> There seems to be no reasonable question that, if language can at all be used to convey sensible meanings, the writer of the account of the Deluge ... definitely intended to record the great fact of a universal, world-destroying Flood, of absolute uniqueness in the entire history of this planet.[80]

The book of these two authors, *The Genesis Flood*, is considered to be a landmark work in the creationist movement. It attained a 50th anniversary edition 50th printing in 2011. Whitcomb and Morris set out the dilemma facing Protestant fundamentalists in straightforward language:

> When confronted with the consistent Biblical testimony to a universal Flood, the believer must certainly accept it as unquestionably true. ... The decision then must be faced: either the Biblical record of the Flood is false and must be rejected or else the system of historical geology which has seemed to discredit it is wrong and must be changed. The latter alternative would seem to be the only one which a Biblically and scientifically instructed Christian could honestly take.[81]

This issue of the Flood is the primary focus of the 'Creation Science' movement. Barry Hankins, an expert on Fundamentalism, defines the movement as follows:

> Creation Science proponents teach that the Old Testament event known as Noah's flood is responsible for the earth's geologic strata, giving the appearance that the earth is ancient when in fact the earth is less than ten thousand years old and was created pretty much as we see it today.[82]

This position on the Flood as being *geographically universal* meets with serious scientific difficulties. For one, how can you get enough rain to cover the entire earth? Whitcomb and Morris note that

> if all the water in our present atmosphere were suddenly precipitated, it would only suffice to cover the ground to an average depth of less than two inches.[83]

Thus, the solution which is now familiar to us becomes necessary, that is, postulating a different set of natural laws for the past:

> The implication seems to be that the antediluvian climatology and meteorology were much different from the present.[84]

In other words, the laws operating on the Earth today cannot be applied to the time of Noah.

Whitcomb and Morris, in their work, propose for future generations the task of constructing a new scheme of historical geology which will both serve the truth of the Bible and correlate with scientific data.[85] It seems that Brown took up their invitation, for he puts forward his own hypothesis, which he calls the 'hydroplate theory'. This theory suggests that the Earth cracked apart and released an enormous volume of subterranean water, which then covered the entire Earth. At the time of the cracking, the Earth was a single, contiguous landmass, but the Flood event caused the separation of the continents and also the ridges, continental shelves, and other features that we observe in Earth's oceans.[86]

Obviously, it is good that these creationists are trying to make sense of the features of the Earth in a scientific fashion. What is wrong is that they are using the Bible as their primary guide in doing so. One of the motivations for Brown to postulate water coming from below is that the Bible describes the waters of the Flood as coming both from the 'fountains of the great deep' and the 'floodgates of Heaven' (see Gen. 8:2). We have already seen how, in the Hebrew conception of the world, the Earth has a roof covered with water and an abyss of water surrounding it. Thus, describing the Flood according to the perception of the senses, the Bible speaks of water as coming both from below and from above. Clearly, this is a popular, not a scientific description. For the creationists, however, a strict literal sense is the only one possible for the passage; thus, a geographically universal flood becomes a divinely revealed truth for them. After that, it merely remains to manipulate all scientific data into the confines of that conclusion.

To sum up the problem with the creationist position, I can say the following:

1. The Bible was written in a popular style, not a scientific style. It was written to communicate religious truths, not facts of physics. As such, it does not speak with scientific exactitude. To impose a scientific sense upon the Bible,

then, is to do violence to the sacred text and the divinely intended meaning.
2. Protestantism, according to its theological blueprint for reaching God, makes use of the Bible alone. Thus, no recourse can be had to an authoritative divine institution either to discover religious truths independently of the Bible, or to discover the religious truths that are in the Bible. This leads naturally to a simplistic, literal reading of all passages, a 'one size fits all' pattern of interpretation.
3. Questions such as the age of the Earth or its position in the universe are essentially *scientific* questions. Thus, there is nothing wrong with arguing them on scientific grounds. What is wrong is to argue them on Biblical grounds or, even worse, to read the Bible scientifically and then make the observations of science conform to that interpretation. The Bible should not be a player in scientific disputes, because it was never meant to be. Similarly, science should not be a player in religious disputes, something I will explain in the last section of the book.
4. We must assume uniformitarianism, or the consistency of natural laws throughout the history of the universe, for historical science to be possible. That assumption can only find its ultimate justification in belief in a Creator outside of the universe who is able to be a lawgiver for it. Creationism, in attacking uniformitarianism, attacks at the same time scientific enterprise and the consistency of the Creator in His own work. It 'creates' problems for both science and theology.

Catholic stances on creationist issues

In an effort to see what was the standard pre-Vatican II teaching in Catholic seminaries on these questions (pre-Vatican II texts would be, if anything, more conservative than post-Vatican II ones), I investigated several manuals. What I found was that not a single manual advocated any of the Protestant fundamentalist

Protestant Biblicism

positions. How could they, given the clear words of Leo XIII above, which were repeated in later encyclicals by Pope Benedict XV[87] and Pius XII?[88] The table below summarises what I found (I don't include geocentrism because the manuals don't speak about it, considering it to be a non-issue; the translations are my own).

Pius XII gave a famous address in November of 1951 to the Pontifical Academy of Sciences, wherein he used the modern findings of science, including those concerning the ancient age of the Earth and the universe, as further evidence of the existence and greatness of God. He gave four points of scientific evidence for the age of the universe being between five and ten billion years old, and then stated the following:

> Although these figures may seem astounding, nevertheless, even to the simplest of the faithful, they bring no new or different concept from the one they learned in the opening words of Genesis: 'In the beginning . . .', that is to say, at the beginning of things in time. The figures We have quoted clothe these words in a concrete and almost mathematical expression, while from them there springs forth a new source of consolation for those who share the esteem of the Apostle for that divinely-inspired Scripture, which is always useful 'for teaching, for reproving, for correcting, for instructing' (2 Tim 3:6).[89]

Thus, for the Pope, the findings of modern science, by pointing to a non-eternal universe, that is, one that began in time, support the Church's dogma of faith, creation in time. Meanwhile, whether that beginning was billions of years in the past or 6,000 affects faith in no way.

Before moving to the scientific argumentation on these controverted questions, I must mention that this analysis in no way means that all Protestants interpret the Bible so literally. In fact, most of them do not. One of the greatest scientists ever, the Lutheran Joannes Kepler, complained about the practice of reading Scripture as a textbook of physics,[90] in an age more likely to do so than our own.

Table 7.4 Catholic Scriptural manuals on the Earth's age and the Flood

Author	Age of the Earth	Flood
Gigot (1903) *Special Introduction to the Study of the Old Testament*, 2nd ed.	p. 187: 'The task of fixing approximate dates for either the Flood or man's creation falls naturally within the province of human sciences, particularly of ethnography and geology ... It is by far the most common opinion that those sciences, while not giving a precise date for those events, have made it necessary to refer them to a period much more remote than the one formerly admitted.'	p. 184: 'The teachings of physical and geological sciences have entirely done away with the conception of an actual Flood which would, at any time since the creation of man, have covered the entire globe.'
Vigouroux (1926) *Dictionnaire de la Bible*	Entry 'Chronologie Biblique': col.718 'We do not find a ready made chronology in the Bible, nor a fixed era or epoch from which we can start the numbering of years, and it is in this sense that we can repeat the sentence that is attributed to Silvester de Sacy: "There is no such thing as a Biblical chronology."' col.719 The Bible 'only says that God created the heavens and the earth "in the beginning", without specifying the era of this beginning.' col. 720 'The sacred text does not determine the origin of man in a manner that is chronologically formal and precise; nowhere does it say: Adam was created on this date.'	Entry 'Le Déluge' col. 1351 'Many commentators and theologians of our day believe that the deluge of Noah should be restricted to the region of the earth which was populated when the deluge happened. According to them, all humans, besides Noah's family, were covered in the waters; but the flood did not cover the whole earth nor destroy all the animals. The universality of the deluge is neither geographical nor zoological; it is only anthropological.' [In col. 1356, Vigouroux adopts this opinion.]
Renié (1945) *Manuel d'Écriture Sainte*, vol. 1, 5th ed.	pp. 459–460: Genesis does not give a chronology, because: • there is no starting point for the reckoning of years • there are gaps in the genealogical tables; various ancient versions of the Old Testament give different ages for the patriarchs • the words for 'son' and 'beget' in Hebrew have a broad meaning such that they can refer to descendants who are more than one generation away. 'The date of the creation of the world is a question for science.'	pp. 441–450: **geographically universal Flood**: it was the majority opinion up to the nineteenth century, but is now universally abandoned because of scientific difficulties **ethnographically universal Flood** (affecting all people): seems the best position because contrary scientific evidence is not sufficient to overturn it **neither geographically nor ethnographically universal Flood**: not a condemned opinion, but needs more proof
Simon-Prado (1955) *Praelectionum Biblicarum Compendium*, 9th ed.	pp. 87–92 Various scientific hypotheses about human pre-history are explored, but ultimately science does not have enough information to provide a solid answer. The Biblical narration about the patriarchs is historical, but chronology is a scientific question.	pp. 97–101 A geographically universal Flood is to be rejected, as it is contradicted by clinching scientific arguments; an ethnographically universal Flood is the most probable opinion, while an ethnographically limited Flood is less probable

What I *am* trying to say is that the Reformation launched a theological paradigm where, on the one hand, philosophical realism could have no place, and on the other hand, the Bible would naturally and logically be interpreted in a strictly literal sense, and so be pitted against reason. Thus, in a sense, modern creationists are more faithful to the founders of their religions than their more liberal co-religionists, who are in the majority today.

The science behind these questions

One of the major problems that one faces in sorting out disputes between believers and atheistic scientists is that most believers do not know science and most atheists have no real understanding of religion. Thus, when atheists use science against religion, believers are naturally very sceptical, and they tend to discount science in general, thinking that the whole lot of it must be bunk.

In point of fact, however, the real findings of science can only tell us about secondary causes; thus, if scientists use those findings against the First Cause, then, first of all, they are speaking as philosophers and not scientists, and, secondly, they are speaking as very bad philosophers. Moreover, as science advances, it progressively unearths a world of stunning complexity and intricacy, finely tuned to an unfathomable degree, ever more mysterious as it becomes more comprehended, and so all the more magnificent. Thus, believers should not fear these real findings, but rather use them to bolster non-metaphysical probabilistic proofs for God's existence, that is, those proofs that do not involve 'being', whose source can *only* be God, but rather involve phenomena whose origin is *best* explained by God.[91]

My purpose in this last section of this chapter is to show that there is solid scientific evidence against the three positions of the biblicists that we have just covered above, namely, their take on geocentrism, the Earth's age, and the extent of the Flood.

Geocentrism

Extend your arm in front of you and raise your index finger. Then close your right eye, followed by your left eye. What do you see? The index finger moves. Why does it move? Because of the distance between your eyes. Looking at your finger with your left eye, you see your finger more to the right; looking at it with your right eye, you see it more to the left. Looking at it with both, you see it in the middle.

If heliocentrism is true, something similar will happen when we view stars at different times of the year from Earth. If the Earth revolves around the sun, then at one month, say January, it will be on one side of the sun, and then six months later, in July, it will be on the opposite side of the sun from where it was in January. The distance from where it was in January and where it is in July will be twice the distance from the Earth to the sun, or 300 million kilometres. So, if E is the position of the Earth on January 21 and E' is its position on July 21, then the distance between E and E' will be 300 million kilometres.

Now, if we consider E and E' as the equivalent of your left eye and right eye, then we can think of a star, star Q, to be distant from the Earth at a distance similar to that from your eyes to the tip of your index finger. When the Earth is at position E, looking at the star will be like closing your right eye, and star Q will appear a bit to the right, if the Earth indeed moves around the sun. Six months later, at position E', star Q will appear a bit to the left, if the Earth moves around the sun. This shifting of star Q is referred to as its 'stellar parallax'.

If we note how much Q shifts when it is observed, first from position E and then from position E', we can easily couple that data with the 300 million kilometre distance between E and E' to measure the actual distance to Q.[92]

The diagram below illustrates how it is just a question of simple geometry.

It turns out that we can observe a parallax shift of all of the stars in the sky that are within 500 light years distance from Earth. Stars that are beyond that distance have a shift that is too negligible to be detected by instruments from Earth. It is like trying to discern how much a billboard that is 100 miles away from you shifts when you close your right eye, then your left eye.

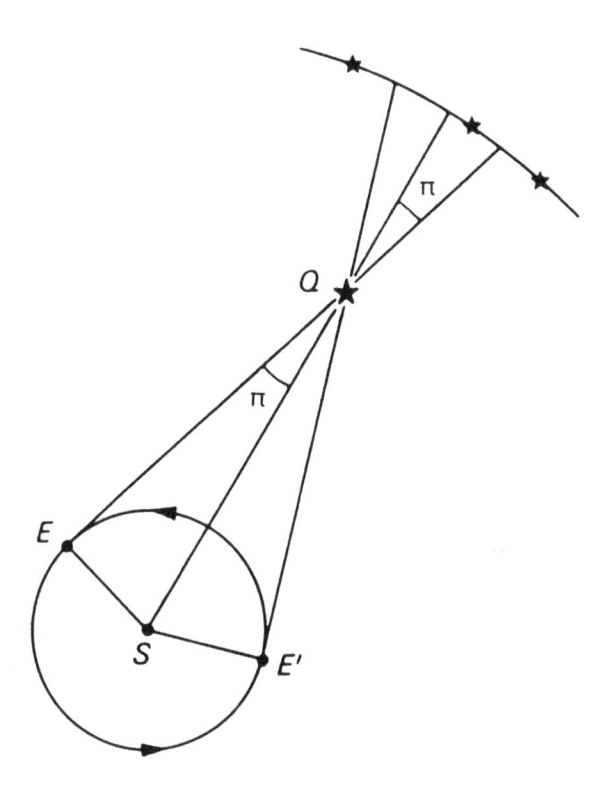

As the Earth (E) rotates around the sun (S), stars seen from the earth, such as star Q, are observed to shift back and forth in the sky. Half the angle of their shift (π) is referred to as their 'parallax' and is used to measure their distance from the Earth.

(Image reproduced with permission from J. Kaler, Stars and Their Spectra (Cambridge: Cambridge University Press, 1997), p. 118)

To get an idea of the distances involved, consider the star 61 Cygni, a star that had its distance measured by parallax, by Friedrich Bessel in 1838.[93] At eleven light years distance, it is one of the closest stars to us. Now, eleven light years might seem like a small number, but a single light year is around 10 trillion kilometres or 10,000,000,000,000km! Light gets around. When 61 Cygni is observed from the Earth 6 months apart, it shifts in the heavens by 2/3 of a second of arc, wherein 3,600 seconds of arc make one degree, and 360 degrees make a complete circle.

To this day, 'tens of thousands of stars have been subject to parallax measurement.'[94] Does this prove that the Earth moves around the sun? At the very least, it provides a strong indication that such is the case.[95] For, why would the stars exhibit this behaviour if the universe were geocentric? The only possible explanation would be that the stars are constantly shifting left and right each year between two different positions, doing a sort of yearly stellar line dance. Why would they dance back and forth in tune to the cycle of our sun? There are certainly no scientific reasons for them to do so.

As Jaki points out, it was not really until a statistically significant parallax shift was observed that heliocentrism was grounded in strict scientific evidence.[96] Up to that time, there were other, less compelling observational arguments, but no clincher. This is an important piece of information for consideration of the controversial 'Galileo case', which is always presented as an instance of the triumph of irrational faith over science and which I must turn to now.

Galileo

Arthur Koestler provides a detailed presentation of the real issues at stake in his *The Sleepwalkers*.[97] The primary problem was that Galileo did not have scientific proof for heliocentrism, yet was pushing Church prelates to accept it as a foregone conclusion and change the Church's understanding of Scripture passages that seemed to advocate geocentrism. This was quite a tall order in the early 1600s, because of the delicate atmosphere vis-à-vis Scripture introduced by the Reformers. The latter put forward their strict literal interpretation as a means of paying the Bible proper respect, which they claimed the Church did not possess. Thus, to protect the Church from this accusation, churchmen began to insist 'on the literal sense in as large a measure as possible'.[98] Enter Galileo.

Protestant Biblicism 283

> [He] took the Church by surprise by claiming that he had demonstrative (experimental) proof on behalf of the earth's motion, and that therefore the teaching of the Church had to be adjusted to the new situation. He did not have the proof, nor did he prove that the Church taught geocentrism as something to be believed. He simply took the Bible's parlance for Church dogmatics. It remained hidden to him that he had merely encouraged biblicism within the Catholic camp.[99]

That does not mean that there was no willingness on the part of the Church to grant Galileo's request. But, as Koestler points out, the essential requirement was that *there had to be scientific proof*:

> 'Propositions which are stated but not rigorously demonstrated,' *such as the Copernican system itself*, were not condemned outright if they seemed to contradict Holy Scripture; they were merely relegated to the rank of 'working hypotheses' (where they rightly belong), with an implied: 'wait and see; if you bring proof, then, but only then, we shall have to reinterpret Scripture in the light of this necessity.' But Galileo did not want to bear the burden of proof; for the crux of the matter is, as will be seen, that he had no proof.[100]

St Robert Bellarmine, who was assigned Galileo's case by the Pope, admitted scientific proof would demand a reinterpretation of Biblical passages that were formerly read in a scientific sense.[101] Galileo, however, failed to bring that proof forward, as Bellarmine stated in a letter:

> Third, I say that, *if there were a real proof* that the Sun is in the centre of the universe, that the Earth is in the third sphere, and that the Sun does not go round the Earth but the Earth round the Sun, then we should have to proceed with great circumspection in explaining passages of Scripture which appear to teach the contrary, and we should rather have to say that we did not understand them than declare an opinion to be false which is proved to be true.

> But I do not think there is any such proof *since none has been shown to me.*[102]

Not only did Galileo not have real scientific proof, but he brought forward obviously bad evidence for heliocentrism: he said that the movement of the tides was caused by the rotation of the Earth, not by the attraction of moon.[103] On Galileo's part, this was 'not a mistake, but a delusion'.[104] He so wanted to prove heliocentrism that he seized on a hare-brained theory which other scientists of his day easily proved wrong.

Armed with his 'proof', Galileo persistently hounded churchmen to intercede with the Pope to make the Scriptural interpretation change that he requested. His aggressiveness at a sensitive time about a delicate issue, combined with his lack of scientific proof, drew down upon him a condemnation of the Church. That condemnation admittedly went too far, but in no way did it involve the Church's infallibility or make of geocentrism a dogma of Catholic belief.[105]

But what are we to say about the heliocentric system itself? Doesn't it contradict the testimony of the senses, which we as realists must accept? After all, we do not feel the movement of the Earth. In answer to this, I do not agree with Galileo who says that Copernicus committed a 'rape of the senses' in proposing heliocentrism.[106] On the contrary, we should not expect the senses to note the Earth's movement in any substantial way.[107] None other than Jean Buridan explains clearly why this is the case:

> If someone is moved in a boat and imagines himself to be at rest, and if he should see another boat which was really at rest, it would appear to him that the other boat is moving, because his eye would be in exactly the same relationship to the other boat whether his own boat was moving and the other was at rest, or the other way around. And thus we might also posit that the sphere of the sun is completely at rest and the earth spins, carrying us along with it. Since we would nevertheless imagine ourselves to be at rest, just as the man on the swiftly moving boat did

not perceive either his motion or that of his boat, therefore it is certain to us the sun would rise and set in the same manner as it does when it moves and we are at rest.[108]

The Earth's Age

I noted in the third chapter that there is a method and discipline of thought whose job it is to investigate quantities. The discipline is exact science and the method is the scientific method. Because quantities fall into science's domain and not religion's, this or that age for the Earth should not be proposed as a matter of religious belief. Moreover, while it is true that the theory of Darwinian evolution, which many use to argue that God is unnecessary, needs vast aeons of time to perform its supposed work, we will see in section three that even 13.7 billion years are not nearly sufficient for it.[109] Regardless, it is impossible for the working of natural processes to make God redundant in a universe to which He has given existence and must sustain in existence at each moment. The point here, however, is that the age of the Earth *has no direct bearing on religious truths.*

That being said, human effort to find solid empirical evidence for the Earth's age took much time and effort, like the working out of heliocentrism. G. Brent Dalrymple, in his 2004 work *Ancient Earth, Ancient Skies*, sketches the failed methods before presenting the successful one. He notes up front the principle of uniformitarianism: 'A fundamental premise of science is that natural laws do not change with time',[110] a principle echoed by Jaki: 'sameness and science are inseparable.'[111] As we have seen, this principle fits perfectly and even exclusively with a belief in Creation by an all-wise, immutable God, as well as with the observations of philosophical realism.

Working on that assumption, scientists prior to 1950 prowled the Earth, looking for some natural clock that might indicate the globe's birth date, sort of like the rings on a tree. Various methods were developed using different physical phenomena: the decline of sea level; the cooling of the Earth; the Earth's tidal effects; the accumulation of sulfate and sodium in the oceans; the accumulation of limestone and sediment in geological structures on land.[112] Each of these methods gave Earth ages in the realm of millions or billions of years, but each of them was ultimately ruled out for one reason or another: the phenomena were not uniform over a long period of time, the phenomena did not change sufficiently to form a measurable record, or the methods relied on false assumptions.

In the end, it was the discovery of the radioactive behaviour of atoms in the late 1800s that provided a path to a reliable dating method. Certain elements emit radiation over a period of time.[113] The reason is that they have too many neutrons in their *nucleus* and, being unstable, periodically emit energy from that nucleus in order to reach stability.[114] When an element does this, it turns into another element, called an *isotope*. Scientists were able to determine this radioactive behaviour of elements, and they found that such decay is extremely constant.

There are two reasons why the decay rate of the elements is uniform (the rate at which energy is emitted from the nuclei of elements):

- an atomic nucleus is extremely small and well insulated by the shells of electrons around it. This insulation
    - keeps the nucleus from changing when the atom hits other atoms
    - prevents changes from external forces taking place anywhere in the atom other than in its outer shell
- the energy required to break down the atomic nucleus from the outside is enormous, much greater than that required for chemical activity between atoms or for separating outer electrons from the atom.

Because atomic nuclei are so well protected, it is practically impossible for outside forces to change them; the only way that the nucleus will change, then, is from within. Thus, unless there has been some undiscovered change in the fundamental nature of matter and energy since the Universe formed, the presumption of constancy for radioactive decay is, for all practical purposes, eminently reasonable.[115]

In other words, unless the laws of nature have changed—because of a God acting arbitrarily, the God behind creationist readings of the Bible—radioactive decay has been constant throughout the history of the universe.

Now, when rocks form, they generally have a certain concentration of radioactive elements within them. The decay of these radioactive elements within the rock over time acts like a clock, indicating the age of the rock from the time of its formation. To explain how this is so, let us look at an example based on Dalrymple.[116] Before starting, however, just a little warning that you are going to need your secondary school algebra to make it through, but no more than that.

First, we have to meet the 'gears' of the 'rock clocks' which count time for us. There are three of them:

- **The parent element**—this is the element that undergoes decay at a known rate. In our example, it is Rubidium 87, ^{87}Rb. The number 87 is Rubidium's *mass number*, the total number of protons (37) and neutrons (50) in ^{87}Rb's nucleus.

- **The daughter isotope**—This is the product of the decay of the isotope of the parent element. When an atom undergoes decay, one of the *neutrons* in its nucleus breaks down into a proton and an electron. The proton remains in the nucleus and the electron joins the atom's outer shell. Because there is now one more *proton* in the nucleus, the nucleus is the nucleus of a new element.

In our example, the new element formed from Rubidium 87 is Strontium 87, ^{87}Sr. It has one more proton (38), but one less neutron (49). The total number of protons and neutrons in the nucleus has not changed, and so the mass number remains 87.

- **The stable isotope**—This is another isotope of the same element as the daughter isotope, but this isotope is not a product of radioactive decay. The isotope is stable because of the number of neutrons in its nucleus. Because it is stable, its mass, and consequently its mass number, do not change.

  In our example, the stable isotope is Strontium 86, ^{86}Sr. To be Strontium, it has to have 38 protons, just like Strontium 87. The difference is that it has one fewer neutron (48), giving it a mass number of 86. That reduced mass number, 86, makes this Strontium atom stable.

Okay, let us say that God did not create the Earth immediately, but rather that the Earth formed by natural processes sometime after God created the universe. When the Earth forms, so do its rocks. If such is what happened, then we would expect that some of the rocks currently on Earth are from the very beginning of the Earth's history. So, we pick up a rock that has certain concentrations of ^{87}Rb, ^{87}Sr, and ^{86}Sr in the hopes of obtaining information about the age of the rock and hence of the Earth. Certain pieces of information that we know up front are going to be crucial in finding the rock's age:

1. The half-life of ^{87}Rb is 48.8 billion years. This means that a rock formed at time 0 with x atoms of ^{87}Rb will have half as many or $x/2$ atoms of ^{87}Rb after 48.8 billion years. The other half will have become ^{87}Sr atoms. Because the half-life of ^{87}Rb is so enormous, there will likely still be some ^{87}Rb left by the time we measure the rock.

2. The daughter and stable isotopes exist in the same proportion throughout the entire rock at time 0. What this means is that *their ratio* is the same at that time, no matter how much or how little of the rock is sampled when it initially forms. With this information, we know something about the *initial condition* of the rock, and that condition works

like hitting the start counter on a stop watch. It tells us that a plot of ^{87}Rb/ ^{86}Sr on the x-axis against ^{87}Sr/ ^{86}Sr at time 0 necessarily yields a horizontal line.

Say we take an ancient rock in our hand at the present moment, and samples in three concentrations: B (bit), P (part) and W (whole). When the rock was formed, the ratio ^{87}Sr/ ^{86}Sr was the same everywhere in the rock, and hence would have given the same value, say 2, for B, P, and W, if we had been able to measure those samples right after the rock formed. From that moment, ^{87}Sr/ ^{86}Sr started increasing at a known rate, the rate of ^{87}Rb's decay, since ^{87}Rb decays into ^{87}Sr. The concentration of ^{87}Sr increases in B, P, and W over time, while that of ^{86}Sr remains the same.

A two-dimensional Cartesian graph helps us visualise the changes that are taking place in the rock. On the y-axis, we plot the *ratio* of the daughter isotope to the stable isotope, or ^{87}Sr/ ^{86}Sr. On the x-axis, we plot the *ratio* of the parent element to the stable isotope, or ^{87}Rb/ ^{86}Sr. At time 0, ^{87}Sr/ ^{86}Sr is 2 for every value of ^{87}Rb/ ^{86}Sr, and thus is a horizontal line on the graph, running through the coordinates for B, P, and W (the y coordinate is the same, no matter what the x coordinate). Over the life of the rock, ^{87}Sr/ ^{86}Sr increases and ^{87}Rb/ ^{86}Sr decreases according to the *rate* of decay of ^{87}Rb. Every time an atom of ^{87}Rb decays, ^{87}Sr/ ^{86}Sr moves up in the same proportion that ^{87}Rb/ ^{86}Sr went down. This causes the horizontal line to rotate upward over time.

The only thing that a measurement of the rock at the present moment will provide us is the *current ratios* of ^{87}Sr/ ^{86}Sr and ^{87}Rb/ ^{86}Sr for B, P, and W. These ratios, however, will enable us to draw the rotated line on the graph. The place where that line intersects the y-axis will indicate the original ratio of ^{87}Sr/ ^{86}Sr. From there, it is a simple mathematical step to find the time that it took the ratio of ^{87}Sr/ ^{86}Sr with respect to ^{87}Rb/ ^{86}Sr to go from being a horizontal line at time 0 to being the diagonal line that it is now on the graph, due to ^{87}Sr/ ^{86}Sr increasing and ^{87}Rb/ ^{86}Sr decreasing over time.

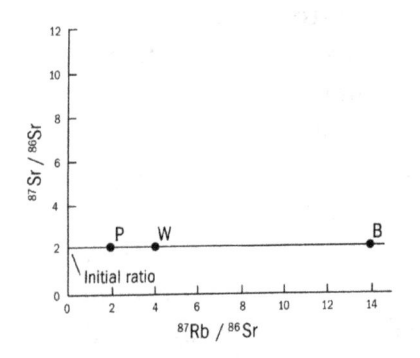

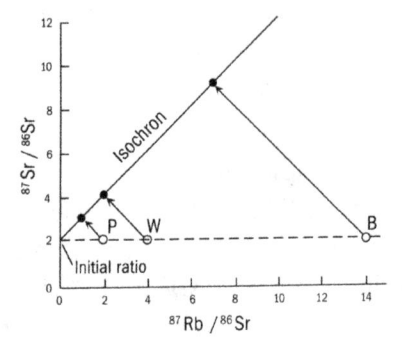

Graph on left: When a rock is formed, the ratio of daughter isotope to stable isotope ($^{87}Sr/\ ^{86}Sr$) is the same for all samples P, W, and B taken from the rock, causing that ratio to yield a horizontal line when it is plotted against the ratio of parent isotope to daughter isotope ($^{87}Rb/^{86}Sr$).

Graph on right: Over time, as the parent isotope (^{87}Rb) decays at a constant rate, producing a greater concentration of the daughter isotope (^{87}Sr), the line running through isotope yields from samples P, W, and B rotates upwards. Since the time necessary for the line to rotate to its position in the right graph is known, the age of the rock at the time samples P, W, and B yield that line can be determined from the line alone.

(Reproduced with permission from B. Dalrymple, Ancient Earth, Ancient Skies (Stanford, California: Stanford University Press, 2004), figure 4.4, p. 70)

Using this method and other isotopes besides the rubidium-strontium pair, certain Earth rocks as well as meteorites landing on Earth from space have been dated to 4.55 billion years old. As Dalrymple points out,[117] it would be a highly improbable coincidence for the rock samples to fall on a straight line in the graph if they had not undergone a constant radioactive decay. Our present measurements yielding a straight diagonal line is confirmation that the straight line is the long-term result of an initial horizontal straight line rotating upwards by a process of constant radioactive decay. Thus, someone wanting to discount the empirical data would have to account for this phenomenon in some other way and, in my mind, it is as difficult as accounting for stars moving left and right in the sky on an annual cycle by a theory other than heliocentrism.

Radioactive decay is not the only reason to assign such an enormous age to the Earth, but is the only one I will give here. I will touch upon star distances and the Big Bang theory in the next section.

The Extent of the Flood

We have already seen how creationists Whitcomb and Morris admit that there is no way to account for a geographically universal Flood other than by God changing the laws of nature. To show why this is the case, I will translate here a summary of the scientific difficulties made by the French Catholic Biblical scholar Vigouroux back in 1926:

> The theory of an anthropologically but not geographically universal Flood appears necessary to some in order to cut short the serious objections raised by zoology and physics against an absolute universality of the Deluge. The placement of all the animal species known to exist today with necessary and vastly different provisions for their upkeep for an entire year in an ark proportionately insufficient; the care which their presence required on the part of only eight persons; the need for animals coming from different regions to accommodate themselves to a uniform climate; the re-populating of the entire world, when the migrations of special animals to America and Oceania, for example, have not left any trace, whereas fauna have always been localised and certain animal species have never existed outside their respective regions; survival of freshwater fish and saltwater fish in the mixing of the waters of the rain and the rivers with the waves of the ocean: all of these things create insurmountable difficulties. On the other hand, in the domain of physics, one can hardly explain the source of the immense mass of water needed to inundate the entire world.

The quantity of known water is insufficient. Even without taking into account the crevices and nooks in the Earth's surface, there would have to be a volume of water above sea level of a depth equal to the highest peak of the Himalayas, a height of 8,839m. Even if the water was sufficient, the simultaneous submersion of the two hemispheres would be physically impossible. Such a submersion would bring about a change in the atmosphere which would modify the conditions of life on Earth. Having recourse to the Almighty divine power in order to explain these impossibilities is to multiply miracles which the sacred narrative does not mention and which the principles of prudent exegesis do not permit to be introduced needlessly.[118]

Conclusion

One who studies carefully and objectively the scientific evidence for heliocentrism, for an ancient Earth, and against a geographically universal Flood discovers the evidence to be compelling. Creationists themselves realise this to be the case and so speculate that nature's laws in past ages were so different that we cannot base scientific inferences about the past on nature's laws as they are today. By adopting this stance, however, creationists create a new notion of God, a God Who cannot be found in the Bible whose literal sense they are so anxious to defend, a God Who is arbitrary and inconsistent, one who delights in placing false clues in His own creation that prevent rational humans from discovering its true history.

By all accounts, the creationists seem to be striking a poor bargain: they slay science and the Christian God in order to purchase a literal, scientific truth of a religious text in which God intended to teach us 'how to go to Heaven, not how the heavens go'. Much saner and safer is it to save God and science by sacrificing biblicism.

Summary of this section (chapters 4–7)

In this section, we have taken a survey of the history of mankind, seeing to what degree various religions have led men to adopt realism or cast it aside. Each of these cultures formulated some idea of an ultimate reality, a God or gods, and allowed that idea to shape their worldview. That worldview, in turn, determined the culture's ability to penetrate reality and know its true causes.

The pre-Christian cultures of chapter 4 saw God as being either the universe as a whole or some part of the universe. The first type of God, the universe-god, is a rather amorphous entity, largely immune to comprehension by rational minds. He is seen as being eternal, as blindly producing a relentless cycle in the universe, and as not being a 'he' at all, but rather an impersonal force. No ancient civilisation, other than the Jews, was wholly exempt from this outlook. Because there was so little for reason to fathom in such a first principle, mythological stories easily wrapped themselves around the worldview, substituting tall tales for causal explanations.

The Indian perspective

Among the Indians, the idea of the universe as an ultimate self-existing and cyclic entity engendered a certain despair, leading them to isolate the powers of sense and intellect, instead of uniting them. For them, the universe's cycle was inevitable and unwholesome. The best option to escape from its fatalistic turning was to withdraw oneself from reality rather than understand it and enrich oneself from it. The result was that the Indians did not adopt realism, did not actively pursue causal knowledge, and did not give birth to a science seeking the natural laws of the physical universe.

The Chinese perspective

The Chinese, working on the same philosophical/theological notion of pantheism, embraced the idea of two impersonal and opposing forces, the Yin and the Yang, as being at the heart of it all, eternally dissolving everything into nothing and making it re-emerge. Because they denied a first principle of the intellect—the principle of non-contradiction—they were not able to establish themselves as realists, not able to build a hierarchy of causal knowledge, and not able to pursue the knowledge of quantitative properties of material bodies.

The Greek perspective

The first recorded culture which set reason free to actively pursue a total causal knowledge of reality was the Greeks'. This pursuit led them to form more sophisticated notions of God, ones wherein God was a cause accounting for reality, not one wherein stories about gods accounted for it. The Greeks set mythology to one side, and let reason seek its own causal explanations of the whole. As a result, schools of philosophy sprouted like mushrooms in the Hellenic world from around 550 to about 350 BC. Each proposed some causal entity within the universe as being a sort of God, an ultimate reason for the universe, and sought to convince others by means of rational argument that their philosophical god was reality's source.

The task was difficult, and Greek philosophers—not knowing yet how to be professional realists—struggled greatly to construct a philosophical system that matched up perfectly with what common sense revealed about reality. The system of each philosophical school was an easy target for criticism, and each group was able to point out the illogicalities in their opponents' worldviews, without being able to fully justify their own. This opened the way for the enemies of intellect and reality—the Sophists—to come close to wrecking the pursuit of causal knowledge.

This is when Socrates appeared on the scene to become the saviour of Greek and arguably Western thought. He powerfully demonstrated the ability of the mind to develop precise definitions about every aspect of the outside world, including most difficult notions such as 'good', 'justice', and 'love'. These concepts were so clear, so well-formed, and so satisfying in their explanatory power that Socrates, or perhaps more properly his foremost disciple Plato, made them the ultimate reality, even the only reality. Making the immaterial Forms gods led Socrates and Plato to embrace the idealist view that sense knowledge has no real value.

Part of the motivation for the Platonic system was a desire to counter the empiricists, who were corrupting the youth with the idea that all is matter and that reality is consequently but a melee of random interactions with no purpose. To defeat them, Socrates and Plato would find purpose all around them, to the point of reducing all reality to purpose, a notion that can only be attained by the intellect and is not accessible to the senses.

Aristotle tried to find a middle ground between the two extremes of Platonism and Sophism, of idealism and empiricism. This led him to formulate epistemological realism as the proper reality mentality. He built a system for investigating causes by use of sense and intellect in tandem, each pulling its own weight according to its precise capacity. Because Aristotle's system exactly fits the way humans are made to know, he was able to apply that system with tremendous effect. By it, he became the first known philosopher to construct a coherent metaphysics, a worldview which proposed as the first principle of reality a God who is an Unmoved Mover, and which was able to prove, by reason alone, that such a God must exist. This accomplishment of Aristotle united sense and intellect, philosophy and religion, man and reality, in a harmonious whole, maintaining each in a single, complex order.

Aristotle's success came from following the *a posteriori* realist paradigm,

- starting with sense data,
- then forming clear notions about reality, and
- finally using those notions in a careful chain of reasoning to arrive at certain conclusions about the whole of reality.

At the same time, Aristotle was not realist enough. On the philosophical side, he did not take sufficient notice of the contingency of being, the dependence of everything around us on another for its existence. Because of this, he was not able to arrive at the notion of creation, without which a complete realist philosophy is not possible. Nor did he take sufficient account of material bodies, and so he sought to explain their movement primarily in terms of final causes, as did Socrates and Plato before him, instead of explaining them in terms of the formal and material causality which they manifest more clearly. What Aristotle had explained of God was true, but it was only a thin slice of God; not being a God who is able to create the universe, it was not a God who could make the universe fully intelligible to human minds.

Medieval Christian developments

The Christians of the Middle Ages were provided, by revelation, the Creator God that escaped Aristotle's reason. The worldview their theology provided led them to embrace Aristotle's realism in philosophy, but also assisted them to formulate a more perfect metaphysics than that of the Philosopher.

St Thomas Aquinas was able to refound and bring to perfection Aristotle's realist metaphysics, through his better notion of God. Aquinas's theology enabled him to discover a way to prove, by reason alone, that God is a creator, endowing creatures with essence and existence, which must be the ultimate components of created being; He is wise, embedding a rational order into all of creation, and so making its utmost recesses intelligible to human minds; He is good, conferring worth on every aspect of the universe, including lowly matter.

Medieval society embodied the balance of Aquinas's realist worldview, by enabling philosophy and theology to dwell together in perfect harmony without coming into conflict. Most theologians were also scientists. They used reason alone to argue about the natural order, and both reason and authority to argue about the supernatural order. Because all aspects of reality were accessible to medieval minds, not being blocked by a narrow worldview or an anti-intellectual society, they were able to explore causal areas that had hitherto been inaccessible.

The prime example of this fact is medieval breakthroughs in science. Thinkers coming after Aquinas turned explicitly to material bodies to investigate their properties. They did not hesitate to reject Aristotle's physics, realising that God could endow inert matter with innate properties, and that matter did not have to be motivated to move. One among them, Jean Buridan, formulated landmark ideas about material movement, which were later used by the great scientists Galileo, Descartes, and Newton. This was the beginning of modern science, and it was built on a realism that derived from a specific theological perspective.

The Muslim perspective

Even though the high Arab civilisation preceded the high Christian culture by two centuries, it was not as successful in adopting realism and drawing from it the ultimate fruits for human intellectual endeavour. The reason was its reliance on the Koran, rather than the Bible. While the Bible presents God as creating in time a universe that is most consistent in its natural workings, the Koran presents Allah as having an inscrutable and supreme will, not bound by any of the consistencies perceived as necessary to reality by human reason, and creating a reality that is at each moment different from the one preceding.

To support the Koran's presentation of the divine, a certain theologism became the gold standard for orthodoxy in Islam. It held to a strictly literal interpretation of the Koran, one that defied reason, and so one that forbade a realism giving full rights to the power of the intellect to know reality. To this day, many followers of Islam follow the dictates of the Koran blindly, even when those dictates oppose basic postulates of common sense.

Some Muslim intellectuals, however, wanted to engage in philosophical pursuits while remaining practising adherents of the Islamic faith. To do this, they had to effect a complete separation between reason and faith in their mind, a division that offends a realism which demands a reality that is one, and therefore a truth that is one. Those Muslim philosophers, while brilliantly elucidating crucial metaphysical distinctions, yet followed Aristotle far too closely, and so conceived of the universe as acting in an absolutely necessary, mechanical fashion. Like their master, they accounted for the motion of physical bodies in terms of final causes, and so tended toward pantheism. As such, they were unable to lend the full weight to the senses which both realism and scientific endeavour require.

The effect of the Reformation

Finally, coming to the time of the Reformation, realism was on the wane in Christendom because of the ascendancy of the ideas of William of Occam. He drove a wedge between faith and reason by means of a radical scepticism that cast doubt on the abilities of the mind to know reality. He could not accept the realist proofs for the existence of God that form the bridge between reason and faith, and so make a unified view of the whole of reality possible. His God was of the same voluntarist mould as Allah, creating wilfully but not intelligently.

The Augustinian order to which Martin Luther belonged taught the ideas of Occam. Luther embraced the spirit of Occam, taking the latter's trajectory to its full consequences, the total rejection of reason. His was a radical theologism, which had no tolerance for metaphysics or natural theology, an intolerance that holds sway to this very day, such that realist syntheses of the whole of reality are not taken seriously.

Wherever the voluntarist God holds sway—whether it be in Islam, in Catholicism, or Protestantism—neither reason nor reality can be accorded their God-given rights. Those who worship a God with will but no reason will believe by an unreasoning act of the will.

In the place of reason and human judgement as the ultimate reference for the choice of one's philosophy and religion, Luther advocated blind adherence to the literal sense of the Bible, as interpreted privately by each individual. This paved the way for the modern creationist movement in America, whose members uphold the literal sense of the Bible in opposition to the findings of science. They deny well-established scientific theories such as heliocentrism and the ancient age of the Earth and universe, and even oppose the very principles which make science possible, that is, the assumption that the universe has acted with uniform consistency throughout its history. Because of this opposition, creationism tends to allow for only one of two options: faith or reason, belief or science, but not both.

Under the creationist outlook, God made a universe inaccessible to scientific endeavour. He created it in a fully formed state, such that it does not have a developmental history, and He periodically interferes with the natural laws that He Himself established in such a major way that the traces of the activity of secondary causes are lost. Thus, when science puts forward theories that can only be probabilistic and can never reach metaphysical certainty, the believer merely points to the gaps in scientific knowledge in order to claim that only a miraculous running of nature by God can explain what we see, instead of holding to a consistent and so rationally discernible running of nature by means of secondary causes.

Now

Today, realism has been reduced to a medieval reminiscence and most minds do not even consider it as a possible solution to the opposition between science and religion introduced by Protestant theologism. They either reconcile them by subordinating philosophy and hence reason to science, or by adopting the intellectually suicidal principle of a double truth, one for faith and the other for reason. Or they say that the two are utterly incompatible, and in such cases, either believers seek to destroy science, or scientists seek to destroy religion. We have seen believers destroying science in this chapter; we now turn to scientists destroying religion in the next section. There, we will encounter the opposite swing of the pendulum introduced by Protestant theologism, that is, a philosophism that refuses to accept as true knowledge anything that cannot be established by scientific fact.

Notes

[1] http://www.evolutionnews.org/2015/03/bill_nye_respon094591.html
[2] Cited in *Ibid.*
[3] Grisar notes Occam's falling out with the Church in his *Luther* (St. Louis: B. Herder, 1914), vol. 1, p. 131, as follows: 'On theological questions concerning poverty [Occam] came into conflict with the Pope, his Sentences were condemned by the University of Paris, he appealed from the Holy See to a General Council, was excommunicated in 1328, protested against the decisions of the General Chapter of the Order, and then took refuge with Lewis of Bavaria, the schismatic, whose literary defender he became. He wrote for him, among other things, his ecclesiastico-political *"Dialogus"*, and even after his protector's death continued to resist Clement VI. Occam died at Munich in 1349, reconciled with his Order, though whether the excommunication had already been removed or not is doubtful.'
[4] See W. Turner, 'William of Ockham' in *Catholic Encyclopedia* (New York: The Encyclopedia Press, Inc., 1913), vol. XV, p. 636.
[5] See pp. 170–173.
[6] See pp. 191–192.
[7] H. Grisar, *Luther* (St. Louis: B. Herder, 1914), vol. 1, p. 147.
[8] *Ibid.*, pp. 133–154.
[9] *Makers of the Modern Mind* (Milwaukee: The Bruce Publishing Company, 1949), pp. 27–28.
[10] *Luther*, vol. 1, pp. 163, 162.
[11] J. Maritain, *Three Reformers* (London: Sheed & Ward, 1944), p. 31.
[12] Grisar, *Luther*, p. 158.
[13] *Ibid.*, pp. 155–165.
[14] *Ibid.*, p. 163.
[15] *Ibid.*, p. 146.
[16] *Ibid.*, p. 148.
[17] *Ibid.*, p. 155.
[18] *Ibid.*, p. 157.
[19] *Ibid.*, p. 161.
[20] *Ibid.*

[21] See pp. 209–213 above.
[22] Grisar, *Luther*, p. 161.
[23] *Ibid.*, p. 256.
[24] Maritain, *Three Reformers*, p. 35.
[25] Neill, *Makers of the Modern Mind*, p. 24.
[26] P. McNamara, *The Neuroscience of Religious Experience* (Cambridge: Cambridge University Press, 2009), pp. 8–9.
[27] Neill, *Makers of the Modern Mind*, pp. 55–56.
[28] To this day, Protestants by and large never use metaphysical First Cause arguments to prove the existence of God, or at least do not see them as providing certainty. Focus on the Family, for instance, in its 'True U' DVD 'Does God Exist?', enlists scientist Dr Stephen Meyer to build a case for God's existence, without having any recourse to metaphysics. To take another case, Protestant metaphysician and apologist William Lane Craig does not seem to use 'being' or vertical causality to prove God's existence, but rather argues that God must exist since science shows the universe had a beginning in time. In his *The Cosmological Argument from Plato to Leibniz* (Eugene, Oregon: Wipf and Stock Publishers, 1980), he finds arguments to God from notions of 'being' to be problematic. Perhaps this is why someone like New Atheist Lawrence Krauss sees the term 'First Cause' as belonging to the Roman Catholic Church, in his *A Universe from Nothing* (New York: Atria, 2013), pp. xxii, 172.
[29] See M. Chaberek, *Catholicism and Evolution* (Kettering, Ohio: Angelico Press, 2015), for a thorough treatment of the revealed truths, pertaining to history, contained in Genesis 1–3, that the Church has her members believe.
[30] See p. 485.
[31] E. Ruffini, *The Theory of Evolution Judged by Reason and Faith* (New York: Joseph F. Wagner, Inc., 1959), p. 69.
[32] *Catholicism and Evolution*, pp. 178–179.
[33] ST, I, q. 68, a.1; my translation.
[34] G. K. Chesterton, *St. Thomas Aquinas* (London: Hodder & Stoughton Limited, 1933), p. 101.
[35] Ruffini, *The Theory of Evolution*, pp. 68–69.
[36] E. Gilson, *History of Christian Philosophy in the Middle Ages* (New York: Random House, 1955), p. 73, emphasis added.
[37] Aquinas spoke of Augustine's theory as 'the one that appeals to me' in his *Commentary on the Sentences*, Book II, distinction XII, q.1, a.2, because it defends Scripture best from the mockery of unbelievers.
[38] *The Theory of Evolution*, p. 87.
[39] *Genesis 1 Through the Ages* (Edinburgh: Scottish Academic Press, 1998), chapter 9.

[40] *Ibid.*, p. 27.
[41] *Manuel d'Ecriture Sainte*, 1960, vol. 1, paragraph 267.
[42] *Genesis 1*, pp. viii–ix.
[43] Cited in Pope Leo XIII, *Providentissimus Deus*, 18. Translation from Denzinger-Hünermann (San Francisco: Ignatius Press, 2012), paragraph 3287.
[44] Pope Leo XIII, *Providentissimus Deus*, 18, emphasis added. Translation from Denzinger-Hünermann, paragraph 3288.
[45] Pope Leo XIII, *Providentissimus Deus*, 19. Translation from Denzinger-Hünermann, paragraph 3289.
[46] *Bible and Science* (Grand Rapids, Michigan: William Eerdmans Publishing Company, 1996), p. 109.
[47] S. Jaki, *Questions on Science and Religion* (Pinckney, Michigan: Real View Books, 2004), p. 49. While my focus in this book is the philosophical notion of God, it would be well to note that a God who is out to confound human minds by writing a Bible that is in contradiction with what they see in his own creation is a God who is theologically out of kilter. It makes no sense for God to endow humans with reason and then see the destruction of that reason as a means for their betterment. One could easily make the argument that this is not the God of the Bible.
[48] Cited in Jaki, *Genesis 1*, p. 146.
[49] E. Gilson, *From Aristotle to Darwin and Back Again* (San Francisco: Ignatius Press, 2009), p. 71.
[50] *Ibid.*, p. 70.
[51] *Ibid.*, p. 69.
[52] *Bible and Science*, p. 110.
[53] Jaki, *Genesis 1*, pp. 150–155.
[54] Two examples among the many Scriptural passages cited by Jaki are the following: 'Your word, O Lord, forever stands firm in the heavens: your truth lasts from age to age, like the earth you created. By your decree it endures to this day, for all things serve you' (Ps 118:89–91). 'When I have no covenant with day and night, and have given no laws to heaven and earth, then too will I reject the descendants of Jacob and of my servant David' (Jer 33:25–26).
[55] *Bible and Science*, pp. 36–39.
[56] See p. 102.
[57] See Aquinas, ST, I, q.19, a.5, ad 2.
[58] Jaki, *Science and Creation*, p. 47.
[59] *Bible and Science*, p. 116.
[60] E. Grant, *The Foundations of Modern Science in the Middle Ages* (Cambridge: Cambridge University Press, 1996), pp. 112–116. See also R. Dales,

Protestant Biblicism

The Scientific Achievement of the Middle Ages (Philadelphia: University of Pennsylvania Press, 1973), pp. 125–138.

61 Grant, *The Foundations of Modern Science*, pp. 115–116.

62 Jaki, *Genesis 1*, p. 144.

63 A. Richardt, *La verité sur l'affaire Galilée* (Paris: François-Xavier de Guibert, 2007), translation mine. For a contrary view on Calvin and science, see E. McMullin, 'Galileo on science and Scripture' in P. Machamer, ed., *The Cambridge Companion to Galileo* (Cambridge: Cambridge University Press, 1998), p. 301.

64 Cited in Jaki, *Genesis 1*, p. 144.

65 See J. Hannam, *The Genesis of Science* (Washington, DC: Regnery Publishing, 2011), p. 30.

66 This quotation and the following ones from Sungenis cited from D. Sefton, 'In this worldview, the sun revolves around the earth', Times-News, 30 March 2006.

67 For a book-long refutation of the so-called 'Copernican principle', the idea that modern science has proved humans to be insignificant, see G. Gonzalez and J. Richards, *The Privileged Planet* (Washington, DC: Regnery Publishing, 2004). See also C. S. Lewis, *Miracles* (Glasgow: Fount Paperbacks, 1947), pp. 53–58; and *God in the Dock* (Glasgow: Fount Paperbacks, 1979 (Glasgow: Fount Paperbacks, 1947), pp. 28–33.

68 *The Everlasting Man* (New York: Dodd, Mead & Company, 1930), p. 1.

69 In *my* mind, Ken Cole did a fine job at http://www.philvaz.com/apologetics/GeocentrismDisproved.htm.

70 John Wilson cited in B. Haskins, *Evangelicalism and Fundamentalism, A Documentary Reader* (New York: New York University Press, 2008), p. 114.

71 W. Brown, *In the Beginning* (Phoenix: Center for Scientific Creation, 1995), paragraph 44.

72 It is obviously possible for God both to create a planet directly *and* for the planet to have a natural history causing it to take on certain features, after its creation by God, over a period of time. Creationists do not have recourse to this scenario because their interpretation of the Bible commits them to a universe that is only 6,000 years old, and 6,000 years is not nearly enough time for current day natural processes, as we know them, to account for the distinctive features of the planets.

73 See p. 102.

74 J. Whitcomb and H. Morris, *The Genesis Flood* (Phillipsburg, New Jersey: Presbyterian and Reformed Publishing Company, 2011), p. xxvii. Biblical catastrophism is to be distinguished from scientific catastrophism, which holds that there have been five mass extinction events in the history of

the Earth, but does not hold that the laws of nature were any different at the times of those catastrophes. See T. Bethell, *Darwin's House of Cards* (Seattle: Discovery Institute Press, 2017), chapter 7.

75. Brown, *In the Beginning*, paragraph 62.
76. *Ibid.*, pp. 158–161.
77. S. Jaki, *The Road of Science and the Ways to God* (Port Huron, Michigan: Real View Books, 2005), p. 42.
78. Brown, *In the Beginning*, p. 160.
79. See, for instance, Whitcomb and Morris, *The Genesis Flood*, p. 369.
80. *Ibid.*, p. 116.
81. *Ibid.*, p. 118.
82. *Evangelicalism and Fundamentalism*, p. 97.
83. Whitcomb and Morris, *The Genesis Flood*, p. 121.
84. *Ibid.*
85. *Ibid.*, p. 119.
86. See Brown, *In the Beginning*, pp. 87–105.
87. *Spiritus Paraclitus*, 22.
88. *Divino Afflante Spiritu*, 3.
89. Translation found in *Catholicism and Modern Science* of The Australian Catholic Truth Society Record, 1961, p. 31.
90. Jaki, *Genesis 1*, pp. 172–173.
91. By this statement, I am not endorsing God of the gaps arguments, which argue from ignorance. Rather, I am endorsing arguments that take certain complexities found in nature, infer the type of cause necessary to produce such complexity, and conclude that no such cause can be found in the natural order.
92. This explanation is adapted from J. Kaler, 'Astronomy: Stars, Galaxies, and the Universe' (Recorded Books, 2004) audio course, lecture 4.
93. Though Kaler, Jaki, and others say he was the first to do this, it was actually Calandrelli in 1806, as W. Wallace notes in *The Modeling of Nature* (Washington, DC: The Catholic University of America Press, 1996), p. 394.
94. J. Kaler, *Stars and Their Spectra* (Cambridge: Cambridge University Press, 1989), p. 118.
95. Foucault's pendulum and the validity of Newton's laws are other ways to disprove geocentrism in empirical fashion. See Jaki, *Questions on Science*, p. 94, and the debate with Sungenis referenced above.
96. *Bible and Science*, p. 117.
97. D. Berlinski's *The Devil's Delusion* (New York: Basic Books, 2009) is not as fair on this question. However, I agree with James Hannam's assessment of Koestler's short treatment of medieval history as being 'woefully

inaccurate'. See *The Genesis of Science* (Washington DC: Regnery Publishing Inc., 2011), p. 354.
98 *Bible and Science*, p. 117.
99 *Ibid.*, p. 113.
100 *The Sleepwalkers* (London: Penguin Classics, 2014), p. 406, emphasis in original.
101 Jaki, *Questions on Science*, p. 98.
102 Cited in Koestler, *The Sleepwalkers*, p. 417, emphasis in original. E. McMullin argues that Bellarmine wrote this passage of his letter only out of professional courtesy, while believing it was impossible to prove heliocentrism, and thus not really meaning what he said in P. Machamer, ed., *The Cambridge Companion to Galileo* (Cambridge: Cambridge University Press, 1998), p. 283. But I find it hard not to take Bellarmine at his word, and think that, if he was presented evidence such as stellar parallax for heliocentrism, he would have followed through with his promised reinterpretation of Scripture.
103 See Jaki, *Questions on Science*, p. 96.
104 Koestler, *The Sleepwalkers*, p. 422.
105 *Ibid.*, p. 425.
106 See S. Jaki, *The Road of Science and the Ways to God* (Port Huron, Michigan: Real View Books, 2005), p. 46; *Questions on Science*, p. 101.
107 See A. Rizzi, *The Science before Science* (Baton Rouge: IAP Press, 2004), pp. 12–14.
108 Cited in R. Dales, *The Scientific Achievement of the Middle Ages* (Philadelphia: University of Pennsylvania Press, 1973), p. 128.
109 See p. 409.
110 B. Dalrymple, *Ancient Earth, Ancient Skies* (Stanford, California: Stanford University Press, 2004), p. 6.
111 *Questions On Science*, p. 163.
112 See Dalrymple, *Ancient Earth*, Table 3.1.
113 *Ibid.*, p. 46.
114 *Ibid.*, pp. 48–49.
115 *Ibid.*, p. 58.
116 *Ibid.*, pp. 68–73. The creationist publication *Grand Canyon Monument to Catastrophe* by Steven Austin (Santee, California: Institute for Creation Research, 1994), pp. 117–119, actually provides a more thorough presentation of the maths behind radioisotope dating than Dalrymple.
117 Dalrymple, *Ancient Earth*, p. 73.
118 F. Vigouroux, *Dictionnaire de la Bible* (Paris: Letouzy et Ané, 1926), vol. II, column 1356.

III SCIENCE

8 SCIENCE SUICIDE

The man of science is a poor philosopher.

Albert Einstein

IN SHAKESPEARE'S *THE Merchant of Venice*, the villain Shylock is intent on destroying his rival merchant, the good and generous Antonio. One reason Shylock detests Antonio is that the latter refuses to borrow or lend with interest and loudly condemns usury. Meanwhile, usurious loans are Shylock's bread and butter.

Shylock believes he has been given an excellent opportunity to exact his revenge on his rival when Antonio comes to him one day to ask for a loan. Antonio, whose three ships are out at sea and whose coffers are empty, is in desperate need of money for a cause of his friend Bassanio. This need drives Antonio to the last extremity of borrowing from Shylock.

Shylock seizes the occasion as a perfect opportunity to force Antonio into acting against his own principles by accepting a loan with interest. Shylock's hatred of Antonio, however, is so great that there is something which he desires even more: Antonio's death. Thus, he proposes to Antonio that the latter not pay interest on his loan, but rather pay with a pound of his own flesh, to be extracted by Shylock, in the event that the loan defaults. Antonio agrees.[1]

What is most interesting in the dramatic events that later unfold in the play is that Shylock believes that all of the steps he is taking are leading to the destruction of Antonio, when they are actually leading to his own destruction. Antonio's three ships are wrecked and so Antonio is not able to pay back the loan.[2] Shylock demands his pound of flesh, even when others step forward and offer to pay Antonio's debt and even more than what was owed. No, says Shylock. I stand by my bond.[3] In a court of trial, he insists over and over again that justice demands he be rendered a pound of Antonio's flesh.[4] Money, persuasion, revilings and threats are of no avail to change Shylock's mind. He will accept nothing less than Antonio's life in payment.

But it turns out that Shylock's stubborn insistence on justice in his own cause is precisely what ruins his own cause. The judge Portia, a disguised female friend of Antonio as well as Bassanio's newly-wed wife, rules that justice be rendered to Shylock—he is to be given a pound of flesh. However, in removing the flesh, Shylock is not to take any blood, for there is no word about blood in the contract. Thus, if he sheds any blood when making incisions in the flesh, his lands and goods will be confiscated by the state of Venice. At this point, Shylock is more than willing to accept the money instead of the flesh! But, no, he has demanded justice, and justice he will have. He *must* take a pound of flesh, but exactly that and no more, not even a hair's weight more, in case of which he will lose his own life.

In the end, Portia allows Shylock to escape with his life and half of his goods, but only by denying him what he had been seeking—instead of strict justice, Shylock gets mercy.

The general framework of this tale is a moral for the conflict between religion and science that we observed in the second section and which will also come to the fore in this third section. Shylock felt threatened by Antonio and sought means to destroy him. But the very means that Shylock pursued to ruin Antonio led, on the contrary, to his own demise.

Similarly, religionists of different stripes and periods felt threatened by the secular knowledge of philosophy and science. Believing that such knowledge posed a threat to belief in God, they sought means to destroy that knowledge. The means was an attack on reason, a means pursued by Al-Ash'ari and Al-Ghazali, by William of Occam, and by Luther, as a way of saving religion. Each of them claimed the right to take a knife to the human intellect in order to do justice to God. Destroying reason, however, did not save religion; it rather ruined it, by making it inaccessible to the human mind. Religion fell into the very pit it had dug for reason and hence realism.[5] Not realising that humans believe by means of their intellect, religionists took out an essential means to religion, thinking they were taking out its primary obstacle.

Once science grew to maturity in the sixteenth and seventeenth centuries, after having been birthed in the Middle Ages, it began to see philosophy as an obstacle to its own legitimate endeavours, attributing to it all of the errors of past ages in science. Scientists started to think that the knowledge gained in their own specific domain could not co-exist with the knowledge provided by philosophy and religion. Feeling threatened by that knowledge, they sought means to destroy it. How would the rights of scientific pursuit be vindicated? Again, it would be by attacking reason, in this case reason in its philosophical function. After destroying philosophy and religion, science would finally be free to pursue and communicate solid truth to the human race.

The problem with this strategy is that science cannot do without philosophy, and specifically realist philosophy. Thus science sought its own death sentence when it set out to wage war against realism. Seeking to become wholly rational, it attacked reason and became irrational, to the degree that much of modern science is as much faith-based as the most superstitious pagan religion of ancient civilisation. Trying to exist without religion, science has become religious, even putting forward as fact theories that are irrational. This has led to science being discredited in the eyes of many. We will see in this third section how a departure from realism is the cause of modern science's self-destruction.

Keeping the balance

It is the realist ideal to achieve a worldview that does not rule out any of the four causes from holding a place in human knowledge. It is a question of mental balance, a worldview which:

1. leaves reality intact with all of its rights
2. keeps each piece of the puzzle in place when new pieces are added
3. refuses to discount true knowledge so as to simplify the problem.

Material causes need not be at war with final causes, yet it is an age-old tendency of the human mind to oppose them. The Ionians held that all was matter and so denied purpose; Socrates responded by denying that matter has intelligible content and laying the entire emphasis of knowledge-seeking on understanding purposes. Aristotle reconciled the impasse by constructing a metaphysics where all four causes played a role. Here at last was a delicate realist balance, but alas, it was still incomplete, for Aristotle's pantheism drove him to leave material causes out of the explanation of physical motion—the quintessential domain of material causes. This mistake left room for the medievals to correct Aristotle's system, insights revealed by God Himself about His own creative activity enabling a more perfect realist synthesis. Once this was achieved in the thirteenth century and the Philosopher's science was finally toppled, there began the work of exploring that realm of knowledge that had been shut off from humanity's mental view for so many centuries.

What would humans do when they found secrets of the universe that had been hidden to all previous ages? What attitude would they adopt when they discovered that even the greatest of the thinkers of the past had been mistaken about the position of the Earth, the size of the cosmos, the innermost components of matter, the nature of heavenly bodies, and countless other scientific data? Would they be able to add these new pieces to the puzzle of reality without discounting the old? Would they maintain that their predecessors had been mistaken about the components and interactions of physical bodies or would they hold them as mistaking the very nature of reality itself?

Science Suicide 313

The answers to these questions are not provided by the medieval period which gave birth to modern science, for while it created a new mental template which would lead to the great scientific discoveries of the modern age, it did not make them itself. The beginning of such discoveries was left for the 'century of genius', the seventeenth, which was directed to 'turning science from a still insecure child into a self-assured adult'.[6] Would this adult, now come of age, be able to learn from the epistemological mistakes of his parents, so as not to repeat them?

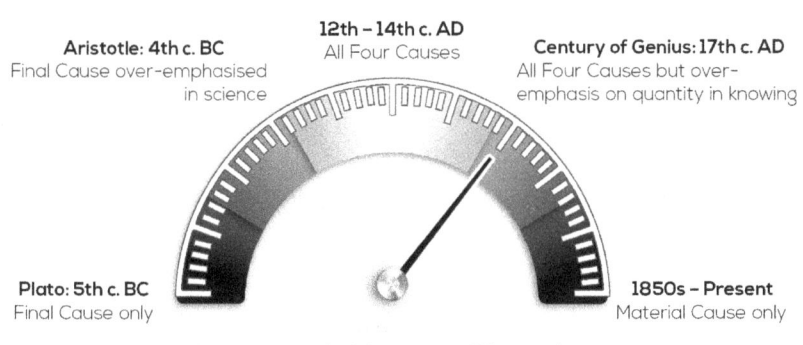

Aristotle: 4th c. BC
Final Cause over-emphasised in science

12th – 14th c. AD
All Four Causes

Century of Genius: 17th c. AD
All Four Causes but over-emphasis on quantity in knowing

Plato: 5th c. BC
Final Cause only

1850s – Present
Material Cause only

History of Western Thought

Unfortunately, no. By the seventeenth century, the Western mind had abandoned its realist philosophical bearings and was drifting in open sea, without a unifying vision of reality.[7] When the wind of scientific discovery started blowing, the slack sails billowed outward, and the epistemological compass was set on the course of empiricism. Science and hence material causes would attempt to be the sole benchmark of true knowledge. Insofar as science tried to steer the ship, however, it undermined the very foundations upon which it rested. *With empiricism as captain, the destination was inevitably set for the shores of irrationality.*

In this chapter, we will look at the players on the transitional stage of the seventeenth century, when science began to shift society's perspective on reality, weakening the value of final causes and over-emphasising that of material causes. As we consider how the empiricist worldview was created, with key notions being re-conceptualised according to its template—ostensibly in order to favour science—we will also indicate five negative effects of the shift on science itself. The new worldview will:

1. eliminate the logical foundation on which any coherent scientific theory must rest
2. render scientific proofs probabilistic at best, incapable of ever being strictly demonstrative
3. radically alter—and for the worse—notions of the universe, God, man, and causality
4. force scientists into choosing between an empiricist theologism or an empiricist philosophism
5. cause scientists to open themselves up to ridicule, by leading them to propose absurd metaphysical views.

Worldview transmogrification

We turn now to history to ferret out examples of 'suicidal science.' When we find scientists adopting an epistemology other than realism, we will also find them committing unwitting hara-kiri. *The Metaphysical Foundations of Modern Science* (1932), E. A. Burtt's classic work, will help us track the transformation of the Western mind's perspective of reality caused by the great thinkers of the Scientific Revolution.

Copernicus and mathematical modelling

Burtt starts with Nicolaus Copernicus (1473–1543), who, despite the work of medieval scientists, was a devoted believer in Aristotelian physics, and is even referred to by Koestler as the 'last of the Aristotelians'.[8] What made Copernicus avant-garde was not so much his heliocentrism,[9] but his construction of a mathematical model to support it. The greater simplicity of this model over the Ptolemaic model of a geocentric universe made it compelling to Copernicus. After all, he reasoned, would not a universe made by an all-wise God be more likely to have a simplicity and order accessible to the human mind rather than being chaotic and inscrutable? Indeed, this was his primary motive for holding that heliocentrism was true of reality, when it could not yet be verified by the senses.[10]

The simplicity of Copernicus' model worked as a spark to gunpowder, attuning scientific minds to the power of mathematics to describe sensible phenomena.[11] If the heliocentric model was so mathematically elegant, the next question to be asked was obvious: *'is the universe as a whole, including our earth, fundamentally mathematical in its structure?'*[12]

Kepler and mathematical metaphysics

Johannes Kepler (1571–1630), for one, certainly thought the answer was 'yes.' He was one of several figures in the genius century pushing the Western worldview away from realism and toward empiricism. Kepler was an accomplished mathematician, making several notable advancements in that field. When he was provided with the vast and carefully recorded astronomical data of Tycho Brahe, he set upon it with the explicit assumption that he would find mathematical harmony permeating the movements of the heavens. To his delight, he found 'scores of mathematical relations',[13] among which were his famous three laws of planetary motion.[14]

Johannes Kepler (Image courtesy of Wikimedia Commons)

Thus far Kepler the scientist. For the fact is that Kepler was not satisfied with discovering mathematical harmonies in the heavens. No, he wished also to go beyond those harmonies to form a metaphysics, that is, he wanted to use his discoveries to make statements about the whole of reality. At this we must not be surprised, for every person naturally seeks to become a metaphysician. It is difficult for the mind of any one of us to rest until it has a coherent picture of the whole of reality.

The coherent picture of reality that we constructed back in chapter 2 was built upon the notion of 'being', and that made sense. If you want to form a notion of the whole of reality, you must use a notion that pertains to reality as such, and 'being' is such a notion: everything that exists, that is real, is a being. What happens, however, when a brilliant mind which has not been formed in realist philosophy seeks to form a synthesis of all reality? Quite simply, he chooses as his starting point that piece of knowledge which seems to be most sure, most compelling, most obvious. For Kepler and many scientists who have come after him, this was mathematics.[15]

We can certainly sympathise with this choice. Mathematical concepts are clearer than any others. This is due to the special nature of the quantities upon which mathematics is constructed. As Aristotle points out[16] and Jaki repeats continually,[17] quantities do not admit of more or less. What this means is that numbers such as 5 or 79 are radically fixed, without having any degrees within themselves. You cannot have more or less of 'fiveness'. Rather, you either have five or you do not. Since there is no wiggle room in our idea of five, that idea is crystal clear. Our mind finds such crystal clear ideas quite appealing, because they leave no room for uncertainty as far as the mind is concerned, no grey area that needs to be explored.

This sort of clarity is not found in metaphysical concepts. 'Being', for instance, is an imprecise concept, as its degrees are practically infinite. We can think of the lowest forms of beings, such as fundamental particles like electrons, then move to entities that have more of being, such as living things like plants, and finally think of God, Who is 'Being itself', the realisation of being in the highest degree possible. The number of ways in which 'being' can be realised between electrons and God is innumerable and this makes the concept 'being' much fuzzier than the concept 'five'. There's only one way to do 'five', but countless ways to realise 'being'.

REALISM
All Four Causes in Balance

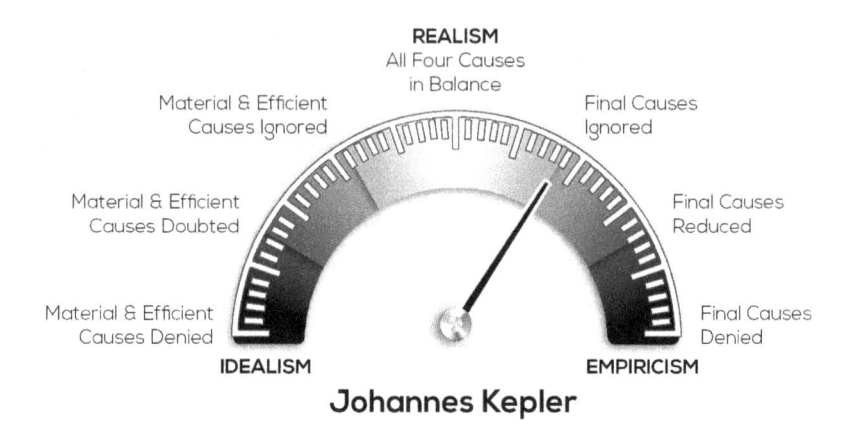

Material & Efficient Causes Ignored

Final Causes Ignored

Material & Efficient Causes Doubted

Final Causes Reduced

Material & Efficient Causes Denied

Final Causes Denied

IDEALISM   **EMPIRICISM**

Johannes Kepler

Aristotle warned in his *Metaphysics* that 'the minute accuracy of mathematics is not to be demanded in all cases'.[18] Rather, the mind must adjust its concepts according to the aspect of reality under study, rather than force reality to conform to this or that type of concept (different methods for different objects). Kepler, however, being enamoured of the mathematical concept, wanted to build his intellectual synthesis of reality upon it.

This is the original epistemological sin of all scientists going back to Pythagoras. It is like someone delighting in the taste of chocolate cake and then deciding to define all food as 'chocolate cake'. Kepler's intellectual palate likes the clarity which numbers provide and decides to define reality as numbers. Instead of starting with reality itself, which presents itself under the imperfectly grasped concept of 'being', Kepler begins with the part of reality which he finds clearest and extends that part to take up the whole of reality.

Of itself, the project is insane. After all, which one of us would want to say that everything is, in its essence, a number? Flowers are numbers, life is a number, love is a number. Perhaps only those who have experienced the exhilaration of solving a complex differential equation can identify with the temptation to form a mathematical metaphysics.

Such was Kepler's metaphysics, and he formed it by adopting a distinction which was proposed in the ancient world and was being revived in his own seventeenth century. On the one hand, there are the *primary qualities*. These are the mathematical objects, which are grasped clearly by the mind, and which provide a knowledge that is certain and consistent, and thus corresponds to what is real. On the other hand are the *secondary qualities*. They consist of all the non-mathematical information presented to the mind through the senses, a knowledge held to be 'obscure, confused, contradictory, and hence untrustworthy'.[19]

Armed with this distinction, Kepler the scientist takes two gigantic philosophical positions:[20]

1. **Reality**—'The real world is a world of quantitative characteristics only; its differences are differences of number alone.'

2. **Knowledge (Kepler's epistemology)**—'All certain knowledge must be knowledge of [objects presented to the senses in] their quantitative characteristics, perfect knowledge is always mathematical.'

Thus, in Kepler's view, God made the entire universe according to a series of mathematical harmonies, and it is those mathematical harmonies which make up reality and actually cause things to be what they are. Meanwhile, God has made the human mind to know reality and that means to know quantity and mathematics, but nothing else. 'Just as the eye was made to see colours, and the ear to hear sounds, so the human mind was made to understand, not whatever you please, but quantity.'[21] Everything else, if not unreal, is at least unknowable.

This was a first step towards the reduction of all knowledge to that which can be described by mathematics, an epistemology today called 'positivism'. The New Oxford American Dictionary defines positivism as

> a philosophical system that holds that every rationally justifiable assertion can be scientifically verified or is capable of logical or mathematical proof, and that therefore rejects metaphysics and theism.[22]

It is a reality mentality which takes all beings and confines them to the narrow field of quantity, a position that 'buys clarity and certitude at the price of mutilating reality'.[23] Other scientists in the 'century of genius' will go further than Kepler in their reductionism.

Galileo

Galileo Galilei (1564–1642) was a contemporary and jealous rival of Kepler. While Kepler 'gave only tantalizing inklings of modernity, [Galileo] kept only occasional ties with pre-modern mentality'.[24] The reason why he, in his writings, sounds like a modern scientist is that he does science in complete isolation from philosophy. Galileo understood the damage that Aristotle's physics had done to the progress of scientific thought, and the *reason* why it did so: its over-emphasis of final causes. The thing to be done, then, was to introduce a new way of approaching reality and writing about it, wherein final causes would be totally ignored. The material realm had to be isolated, disencumbered of philosophical presuppositions and left to speak for itself in the bare nudity of its facts.

Galileo exemplified this new procedure in his first scientific work, *Messenger from the Stars*. In the short folio, he set forth his discoveries of features on the Moon, the satellites of Jupiter, and innumerable previously unseen stars, by means of an improved telescope he had developed. But this work

> not only contained news of heavenly bodies 'which no mortal had seen before'; it was also written in a new, tersely factual style which no scholar had employed before ... devoid of all philosophy.[25]

Galileo Galilei (Image courtesy of Wikimedia Commons)

Galileo did not just speak of material bodies as if nothing more was to be said of them than their physical properties; he also believed that such was the case. Like Kepler, he embraced the distinction of primary and secondary qualities, relegating the latter to the realm of illusion. The only real aspects in the bodies we observe are quantitative ones; all the rest, including and especially purpose, are illusory. Burtt summarises Galileo's reduction as follows:

> The scholastic substances and causes, in terms of which the fact of motion and its ultimate *why* had been accounted for teleologically, were swept away in favour of the notion that

bodies are composed of indestructible atoms, equipped with none but mathematical qualities ... Galileo conceived the whole physical universe as a world of extension, figure, motion, and weight; all other qualities which we suppose to exist *in rerum natura* really have no place there but are due to the confusion and deceitfulness of our senses ... all immediate causality is lodged in quantitatively reducible motions of its atomic elements, hence only by mathematics can we arrive at true knowledge of that world.[26]

REALISM
All Four Causes in Balance

Material & Efficient Causes Ignored

Formal & Final Causes Ignored

Material & Efficient Causes Doubted

Formal & Final Causes Reduced

Material & Efficient Causes Denied

Formal & Final Causes Denied

IDEALISM

EMPIRICISM

Galileo Galilei

The beauty of the rose, the shimmering of the sea, nay, the totality of the world's poetic aspects, are mere illusions without actual real existence. When push comes to shove, roses are mathematical objects of a certain weight, mobility, and dimension, nothing more, nothing less. Such is Galileo's perspective, our second example of a scientist shrinking reality to the confines of his own field of study, so as to render it investigable by the scientific method alone.

While it is true that a keen focus on purely quantitative aspects of bodies aids science greatly by enabling the discovery of physical laws, yet saying that what the scientific method discovers is all that exists only harms science in the long run. We are now ready to consider empiricism's five negative effects on science.

1. Incoherent science

The first of our science injuries—making scientific theory incoherent—comes from the relegation of quality to the realm of illusion. The scientific method relies on observation and experimentation. But our eyes do not observe quantities as such; rather they observe qualities: colours and shapes, not numbers. The numbers come from the mind quantifying what the eyes have observed. In other words, the numbers obtained by the scientific method rely on the actual existence of the qualities that certain lovers of the scientific method hold to be illusory.

Feser perfectly expresses the reason why the denial of qualities makes all scientific theories illogical:

> It is only through observation and experiment—and thus through conscious experiences defined by ... qualitative features—that we have evidence for the truth of the scientific theories in the name of which we would be eliminating the qualitative. Such eliminativism is incoherent.[27]

In the end, scientific theories are a construct of the mind—ideas—that are at a certain remove from the data of the senses. The fact that they are most often expressed in terms of abstract mathematical formulas testifies to this. Certain scientists, however, somehow conflate the quantitative with the sense data from which they derived their formulas. On the contrary, they are not the same, and the last thing a scientist should want to do is relegate that sense data on which his theories rest to the realm of illusion. This is exactly what is done by empiricists whose 'working notion of matter is one that has, by definition, extruded the qualitative from it'.[28]

2. Probabilistic science

A second problem results from the tendency of the figures of the Scientific Revolution to mathematise reality, not just by describing physical movement in terms of mathematical formulas, but also by implying that the material quantities covered by those formulas are all that exists in reality. Their motive was to do away with final causes, but this step inevitably took out formal causes as well. Formal causes are the essences of things, their natures, and they are not material nor are they quantities. One holding that material bodies are *only* quantitative extension, then, will not see those bodies as possessing this or that nature. *Empiricism commits a mind to the denial of both formal and final causes.* A major aspect of this section is the investigation of the ultimate intellectual consequences of this double denial in various scientific fields.

When formal causes are 'removed' from reality, scientific proofs can only be probabilistic at best. Recall that Aristotle held that one possesses 'science' when one knows with certainty the causes of a given thing, 'opinion' when one has probable arguments for the cause of an effect, and 'belief' when one has rhetoric to support one's proposition.

The point we need to establish here is that, when modern science does away with formal causes, it is not able to provide certain knowledge. Science cannot give science; it can only give opinion. The reason is that, *to establish that there is a necessary connection between a cause and an effect, you must show that it is in the very nature of a cause to produce such an effect.*

Once one holds, however, that physical bodies are *only* quantitative extension, and so do not have any intrinsic nature, it becomes impossible to establish a necessary connection between water and wetness. The best that one can do is say, 'In all of the instances that we have observed up to this point, wetness has accompanied water. Thus, it is *probable* that whatever water touches will be wet.'

Wallace's magisterial work on realist science, *The Modeling of Nature* (1996), is the one-stop book for this discussion. In it, he indicates how scientists before the modern era considered themselves capable of providing demonstrative and so absolutely certain proofs of various scientific propositions. One of them was Galileo.

Galileo did studies in philosophy, and notably logic, under Jesuit teachers at Pisa. Jesuits of the sixteenth century at the University of Padua had developed a realist mode of argumentation, tailored for the scientific method, by which scientists could put forward demonstrative proofs of their discoveries. They called the methodology the 'demonstrative regress'. It has the scientist start with sense data and, from that sense data, know the cause of a given effect in a confused way. Then, the scientist embarks on an intense examination of the cause in order to know it more distinctly. If he is able to ascertain a necessary connection between the cause and the effect, then he is able to claim certain knowledge and make a demonstrative proof.[29]

While 'the vast majority of arguments based on scientific research yield at best probable conclusions',[30] yet science is, at times, able to discover the natures of things through the scientific method, and so give demonstrative proofs of scientific conclusions. Galileo recognised this and proposed, during his career, nine of his discoveries as capable of demonstrative proof, though he ended up realising that, for five of them, he did not have sufficient evidence to argue a necessary connection between cause and effect.[31]

Wallace sets out in detail Galileo's demonstrative arguments that there are mountains on the moon, that Venus rotates around the sun, and that Jupiter has moons,[32] each argument indicating a necessary connection between a given cause and effects observed. The arguments rely on material objects possessing natures and the ability of the mind to grasp those natures.

What Galileo did not realise was that his views on the nature of material bodies undermined the 'necessary demonstrations' he was using to establish his scientific conclusions. Later scientists did see the full philosophical implications of the distinction between primary and secondary qualities, including it preventing science from providing scientific proofs. This realisation, however, instead of leading them to flee empiricism and embrace realism, only led them to abandon all hope of gaining certain knowledge through their trade.

Today, a form of reasoning called 'hypothetico-deductive' is considered to be the gold standard for scientific methodology.[33] It consists of formulating hypotheses which can be empirically tested, and which grow in certainty to the degree that they are confirmed by experimentation. When a sufficient number of confirming experimental instances has been reached, the hypothesis is held to be worthy of 'justified true belief', thus not even reaching the level of probabilistic opinion![34] Ironically, today's scientists still instinctively use the realist demonstrative regress to argue their conclusions, 'although rarely are claims made for their apodictic character',[35] because empiricist epistemology does not allow it.

Many moderns have tried to find a way to provide stronger certitude to scientific conclusions, while maintaining the empiricist reduction of reality. But whether one follows Carnap's verification theory or Popper's falsification theory as the true litmus test for scientific certitude, the conclusions are still necessarily probabilistic, and so at best can be said to approach the truth.[36]

Meanwhile, other twentieth-century thinkers have practically emptied science of the ability to be objective or truthful. Notably, Thomas Kuhn reduces science to adopting paradigms in order to solve puzzles, paradigms that 'are not closer approximations to the way things are, nor are they closer approximations to the truth'.[37] Even Popper and his followers end up emptying science of all rationality, as Stove has shown in his devastating essays.[38]

The seventeenth-century scientific geniuses did not realise that, while they were breaking ground with their scientific discoveries, they were at the same time removing the ground underneath science by the philosophy they imposed on top of their discoveries. We are today witnesses of the long-term damaging effects of empiricism on science itself, and we can only hope that one day, realism will come to science's rescue. There is no reason for science to do away with the ability of the mind to know the natures of things, as Wallace says:

> It is important to note that there is nothing in the training of scientists that requires them to negate their powers of intellect or profess an inability to form a universal or to grasp a causal connection.[39]

3. Unreasonable world

We have tarried on the weakening of scientific certitude, and now must return to the transformation of worldview implicit in the ideas of the seventeenth-century scientists. Their starting point, as we saw, is not 'being', but rather an assumption about the world, namely, that it is a purely quantitative realm of mathematical objects. We have seen how this eliminates qualities and natures from material entities. We now must consider what notions of causality, man, and God necessarily result, if we begin with an empiricist vision of the universe—notions that hinder science rather than aid it.

Empirical causality

Let us take causality as our first example. We begin with our assumption that the universe is composed only of quantities. As such, things are to be described solely in terms of their material components (their quantitative makeup), and their interaction is to be explained solely in terms of efficient causality. Natures or essences (formal causes) and purposes (final causes) can have no place in the knowledge of such a purely material, mathematical realm. We can speak of what things are made of (material cause) and the physical forces by which they interact (efficient causes), but we cannot say what they are (formal cause) nor why they act in the way they do (final cause).

What does God do, we may ask, in such a system? Recall that God only acted as a final cause in Aristotle's metaphysics, being the good towards which all things strove. Christians found this notion of God incomplete, since they knew Him to be a Creator, and so they spoke of Him as also being the efficient cause of the universe. Thus, God is both the source of all reality (efficient cause) and the purpose for which it was made (final cause). But Galileo and the scientists following him are finished with final causes, all of them. Extending this principle to God Himself means that 'God [] ceases to be the Supreme Good of the universe in any important sense';[40] He is not the good toward which all things strive, directly or indirectly.

To repeat our question, then, what does God do in this system? He is left with being a Creator, an efficient cause, but a severely reduced one. Since the universe is merely a conglomeration of material components interacting according to a set of pre-determined laws, God 'is a huge mechanical inventor, whose power is appealed to merely to account for the first appearance of the atoms'.[41]

Is that it? What about sustaining things in being? What about the domain of primary causality? Quite simply, these considerations no longer have any place in a system which only sees beings in terms of their material components. There is no reason even to speak of a concept such as 'being', as 'being' cannot be formulated in mathematical terms and is not something material. To exist is not to be made of this or that matter; it is to stand outside of nothing.

Material things, as conceived by empiricists, have what Feser refers to as 'existential inertia', namely, they 'have the capacity to remain in being on their own'.[42] This follows directly from existence not being conceived of as part of their being. The only thing that exists, as it were, is quantitative extension. Once God provides this extension to bodies, they have no need of Him any longer. He is a Creator of beings, but not their Conserver.

Science Suicide

Table 8.1 *Three views on God's causality in the universe*

Thinkers	Is God Creator of the universe? (first efficient cause)	Is God Supreme Good of the universe? (first final cause)
Aristotle	NO	YES
Aquinas	YES	YES
Galileo	YES	NO

It should not surprise us that Galileo was tempted to relegate to the realm of the unknown 'the fundamental questions of the creation of the universe and its first cause'.[43] For causality, in an empirical system, is not merely reduced to efficient causality, but *secondary* efficient causality. When we ask for an explanation of the cue ball thumping into the eight ball, 'motion' and 'force' are the only causes which can be given in answer. 'Atomic motions are treated [] as secondary causes of events, the primary or ultimate causes being conceived always in terms of force.'[44] In chapter 2 on the four causes, we would have said that speaking of motion and force is insufficient, since our mind perceives that they do not give a complete explanation for what takes place on the pool table. For instance, we could easily ask a *why* question, such as 'Why does the cue ball act in the way that it does?', since the language of 'forces' only describes *what* the ball does, forcing us to find a different type of answer to the *why* question, one relating to formal or final causality. We might say, 'The cue ball has an intrinsic nature (formal cause) which determines the way that it acts' or 'The body of the cue ball pursues the laws which have been established for it (final cause)'.

The scientist positivist empiricist, however, is not willing to allow such explanations to count for anything, since they invoke causes outside of matter, causes that cannot be directly observed by the senses. Having decided that only the observable is knowable, the empiricist proceeds to hold that only the observable is what really exists. All is matter. From this premise, the reduction of all explanation to the giving of efficient causes follows directly:

- the objects outside of us are wholly material and so must be explained only in material terms
- consequently, in all events, that which is happening at the material level is the movement of atoms by means of forces
- consequently, all causation in the world around us is to be explained in terms of the movement of atoms by means of forces.

Man in the empirical universe

God creates billions of atoms, which interact according to rigidly determined mathematical laws. Such is the universe as we know it, say the empiricists. Where does man fit in all of this, we may ask? Aristotle thought that the universe was composed of a hierarchy of beings, ordered from top to bottom, everything connected in a great interlocking chain, with man being lower than heavenly objects and higher than the rest of earthly objects. The empiricists, however, have tossed out the very notion of being and are treating quantified matter as the highest concept; there is no order (final causality), just movement (efficient causality). A human is left with one of two choices when trying to locate himself in such a world:

- either I am one with that world and so just a soulless clump of mere matter following mathematical laws like everything else, or
- I am a spiritual mind existing outside the world but somehow imprisoned in it for the duration of my life.

Once it is decided that the outside world is mere matter, man can either hold that he is part of that world and so mere matter too, or not a part of that world and so mere spirit, but he can no longer hold that he is spiritual and material, soul and body, AND part of this world at the same time.

For realists, reality is both material and immaterial: the material aspect is presented to our senses/body and the immaterial part to our mind/soul. We are compatible with the world around us in both our being and knowledge. Both our senses and mind provide true information, and both the material and immaterial aspects of reality really exist. But the empiricist has ruled out the immaterial aspects—essences and purposes, formal and final causes—as being misleading detours on the road to knowledge. The only thing which really exists and so which the mind really knows is the material. The mind itself, however, is immaterial.[45] How, then, does it know that with which it is incompatible? A consistent empiricist can only answer that the mind, in the end, does not know reality.

Summary of the transition in worldviews

Having tracked the shift from one worldview to another, in their most important notions, it will be helpful to review the starting and ending points of the shift. At point A, you have the medieval view of the world, wherein all is in harmony. A benevolent God creates a material universe which is ordered, knowable, and serves the interests of man. Man looks out at the world around him and, using reason alone, perceives a hierarchical chain of being:

- at the bottom of the chain are inert, non-living things, such as rocks, of greater or lesser complexity
- then come living things, with plants at the bottom, then animals, then man
- at the top is God, ultimate foundation for the ordered universe, as well as its purpose.

Reality is of one piece, each being occupying a determined level of reality and having some connection with the other beings in their respective levels.

At point B is the empiricist view developed in the seventeenth century. The universe is a conglomerate of physical bodies, that consist solely of quantitative extension. God invents the material bodies and starts them on their journey, but is not responsible for their continuance in being, as they are able to run by means of mathematical laws alone. Man looks out at the world and does not see being, but only mechanical motions, quantities and formulas which represent them. As for himself, man does not really know where he fits in the machine, nor can he explain philosophically how it is that he can know it, whether he decides that he is part of the machine or not.

It is a reality wherein the players have no proper roles and so cannot be on the stage together acting out a single performance. God has no transcendent, primary causality; man has no lordship over the material world; the material world is a standalone unit, neither purposefully directed towards God's glory nor man's use.

In short, empiricism projects a reality that is incoherent from top to bottom, unknowable by humans, who find themselves in a foreign world, which is impervious to coherent scientific endeavour.

Table 8.2 *Transition in worldviews*

	Point A Medieval realism	Point B Seventeenth-century empiricism
Universe	The universe possesses aspects of all four causes, which can all be known by man.	The universe is a purely quantitative entity, known only by means of mathematical laws.
God	God, as Creator and Conserver, gives being to all creation and maintains it in being.	God creates material bodies, but does not sustain them in existence.
Man	The universe is for man, and man is for God.	Man is either a purely material component of the universe, or entirely separate from it.
Causality	Matter, form, agency, purpose	Matter and agency only

4. Mental confinement exercised by empiricism

This brings us to the fourth scrape into which science is pinned by an empiricism that supposedly serves it. Recall the starting point of empiricism, its original error: the world outside of us is purely material. Recall that the original error of religionists was a similar extreme: the world outside of us is purely spiritual, that is, it is only the action of God (occasionalists), or at least only what God tells us it is through revelation (creationists). Now, *what is interesting about these two diverse starting points is that they lead to the very same ending points.* Just as religious idealism led to theologism and philosophism, so too does empiricism, in a certain way. How so? Because both positions divide humans in two, making them choose between body and soul, earth and heaven, matter and mind, reality and God—without making it possible for a person to keep both.

If we start with the premise that the outside world is purely material, then we are left with two choices:

1. **Empiricist theologist (soul only)**—the human immaterial mind is incompatible with the purely material world outside of it
   - consequently, human ideas do not come from the outside world, but from within
   - consequently, the only way for me to know that the outside world exists is if God reveals it to me
   - consequently, all that I know comes directly from God
   - consequently, all that is real for me comes directly from God.

2. **Empiricist philosophist (body only)**—the human mind knows the outside world, which is purely material
   - consequently, our minds are purely material
   - consequently, humans are mere conglomerations of atoms
   - consequently, all spiritual realities, such as free will, design, God, causality, reason, are non-existent
   - consequently, everything is meaningless.

It was René Descartes (1596–1650) who set empirical thinkers off on the first path. He held, among other things, that the methods of mathematics were to be applied to all reality (empiricism), instead of there being a different method appropriate for discovering different aspects of reality (realism).[46] The torch was passed down this path by such thinkers as Leibniz, Spinoza, and Malebranche, being brought to its final terminus by Berkeley, who held that ideas and spirits make up the whole of reality.

While the journey down the road of empiricist-driven idealism (!) is fascinating in its own right, you might find Gilson's masterful guided tour in chapters 6 and 7 of his *The Unity of the Philosophic Experience* a useful first exposure. In it, he cites Faydit's pithy summary of the entire movement: 'He who sees all in God, there, sees not he is mad'.[47]

More germane to our direction in this section is the philosophist path engendered by the empiricist first principle, the path whose principles ultimately triumphed in the Western world and reign today. One of its torchbearers was Sir Isaac Newton (1642–1727), and he will showcase the fifth empiricism-inflicted injury on science: leading scientists to become absurd metaphysicians.

5. Newton and empiricist metaphysics

Alexander Pope quipped of Newton that 'God said, Let there be light. And then there was Newton.' There is no question that he was a genius of the first rank, even towering above other figures in a century of geniuses. The insight leading him to assimilate the movement of bodies on Earth to those in the heavens, and formulate a law for all of them—that insight alone was sufficient to render his name immortal.

Jaki is at pains in his Gifford Lectures to show that Newton, when working as a scientist, was a realist.[48] Sir Isaac was engaged in a 'gigantic struggle for truth about physical reality';[49] he upheld the validity of forming concepts from sense data;[50] and he insisted on squaring those concepts with observations made by the senses.[51]

This realism is certainly true of Newton, and indeed of all scientists, as Jaki shows exhaustively in his many books. After all, it is impossible to do science without being a realist, because it is impossible to know anything without being a realist. Humans are created realists and only sidestep their ontological makeup by playing a part. Thus, we should not be surprised to find Newton trusting the abilities of both his senses and intellect when formulating his great physical theories.

Isaac Newton (Image courtesy of Wikimedia Commons)

What I am aiming to highlight in this book, however, is intellectual inconsistency and its nefarious effects. We are not so much concerned with thinkers in this or that aspect of their intellectual endeavour, but rather their theory of knowledge as a whole—their epistemology. When we come to Newton, we find that he was a fantastic realist when wearing his scientific hat, but terribly unrealistic when he switched to philosophy. The reason is quite simple: he decried philosophy and then proceeded to philosophise.

Firstly, while Galileo ignored philosophy, Newton abhorred it. What moved him to this revulsion was his attached-at-the-hip relationship to the scientific method.[52] As we saw in chapter 3, that method requires that theories be constructed solely from experimental data—no hypotheses are to be framed which are not subject to direct experimental, quantitative verification.[53] But no philosophical position—realism included—is subject to scientific measurement. Thus, if, as was the case with Newton, you only accept that which can be revealed by the scientific method, you will tend to discredit philosophy.

Newton had been so successful in formulating physical laws directly from experimental phenomena that he decided to make that method the benchmark for truth.[54] Any proposition not constructed by means of it he disdainfully referred to as an hypothesis, in the same breath disassociating himself from engaging in such disgraceful mental behaviour. *'Hypotheses non fingo'* was his famous dictum ('I don't come up with hypotheses'). It was another case of a brilliant mind taking his favourite mode of finding truth and requiring that all truth be found that way.

There is at least one major problem with this, however: it leaves no room for the ideas upon which science rests. For instance, nothing can be said about reality as such, nor 'about the nature of the universe at large.' Newton is assuming that 'it is possible to acquire truths about things without presupposing any theory of their ultimate nature; it is possible to have a correct knowledge of the part without knowing the nature of the whole'.[55] No such thing is possible, however: one cannot discourse on quantitative aspects of beings without first presupposing that they are beings.

Newton thought that he could go ahead and do science without taking anything from philosophy and even while denouncing philosophy as a legitimate avenue to truth. This position, however, is itself a philosophy, an epistemology, and eventually, a metaphysics. Newton sets out his positivist exclusion of philosophy and, in doing so, is caught philosophising.

> The attempt to escape metaphysics is no sooner put in the form of a proposition than it is seen to involve highly significant metaphysical postulates ... The only way to avoid becoming a metaphysician is to say nothing.[56]

Science Suicide 337

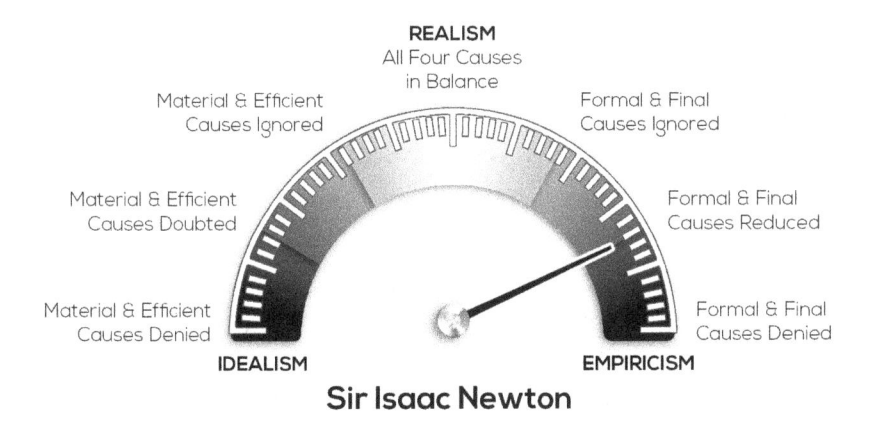

REALISM
All Four Causes in Balance

Material & Efficient Causes Ignored — Formal & Final Causes Ignored

Material & Efficient Causes Doubted — Formal & Final Causes Reduced

Material & Efficient Causes Denied — Formal & Final Causes Denied

IDEALISM — EMPIRICISM

Sir Isaac Newton

Thus, a scientist becomes a philosopher the moment he extends his scientific method to the entire realm of knowledge. What kind of philosopher? The worst kind, those who are philosophers without realising it, formulators of philosophical systems without systematic thinking.

> What kind of metaphysics are you likely to cherish when you sturdily suppose yourself to be free from the abomination? Of course it goes without saying that in this case your metaphysics will be held uncritically because it is unconscious.[57]

Philosophising with your eyes shut is dangerous activity, because the willy-nilly philosopher is unable to see the ultimate consequences of his position or think outside of it. Burtt lists three characteristics of the philosopher who denounces philosophy, before applying them to Newton:[58]

1. He will hold the ideas of his age on ultimate questions.

2. He will tend to make a metaphysics out of the method he uses in his particular field of study, supposing 'the universe ultimately of such a sort that his method must be appropriate and successful.'
3. When he deals with ultimate questions, because he has 'refused to school [himself] in careful metaphysical thinking, [his] ventures at such points will be apt to appear pitiful, inadequate, or even fantastic.'

With regard to the first, Newton 'took over without criticism the general view of the physical world and of humanity's place in it which had developed at the hands of his illustrious predecessors'.[59] He swallowed whole the idea of his day that secondary qualities are purely subjective impulses produced in our brains, not possessing any extramental reality.[60] He also latched onto a popular interpretation of Descartes' writings, which held that 'the human mind is a unique but small substance imprisoned in the brain'.[61]

Meanwhile, Newton's discovery of three laws of physical motion, experimentally verifiable, unknown to past ages, universal in scope, and in opposition to the physics of the great Aristotle, turned him into a demi-god of knowledge in the eyes of his contemporaries. Seeing him a giant in science, they assumed a like stature of him in philosophy, when he was actually a metaphysical midget. With realism in desuetude, impotent to command the attention it formerly had, the seventeenth-century popular mind clung to Newton as to an oracle of learning, able to sweep aside the old, pre-scientific worldview with one hand, and usher in a new, scientific one with the other. But Newton did not discover a worldview; he only discovered laws of motion pertaining to physical bodies. He was capable of replacing Aristotle's physics, but not his metaphysics. Yet it seemed almost natural for Newton to move from exposing his universal law of gravitation to discoursing on the universe and reality as a whole, and for the whole world to follow him.

Science Suicide

The impact on the human psyche from selecting Sir Isaac as the Western world's Delphic voice was devastating:

> [N]ow the great Newton's authority was squarely behind that view of the cosmos which saw in man a puny, irrelevant spectator ... of the vast mathematical system whose regular motions according to mechanical principles constituted the world of nature ... The world that people had thought themselves living in—a world rich with colour and sound, redolent with fragrance, filled with gladness, love and beauty, speaking everywhere of purposive harmony and creative ideals—was crowded now into minute corners in the brains of scattered organic beings. The really important world outside was a world hard, cold, colourless, silent, and dead; a world of quantity, a world of mathematically computable motions in mechanical regularity.[62]

The second characteristic of philosophy eschewing metaphysicians—their tendency to find the method of their field of study appropriate for all reality—we have already seen in Newton, mentioned in passing about Descartes, and applied to just about every figure mentioned in this book deviating from realism. Thus, we turn to find the third characteristic in Newton: bumbling in natural theology.

The first thing to be noted on this score is that, though Burtt speaks of Newton as a 'pious, believing Christian',[63] Newton neither believed in creation in time nor in the divinity of Jesus Christ, two dogmas which, as we saw in chapter 5, provided the vital insights needed to overthrow Aristotle's pantheism-motivated physics. Failing belief in those two propositions, Newton was open to a reversion to the science stifling pre-Christian ideas of an eternal universe and a deity barely separate from that universe. Without a realist metaphysics to balance him, Newton went beyond openness to such a reversion to actual reversion.

When Newton turned to extend his physics to all of reality, a sizeable difficulty awaited him: what sort of universe exists for one who is both an empiricist and a theist at the same time? After all, empiricism conflicts with theism. The former holds that all true knowledge is knowledge of material things. God, however, is not material. Thus, God is not knowable for an empiricist.

Getting rid of God was not an option for Newton, and he left that task to his empiricist successors. As for himself, he could not tolerate a godless universe. Newton would keep God by constructing *hypotheses* about God outside the strict confines of the scientific method—the very thing he said he did not do. At the same time, Newton would construct a God closely wed to the mathematical universe he had discovered. Being so smitten by the wonder that all material objects obeyed geometrical laws, Newton decided that those laws were the ultimate end of reality, and made God their servant. His God was a quasi-scientific God, not in charge of metaphysics—being—but in charge of mechanics—becoming. In the end, *Newton moved the universe toward God and God toward the universe*, in two ways:

1. Newton wanted an absolute reference point for all motion, so that the universe would be mathematically simple. For this to happen, the universe had to be *infinite* in space and time.[64] From this perspective, though, 'the world outside of man appeared nothing but a huge machine—God appeared to be swept out of existence and there was nothing to take his place but these boundless mathematical beings'.[65] In order to keep God, then, Newton made the divine consciousness 'the ultimate centre of reference for absolute motion'.[66] God does the universe service, providing a fixed point from which mathematical calculations can be done. Meanwhile, with the universe becoming infinite, its infinity could easily be identified with God's infinity. Later thinkers, in fact, would hold to an infinite universe without an infinite God.

2. Newton recognised that there were certain irregularities in the cosmos and that it would eventually break down if it were not periodically corrected.[67] Wanting to preserve the smooth running of the universe, and hence its infinity and

mathematical regularity, Newton assigned to God the task of keeping the universe in tune. In this way, God was not conceived of as exercising a primary causality over being, but rather as exercising a difficult secondary causality, the periodic re-calibration of universe's energy. Later thinkers would attribute this tuning of the universe to merely natural causes. In this system, God is no longer in charge of being, of providing that fundamental layer of causality without which nothing exists. He is rather a 'God of the gaps', jumping in when necessary to correct irregularities perceived by scientists on Earth, enabling them to explain why the universe has continued forever in such good working order.[68] He is a toiler on the level of secondary causality just like the rest of Creation, only on a broader scale than us mere mortals. He keeps us reassured that the cosmos will not lack the attention it needs, for the divine eye is 'constantly roaming the universe on the search for leaks to mend, or gears to replace in the mighty machinery'.[69]

Now, it is clearly absurd to maintain that God exists for the universe that He Himself created, that His job in life is to maintain a cosmic planetarium in good working order. Yet such was the metaphysics which Newton formed under the hypnotic influence of his physical laws. Furthermore, in the view of this metaphysics, the only reason that God is needed at any given moment is to make sure that the universe stays on track. It did not seem to enter into Newton's mind that God could be okay with the universe dissipating its energy over time, and so he assigned God the job of intervening as necessary with acts of His will to re-calibrate the cosmic cogs so they can run forever.

But 'to stake the present existence and activity of God on imperfections in the cosmic engine was to court rapid disaster for theology'.[70] For what if the irregularities that Newton perceived were not irregularities at all, but part of the running order of the universe-machine? What need would there then be of a cosmic mechanic? Would it not then seem as if the universe had no need of God, at least of the Newtonian breed of deity?

The fundamental problem is that, *when God is made a secondary cause, He is placed in competition with His own creation for causal activity.* Reality is seen as having only one layer of explanation, the area of secondary causality. Once a secondary cause is given for a certain effect, nothing else is to be said. Thus, only natural causes or God can be responsible for this effect, but not both. If both God and nature exist in reality, it can only be because they exercise causality over different sections of reality. 'Over here, we have nature working, and over there, God is working. Yes, we have found natural causes to explain the universe running all by itself, but don't worry! There is still something for God to do; He periodically adjusts that running.'

The scientists succeeding Newton made his secondary-causality God non-existent, showing that the universe's irregularities are not corrected at all. Thus, Newton's 'cherished theology was rapidly peeled off by all the competent hands that could get at him, and the rest of his metaphysical entities and assumptions, shorn of their religious setting, were left to wander naked and unabashed through the premises of subsequent thought'.[71]

Philosophers coming after Newton, especially Kant (1724–1804), thought they could not return to realism, for it was Aristotelian and so seemed to be wedded to the Stagirite's false physics. The only thing to be done was construct a better metaphysics on top of Newton's physics than Newton himself had done, while maintaining Newton's empiricist epistemology. That epistemology, however, led straight to critical doubt about the ability of the mind to form correct ideas about reality. Moreover, with God no longer in existence to help human knowledge, the only possible conclusion was that 'certainty of knowledge is decidedly and closely limited, if indeed the very existence of knowledge at all is possible'.[72]

By the nineteenth century, none of the philosophical currents could account for the elements upon which all science rests:

being, causality, God, universe. Each of those notions had been remade to serve a reality assumed to be solely quantitative. Only the original meanings of those words, however, could give logical support to scientific endeavour. Thus, by demanding that its own methods be applied to the whole of reality, science had destroyed its own presuppositions. Refusing to receive its fundamental notions from realism, it established itself on incoherence.

Chapter summary

The medieval Christian worldview wedded to realist philosophy engendered a vision of a reality that was ordered, knowable, accommodated to human nature's intrinsic makeup. This worldview, however, dissolved under the pressures of Church corruption, Scholastic decadence, and the advent of Protestantism. Realism continued on as a fundamental disposition of Catholic minds, more as a subconscious instinct than a Church dogma. The world at large, though, was philosophically adrift, ready to latch onto whatever *Weltanschauung* (worldview) the *Zeitgeist* (spirit of the times) would breath forth.

In the seventeenth century, the *Zeitgeist* was decidedly scientific. The ordered balance which the medieval mind had established toward the material world finally led to a full application of the scientific method in probing reality. The method was practised by experimentation and its findings were expressed in the language of mathematics. They were findings that left the world speechless.

The new scientists themselves were most stricken and hastened to stretch their scientific method to the whole of reality. They set about relating all being to the movement of material bodies. All else, in their mind, was only in the mind. If you are not a quantity or at least relative to one, you don't count.

This primal metaphysical assumption on the part of philosophy-eschewing scientists begot new notions of God, man, universe, and causality. The universe became a purely material machine, God its designer and fixer-upper, man its resident alien, and causality only that which makes bodies move. A wedge had been firmly driven between qualities and quantities, form and matter, soul and body. Knowledge and even reality could now only belong to the latters, not the formers.

Exact science, like a brute giant waking from aeons of slumber, roared out its neglected rights with deafening din, practically drowning out the voice of all other intellectual disciplines in the ears of the academic elite. The stature of wisdom passed down through ages in the Western tradition seemed to shrink down to a Lilliputian littleness, scarcely to be descried in science's shadow.

Like so many giants of yore, the newly born science turned out to be an overgrown ogre, pulverising reality into little quantitative bits and confining its most ardent devotees into a dark intellectual prison, from which cell countless discoveries would come forth, but only combined with an incoherent cacophony of ravings about the world outside the gaol of quantity.

Just as tyrants are the ones who suffer most from their own tyranny, so too an oversized science, swollen into a metaphysical system, ultimately commits self-slaughter in overstepping its bounds. It empties its own method of consistency, atrophies its own proofs, and cripples the minds of its practitioners, by forcing them to hold false notions about non-scientific entities, choose either the poison of empiricist theologism or empiricist philosophism, and babble nonsense in metaphysics.

Seemingly, the reduction of reality to a series of bodies jostling according to Newton's laws would be a most dissatisfying outlook for an age and culture. Not so. The centuries following the seventeenth, far from keeping Newtonian physics while jettisoning his metaphysics, ran with both. Where did they run with them? Into all manner of irrationality.

Having seen the general types of trouble science gets into with an empiricist mindset, we will consider, in the next chapters, particular species of contradictory conclusions officially described as scientific. Chapter 9 will target empiricist physicists; chapter 10, empiricist biochemists; and chapter 11, empiricist evolutionary biologists.

Notes

[1] Act I, scene 3.
[2] Act III, scene 1.
[3] Act III, scene 2, 272–282.
[4] This and what follows in Act IV, scene 1.
[5] See Ps 7:16; 56:7; 93:13.
[6] *The Road of Science and the Ways to God* (Port Huron, Michigan: Real View Books, 2005), p. 50.
[7] C. S. Lewis, in his *Miracles* (Glasgow: Fount Paperbacks, 1947), p. 46, says that during the sixteenth century, 'men of science were coming to be metaphysically and theologically uneducated', thus leaving them without a means to correct the naturalistic bent of their scientific minds.
[8] *The Sleepwalkers* (London: Penguin Classics, 2014), p. 174.
[9] In *Ibid.*, p. 186, Koestler notes that 'Cosmology at the end of the Middle Ages was saturated with vague notions of a spinning and moving earth'.
[10] Jaki, *The Road of Science*, p. 46.
[11] See S. Jaki, *Questions on Science and Religion* (Pinckney, Michigan: Real View Books, 2004), p. 186.
[12] E. Burtt, *The Metaphysical Foundations of Modern Science* (Mineola, New York: Dover Publications, 2003), p. 52, emphasis in original.
[13] *Ibid.*, p. 62.
[14] The laws are so famous that they even appear in dictionaries such as *The New Oxford American Dictionary* (Oxford University Press, Inc., 2005), under 'Kepler's laws': 'The first law states that planets move in elliptical orbits with the sun at one focus. The second states that the radius vector of a planet sweeps out equal areas in equal times. The third law relates the distances of the planets from the sun to their orbital periods.'
[15] Burtt, *Metaphysical Foundations*, p. 68.
[16] *Categories*, 6a20.
[17] See, for example, *A Mind's Matter* (Grand Rapids, Michigan: William Eerdmans Publishing Company, 2002), p. 172; *The Mirage of Conflict* (New Hope, Kentucky: Real View Books, 2009), p. 45.
[18] 995a15; translation R. McKeon, *The Basic Works of Aristotle* (New York: Random House, 1941), p. 715.
[19] Burtt, *Metaphysical Foundations*, p. 67.
[20] *Ibid.*
[21] Cited in *Ibid.*
[22] Oxford University Press, Inc., 2005.
[23] Jaki, *The Road of Science*, p. 66.

[24] S. Jaki, *Science and Creation* (New York, Science History Publications, 1974), p. 276. See also his *The Paradox of Olbers' Paradox* (Pinckney, Michigan: Real View Books, 2000), p. 35.
[25] Koestler, *The Sleepwalkers*, p. 335.
[26] *Metaphysical Foundations*, pp. 203–204.
[27] *Scholastic Metaphysics* (Heusenstamm, Germany: Editiones Scholasticae, 2014), pp. 15–16. For a careful treatment of measurement being a measuring of qualities, see H. Relja, *Il Realismo di S. L. Jaki* (Rome: Ateneo Pontificio Regina Apostolorum, 2008), pp. 51–57.
[28] Feser, *Scholastic Metaphysics*, p. 17.
[29] W. Wallace, *The Modeling of Nature* (Washington, DC: The Catholic University of America Press, 1996), pp. 300–301.
[30] *Ibid.*, p. 282.
[31] W. Wallace, 'Galileo's Pisan studies in science and philosophy' in P. Machamer, ed., *The Cambridge Companion to Galileo* (Cambridge: Cambridge University Press, 1998), p. 49.
[32] Wallace, *The Modeling of Nature*, pp. 334–350.
[33] *Ibid.*, p. 247.
[34] *Ibid.*, p. 264.
[35] *Ibid.*, p. 416.
[36] *Ibid.*, pp. 248–249.
[37] *Ibid.*, p. 219.
[38] See the three essays on 'The Cult of Irrationalism in Science' in *Against the Idols of the Age* (Transaction Publishers, 1999).
[39] Wallace, *The Modeling of Nature*, p. 422.
[40] Burtt, *Metaphysical Foundations*, p. 99.
[41] *Ibid.*
[42] *Neo-Scholastic Essays* (South Bend, Indiana: St. Augustine's Press, 2015), p. 71.
[43] Burtt, *Metaphysical Foundations*, p. 103.
[44] *Ibid.*
[45] This fact that the mind is immaterial is traditionally proved by stating that everything material is composed of parts, but, for the mind to form notions of things, it cannot have material parts. See Aquinas, SCG, Book II, chapters 49–50. See also how Gödel's theorem on the inability of mathematics to supply its own consistency can be used to prove the immateriality of the mind in H. Relja, *Il Realismo*, p. 131. For a more popular proof, see D. Axe, *Undeniable* (New York: HarperOne, 2016), pp. 237–242.
[46] Jaki, *The Road of Science*, p. 66.
[47] Cited in E. Gilson, *The Unity of the Philosophic Experience* (London: Sheed

and Ward, 1938), p. 196.
48 *The Road of Science*, pp. 83–90.
49 *Ibid.*, p. 85.
50 *Ibid.*, p. 86.
51 *Ibid.*, p. 84. See also Wallace, *The Modeling of Nature*, pp. 360–361, for Newton's realist assumptions.
52 Burtt, *Metaphysical Foundations*, pp. 225–226.
53 See p. 77.
54 M. Heller remarks in his *Ultimate Explanations of the Universe* (Heidelberg: Springer-Verlag, 2009), p. 146, that 'nothing crystallizes a scientist's philosophical opinions as strongly as his own scientific achievements'.
55 Burtt, *Metaphysical Foundations*, p. 227.
56 *Ibid.*, pp. 228, 227.
57 *Ibid.*, p. 227.
58 *Ibid.*, p. 229.
59 *Ibid.*, p. 231.
60 *Ibid.*, p. 236.
61 *Ibid.*, p. 237.
62 *Ibid.*, pp. 238–239.
63 *Ibid.*, p. 285.
64 *Ibid.*, p. 256.
65 *Ibid.*, p. 258.
66 *Ibid.*, p. 261.
67 Jaki indicates these irregularities in his *Science and Creation*, p. 287: 'That the present course of Nature could not go on indefinitely was traced by Newton to two causes: friction in the ether and the mutual disturbance of the planets ... In 1713 ... Newton speculated about a third cause, the gradual loss of light and heat of the sun and stars.'
68 For Newton's theories setting up God of the gaps arguments, see M. Heller, *Ultimate Explanations*, pp. 148–149.
69 Burtt, *Metaphysical Foundations*, p. 298.
70 *Ibid.*
71 *Ibid.*, p. 299.
72 *Ibid.*, p. 301.

9 GODLIKE UNIVERSE

When I think what an Elixir is this Nothing I am for putting up a statue nowhere, on a pedestal that shall not exist, and for inscribing on it in letters that shall never be written:
TO NOTHING
THE HUMAN RACE IN GRATITUDE.

Hilaire Belloc

AS LATE AS the first decades of the 1900s, the human race still thought of the universe as consisting of a single galaxy, our own Milky Way. Telescopes were not yet able to peer keenly enough into the night sky to distinguish deep space objects from near space ones, and there was no good means for determining the distance of the objects viewed.[1] This all changed through the work of three astronomers: Henrietta Leavitt (1868–1921), Vesto Slipher (1875–1969), and Edwin Hubble (1889–1953).

Leavitt discovered a way to measure the distance to certain stars called Cepheid variables. Her job was to examine numerous photographs of the night sky taken on different days. She began to notice that variable stars, whose brightness in the sky varies over time, follow regular cycles of bright-dim-bright. Moreover, the *time* which it takes them to complete the cycle is correlative with the *amount* of light they emit. Thus, once Henrietta knew how long it took a variable star to complete its cycle, she also knew how bright it was in itself, regardless of its apparent brightness here on Earth. Then, she could use the apparent brightness of the star to us and its actual brightness in itself to calculate the star's distance. Leavitt went on in 1908 to publish a study of 1,777 variable stars whose behaviour she had tracked. This work became the basis of using Cepheid variables as a 'standard candle' or standard for the measurement of astronomical distances. Whenever such a star is located in a galaxy, its distance can be used to know the distance of the galaxy itself.[2]

Henrietta Leavitt (Image courtesy of Wikimedia Commons)

While Leavitt conquered *distance* calculation of remote stars, Vesto Slipher tackled *speed*.[3] He would take visible light from stars and nebulae, and measure the wavelength of that light. Objects moving *away* from us, he found, cast off light of a *longer* wavelength, because the light is being stretched by the motion of its carrier. Conversely, objects moving *towards* Earth emit light with a *shorter*, compressed wavelength. How does this relate to speed? Well, to the degree that the light's *stretching* is greater, so is the *speed* of its corresponding star greater. In addition, Slipher found that practically all of the objects in the sky emit longer wavelength light and so are moving away from us (no doubt a comforting thought).

The first person to get a good look at stars within galaxies other than our own was Edwin Hubble. In 1919, he started to make systematic use of the recently built 100-inch mirror telescope on

Mt. Wilson Observatory near Los Angeles, gazing into the will-o'-the-wisp cloudlike patches of the night sky known as nebulae. After locating Leavitt's Cepheid variables in these nebulae, he measured their distances in the millions of light years, a number far too great to include the nebulae in our own galaxy. This led him to conclude that the nebulae were themselves galaxies in their own right, and that our universe is composed of a veritable forest of galaxies, separated by vast reaches of empty space.

Edwin Hubble (Image courtesy of Wikimedia Commons)

But Hubble also knew the speed of clumpy sky objects by means of Slipher's work, and he was in a position to be the first to compare the distance and speed of the objects. What he discovered is that they have a precise mathematical relationship: they are directly proportional, that is, *the distance of galaxies from us is greater in proportion as their speed is greater.* Thus, 'if we look at two galaxies and one is twice as far away from us as the other, then the farther galaxy will be moving away from us twice as fast as the closer galaxy'.[4]

The astounding conclusion that follows from night sky objects moving away from us, and at greater speeds when they are farther away, is that the universe is expanding.[5] In addition, if the universe has been *consistently* expanding throughout its history, then going back into the past of the universe's history is simply a question of contracting it. Thus, it had to be more compact 100 years ago, more compact than that 1,000 years ago, and so on, until the universe, at a given point of time in the past, was the size of a mere point, that is, no size at all. The first person to propose this idea was a Belgian priest, Fr Georges Lemaître. He had solved the equations for Einstein's theory of general relativity and found they predicted that the universe was expanding. Lemaître then steered the universe backwards in time and held that the whole thing started as what he called a 'primeval atom',[6] a beginning for the universe to which Fred Hoyle gave the derogatory label 'big bang'.[7]

Fr Georges Lemaître (Image courtesy of Wikimedia Commons)

What is important to note is that both Hubble and Lemaître had found scientific evidence pointing to the universe having a beginning in time, before which point—to all appearances—there was nothing of the universe. In a Christian age, this would have been a stimulus for proclaiming all the more the glory of the Creator (Pope Pius XII actually did just that in the 1951 address quoted in chapter 7, wherein he gave support to the Big Bang Theory).[8] For scientists set on a purely materialistic explanation of the universe, however, evidence that it had a beginning could only provoke disturbance. At the very least, a godless universe must be an eternal one, not one so radically contingent as to be brought into being in a moment of time. Yet here was science itself casting stark evidence of its own createdness in the face of atheistic scientists, and so providing indirect evidence of a Creator. None of this was lost upon the late NASA astronomer Robert Jastrow. He famously commented on the impact of science's proof of the universe's beginning on himself and other strict empiricists as follows:

> For the scientist who has lived by his faith in the power of reason, the story ends like a bad dream. He has scaled the mountain of ignorance; he is about to conquer the highest peak; as he pulls himself over the final rock, he is greeted by a band of theologians who have been sitting there for centuries.[9]

The solution for Jastrow, it would seem, is simple: If science is pointing to God, and you believe in science, then why not believe in God? But it was not simple at all. In the end, it was impossible for Jastrow to reconcile to science what science itself was teaching him, as he himself confessed in 2004, four years before his death:

> Just as I can't believe that there is a Creator, I can't believe that this all happened by chance, which implies there was a Creator. So, you see, I'm in a completely hopeless bind. And I stay there. Again, I find it hard to believe that this is all a matter of atoms and molecules. And so, I try to fit into my model of the world the conclusion that there is a

larger force of some kind ... But I can't accept that. I'm what's called a materialist in philosophy. It means that I believe the world consists entirely of material substances. And when you specify those substances, the atoms and molecules and the laws by which they interact, you've done it all. There isn't anything more to be said or inserted in your model of the universe. That's what my science tells me ... but I find it unsatisfactory. In fact, it makes me uneasy. I feel that I'm missing something. But I will not find out what I'm missing within my lifetime.[10]

Thus, instead of following the evidence to its logical conclusion, Jastrow's will forced his intellect to stop short of judging that God is at the origin of what science investigates. In his empiricism, Jastrow had elevated science to a deified metaphysics, alone capable of yielding knowledge and ultimately capable of explaining all. Science, refusing Jastrow's deification, had produced astounding evidence that, instead of being able to provide ultimate causal knowledge, science itself relies radically on an ultimate, ineffable, transcendent First Cause. That, at least, was the reasonable conclusion to be drawn. Reason, however, was being blocked, arrested in its pursuit of ultimate fulfilment, by an ideology acting as a religious faith, requiring its conclusions to be maintained blindly, even when all the evidence rendered them untenable.

In this chapter, we must consider how empiricism defeats reason in those scientists, the physicists, who seek to give ultimate explanations of the universe through physical laws alone.

Making the universe unreasonable

We tend to think of scientists as the most objective people in the world, because it is their duty to inspect the hard facts of reality. Our imagination turns to the hallowed clean room where dutiful and meticulous droves of researchers carefully conduct their experiments, taking down data under the sagacious eye of the lab master, a wizened old man with Einsteinian hair, upright in his bleached lab coat, easily abstracted into a fit of mathematical calculations, relentlessly following the evidence wherever it leads. How could such an environment yield anything but pure truth?

But the fact is that scientists are much more than computing machines; they are human beings. What this means is that it is impossible for them to show up at their job as detached, disembodied intellects. Rather, like the rest of us, they apply themselves to their work as persons, with all the complexity that personhood implies. They do not crunch numbers or reason in a vacuum, but according to the complete manifold of their individual characteristics, the totality of what they are, both the good and the bad.

At the end of the day, sense data does not speak for itself. It needs a mind to interpret it and, in the case of scientists, to construct a mathematical model to fit it. Moreover, the *way* that this mind or that mind will read into the data depends on many more factors than their education and intellectual ability. Indeed, one of the most important of those extra factors is the worldview by which the scientist as *person* tends to regard the whole of reality.

In this chapter, I would like to perform a case study of scientists who, by and large, have a materialistic worldview, that is, a 'philosophical belief that the material world is the only reality that exists'.[11] By no means do I wish to imply that all scientists are materialists; theistic scientists have far outnumbered atheistic ones in the history of mankind. I leave believing scientists to the side, however, because they do not adopt that radical rejection of realism which is empiricism as their dominant narrative. We must here investigate empiricism and its corrosive effects on human reason, and atheistic scientists are perfect examples of its irrational endgame. By definition, empiricism demands at least agnosticism, for it claims that everything not falling under the senses is unknowable. And the senses certainly cannot perceive God.

REALISM
Both Spirit & Matter Exist

IDEALISM
Only Spirit Exists

EMPIRICISM
Only Matter Exists

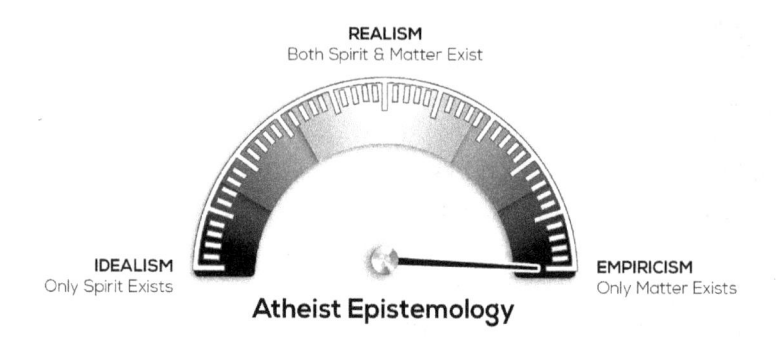

Atheist Epistemology

The task that empiricists set for human reason is most difficult: explain all of reality by means of material causes alone. It is like one of those MacGyver episodes where the lead has to save the world and the only tools he has available are a pocket knife and duct tape. We say to the hero, 'Okay, you ready? Here's your toolkit with subatomic particles and the laws of their interactions. By the end of the program, you have to use it to explain the whole of reality. Go!' After suffering through the program and the commercial breaks, G. K. Chesterton announces to a crestfallen MacGyver, 'I admit that your explanation explains a great deal; but what a great deal it leaves out!'[12]

We do not have space to consider all of the desperate attempts of atheistic physicists to stretch atoms wide enough to cover the nakedness of a godless universe, and so we will limit ourselves to four. To be precise, we will consider their attempts to explain four aspects of the universe without having recourse to divinity or any concepts that lead to divinity, especially formal and final causes. The key pattern that will develop in the course of the analysis is that *atheistic scientists, in order to cling to their worldview, are ineluctably led to remove intelligibility from the universe. They attack reason instead of changing their faith.*

The table below anticipates the positions to be taken by godless scientists on the four aspects of the universe. Now, we must consider those aspects one at a time.

Table 9.1 Two views on the universe

Aspects of the universe	The theist realist's view on each aspect	The atheist empiricist's view on each aspect
Size	Finite	Infinite
Change	Universe gets older	Universe stays the same
Configuration	Fine-tuned	Homogeneous
Cause	God	Nothing

The size of the universe

Types of infinity

We saw in the last chapter that Newton conceived the universe as being infinite in order to attribute to it a mathematical simplicity.[13] God's job was to serve as an absolute reference point for all movements within the mathematical universe, to provide that simplicity. Atheist scientists, latching onto Newtonian ideas, thought they saw in them a way to bump God out of the way. The reason is that an infinite universe *can appear* not to have need of a deity. Thus,

> those, mostly philosophers, who endorsed the idea of an infinite universe almost invariably saw in it a convenient excuse for dispensing with a truly transcendental God.[14]

The reason for this false appearance is that infinity is clearly an attribute of Deity. Whatever is finite can make no claim to being God. Thus, an atheist might argue, if infinity belongs to God, and the universe is infinite, then the universe must be God. The problem with this argumentation, besides committing the fallacy of the accident, is that the word 'infinite' is being used in two different senses. For surely, if God is infinite, He is so by an *immaterial* infinity, while if the universe is infinite, it is so by a *material* infinity.

To qualify as being infinite, it is necessary not to have any boundaries or limitations, anything closing off or confining. Now God is infinite, as Aquinas explains, because 'God's existence is not received into anything, but He is His own subsisting existence.'[15] What this means is that God is a self-existing being without having any container or essence to constrain His existence in any way, to put limits on it. In other words, the absence of limits or infinity that pertains to God is at the level of being. He is infinite as 'a being without limits.'

Now, it is quite clear that the universe cannot be infinite in this way. For one thing, the universe must be limited in being, by the very fact that it is spread out in space. It does not act from a single point, with a single, unlimited power, but rather over a vast range of space in which very limited and determined powers are exercised. For instance, one thing heats in this place and another thing cools over there, but nothing in the universe both heats and cools at the same time, from a single point. The matter of the universe, then, does not have a single, unified power, but one that is divided, being broken into many limited segments. This indicates that the being of the universe as a whole must be limited. Besides, as Jaki insightfully points out, even if we could ascribe an infinity to the universe, we would still have to ask: Why are there finite things at all?, a question certainly not answered by an infinite universe.[16]

But anyway, the universe is not even a substance! In other words, it is not a single, subsisting, unified being, but is rather a composite of a vast array of material beings. It is not an individual existing thing, but a conglomerate of all individually existing material things.

So much for the universe's bid for a divine infinity. Given that many atheists satisfy themselves with an apparent reasoning, however, we should still ask ourselves whether the universe has a non-divine material infinity, an infinity in size. Such a universe would not have any limits in space: it would go on forever in every direction. The first thing to be noted is that an infinite quantity is a contradiction in terms. It is the equivalent of an infinite number, a number without limits. No such number can ever exist, since every number has a specific limit just by being a number. To see this, say we pick any number, like 58,921,752,839,201. It is a big number, but one that indicates a specific and limited sum of units. We could choose a bigger number but it would have the same problem. Even if I typed out a number that occupied the next 50 pages of this book, the final product would still be a finite number, since I would have stopped. The bottom line, then, is that quantities by their very nature have limits, and what has limits cannot be infinite. But the universe is a material quantity. Thus, the universe cannot be materially infinite.[17]

This sort of realist reasoning, which takes seriously our concepts formed from reality, does not have traction with empiricist types, and so scientists took another idea quite seriously for three centuries: the idea that the universe is infinite in space. We already saw in the last chapter that scientists easily make bad philosophers and thus we should not be surprised that they pursued a philosophically irrational idea for hundreds of years.[18] Rather, what should surprise us is that *an infinite universe was also a scientifically bad idea, yet its scientific problems were largely glossed over until overwhelming evidence against it appeared in the twentieth century.*

Belief in an infinite universe

Jaki tracks this tale with great thoroughness in his book *The Paradox of Olbers' Paradox*. He points out that the Anglican minister Richard Bentley (1662–1742) was the first to point out, on empirical grounds, a problematic paradox with an infinite universe.[19] Between 1692 and 1693, Bentley exchanged a series of letters with Newton, after reading the latter's *Principia*, wanting to assure himself that arguments he was going to make on behalf of a finite universe were sound.

What the *Principia* provided Bentley was the notion of a law of gravitation that works throughout the universe. If the universe is infinite in space and time, however, then gravity must have been working on the heavenly bodies *forever*. When gravity works on bodies forever, one of two things must happen:

- If all matter is in perfect equilibrium: no matter can coalesce and form large bodies, since all gravitational forces cancel one another out.
- If all matter is not in equilibrium: all pieces of matter will exercise gravitational pull, such that heavier bodies will draw in lighter bodies, and they must eventually coalesce into a single mass.

Since both scenarios contradict what we currently observe, it is impossible for the universe to be infinite, at least if Newton's law of gravitation holds true.

Newton did not believe this paradox carried much weight, but he did not have much to refute it either, and Bentley went on with his lectures supporting a finite universe in order 'to defend the cause of religion in the face of the growing rationalistic if not atheistic trends eager to exploit science'.[20]

The gravitational paradox was not the only scientific argument that could be set against an infinite universe. There was also the optical paradox, first put in print by Edmund Halley (1656–1742), of Halley's comet fame. Halley wrote two papers in support of an infinite universe, and addressed in them objections against his thesis. Besides the gravitational paradox, says Halley, some have urged him that the night sky would not be dark if the universe were infinite.[21] The reason is that an infinite universe would have stars throughout it in every direction and light from those stars would reach Earth in such a way that the entire sky would be lit up, just as it is when the sun is up. Night would be day, and so there would be no night.

Jaki laments the lack of seriousness with which Halley addressed the gravitational and optical paradoxes. He did not 'follow mathematical rigor' in regard to the former and, as for the latter:

Godlike Universe 361

> The obviously confident tone with which Halley disposed of the paradox is worth noting. It shows clearly the inhibitory role played by an almost blind faith in infinity. It fatally predisposed even the best scientific minds against considering in depth some problems of the infinity of the universe.[22]

Interestingly enough, blind faith in the infinity of the universe also afflicted believers in God. As telescopes improved, they peered deeper and deeper into space, and what did the scopes reveal but more and more stars? This scientific fact worked on popular imagination as overwhelming support for an infinite universe, and there was no philosophical realism to stand in the way. As such, 'it served as an implicit matrix of scientific thought throughout the eighteenth century'.[23] Moreover, since philosophy built off empiricism, not philosophy built off reality, was now driving worldviews, the only thing for a believer to do was to hold that an infinite universe gave glory to an infinite God. Kant even went so far as to say that such a universe was the only one 'that could come forth from the hands of the Creator with infinite powers',[24] an idea refuted in several places by Aquinas.[25]

With both scientists and believers unable to topple the idea of an infinite quantity by realist philosophical arguments (with exceptions, of course[26]), the idea maintained its grip on them for centuries. Even the scientific difficulties were unable to engender a sufficiently healthy anxiety. One sign of this is that the name affixed to the stellar light paradox—that of Wilhelm Olbers (1758–1840)—was not the name of its original proposer, but of one who wrote a paper on it 100 years later, in 1823.[27] Olbers, who was a theist, thought that light from the stars was absorbed in space in the proportion of 1/800, and this was sufficient to account for the sky's night-time darkness,[28] despite thermodynamics arguing that this cannot happen.[29]

Thus, the notion of an infinite universe traipsed its way through the centuries, leading whole civilisations in its train, while the universe itself, happily ensconced in its finitude, watched and waited for a wake-up call. It came with Einstein's Theory of Relativity and not a moment too soon. Around that time, you had figures like Lord Kelvin stating that '*finitude* is incomprehensible, the infinite in the universe is comprehensible ... apply a little logic to this';[30] Bertrand Russell holding the 'homogeneity of an infinite universe as a scientific principle' to be 'established forever';[31] and astronomer William MacMillan finding the idea of a finite universe 'repugnant to most minds that have dwelt upon the subject'.[32] Clearly, it would take an object of enormous weight to knock minds so religiously and irrationally attached to material infinity out of their trance.

Einstein roundly defeated material infinity, by scientific means, because his General Theory of Relativity requires that the total mass of the universe be finite, a mass for which he himself gave a formula.[33] If the weight of the universe as a whole is finite, then the universe itself must be finite. You would have thought that the scientific community would have breathed a sigh of relief, realising that the universe went from being a divine, uninvestigable entity, to being a finite, quantifiable one.[34] Indeed, those were the two alternatives for science. An infinite universe is beyond the reach of empirical investigation, while a finite one is not. Not surprisingly, striking calculations concerning the entirety of the universe have been made since Relativity.

Far from breathing a sigh of relief, however, scientists either took no notice of the restoration of 'the old notion of a finite closed world'[35] or lamented it, because now physicists would be able to figure the entire universe out and so lose interest in science![36]

Needless to say, after being converted from an idea that was stifling science to one that fosters it, scientists have not returned to the philosophical realism or Christian theism that gave birth to science in the first place.

The sameness of the universe

The tendency of the post-realist Western mind to fall back into pantheistic notions of the universe is not restricted to the aspect of its *size*, for it also comes into play in regard to its *sameness*. Again, it is a question of applying to the universe an attribute belonging to Deity, in this case immutability.

It is clear that God, to be a Supreme Being, must not change. For when one changes, it is either for better or for worse. But if God changes:

- **For the better:** God changing for the better means He is not a perfect being but an imperfect one, since He becomes better by changing. If He is improved by something else, however, that something else must be greater than Himself.

- **For the worse:** God changing for the worse means He possesses the attribute of corruptibility, wherein He can become more imperfect in His being. Just His being able to become imperfect would mean that He was not perfect in the first place.

In the words of Aquinas, 'Since God is infinite, containing in Himself the complete fullness of perfection of being itself, He cannot acquire anything, nor attain something that He had not previously attained.'[37] God is at the apex of perfection *in His very being*, such that any change whatsoever would necessarily be a step down from that perfection.

The materialist MacGyver, then, is faced with another enormous task in deifying matter: he has to make it unchanging. This is a tall order indeed, because matter is the very principle of change, as we saw in chapter 3.[38] We also saw that the ancients considered the heavens to be like unto the divine by moving in perfect, unchanging circles, and how the idea of eternal cycles was the greatest atrophying agent of science in human history. From this, it would seem that modern scientists would avoid similar ideas like the plague. Not so. The heavens must not declare the glory of God anymore, but their own—and our own—divinity.

Steady-State sameness

How are we to proceed? By means of the intrepid proponents of the Steady-State Theory. These were scientists of the first half of the twentieth century who were desperate to make the universe godlike in spite of all the scientific evidence pointing in the opposite direction. One of its champions was Herman Bondi, and he lists the assumptions of the theory as follows:

1. The average distance between stars and the average luminosity of each star are more or less the same throughout the universe. In other words, the universe is *homogeneous* when viewed on a large scale.

2. The general character of the universe is not only the same at all places but also at all times ... In other words the universe is *unchanging* in time when viewed on a large scale.

3. On an average, the relative velocity of any two stars vanishes, so that there are *no major systematic motions* in the universe.

4. The laws of physics as derived from our terrestrial experience apply throughout the universe.[39]

We hardly need to remark that the fourth assumption is that of uniformitarianism, an assumption which has a rational basis only if one believes in a Being transcendent to the universe able to legislate that it act in a strictly consistent fashion. The sameness of physical laws is a dependent, contingent, created sameness, wholly insufficient to ascribe divinity to the universe. Bondi, then, adds the first three assumptions to bolster that case. These assumptions, going beyond the attribution of a sameness in behaviour to the material components of the universe, attribute a sameness to the universe as such. In the minds of the Steady-State theorists, the universe *as a whole* has a sameness in time, place, density, and motion. Clearly, this is not an immutability in *being*, yet at the same time the universe is being treated as if it were a being and as if that being possessed many immutable aspects.

The amount of science that had to be studiously ignored for scientists to propose and stick to this theory was immense. Steady-State theorists had to admit from Hubble's observations that the universe was expanding, which in turn meant that the density of matter was necessarily decreasing. Instead of accepting, however, that the universe's matter is becoming thinner over time, they assured the world that it was remaining constant. How? By one hydrogen atom per cubic metre of the universe being created *from nothing* every 300,000 years.[40]

Now, by *nothing*, they were meaning non-being, the total absence of existence. Back in chapter 4, we quoted Democritus as saying 'Nothing can come into being from that which is not', and pointed out that the denial of this principle spells the destruction of reason.[41] The reason for this is clear: if non-being can act, then non-being is not nothing but something. Non-being is being. And if the negation of a thing is the same as the thing itself, then any attempt we would make to understand a being as being what it is would necessarily involve us in not understanding it. All reality would be unintelligible.

Epistemological realists and Biblical Christians hold that God is an all-powerful Creator, while these scientists were saying that nothing is a Creator. The former belief is firmly based upon reason, the latter on an utterly irrational faith. The contrast could not be greater, when one considers the hubris of so many members of today's scientocracy who cast disdain on religious belief as being irrational. This sort of hubris was also being exercised by the most famous name of the Steady-State theorists, Fred Hoyle. For him, the creation of all by God at one moment was 'an irrational process that cannot be described in scientific terms', while '[Hoyle's] continuous "creation" of hydrogen atoms was rational and scientific because "it can be represented by mathematical equations whose consequences can be worked out and compared with observations"'.[42] God creating with power proportionate to effect is irrational; Fred creating from his own imagination is rational.

Great damage is done to science by such scientists, for two reasons:

1. they expose the entire scientific enterprise to ridicule and mistrust on the part of the general public
2. they insert wilful and false ideology in the path of science's advance. As an example of this, consider that satellites went off looking for radiation predicted by Steady-Staters in the mid-1960s, but of course found nothing.[43]

Abandonment of Steady-State

In the end, such overwhelming evidence came in for the Big Bang Theory, ridiculed by Hoyle, that it became scientific orthodoxy. The universe was manifesting that, far from keeping itself in a constant equilibrium, it was headed in a certain direction, a one-way direction. This was pointed out in a criticism of the Steady-State Theory by astronomer H. Dingle in 1953:

> Every process we know, on the small or the large scale, is a one-way process, showing a preference for one direction over the opposite. The system of nebulae expands and does not contract, gravitation is an attraction and not a repulsion, the entropy of a closed system increases and does not decrease, every chemical process tends towards a state of equilibrium from which the substances concerned do not of themselves depart ... and so on. There is nothing whatever in nature that indicates that any course of events is reversible.[44]

The universe, then, was showing itself to be finite, expanding, with a beginning in time and a succeeding linear history, all characteristics lining up with the Big Bang Theory, as well as the Christian doctrine of Creation in time. Far from being in a steady state, the universe ages, having a life cycle like unto that of a human being. From a scientific perspective, it began its infancy at time 0, 13.72 billion years ago, it is now in its middle age, and it is heading toward old age billions of years in the distant future.

The triumph of the Big Bang Theory was a triumph for science, for the universe corresponding to it can be explored by the scientific mind to an astonishing level of detail. It is a universe with arms wide open to scientific discovery. Hoyle's godless universe-god, however—timeless, unchanging, homogeneous— can no more be explored than the inner life of God.

Let us turn to some astonishing features of the universe, revealed by Big Bang insights, that further confound all attempts to deify it.

The specificity of the universe

Inferring design in general

When engineers design an aeroplane, they must carefully specify every detail of its makeup:

- the materials and dimensions of its respective parts
- the exact location of each of those parts
- precisely how the parts are to be joined together
- and so on.

Someone coming along after the construction of the aeroplane can inspect it and see that its matter has been very carefully crafted so that it can be an aeroplane. He can even take measurements in order to 'reverse engineer' the aeroplane, so as to construct one for himself. Regardless, the need for innumerable details to be carefully chosen for the aeroplane to be able to function clearly indicates that some mind was behind its design. Only minds can conceive an abstract goal like 'flying machine', conceive the specific means required to realise that goal in the distant future, and then execute the mental plan by amassing the parts and assembling the product.

The process by which someone is able to infer that an aeroplane has been designed is a realist process. The senses testify to the many unique details present in the aeroplane's configuration; the intellect understands that those details are all directed to the accomplishment of a single purpose and that only abstracting minds can adapt many means to a single end.

The proponents of the Intelligent Design movement support this realist path to inferring design, though they use a different language when explaining it. They speak of the ability of the mind to distinguish *specified* complexity from *mere* complexity, and define their terms as follows:[45]

- **complexity**—sequences of information that 'exhibit an irregular, nonrepeating arrangement that defies expression by a general law or computer algorithm'
- **mere complexity**—a complex sequence of information that *is not* specifically arranged to perform a function
- **specified complexity**—a complex sequence of information that *is* specifically arranged to perform a function

According to Stephen Meyer,[46] an example of *mere complexity* would be the normal arrangement of flowers on a hillside. *Specified complexity*, however, would exist if the flowers were arranged to spell something like 'Welcome to Victoria'. In the latter case, the arrangement serves a specific, functional purpose—communication—while in the former, no such function exists, though the arrangement is complex, according to the definition of complexity given above.

Inferring the design of the universe

All of this is a lead-in to consider what impressions the universe might make on our minds when we make discoveries about it. Here are three aspects it could present and the conclusions we would naturally draw from those aspects:

- **homogeneous universe**—This would be a universe with great sameness and little diversity. It would be a universe with few and simple laws, making each individual thing much like other things. Given those laws, it would seem that this was the only universe possible, that there is no other way for a universe to exist. Such a universe would present itself to our minds as being undesigned and *necessary*, that is, uncreated and with no possibility of being anything other than it is.

- **merely complex universe**—This would be a universe with little sameness and great diversity. Everything would seem to be chaotic and random, not made for any purpose or going in any particular direction. Each individual thing would be different from everything else, and nothing would be arranged in any particular pattern, in order to work in harmony for the accomplishment of a function. There would not seem to be any laws, and so no particular reason why the universe is what it is. It would appear that a universe could be anything whatsoever. Such a universe would present itself to our minds as being undesigned and *chance*, that is, uncreated and unintelligible.

- **specifically complex universe**—this would be a universe with both sameness and diversity. On the one hand, there would be universal laws holding true for all material things. On the other hand, great diversity in individual things would result from the deployment of those laws. Moreover, the great diversity would clearly be directed to specific functions, performed within each individual organism (intrinsic finality) and by many organisms working together (extrinsic finality). Because of the specificity, it would be clear both that many other universes would be possible and that such universes would not be functional. Such a universe would present itself to our minds as being designed and *contingent*, that is, created and directed to most specific ends.

Table 9.2 Possible universes

Type of universe	General sameness	Individual diversity	Appearance	Possible universes
Homogeneous	Great	Little	Necessary, uncreated	One
Merely complex	Little	Great	Random, uncreated	Infinite
Specifically complex	Great	Great	Contingent, created	Innumerable, but extremely few useful ones

When things are set out this way, we can see why Steady-State empiricists would want the universe to be homogeneous. Such a universe would have the *appearance* of being uncreated, not just because it would be unchanging, but also because it would be undesigned. On the other hand, a universe having great specific complexity would indicate that it had been configured it in its finest details to pursue specific functional goals by a being outside of it.

SPECIFIED COMPLEXITY
Innumerable Possible

HOMOGENEITY
One Possible

MERE COMPLEXITY
Infinite Possible

Possible Universes

The actual universe

Now, the Big Bang Theory was an absolute nightmare for the universe-deifying types, not only because it pointed to a specific beginning of the universe, but also because it led to the discovery of a mind-boggling *specificity* built into the universe's configuration, necessary for the universe becoming habitable by living beings.

To illustrate this, let us consider the prediction and discovery of Cosmic Microwave Background Radiation (CMBR). After Hubble and Lemaître started to convince the scientific world that the universe had a beginning in time, scientists constructed models of the development of the universe from that beginning. All matter would somehow start expanding from a single point, developing according to the known laws of physical forces. At first, matter would be too dense to release any radiation. Over time, however—380,000 years, to be precise—pressure would drop sufficiently such that radiation could be released in the form of photons. The photons from this release event would permeate all of space and would travel throughout it from that time forward. Thus, if the Big Bang Theory were true, we would expect to be able to find *today* a radiation left over from the Big Bang permeating all of space. This was the very prediction made by Ralph Alpher, George Gamow, and Robert Herman in the late 1940s.[47]

On the face of it, this prediction seems speculative at best and far-fetched at worst. A pack of scientists are taking many and complex physical properties of matter, assuming that those properties have held true for all time, simulating what that matter would do if the entire universe originated in a single energetic point in a distant past, telling us that it would release radiation after 380,000 years, and predicting that the radiation is still around 13 billion years later in all of space. Crazy? No, for the radiation was found in 1965 by a pair of engineers at Bell Telephone Lab in New Jersey. What they discovered was a black body radiation in the microwave part of the electromagnetic spectrum which permeates space and gives it a uniform temperature of 2.73°C above absolute zero.

But is this radiation truly from a time-distant cosmic event? It seems so, for the photons of the CMBR do not match the current state of the universe. They could only have been produced when the universe was much denser and hotter than it is now. Thus, the CMBR 'has turned out to be a sort of cosmic "Rosetta stone" on which is inscribed the record of the Universe's past history'.[48] That is not all, for the CMBR has subtle fluctuations which have been carefully measured by space probes, providing scientists with a detailed temperature map of space.[49] From this data, 'cosmologists can extract at least ten cosmological parameters'.[50]

In a large part by means of the insights delivered by the Big Bang model, scientists have been able to discover what is referred to as the 'fine-tuning' of the universe, its specific configuration to perform the function of providing a habitable place for life forms. They start the clock at time 0 and then run it forward, seeing what events were necessary to transition from raw energy to subatomic particles to atoms to the clumping of matter to the formation of stars and galaxies to the formation of heavier elements to the formation of our own solar system. What they find is that the known configuration of the universe, in its physical laws and constants, had to be very precisely what it is and nothing else for our planet and sun to be what they are. In other words, the chemical (not biological!) evolution of the universe had to be very *specifically* configured to become what it is now. Only slight modifications in that specificity would have rendered our universe uninhabitable.

Matter vs. antimatter

Consider, as an example of this, the relationship between matter and antimatter. The Oxford Dictionary of English defines 'antimatter' as 'matter consisting of elementary particles which are the antiparticles of those making up normal matter.' Thus, in the totality of physical bodies, there is matter and antimatter, and the two are symmetrical in such a way that when a particle of matter interacts with a particle of antimatter, they cancel one another out, both returning to a raw energy state. For instance, corresponding to the matter particle called a 'proton', there is also an antimatter particle in the universe called an 'antiproton.' When the two come together, they lose their organised state and are reduced to raw energy. What is interesting is that, while antimatter exists, yet the stuff in the universe as it is *today* consists almost entirely of matter—subatomic particles like protons, electrons, and neutrons. There is almost no antimatter around: antiprotons, antielectrons, and so on. The question then arises: Where did the antimatter go? Why is there only matter around?

If the universe got started with equal portions of matter and antimatter, then the matter and antimatter would have cancelled each other out, and the universe today would only consist of raw energy. Atoms and stars and galaxies and suns and planets would never have formed. The material ingredients for complex life would certainly not be around. Matter, however, won out over antimatter and the CMBR tells us the proportion in which it did so. According to the background radiation, 1,000,000,001 matter particles developed from raw energy in the early universe for every 1,000,000,000 antimatter particles that developed.[51] Matter was able to win out only because the laws for the development of energy into particles are so specifically configured that one more matter particle than antimatter particle came out of the Big Bang for every billion of each. This imbalance was at work in 'the trillionth of the first second' of the universe,[52] and the universe would not be habitable today without it.

The slight matter-antimatter asymmetry is just one of dozens of fine-tuning conditions necessary for the universe to develop as it did from the Big Bang onwards. The book *The Privileged Planet* has a most helpful image to illustrate how delicate this fine-tuning is.[53] The authors have us imagine a Universe Creating Machine with innumerable dials to set mathematical values for the fundamental laws, constants, and initial conditions of the universe, such as mass density, weak nuclear force, gravitational force, cosmological constant, and so on. It turns out that all of the dials would have to be very precisely set for the universe to attain a state where it could be inhabited by humans. Take as an example the cosmological constant, which determines the rate at which the universe expands:

> [The cosmological constant] refers to the balance of the attractive force of gravity with a hypothesized repulsive force of space observable only at very large size scales. It must be very close to zero, that is, these two forces must be nearly perfectly balanced. To get the right balance, the cosmological constant must be fine-tuned to something like *1 part in 10^{120}*. If it were just slightly more positive, the universe would fly apart; slightly negative, and the universe would collapse.[54]

There are at least 22 such values that must be most precisely configured for a universe starting from a Big Bang to be able to support complex life. For this reason, almost all of the innumerable universes produced by such a Universe Machine would be uninhabitable. In the face of such incomprehensibly detailed fine-tuning, even such a hardened atheist as Hoyle had to admit,

> A commonsense interpretation of the facts suggests that a superintellect has monkeyed with physics, as well as chemistry and biology.[55]

Because the universe presents itself as so finely tuned to obtain a long-term result—a habitable world—it also presents itself as having been designed and so having a radical dependency on the mind of another.

Let us now turn to science's say on the universe's cause.

The cause of the universe

Back in chapter 2, I set out realist reasoning for a First Uncaused Cause of the universe, explaining that the only way to account for the things around us existing at each moment is by some uncaused Being sustaining them in existence. God being uncaused means that He is not dependent in His Being in any way on the being of another. He does not receive anything from anybody.

Atheists realise that, if they are going to convince us that God does not exist, they must prove to us that either the universe as a whole or some part of it is both uncaused and the cause of everything else within the universe. In chapter 4, I called the first position 'crass pantheism' and the second 'elaborate pantheism'.

Given the immense difficulty of demonstrating that something purely material is an uncaused cause of all material things, atheists generally resort to a shortcut strategy to reach their goal: define all true knowledge as wholly and exclusively scientific knowledge. Then investigate reality, return from your exploration, and announce that the universe is the only thing that exists. This is what New Atheist Lawrence Krauss does when tells us that 'there is no *observable* evidence whatsoever' for divine intelligence,[56] expecting us to be able to look at God's mind through a telescope!

Lawrence Krauss (Image courtesy of Flickr/Mal Vickers)

But the empiricist contradicts himself as soon as he declares himself an empiricist. The moment he puts forward as true the proposition that 'only scientific knowledge is true knowledge', he has gone beyond the limited area that he has set for human knowledge, because his proposition is not a scientific, empirically verifiable one, and yet he is asserting it to be true knowledge.[57] At the end of the day, the scientistic position is self-refuting, because it is not a scientific stance; it is a philosophical one.

Arguments for an uncaused universe

It gets more interesting when atheist scientists try to explain how the universe is uncaused. The task has become extremely challenging after the acceptance of the Big Bang, which even someone like Krauss says 'is too firmly grounded in data from every area to be proved invalid in its general features'.[58] A Big-Bang beginning to the universe points to a cause outside of it, as shown by the *kalam* cosmological argument of Al-Ghazali:

> Everything that begins to exist requires a cause for its origin.
> The world began to exist.
> Therefore, the world had a cause for its origin.[59]

Krauss thinks that he has a solution to this difficulty: the world does have a cause, and that cause is nothing. By 'nothing', he does not mean non-being, but rather a body of empty space. Physicists like Krauss have found that such empty space *weighs* something,[60] which means that it contains energy. Now, Krauss admits that 'we understand virtually nothing' about that energy,[61] yet he believes that that energy is the source of the universe. How so? Well, there are fluctuations in the energy of empty space which cause subatomic particles to form periodically and also be reduced back to raw energy, in a 'time frame determined by the Uncertainty Principle'.[62]

Okay, so how does that explain the universe? Well, it doesn't, but let us set it out again, this time exposing all the steps of the process, for Krauss' sake:

1. In the beginning, there is empty space, that is, 'nothing', also known as the 'quantum vacuum'.
2. That nothing fluctuates and periodically produces particles.
3. Our entire universe came from those fluctuations.

In this view, the universe is uncaused in that the empty space is assumed to be there already, and that empty space would be the initial universe. The Big Bang would simply be an unfolding of complexity from an already existing universe of empty space by fluctuations of the quantum vacuum.

REALISM
All Four Causes in Balance

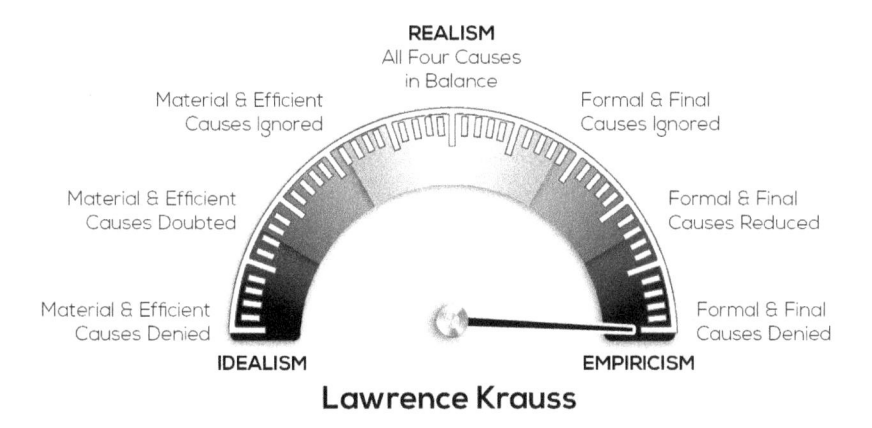

Material & Efficient Causes Ignored — Formal & Final Causes Ignored

Material & Efficient Causes Doubted — Formal & Final Causes Reduced

Material & Efficient Causes Denied — Formal & Final Causes Denied

IDEALISM — **EMPIRICISM**

Lawrence Krauss

Krauss was not satisfied with the quantum vacuum 'nothing' and wanted to make it a little bit less than it was, more nothing than before, ostensibly because nothing is more powerful the less it is. He wanted to have a nothing that did not even contain empty space, but still contained the quantum vacuum somehow. Luckily for him, eminent scientists Stephen Hawking and Jim Hartle had done the work for him, by removing space and time from nothing, and so he could just quote their conclusions directly:

1. In quantum gravity, universes can, and indeed always will, spontaneously appear from nothing. Such universes need not be empty, but can have matter and radiation in them...

2. In order for the closed universes that might be created through such mechanisms to last for longer than infinitesimal times, something like inflation is necessary. As a result, the only long-lived universe one might expect to live in as a result of such a scenario is one that today appears flat, just as the universe in which we live appears.[63]

Krauss summarises as follows:

> The lesson is clear: quantum gravity not only appears to allow universes to be created from nothing—meaning, in this case, I emphasize, the absence of space and time—it may require them ... Moreover, the general characteristics of such a universe, if it lasts a long time, would be expected to be those we observe in our universe today.[64]

But even after reducing nothing so close to actual nothing, Krauss still has scruples: what about the laws of quantum gravity that spontaneously create the universe? Where do they come from? Needless to say, Krauss finds a way to source them from nothing as well. I will spare you his absurd arguments, leaving you only with his conclusion:

> One thing is certain ... The metaphysical 'rule', which is held as an ironclad conviction by those with whom I have debated the issue of creation, namely that *'out of nothing nothing comes,'* has no foundation in science.[65]

No, it seems that science is telling us the opposite: out of nothing everything comes. 'All Being is Becoming; and is but the evolution of Not-Being by the law of its Being'.[66] Entire universes just pop spontaneously into existence. Nothing is God, and so God is nothing. I suppose that Krauss' book is not called *A Universe from Nothing* for nothing. Then again, I could be mistaken about that. Regardless, he could well wax lyrical about his sweet nothing with Belloc:

> Nothing is too great for any man who has once embraced it to leave it alone thenceforward for ever ... the dignity of Nothing is sufficiently exalted in this: that Nothing is the tenuous stuff from which the world was made.[67]

Krauss seems to think that if he describes how one thing comes from another, probing into smaller and smaller things, he will eventually come to nothing at the bottom of it all, as the cause of it all.[68] But talking about how some things come from other things says nothing about how they can come from nothing, as Chesterton remarks:

> Nobody can imagine how nothing could turn into something. Nobody can get an inch nearer to it by explaining how something could turn into something else.[69]

Is he for real?

We might rightly scratch our heads, asking if Krauss expects to be taken seriously. Indeed he does, to such a degree that he believes his position as a 'rational scientist' enables him to make moral judgements on the value of religion for society. Krauss, for instance, opposes religious education for children.[70] For him, religion is irrational, while science is rational. Children should be taught the reasonable scientific arguments which show they came from nothing and their minds must not be corrupted with the non-scientific idea that they came from God.

It is fashionable among scientists to take a smug glance at ancient peoples, despising them for their ignorance of natural causes, pitying them for their fear of divine powers, mocking them for their captivity to superstition. When we look up the definition of superstition, however, we find that it is the false attribution of divine powers to a mere creature. It is a causality problem. This or that person believes that a broken mirror can cause him seven years' bad luck, but broken mirrors do not have such causal power. Behind this superstitious belief is the acknowledgement that some power higher than humans is in control of reality. It is the location of that power in silly events that makes for superstition.

But what are we to say of the idea that everything comes from nothing? Before, it was a black cat or a salt shaker knocked over that would have momentous consequences, and a frenzied dance or ritual sacrifice was needed to ward off the evil spirits. Now, it is nothing, non-being, that is the most momentous cause in existence. Before, lowly beings were falsely attributed superhuman powers. Now, that which has no power at all and even no existence is said to be omnipotent. In my judgement, then, Krauss and his ilk have reached an extremity of superstition and hence irrationality far beyond that of ancient times and one that cannot be surpassed.[71]

If Krauss were just an isolated crank, then we could just shrug off his nonsense. While he is isolated in his militant atheism, *he is, however, considered mainstream in his science.* The scientific community listens willingly to ideas about the universe originating from nothing, allowing them currency in the public academic forum. Krauss' book has an endorsement from the prestigious magazine *Nature,* saying that 'unstable nothingness, as described by Krauss ... is [] invigorating for the rest of us, because in this nothingness there are many wonderful things to see and understand.' *New Scientist* raves: 'Space and time can indeed come from nothing; nothing, as Krauss explains beautifully, being an extremely unstable state from which the production of "something" is pretty much inevitable.'

Other nothing-lovers

Set Krauss aside and pick up the book *Nothing,* a collection of *New Scientist* articles on nothing edited by Jeremy Webb. In it, you will find other instances of mainstream scientists denying the first principles of reason. For instance, Paul Davies, who for all that seems to be a reasonable man, has this to say on page 50:

> One may say quite generally that once space and time are made subject to quantum principles, the possibility immediately arises of space and time 'switching on,' or popping into existence, without the need for prior causation, entirely in accordance with the laws of quantum physics.[72]

Another physicist informs us on page 211: 'According to quantum mechanics, a particle can exist in many places at once and move in more than one direction at a time.' The statement is contrary to reason, but scientists do not seem to feel any duty to pay homage to the first principles of their own thinking when they have their science hat on.

What is ironic is that arguing to nothing as cause of everything is permitted among the vetters of scientific orthodoxy, but arguing to intelligence as cause of everything is not.[73] It is illogical to do science while holding that nothing is at the source of everything, while it is perfectly logical to do science while holding that intelligence is at the source of everything. The same Paul Davies who believes that space and time can pop into existence without cause admits that science has to be monotheistic in its assumptions in order to be science:

> The worldview of the scientists, even the most atheistic scientists, is a view of monotheism. It is a belief which is accepted as an article of faith that the world is ordered in an intelligible way. Now, you couldn't be a scientist if you didn't believe these two things. If you didn't believe there was an underlying order, you wouldn't bother to do anything, because there would be nothing to be found. And if you didn't believe it was intelligible, you'd give up, because there's no point, if human beings can't come to understand it. Scientists do, as a matter of faith, believe that the universe is ordered and, at least partially, intelligible to human beings, and that's what underpins the entire scientific enterprise. And that is a theological position. It's absolutely clear, when you look at history, that it comes from that theological worldview.[74]

On the one hand, then, scientists must be monotheistic in their assumptions; on the other hand, they must be atheistic in their conclusions. But if the conclusions rely on the assumptions, how can they not be consistent with them? Only by an act of the *will* which has chosen beforehand the conclusions to be reached. Such is the sorry state of modern science, which has sold itself in bondage to a fideistic empiricism, in the supposed interests of science, while performing a science that relies on epistemological realism and monotheism.

Before we conclude this chapter, we must consider briefly two other strategies scientists use to avoid the obvious conclusion that the universe is caused by a supreme intelligence: the notion of the multiverse and the denial of the principle of causality.

The Multiverse

To remove the hallmarks of design from the universe, the atheist must get rid of *specificity*. Getting rid of specificity means getting rid of fine-tuning. Clearly, this cannot be done with our own universe; the evidence is too overwhelming even for our intrepid God-refusers. The thing to be done, then, is to go *outside* of the universe to show that there are innumerable other universes with bad configurations, while our universe is one of the very few with a good configuration. This entire collection of such universes is called a 'multiverse'.[75]

Imagine that the Universe Creating Machine of above produced a universe for all of its possible settings. The number of universes would be astronomical—no pun intended—but not infinite. Because of the most delicate conditions required for a habitable universe, the vast majority of them would not be able to sustain life. Our own universe, then, would just be the lucky outcome of a *chance* configuration of the universe generator. In this scenario, so the narrative runs, no intelligence is needed to design our universe.

This ingenious scenario, however, is not compelling for minds unenslaved to empiricism, for the following reasons:

1. **No science is involved.** A multiverse, by definition, is beyond the reach of scientific observation.[76] For either the other universes are part of our own universe, in which case they are not different universes at all, being one with our own; or they are indeed separate from our universe, in which case there is no possibility for us making contact with those universes.[77]

2. **The multiverse solves nothing.** The multiverse hypothesis does not provide the ultimate explanations which the rational mind is looking for, but only puts them off.[78] For

once the multiverse is accepted, there is another question to ask: Where does the multiverse come from, or the force that makes universes? And, of course, the question of causality in the vertical chain can never be escaped: Why does anything around us exist at all at each moment?[79]

3. **Chance is not an explanation.** 'For well over two millenia', says Jaki, 'the chief spokesmen of Western thought took the word *chance* for an ignorance of true causes.'[80] The reason is that chance is not the expression of a cause-effect relationship. It does not indicate *why* this or that happened, but just reaffirms that they happened. Thus, to say that our universe is the chance product of a universe lottery still leaves us looking for its proper cause. All chance, in the end, relies on non-chance.[81] This third problem is simply a re-phrasing of the second problem in different terms.

Denial of causality

A final way for atheists to avoid the difficulties (for them) presented by a universe pointing to a First Cause is to say that effects do not need to have causes. Thus, those who are searching for an ultimate reason for the existence of the universe are troubling themselves needlessly: there is no reason.

Such a position is just as desperate as the one which makes nothing a cause, for it destroys the validity of all reasons. If effects need not have causes, then causal explanations are useless, whether they fall in the category of material, formal, efficient, or final causes. At one fell swoop, the entire edifice of human sciences and learning comes down with a crash.

The reasons given to doubt causality are scientific ones. As technology advanced in the early 1900s, our ability to probe into the ultimate components of matter grew enormously. Scientists soon realised, however, that no technology, no matter how sophisticated, could probe matter all the way to the bottom. This limitation comes from the human eye and that by which it sees, visible light. Visible light has a wavelength of 10^{-7} metre, while the size of atoms is 10^{-10}, protons 10^{-15}, and quarks 10^{-20}. What this means is that visible light is not small enough to illuminate atoms, protons, and quarks (the ultimate components of protons), and so *the human race will never be able to see them*. The only way for us to detect and measure atoms and their components is by hitting them with something and noting their movement by means of some device.

While this method has been extremely successful—witness all of the valuable information coming from the massive particle accelerators built in the USA and Europe—it is yet subject to limitations. Since the proton, or electron, or whatever, is being hit while it is being measured, its true behaviour is being modified. To be precise, its velocity is changed by the hit. Thus, we may get a good reading on our device as to the *position* of the particle, but we will get a false reading as to its *speed*.

One way to remedy this situation is by hitting the particle more gently. The measuring beam is reduced to a lower energy and hence a longer wavelength. Particles struck by it maintain their normal velocity, which can then be measured accurately. At the same time, we are no longer able to determine the particle's *position* with any accuracy. The reason is that the reduced wavelength of the beam makes it take up a broader space. The particle is known to be somewhere within that space, but not with any precision.

Here, then, is the dilemma facing scientists: the *velocity* and *position* of particles can be measured accurately, *but never at the same time*.[82] Thus, 'there is an inherent limitation to the accuracy that can be achieved in measurements'.[83] The physicist Werner Heisenberg was able to develop a law which expressed in mathematical terms the degree of measurement uncertainty that is bound to exist in his famous Uncertainty Principle. So far so good. We get excited when science makes these amazing breakthroughs.

The problem arrives after the science when scientists become philosophers and use the Uncertainty Principle, which concerns humans' ability to measure the position and speed of subatomic matter, to make statements about reality as a whole. According to Heisenberg and the Copenhagen school, 'an interaction that cannot be measured exactly cannot take place exactly'.[84] In other words, because we cannot measure accurately both the position and velocity of particles, then they do not have any set position and velocity, in themselves. There is, in reality, no determinate relationship between what these particles are (cause) and how they behave (effect). *The particles, then, do not adhere to the law of causality.*

Such was the reasoning which led Heisenberg to announce that his Uncertainty Principle definitively disproved causality, and which led Jaki to remark that he was 'selling the idea that doing very good science justifies doing philosophy very badly'.[85]

This 'decline and fall of causality', as Waismann put it,[86] was the end result of the change wrought on the notion of causality by the seventeenth-century scientists. As we saw in the last chapter, they reduced causality to the interaction of material forces according to strictly determined mathematical laws.[87] If such is your conception of causality, then what do you say when you find that matter does not interact according to strictly determined laws? Or, at least, that no such laws can be observed? Quite simply, you pronounce the end of causality, for, at that point, what empiricism defines as causality, science is unable to observe.[88]

Did the scientific community denounce this attack on causality as an attack on science? Did it rush to the defence of reality, rationality, and the ultimate foundations of human knowledge? No, on the contrary, it embraced the idea that, because we cannot see or measure what particles are doing, they must not be obeying the law of causality. Dr Richard Wolfson stated in 2000:

> Most physicists subscribe to the *Copenhagen interpretation* of quantum physics. This view grows out of logical positivism, with its claim that it makes no sense to talk about what cannot be measured. In the Copenhagen interpretation, not only can one never measure the velocity and position of a particle simultaneously, but it also makes no sense to say that the particle *has* a velocity and a position.[89]

It is this interpretation of the Uncertainty Principle that is actually behind the ravings of physicists about particles popping in and out of existence from nothing, as well as universes. For if particles do not obey causality, then they can exist as effects without there having been any pre-existing cause. 'Compared with this,' says Jaki, 'the pulling of rabbits out of a hat should seem rationality incarnate'.[90]

Armed with the Uncertainty Principle, scientists not only felt themselves capable of deifying the universe, but also of passing their time bringing universes in and out of existence.

Chapter summary

Medieval Christendom gave birth to modern science by overthrowing the pagan pantheistic view of the universe, which considered the universe to be the ultimate reality, uncreated and eternal. For Christians, God brought the universe into being, designing it for specific purposes and giving it a specific configuration to accomplish those purposes. The universe is temporal, finite, limited, and hence eminently knowable.

The science born in the medieval period came to full maturity in its tools and methods after the Christian worldview had given way to a radical humanism during the time of the so-called Enlightenment. Astounding discoveries were made about the laws of the universe, the nature of heavenly bodies, and the utmost composition of matter. These scientific advancements, however, were no longer accompanied by a philosophical and theological environment which could fit them into a coherent picture of reality. Philosophy was drifting aimlessly and theology was shattered into countless pieces. Newly-matured science was now an orphan and decided to rule the world as his parents had once done.

But the only way for science to be all that philosophy had been was for it to make its particular object of study count for all reality. The material world had to become God once more, as it had been in pagan times. After the universe had been reduced to a finite creature by the scholastics, modern scientists set out to raise it back up. And so they made it infinite, eternal, unchanging, homogeneous, purposeless. How did they do so? By removing from it all rationality. Neither it nor anything in it had a cause. Thus science, which is the knowledge of causes, could no longer be pursued by human minds. Self-deified science destroyed itself. It was a suicide deicide.

Fortunately for science, the universe would not tolerate its own deification. As its secrets were probed more deeply, the universe time and again shouted out its radical contingency, finitude, temporality, creatureliness, specificity.

In a fairy tale, the whole of the intellectual world would have licked its chops, learned its lesson, and returned to philosophical realism and Christian theism. In the real, fallen world, however, no lesson was learned, no worldview was overturned, and the irrational marriage between the facts of modern science and the artificial atheistic worldview which misinterprets those facts continues.

Today, scientists make brilliant discoveries and breakthroughs in the penetration of material reality, while spouting irrational nonsense when speaking about reality as a whole. Worse, they hold to be backwards and unscientific those who do not join with them in denying the first principles of reason, using the immense clout of scientific opinion to shout out of academic hearing those who see intelligence behind the intricacies of the universe. It is as if irrationality has been defined as the precondition for modern science.

We here come back face to face with the premise of this entire book: human understanding of reality is an all or nothing proposition. You either take reason with realism, science and religion all together, or you reject them all. Many modern scientists rejected realism, clamped themselves tightly to empiricism and, inevitably led by it on its natural course, embraced anti-science, atheism, and irrationality.

Notes

[1] J. Trefil, *Space Atlas* (Washington, DC: The National Geographic Society, 2012), p. 266.
[2] *Ibid.*, pp. 194–197.
[3] L. Krauss, *A Universe from Nothing* (New York: Atria, 2013), pp. 9–10.
[4] Trefil, *Space Atlas*, p. 269.
[5] It should be noted that the Earth is not at the centre of the expansion, as all astronomers know. The reason is that everything in the universe is moving away from everything else, instead of one item staying put and the rest moving away from it. For instance, if all seven billion people on the Earth were shrunk to the size of ants, and the Earth in like manner, after which the Earth was expanded outward, then each of the seven billion persons would see the others moving away in the midst of the expansion while seeming to be in the centre of the expansion, while not actually being so. So it is with our position in the expanding universe. See Krauss, *A Universe from Nothing*, pp. 11–14.
[6] Krauss, *A Universe from Nothing*, p. 5.
[7] M. Heller, *Ultimate Explanations of the Universe* (Heidelberg: Springer-Verlag, 2009), p. 49.
[8] See p. 277.
[9] *The Enchanted Loom: Mind in the Universe* (Simon & Schuster, 1981), p. 19.
[10] DVD *Privileged Planet* (Illustra Media, 2004), bonus feature 'Questions & Answers', 6.
[11] G. and H. Kemper, C. Luskin, *Discovering Intelligent Design* (Seattle: Discovery Institute Press, 2013), p. 22.
[12] *Orthodoxy* (London: William Clowes and Sons, 1908), p. 32.
[13] See p. 340.
[14] S. Jaki, *God and the Cosmologists* (Fraser, Michigan: Real View Books, 1998), p. 8.
[15] ST, I, q. 7, a.1; my translation.
[16] *The Paradox of Olbers' Paradox* (Pinckney, Michigan: Real View Books, 2000), p. 257.
[17] See Aquinas, ST, I, q.7, a.4, for this reasoning.
[18] See p. 337.
[19] *The Paradox*, pp. 59–62.
[20] *Ibid.*, p. 58.
[21] *Ibid.*, p. 77.
[22] *Ibid.*, p. 79.

[23] *Ibid.*, p. 94.
[24] Jaki, *God and the Cosmologists*, p. 12. See also Jaki, *The Paradox*, p. 135.
[25] See, for example, ST, I, q. 25, a.2, ad 2.
[26] See Jaki, *God and the Cosmologists*, p. 10.
[27] Jaki, *The Paradox*, p. 133.
[28] *Ibid.*, p. 139.
[29] *Ibid.*, pp. 151, 164; Jaki, *God and the Cosmologists*, p. 13.
[30] Cited in S. Jaki, *God and the Cosmologists*, p. 14; S. Jaki, *The Paradox*, p. 174.
[31] Cited in S. Jaki, *The Paradox*, p. 227.
[32] Cited in *Ibid.*, p. 236. See also S. Jaki, *Science and Creation* (New York: Science History Publications, 1974), p. 337.
[33] Jaki, *The Paradox*, pp. 217–218.
[34] See *Ibid.*, p. 262.
[35] George Sorel cited in Jaki, *God and the Cosmologists*, p. 15.
[36] Bertrand Russell cited in Jaki, *The Paradox*, p. 229.
[37] ST, I, q.9, a.1; my translation.
[38] See p. 76.
[39] Cited in Jaki, *The Paradox*, pp. 242–243, emphasis added.
[40] *Ibid.*, pp. 238–239.
[41] See p. 125.
[42] S. Jaki, *The Road of Science and the Ways to God* (Port Huron, Michigan: Real View Books, 2005), p. 435. See also Jaki, *God and the Cosmologists*, pp. 68–75; *Science and Creation*, pp. 347–350; *The Road of Science*, pp. 269–271.
[43] Jaki, *Science and Creation*, pp. 270–271.
[44] Cited in *Ibid.*, p. 348.
[45] S. Meyer, *Signature in the Cell* (New York: HarperOne, 2009), pp. 106–107.
[46] *Ibid.*, p. 353.
[47] G. Gonzalez and J. Richards, *The Privileged Planet* (Washington, DC: Regnery Publishing, 2004), p. 175.
[48] Cited in *Ibid.*, p. 176.
[49] Trefil, *Space Atlas*, pp. 262–263.
[50] Gonzalez and Richards, *The Privileged Planet*, p. 175.
[51] Krauss, *A Universe from Nothing*, p. 158.
[52] Jaki, *God and the Cosmologists*, p. 48.
[53] Gonzalez and Richards, *The Privileged Planet*, p. 196.
[54] J. Richards, 'List of Fine-Tuning Parameters', p. 286, from http://www.discovery.org/f/11011; emphasis in original.
[55] Cited in Gonzalez and Richards, *The Privileged Planet*, p. 263.

56 Krauss, *A Universe from Nothing*, p. 118, emphasis added.
57 See E. Feser, *Scholastic Metaphysics* (Heusenstamm, Germany: Editiones Scholasticae, 2014), section 0.2.1 for a detailed argument.
58 Krauss, *A Universe from Nothing*, p. 118.
59 W. Craig, *The Cosmological Argument from Plato to Leibniz* (Eugene, Oregon: Wipf and Stock Publishers, 1980), p. 104.
60 Krauss, *A Universe from Nothing*, p. 58.
61 *Ibid.*, p. 136.
62 *Ibid.*, p. 163.
63 Cited in *Ibid.*, pp. 169–170.
64 *Ibid.*, p. 170.
65 *Ibid.*, p. 174.
66 G. K. Chesterton, *St. Thomas Aquinas* (London: Hodder & Stoughton Limited, 1933), p. 181.
67 *On Nothing and Kindred Subjects* (London, Methuen & Co., 1908), p. xvi.
68 Alister McGrath makes a similar remark about Krauss' co-religionist Richard Dawkins at the 56 minute mark of the documentary *Expelled*: 'Dawkins seems to think that scientific description is an anti-religious argument. Describing how something happens scientifically somehow explains it away. It doesn't, but the questions of purpose, of intentionality, the question "why", still remain there on the table.'
69 *The Everlasting Man* (New York: Dodd, Mead & Company, 1930), p. 3.
70 See http://www.rawstory.com/2014/11/theoretical-physicist-lawrence-krauss-religion-could-be-gone-in-a-generation.
71 This is why Edward Feser named his book against them *The Last Superstition* (South Bend, Indiana: St. Augustine's Press, 2008). See pp. 14–20 in that work. See also Jaki, *God and the Cosmologists*, pp. 246–247.
72 P. Davies, 'The day time began' in J. Webb, ed., *Nothing* (New York: The Experiment, 2013), p. 50.
73 See J. Wells, *The Politically Incorrect Guide to Darwinism and Intelligent Design* (Washington DC: Regnery Publishing, 2006), chapter 16.
74 DVD *Privileged Planet*, bonus feature, 'Questions & Answers', 1.
75 Trefil, *Space Atlas*, p. 295.
76 See Heller, *Ultimate Explanations*, pp. 96, 121.
77 See S. Jaki, *Questions on Science and Religion* (Pinckney, Michigan: Real View Books, 2004), p. 77.
78 See Heller, *Ultimate Explanations*, p. 120.
79 See S. Jaki, *God and the Cosmologists*, p. 244.
80 *Ibid.*, p. 149.
81 See E. Feser, *Neo-Scholastic Essays* (South Bend, Indiana: St. Augustine's

Press, 2015), p. 140.
[82] See R. Wolfson, *Einstein's Relativity and the Quantum Revolution: Modern Physics for Non-Scientists* audio course (Chantilly, Virginia: The Great Courses, 2000), lecture 19.
[83] Jaki, *God and the Cosmologists*, p. 125.
[84] *Ibid.*, p. 139.
[85] *Ibid.*, p. 124.
[86] W. Wallace, *Causality and Scientific Explanation* (Ann Arbor: University of Michigan Press, 1974), vol. 2, p. 163.
[87] See p. 330.
[88] *Ibid.*, p. 164. Unfortunately, Pierre Duhem, despite his brilliance in the history of science, was one of those who adopted the majority view of contemporary science that science is not able to know causes. See *Ibid.*, pp. 177–180.
[89] Wolfson, *Einstein's Relativity* audio course, course guidebook, p. 100.
[90] Jaki, *God and the Cosmologists*, p. 247. See Jaki, *Questions on Science*, pp. 74–76; S. Jaki, *Impossible Divide* (New Hope, Kentucky: Real View Books, 2008), pp. 92–94; S. Jaki, *The Mirage of Conflict* (New Hope, Kentucky: Real View Books, 2009), pp. 74–76.

10 INORGANIC LIFE

An honest man, armed with all the knowledge available to us now, could only state that in some sense, the origin of life appears at the moment to be almost a miracle.

Francis Crick, Agnostic Discoverer of DNA's Structure

IN THE 2008 documentary *Expelled,* Ben Stein goes on an exploration of the repercussions falling on academics who dissent from the standard conclusions of modern empiricist science. While this is the main focus of the documentary, it has for its leitmotiv the investigation of origin of life explanations. The standard position is that life emerged by chance processes in the early history of the Earth. Some scientists, however—notably those of the Intelligent Design (ID) movement—believe that the very methods of science point to intelligence as the best explanation of life's origin. Ben finds out that their opinion, when expressed publicly, is met with severe academic sanctions, including loss of professorships. Then, he asks himself the question: is the idea that life originated from non-life so solidly scientific, that questioning it is like saying that the Earth is flat? He begins by getting the opinion of some New Atheist scientists on ID theory. They come up with the following:

- Biologist Richard Dawkins: 'Intelligent Design people are not genuine scientists.'
- Biologist P. Z. Myers: 'Intelligent Design is a racket.'
- Philosopher Daniel Dennett: 'It's just propaganda.'
- Philosopher of science Michael Ruse: 'It's really very stupid.'

After hearing such strong reactions, Ben explores the arguments given by the scientific establishment for the origin of life and compares them with those given by the ID theorists. He is more than willing to grant that irrational theories should not be provided public discussion time and wonders if, indeed, the common scientific opinion is rational while ID is irrational. This, at least, would lend a certain credibility to the ruthless suppression of ID by the scientific community. So, what sort of scientific evidence underpins the opinion that life originated from non-living matter?

Ben's first attempt at an answer is provided by the documentary 'Cosmic Origins.' It says the following:

> The chemical elements essential for life—hydrogen, oxygen, carbon, and nitrogen—were now in place. What was needed was a way of combining them. Perhaps the energy came from lightning. Whatever it was, energy managed to arrange these chemical ingredients in just the right way.

This hypothetical scenario only seemed to be an admission of ignorance, so Ben asked Dr Michael Ruse for his explanation of the origin of life:

> Ben: How do you get from the inorganic world to the world of the cell?
> Michael Ruse: Well, one popular theory is that it might have started off on the backs of crystals. Molecules piggybacked on the back of crystals forming and this led to more and more complex... But of course the nice thing about crystals is every now and then you get mistakes, mutations, and this opens the way for natural selection.
> Ben: But at one point there was not a living thing, and then there was a living thing. How did that happen?
> Michael Ruse: I've just told you!

Not satisfied by piggybacking molecules, Ben turns to New Atheist superstar Richard Dawkins to find a scientific explanation for the origin of life.

> Ben: How did it start?
> Dawkins: Nobody knows how it started ... We know the sort of event that must have happened for the origin of life. It was the origin of the first self-replicating molecule.
> Ben: Right. How did that happen?

Inorganic Life

Dawkins: I've told you. We don't know.
Ben: So, you have no idea how it started?
Dawkins: No, no. Nor does anybody.

Since no one knows how life got started, it would seem that there is no scientific consensus on the question. Why, then, should those who argue scientifically for ID not be allowed to have a voice?

Ben: What do you think is the possibility that Intelligent Design might be the answer to some issues in genetics or Darwinian evolution?

Dawkins: Well, it could come about in the following way. It could be that, at some earlier time somewhere in the universe, a civilisation evolved by Darwinian means to a very, very high level of technology and designed a form of life that they seeded perhaps onto this planet. That is a possibility, and an intriguing possibility. I suppose that it's possible that you might find evidence for that if you look at the details of biochemistry ... You might find a signature of such a designer.

Dawkins, then, is willing to admit an intelligent designer, but only if that intelligent designer received its intelligence and life from non-life. This idea of life being seeded on Earth by aliens— 'directed panspermia' it is called—is acceptable in the scientific community, because life still takes its ultimate origin in non-life.

Richard Dawkins (Image courtesy of Flickr/Luiz Munhoz)

In today's climate, then, it is considered to be rational and scientific when some material cause is ascribed to the origin of life: lightning, molecules on crystals, aliens who came from non-life. Ascribing a non-material cause to life's origin, such as intelligence, on the other hand, is said to be irrational and unscientific. Intelligence is unintelligence, because only non-intelligence can be intelligent. This is another example, in origin of life studies, of how empiricist science leads to irrationality, the denial of the very principles of reason. The purpose of this chapter is to expose that irrationality.

Biology and finality

In the last chapter, we saw that *physicists* wanting to make science capable of explaining the *universe* inevitably were led to bestow the attributes of God upon the universe. Now, we must consider to what lengths *biologists* must extend themselves, when they likewise want science to explain everything about *life*.

Back in chapter 3, we saw some key differences between the life sciences and physical sciences.[1] Revisiting and performing a deeper analysis of those differences here will help us understand why finality or purpose, a reality denied by empiricists, is much more evident in life sciences than physical ones.

Differences between living and non-living

The proper object of biology's attention is living bodies, while that of physics is material bodies in general. Moreover, life processes, being inherently different from inorganic processes, demand a different method of investigation, according to our realist principle 'different methods of study for different objects of reality.' Materialists maintain the same method of study for all reality—the scientific method—because they believe that there is only one object in reality: matter. For them, life is only *quantitatively* different from non-life and not *qualitatively*

Inorganic Life

different,[2] and so is equally accessible to the methods of science. This is not the case.

Let us distinguish the organic from the inorganic by making reference to their four causes. To start with non-living things, they

1. (material cause) have a high degree of homogeneity in their material constitution
2. (efficient cause) are inert, and so interact with other things only in being moved by outside forces, not by their own internal impetus
3. (formal and final causes) possess a simple unity, from which few activities flow, which activities are directed to an obscure goal.

Living things, on the other hand,

1. (material cause) have bodies consisting of quite heterogeneous matter
2. (efficient cause) interact with other things by means of an internal principle
3. (formal and final causes) function as a complex unity, directing many functions of diverse matter to a clear goal, life.

These distinctions are summarised in the chart below, and are inspired by Aristotle,[3] yet improve somewhat on his perspective, as he thought that non-living bodies possess matter that is entirely homogeneous.[4]

Table 10.1 *Differences between the living and non-living*

Types of beings	1. Parts/Body (material cause)	2. Interaction (efficient cause)	3. Unity and Purpose (formal and final causes)
Non-living	More homogeneous – mainly the same type of matter	Moved by things outside of them	Simple: few types of matter → few functions → obscure goal
Living	More heterogeneous – many diverse types of matter	Moved from within	Complex: diverse types of matter → diverse functions → clear goal

We are not able to make as stark a distinction between non-living bodies and living ones as Aristotle did, by saying that the former have homogeneous matter and the latter heterogeneous matter.[5] What we can say, though, is that living bodies are heterogeneous *to a much greater degree* than non-living ones.

Studying the living

Once one realises the greater complexity of living things, the question arises: does that complexity demand a different and higher level of explanation than that given to mere material processes? Aristotle answers 'yes' to this question in his *On the Parts of Animals*,[6] and it seems obvious to him, for all that. His predecessors spoke of animals merely in terms of their homogeneous matter and how that matter interacted—they spoke only in terms of material and efficient causes. But this is to treat living beings as mere *mechanisms*, as if they were simply a random combination of moving parts, much like a sea of atoms moving around in space, without order, without direction, without any special unity—without, in other words, formal or final causes.

When we have described the movement of living beings and their material components, our work is not done. They present realities that are out of the reach of those explanations, namely, the organisation and coordination of many heterogeneous components, and the direction of that vast variety of matter towards the service of a complex purpose. The unifying principle that organises life forms is called the 'soul' and it is the formal cause; the purpose towards which everything is directed is called 'life' and it is the intrinsic final cause. Neither of these causes are directly observable by the senses and so neither of them falls within the scope of the scientific method. Yet they are the only coherent explanations for the unique facts that we observe in regard to living things.

By intrinsic final causality, we mean the direction of all the parts of living things toward the perfection of their nature, rather than toward goals imposed from the outside.[7] Though everything

Inorganic Life

in nature pursues goals and so has final causality, yet non-living things pursue goals only by being moved by forces outside of them, while living things do so by self-movement: they direct themselves to the intrinsic goal of their nature.[8] Since non-human life forms do this unconsciously (even many of the life functions of humans are not directed by them), we are moved to wonder where their intrinsic direction towards life's goals originated. Clearly, it must be in a mind building that design into plants and animals, a mind typically referred to as their extrinsic formal cause or their *exemplar* cause.

To return to the difference in the object of the physical sciences and the life sciences, its existence demands a corresponding difference in methods investigating those objects: non-living things should be considered more from the side of efficient causality, and living things more from the side of final causality. Non-living things can be said to act *mechanically*, in that they do not move on their own in pursuing their end. Thus, one studying their activity should focus on the agents acting upon them, the efficient causes which initiate this or that activity in them. Living things, on the other hand, act *dynamically*, moving themselves to pursue the purposes of life. Rather than only operating automatically based on forces being exercised from outside them, living things have an intrinsic, immaterial principle—something Aristotle called a 'soul'—by which they move their parts to act on the outside world. The superiority of living things to non-living ones makes their finality more manifest to human minds, but their functionality and material components are more complex and hence less investigable by human minds.[9]

I am not saying that *only* material, formal and efficient causes should be used to explain non-living things, and *only* final causes should be used to explain living things. On the contrary, all four causes must be used to account for every single one of the beings in our universe, as we saw in chapter 2.[10] What I am saying is that final causes will play a more preponderant role in grasping and explaining living things than material/formal and efficient causes, whereas the reverse is true in grasping and explaining non-living things.

I noted in chapter 4 how Aristotle over-emphasised finality in inanimate beings, leading him to make mistakes in physics. There is, however, no over-emphasis of finality here, in the realm of the living. Because of their manifest purposefulness, life forms must not be considered primarily in the activity of their parts—how one part moves another moves another, in mechanistic fashion—but more according to their purpose, how the parts are organised among themselves to work together for the achievement of a single end that is greater than the activity of the parts taken individually.

Illustration

Let us take an example to illustrate these differences between non-living and living things, and their explanation. On the one hand you have our sun, an enormous non-living body of largely homogeneous matter. The individual parts of the sun are not being directed to a purpose higher than themselves by some unifying form pervading the whole. Rather, an immense number of hydrogen atoms randomly bump into one another, generating heat and decaying into helium, following the blind processes of nature, in a rather mechanical fashion. Using such interactions alone, we are able to provide a satisfactory account of the formation of the star and its 'life' cycle. Moreover, these simple processes are easily translated into the language of mathematics. This is the proper domain of physics, and we don't need to leave the realm of material, formal, and efficient causality to achieve a satisfying explanation of the sun's processes. It is true that final causality is also present, but the material homogeneity of the sun and its simple functioning renders that finality obscure. In the end, the sun is a subject most fit for the investigations of exact science.

On the other hand, you have an eagle. The individual parts of the bird—beak, feathers, eyes, brain, heart, claws, and so on—are composed of quite different materials and have their own specific functions. While they are different in their composition and their activity, we yet do not find them functioning independently of one another, as did the hydrogen atoms in the sun. Rather, they all work together as a team, in a complex harmony, cooperating to attain a goal that is outside of their own respective spheres. This goal—life—is readily apparent and easily studied. Claws are for grasping, but here claws are being used to grasp twigs for building nests, here branches to keep from dropping to the ground, here prey to provide food for the body. Feathers are for flying, but these feathers are being used to escape dangers, locate food sources, and attain secluded places. Both the claws and the feathers, then, are being directed to perform their activities in the interest of a single goal, the maintenance and continuance of the life of the eagle. And so it is with the rest of the components of the eagle's body—each of their functions are being co-opted to serve the life of the eagle. Moreover, they are being co-opted by the eagle itself, that is, the eagle is a single reality directing all of its diverse matter to a unique goal. This fact, along with others, points to a reality that cannot be explained merely in mechanical terms, a reality called purpose. That reality is not subject to mathematisation, is not quantifiable, and so is not within the proper limits of science. Yet it can be explained in terms of its own proper causality—final causality—in the field of natural philosophy.

Life explanation choices

To give a full account of the fact of life, then, the realist or the thinker or whoever must answer questions about all four causes:

1. (material and efficient causes) What matter is present and how does it act?
2. (intrinsic formal and intrinsic final cause) Why do the parts of living bodies work together to serve life?
3. (extrinsic formal or exemplar cause) Who designed the life forms to work that way?

The first question can be asked of both inorganic and organic things, but the second and third are tailored to address the purposefulness that is so obvious to us in life forms.

We must consider how four different parties respond to these questions:

- the mechanists
- Aristotle
- the Intelligent Design movement
- realists

By mechanists, I refer to the empirical scientists who believe that they can reduce all explanations to material and efficient causes. I am in no way implying by this that mechanical explanations are wrong; material and efficient causes really exist and so need to be part of our understanding of natural bodies. By the word 'mechanists' in this context, I am referring to epistemological empiricists who reduce *all* explanations of living things to mechanical ones, the mere movement of parts.[11]

The empiricist mechanist position is largely one of denial. It is easy to find mechanists who deny teleology/finality, but hard to find finalists who deny mechanism.[12] The typical mechanist answer to question 2 would be 'They don't work together to serve life', and to question 3, 'No one designed life forms.' Quite simply, empiricists refuse to find either order or design in living things, though it stare them in the face ever so clearly. For them, the evidence for design is a trick, a deception foisted on us by our gullible intellects. Thus, Richard Dawkins defines biology as 'the study of complicated things that give the appearance of having been designed for a purpose'.[13]

Inorganic Life

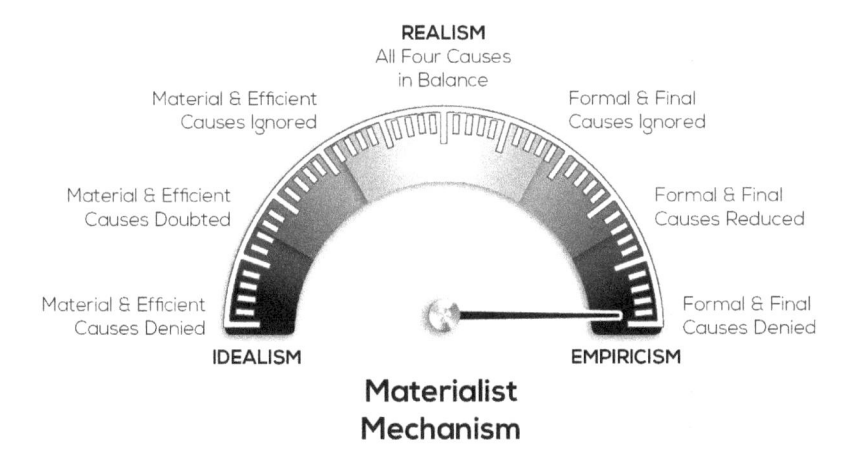

```
                    REALISM
                 All Four Causes
                   in Balance
  Material & Efficient              Formal & Final
  Causes Ignored                    Causes Ignored

  Material & Efficient              Formal & Final
  Causes Doubted                    Causes Reduced

  Material & Efficient              Formal & Final
  Causes Denied                     Causes Denied
       IDEALISM                       EMPIRICISM
                   Materialist
                   Mechanism
```

Such empirical scientists existed in Aristotle's day and he attacked one of them—Empedocles—in his *On the Parts of Animals*. Empedocles 'said that many of the characters presented by animals were merely the results of incidental occurrences during their development; for instance, that the backbone was divided as it is into vertebrae, because it happened to be broken owing to the contorted position of the fetus in the womb'.[14] There is no special purpose in the vertebra's configuration; it is the result of mere chance. Thus, it is neither directed towards the life of the organism, nor designed for that purpose.

Aristotle strongly disagreed with Empedocles, pointing out that children are obviously not the product of chance; rather, they come from the seed of their parents. That is why they take on the bodily characteristics of their parents. Moreover, it is clear that children somehow pre-exist physically in their parents, since they are produced from them. Thus, far from generation being a random process, it is rather one with a very definite direction and goal, a goal directed by nature.

Aristotle answers the second question, then, with final causality, saying that the material parts pursue a goal because of their intrinsic finality. They are directed to that goal by the soul of the life form, its formal cause. Who set all of this up (question 3)? Here, Aristotle falls a bit short, only speaking of 'nature' in the abstract as bestowing purpose on living things. The reason was his inability to consider God as a creator of the universe, the same shortcoming that caused him to over-emphasise finality in physics, as we saw in chapter 4.[15] Thus, Aristotle 'appears to rest content ... with the surely unsatisfactory notion of purpose which is not the purpose of mind'.[16]

This is where the Intelligent Design theorists come in. They tend to ignore (but not deny)[17] the intrinsic finality which is the logical answer to the second question. The reason is that they bind themselves to start with a scientific mode of reasoning and see where it leads them. We will see this in more detail later in the chapter, but suffice it to say here that it leads them to conclude that an intelligent designing mind—an exemplar cause—is the best explanation for the complexity that we observe in life forms.[18]

The realist philosopher will embrace the material explanations of the empiricists, the immanent finality explanations of Aristotle, and the extrinsic design explanations of ID scientists. Each of them has its role to play in accounting for the complex reality of life, and the realist is never one to eliminate this or that causal explanation, when it accounts for a distinct aspect of reality. None of those explanations, however, seeks to assign a cause for designing the essential aspects of the being of life forms, leaving the realist to perform that mental work himself.

By the essential aspects of life forms, I mean those aspects that place them into a different level of being than other things. For instance, animals such as starfish, which only have the sense of touch, are at a lower level of being than dolphins, which have all five senses. This difference makes for an ontological divide between them, and so a divide which cannot be bridged by secondary causes. No secondary cause can make new sense powers come into being from old sense powers, turning touch into hearing or smelling. A technical philosophical explanation of the reasons why secondary causes cannot do this would take us too far afield,[19] but suffice it to say here that only the cause of being, God, can bring into existence beings of an essentially higher level than the beings which currently exist. But once God has created, for instance, animals with all five senses like dolphins, then secondary causes—such as dolphins, natural selection, humans, and even good and bad angels—can modify dolphins to make other animals that are new to some degree.

When atheists hear talk of a benevolent God being responsible for life, in its major lines, they believe they have an argument against Him. Looking around at the biological world, they find it to be full of killing, 'red in tooth and claw'.[20] What they fail to see is that physical evils can be good, not as such, but in that they serve a greater good. There are strong arguments to support the idea that God uses physical suffering, on both the part of animals and men, as a means for them to attain higher purposes.[21]

Rizzi suggests that angelic interference might help explain diseases, so that they need not be attributed to God.[22] While such an explanation might provide a passing assistance to a theologian attempting to account for something like the evident intentional design of malaria that Behe has us ponder long and hard,[23] it is nevertheless entirely speculative. The most philosophy can say is that life, in its grand lines, must be designed by God; the most science can say is that certain micro-evolutionary changes take place of themselves in nature; and the most theology can say is that God loses none of His benevolence by including physical evils in the natural order. Beyond this, we do not currently have any intellectual resources to provide further detail about macro-evolutionary changes and so must be content to leave that question open until more information becomes available.

The table below gives the respective answers of our four parties to the three questions concerning living things.

Table 10.2 Answers to questions about the causes of life

Causes of life	1. What are living bodies made of and how do they act?	2. Why are the parts of living things ordered toward life?	3. Who designed life forms?
Mechanists	Description of material processes	They are not ordered toward life.	No one; they are not designed.
Aristotle	Description of material processes	By reason of their soul and their intrinsic finality	Nature in the abstract
ID	Description of material processes	Question not considered	An intelligent designer
Realists	Description of material processes	By reason of their soul and their intrinsic finality	God, at least in their major lines

Having explored the general epistemological territory of biology, we will now try to explain the mechanist account in more detail. Specifically, we will try to show how the mechanist refusal to yield any explanatory territory to final causes, in an effort to keep everything for science, leads its proponents straight into irrationality.

Away with purpose

Modern scientists just don't like final causality. For one thing, focusing too much on purposes held back science for centuries. For another, final causality cannot be detected by the scientific method, which is supposed to be able to 'shed light on every and any concept'.[24] Not least is that questions of purpose lead straight to God, and many scientists would rather lose purpose if that's what it takes to get rid of God, rather than having to keep the both of them.

So, onward with the attack on purpose! Lawrence Krauss finds 'living in a universe without purpose to be amazing'.[25] He explains that '"Why?" is not really a sensible question in science because it usually implies purpose' and what science does, as it progresses, is change 'why' questions to 'how' questions.[26] So, if you are starting to wonder about purpose, don't even ask! For Peter Atkins, 'the question of the purpose of the universe is an invention of human minds, and has no significance'[27] and 'ultimately everything is junk'.[28]

In all of their purposeful efforts to destroy purpose, these scientists seem to understand what they are about. We do have to wonder why men committed to ultimate meaninglessness write books, and probably more why those books are even printed and read. For, if there is no purpose, there is no reason to do anything at all. Reason and meaning come from purpose.

None of this impedes our empiricist scientists, for they have fixed themselves on the firm purpose to eliminate from human understanding anything that does not fall under science's limited scope. What strategy must they employ, then, to claim that life forms are without purpose? To convince their public, they must attempt to show that *the complexity of living things is not the product of intelligence, but rather of random or mindless processes.*

This is as much as to say that plants and animals are really no more than the sum of their parts. There is not in reality a greater whole called 'life' to which all of the physical processes of living things are directed. 'Life' is just a convenient concept for our minds to speak about the totality of the activity of the clump of matter before us. That clump does not have any real unity; it is a mere set of individual chemical components, randomly juxtaposed. Don't let your mind fool you into believing that your pet chihuahua is ontologically higher than baking soda.

But say our biological reductionists could establish their thesis that life forms are the result of mindless processes. Would that prove that living things are purposeless? In fact, no. Would it give the appearance of proving it? Yes. The reason why it would not prove that living things are purposeless is that *every existing thing, whether living or non-living, expresses purpose by its very activity.*[29]

Imagine a drop of water rolling onto a sponge. A million things *could* happen: it could bounce off, explode, freeze into an ice cube, turn into a spotted leopard, and so on. But none of those things happen. Only one thing happens: the water is absorbed by the sponge. Why so? Because the water is not indifferent to the million possibilities. Water, by its very nature, *inclines* towards one eventuality to the exclusion of all other possible eventualities.

This inclination, this determination to one outcome out of all possible outcomes, is the 'pursuit' of an end, and so is a manifestation of purpose. If the water had no end, it would not incline to be absorbed by sponges or to anything else. It would not tend toward any one thing over any other; all possible activities would be indifferent to it. As such, it would not act at all. But it does act. Therefore, it must have finality or purpose.

By the fact, then, that a being does this rather than that, it is manifesting finality. It is for this reason that the final cause enters into the ontological structure of all beings, and so also their explanation, as I indicated in chapter 2. Thus, we merely need this or that being to act to show that it manifests purpose.

Scientists don't realise this, and you would be hard pressed to find mention of it anywhere. That's one of the reasons why many are taken in when empiricists put forward technical arguments to show that animals are undesigned. They don't realise that every non-self-existing entity must be designed, from the fact alone that it acts.

Let us now turn to the technical arguments of the empiricists, to see if they have any value.

Life is so complex

What our mechanist biologists must do is indicate to us that the heterogeneous parts of life forms all came together, started working in all of their functionality, and started working in harmony with one another for the growth, nutrition, and reproduction of the organism—all of this by merely random processes. In essence, they have to show us that plants and animals came together in the same way that stars and galaxies came together— by gazillions of atoms just doing their thing, without any special help beyond the kick start given to a finely tuned universe. The technical term for this is *abiogenesis*, the generation of life from non-life.

In this chapter, we consider whether it is possible, given the laws of our universe, for a life form to be assembled from scratch by random processes; in the next, we consider the possibility of one life form randomly changing into another.

Forming a place for life

How do you take the known laws of nature, the 13.7 billion years science assigns as the age of the universe, the raw atomic stuff in that universe, and make a plant? Well, let us just say that a lot of stirring does not get us anywhere, but we are going to give it the old college try.

For one thing, you are going to need a third generation solar system containing complex elements, like our own. The reason is that all life is carbon-based. Only the bonds of the carbon atom are sufficiently stable to sustain life forms; silicon is the closest runner-up, but it does not do the job.[30] Okay, so how do you get carbon if you start with a Big Bang? As follows:

> The Big Bang produced hydrogen and helium and little else. Over the next 13 billion years, this mix was cooked within many generations of stars and recycled. Beginning with the fusion of hydrogen atoms, massive stars make ever-heavier nuclei deep in their hot interiors, building on the ashes of the previous stage and forming an onion-like structure. Exploding as supernovae, the massive stars eventually return atoms to the galaxy. But they return them with interest, by producing heavy elements that didn't exist before.[31]

So, only massive stars form heavier elements like carbon and oxygen. They complete their life cycle, and eject the heavier elements into space. New stars form and also planets with the heavier elements in the mix. This cycle would have to take place at least twice before our sun and planet Earth could be formed if that formation took place 4.55 billion years ago. The cycles would produce the carbon, nitrogen, oxygen, iron, and many other heavy elements that are needed for life's delicate conditions here on Earth.

There are innumerably more complexities involved to provide the conditions for a habitable planet—so many that it seems likely that Earth is the only one in the universe[32]—but we grant that our planet could have formed by merely natural processes without a direct intervention by God or an immaterial intelligent agent. The theory has reputable, mathematical models behind it, something the formation of life will never have. Our focus here is more on the time question, which is important for naturalistic scientists. If life was to develop anywhere in the universe by purely random processes, it would have to be at the later end of the universe's history.

Formation of cells

As for the Earth, life had to get started quite soon after the planet's formation. Scientists have discovered fossils of algae in rocks dated to 3.5 billion years.[33] Subtracting that from the 4.5 billion years they assign as the Earth's age leaves only 1 billion years of atomic stirring to get the life spark ignited. That's an awful lot of time, surely enough for a nice, simple, little life form, like a bit of mould or a clump of algae or a juvenile protozoa.

It is here that, with the help of twenty-first-century science, a point needs to be made loud and clear: *there is no such thing as a simple life form.* The difference between the formation of a star and the formation of a life form is as the difference between the setting off of an avalanche and the Manhattan Project. In the words of Michael Denton:

> We now know not only of the existence of a break between the living and non-living world, but also that it represents the most dramatic and fundamental of all the discontinuities of nature. Between a living cell and the most highly ordered non-biological system, such as a crystal or a snowflake, there is a chasm as vast and absolute as it is possible to conceive.[34]

Inorganic Life 411

Because the cell is common to all life forms and it is the most basic building block of life, mechanists try to think of ways in which a self-replicating cell could have arisen by merely natural processes. The first thing that they need is a pre-biotic soup, or a body of liquid in the Earth's past that would contain the ingredients necessary for forming a cell. There is no evidence that such a soup could exist in the Earth's early aeons, but its existence is generally taken for granted.[35]

Besides this, the complexity of a single cell is staggering and hence an immense coincidence of forces would be necessary to form one. The one-stop source for this discussion is Stephen Meyer's magisterial work *Signature in the Cell*. Recall his distinction between 'mere complexity' and 'specified complexity' that I considered in the last chapter. Meyer uses the phrase 'specified complexity' in a roughly equivalent way to my use of 'order' and 'coordination of heterogeneous parts to perform a higher function', following the traditional philosophical language of Aristotle.

Meyer begins by explaining the makeup of the cell that needs to be accounted for, and then he considers all of the naturalistic theories that have been put forward to justify its spontaneous formation. Even better, he explains the concepts involved in the discussion, along with the logical processes that are being used to draw conclusions.

It is impossible to detail all of the cell's complexity—not just for me, but for anyone, as its complexity exceeds the greatest feats of human technology by many orders of magnitude—and so I will just give a mechanical explanation of three of its aspects to illustrate a small facet of that complexity:

1. **Proteins**—there are thousands of protein types and they perform innumerable tasks in the cell, such as building cellular machines, delivering cellular material, catalysing cellular reactions, and processing genetic information.[36] They are composed of a string of amino acids, typically 150 of them. There are 20 types of amino acids and each can be right-handed or left-handed. Specific proteins are *only*

formed from left-handed amino acids and *only* when the 150 acids are of the right type and in the right sequence. The simplest known cell requires 482 different proteins composed of these specific sequences of left-handed amino acids.[37]

2. **DNA**—deoxyribose nucleic acid is the genetic code of life forms, containing the instructions for the activities of the cell, among which is the assembly of proteins, a process called 'protein synthesis.' That process has two steps:

   a) **Transcription**[38]—this is the process of copying the DNA information onto a strand of RNA (ribonucleic acid). There are four types of bases in DNA (A, C, G, T) which are arranged in a very specific order on the DNA's double-helix structure; that arrangement is the genetic code of the organism. When transcription takes place, the exact portion of DNA to be copied is identified, the double-helix is unwound, the RNA is matched up with the part exposed, the copying is performed, and finally the RNA is trimmed and spliced back together, now containing the code from the given portion of DNA. This process requires 12 proteins.

   b) **Translation**[39]—the RNA goes to a ribosome, a molecular machine that acts like a data processing unit. The ribosome splits into two, with the RNA binding to one side. The first section of the RNA contains a command for translation, which is read by another type of RNA. The reading of that command brings the other half of the ribosome back to begin the translation work. Translation involves summoning the amino acids of the target protein based on the DNA code contained in the RNA. The code is read by examining three DNA bases at a time (examples of DNA triplets would be sequences like TCT, AGA, CGT, and so on). *Based on the order alone of the triplets and not on a chemical* *reaction*, this or that amino acid is summoned. The acids are placed in a row on a peptide chain until the translation is finished. Then the chain is cut and the string of amino acids goes away, forming itself into the right protein. This process requires 106 proteins. The simplest known cell needs 562,000 bases of DNA to assemble the proteins.

3. **Mutual dependency**—the complexity of proteins and DNA is daunting enough, but their challenge to empiricists is exacerbated a thousandfold when we note that *proteins are involved in the protein-making process*. In Meyer's words, this poses a 'chicken and egg' dilemma:

> The cell needs proteins to process and express the information in DNA in order to build proteins. But the construction of DNA molecules (during the process of DNA replication) also requires proteins. So which came first, the chicken (nucleic acids) or the egg (proteins)? If proteins must have arisen first, then how did they do so, since all extant cells construct proteins from the assembly instructions in DNA.[40]

This is just a tiny look at the cell's complexity, but it is enough for us to see that our materialist mechanists have a terrible problem on their hands. Following Meyer, we will consider two classes of explanation that they put forward to convince us that the cell arose by unguided processes: chance and necessity.

Chance—stuff just happens

The chance proponents hypothesise that chemicals floated around in some pre-biotic soup with sufficient opportunities for them to combine and recombine until they hit the 'cosmic jackpot', that is, the chance conglomeration of the building blocks of life to form the first self-replicating cell.[41] Before I explore the plausibility of this hypothesis, I just want to reiterate that chance is not a proper cause, and thus to say that chance made life is to say that nothing made it. It is the same as saying that there is no intelligible cause to be discovered by the mind to explain the phenomenon of life.

Okay, so what are the chances for chance? First of all, we need proteins and lots of them. But even if we had tons of amino acids in a puddle and started stirring it and striking it with lightning, the chances of us getting any functional protein would be 1 in 10^{164}.[42] That number represents the proportion of functional, bonded amino acid sequences—the ones that turn into proteins—to total possible amino acid sequences. We have to hit that jackpot 482 times in short order to get some of the raw material for the simplest cell on Earth.[43]

It might help to note here—to satisfy those who think that any chance is still a chance—that around 10^{17} seconds have elapsed since the beginning of the universe (assuming the Big Bang model to be true), that the number of interactions of elementary particles per second is at most 10^{43}, and that there are around 10^{80} elementary particles in the universe. This means that there have been at most 10^{140} particle events since the beginning of the universe (multiplying the three numbers by adding their exponents, $10^{17} * 10^{43} * 10^{80} = 10^{140}$).[44] Dividing 10^{140} by 10^{164}, we are left with a 1 in 10^{24} chance of generating a single functional protein 'if every event in the universe over its entire history were devoted to producing combinations of amino acids of the correct length in a prebiotic soup (an extravagantly generous and even absurd assumption)'.[45] That's 1 in 1,000,000,000,000,000,000,000,000.

We also need DNA, which is to say that we need a computer code in nucleic bases to arise spontaneously by blind natural forces. Meyer did not run the numbers on those chances, but I am thinking they are less than zero.

Even if that happened, we would still only be at the point of raw materials. We would still need some way of initiating the whole factory process of protein synthesis, gene expression and DNA replication, for what good are raw materials if they are not arranged to work together, ordered to a given goal? And we need

Inorganic Life 415

all of this to work flawlessly, for with cells, it is all or nothing. There is no such thing as a half-functioning cell. 'A cell burdened with inefficient proteins, an error-prone code, and choked with junk would grind instantly to a halt'.[46]

In the face of all this evidence, it would seem embarrassing to ask an intelligent, reasonable person to believe that a cell magically came together some time in the distant past.

Necessity—it had to happen

Necessity theorists call upon a certain 'biochemical predestination' to explain the origin of life. By this, they mean that certain laws of nature automatically lead to greater order and, eventually, the order and information needed for a cell.[47] They are not aware of the metaphysical impossibility of blind forces constructing an intricate order, the violation of the principle of causality contained therein. The blind forces have nothing of the complex order found in life forms, and so it is impossible for those forces the make such an order. You cannot give what you do not have. To expect order to spontaneously arise from disorder is the same as expecting something to come from nothing. That is why our friend from chapter 9, Fred Hoyle, said that a nonorganic origin of life is like a 747 being assembled from a tornado in a junkyard.[48] It is obvious to us that tornadoes do not have such causal abilities, and so it is irrational, even superstitious, to attribute such powers to them.

The scientists appealing to necessity thought that there might be processes of self-organisation in nature, such that there would be 'a spontaneous increase in the order of a system due to some natural process, force, or law'.[49] For instance, it could be possible that amino acids, by their very chemical properties, have an inclination to bond together and form proteins when they are in close proximity. If such were the case, it would make the formation of proteins practically inevitable, certainly much more probable than when invoking chance.

Dean Kenyon and Gary Steinman investigated this possibility in the late 1960s. What they found is that amino acids do have preferences in how they interact with each other, and this affinity for chemical interaction is determined by their chemical structure, and makes certain sequences more likely than others. This finding established Kenyon as a leading researcher in his field and held the attention of the scientific community for two decades. In the late 1980s, however, it was discovered that the amino acid affinities do not match up with the very specific arrangements that lead to the formation of proteins. It is as if amino acids, if they would have their druthers, would prefer not to form proteins. This makes it clear, then, that the only viable way for proteins to arise in nature is through the specific information contained in the DNA molecule that all life forms possess.[50]

This specific information brings us back to the original point of the impossibility of the order of the cell arising by purely natural forces. The complexity of the cell is unique in the whole of nature because it does not work primarily by means of chemical interactions, but rather via the computer-like code embedded in DNA. As mentioned, DNA contains four different types of bases to which biologists have assigned the letters A, C, G, and T. These bases act like a four-letter alphabet, such that their specific arrangement *spells* instructions which the machinery of the cell is able to read and execute. This is the equivalent of saying that there is a single language for life 'understood' by the cells of all life forms.[51]

This unique complexity of living things is not just greater in *degree* to that of non-living things such as stars, but it belongs to an entirely different *order* of complexity. Raw material forces are intrinsically incapable of producing such complexity; such a production completely exceeds their causal powers. *This complexity, then, is beyond the reach of the scientific method.* It is the complexity of an order that is immaterial, that is based on concepts such as those from which all language derives, and so falls outside the mechanical workings of matter.[52]

Modern science, then, has confirmed in a striking way what Aristotle knew all along, that the complex ordering of heterogeneous material parts in service of a higher unified function can be explained only by formal and final causality.

Meyer sums up his own analysis of self-organisational necessity models as follows:

> Self-organizational forces of chemical necessity, which produce redundant order and *preclude* complexity, preclude the generation of specified complexity (or specified information) as well. Lawlike chemical forces do not generate complex sequences. Thus, they cannot be invoked to explain the origin of information, whether specified or otherwise.[53]

Irrational attachment to unintelligence

My treatment of naturalistic explanations for the origin of life would not be complete unless I linked it to a key idea in this book, namely, that *errors in epistemology lead to irrationality*. Just as religious idealists can refuse the obvious evidence of their senses because of supposed revelations contained in a sacred text, so too scientific empiricists can refuse the obvious evidence of their intellect because of their deification of science.

The fact is that evidence for a non-material origin of life is overwhelming. The metaphysical argument of the inability of mere matter to produce complex order *ex nihilo* is a clincher. But even to the common man not attuned to philosophical arguments, it is plainly obvious, based on modern science's revelation of life's fascinating complexity, that life cannot have emerged from a pre-biotic, chemical womb. We could ask ourselves, then, if it is at all intellectually reputable to maintain that life rose from non-life.

Needless to say, such an opinion is not only considered reputable, but unquestionable, by many in the scientific community. Given that they are experts and so are much more familiar with the complexity of life than the general public, we can only conclude that the universe of evidence against a mechanistic origin of life is getting overturned by something outside the realm of science. For surely it takes a blind faith to believe in something that is not only unfathomably improbable, but runs contrary to reason. Only blindness can mistake the fundamental difference between complex order and raw matter, lumping them both into a flattened landscape of reality. It is a specific type of blindness, a seeing blindness, which is constantly putting its hand over the eyes of the intellect, which are ever inferring the fact of intelligent design and not its mere appearance.

Dawkins' explanation

Consider how Richard Dawkins—the preeminent spokesman for naturalistic biological explanations—tries to convince us that life comes from non-life. In chapter 8 of his *The Greatest Show on Earth*, he speaks of the protein function of accelerating cellular reactions, trying hard to reduce everything to the chemical level.[54] He repeats incessantly that it is just a question of chemicals following local rules; there is no over-arching order or design. The proteins just start folding, like self-constructing origami. Assuming that we are convinced by his analogy, he moves to justify a naturalistic construction of human genetic code. We are all expecting an intellectual slam dunk powerhouse of an argument from the materialist poster child—and believe me, Dawkins would give it if it existed—but this is all we get:

> Haldane's interlocutor found it implausible that natural selection could put together in, say, a billion years, a genetic recipe for building her. *I find it plausible, although of course neither I nor anybody else can tell you the details of how it happened.* The reason it is plausible is precisely that it is all done by local rules ... Nobody understands the whole picture, and nobody needs to understand it in order to accept the exquisite plausibility of natural selection ... The whole picture emerges as a consequence of hundreds of thousands of small, local interactions, each one comprehensible in principle ... The whole may be baffling and mysterious in practice, but there is no mystery in principle

Inorganic Life 419

...Haldane's questioner was wrong. It is not in principle difficult to make something like her.[55]

The best that we can say about this is that it is disingenuous, hiding a whole world of insuperable metaphysical, mathematical, and biological difficulties. It is the assertion of a plausibility without providing a shred of scientific evidence that the plausibility is an actuality. Let Dawkins specify the small, local interactions—just one hundred out of the hundreds of thousands—and let him point to them happening in nature. Then we will be able to speak about the beginning of a scientific argument. Otherwise, he is believing in a creation myth far more far-fetched than anything believed by creationists. They have a Creator, who is omnipotent. Dawkins has 'nothing', just like his close friend Krauss. He has non-life, he has non-order, he has non-function, and it is with these that he has to construct the exquisite order of life forms.

New Atheist Peter Atkins is more honest when he says, 'My own faith, my scientific faith, is that there is nothing that the scientific method cannot illuminate and elucidate'.[56] Fair enough, but should it not be stated that a faith is outside of the scientific method? That his faith is an expression of an epistemology, and an epistemology that wilfully hinders the mind from knowing certain aspects of reality? That it is a faith that brings in its train a coterie of devastating dogmas, wrecking the mind and human life?

Empiricism wrecking society

If the scientific method is the only possible source of knowledge, then there is no reality called 'purpose.' If there is no reality called 'purpose', then life has no meaning and should not be valued. If life should not be valued, then abortion, euthanasia, and even homicide in general lose their negative connotations.

If local laws are the only laws, then each one is a law unto himself. Recall from chapter 4 that this was the very dictum of the materialists of Socrates' time. Permit me to quote again the relevant passage from that chapter to demonstrate the kindred affinity existing among empiricists of all times:

> [A]s the Sophist Protagoras famously put it: 'Man is the measure of all things—of the things that are, that they are; of the things that are not, that they are not ... Each and every event is for me as it appears to me, and is for you as it appears to you'. From such a perspective, each man is master of his own reality and cannot be imposed upon by any norm external to himself. There is no truth or real knowledge, and so no moral standards.[57]

If you start off with a worldview such as 'empiricism' or 'realism' or 'idealism', you are inevitably led to hold the logical derivatives of that worldview, to the degree that you are consistent. Empiricism demands the denial of final causes and so has purposelessness as one of its necessary logical offshoots. It demands that the only forces working in the universe be ones without intelligence, and so leaves humans to make their own rules, their own meaning, their own destiny, in the face of a reality inherently hostile and uncomprehending of their aspirations.

But instead of interpreting the empiricists' worldview for themselves, let us have one of their twentieth-century leading lights—Bertrand Russell—speak eloquently on their behalf, telling us the scientific way to view the world. He starts by making reference to a world created by a heartless and capricious being, then continues:

> Such, in outline, but even more purposeless, more void of meaning, is the world which Science presents for our belief. Amid such a world, if anywhere, our ideals henceforward must find a home. That man is the product of causes which had no prevision of the end they were achieving; that his origin, his growth, his hopes and fears, his loves and his beliefs, are but the outcome of accidental collocations of atoms; that no fire, no heroism, no intensity of thought and feeling, can preserve an individual life beyond the grave; that all the labours of the ages, all the

devotion, all the inspirations, all the noonday brightness of human genius, are destined to extinction in the vast death of the solar system, and that the whole temple of Man's achievement must inevitably be buried beneath the debris of a universe in ruins—all these things, if not quite beyond dispute, are yet so nearly certain, that no philosophy which rejects them can hope to stand. Only within the scaffolding of these truths, only on the firm foundation of unyielding despair, can the soul's habitation henceforth be safely built.[58]

'Unyielding despair' does not appear to me to be a suitable rallying cry for any people, much less a higher civilisation.

The search for aliens

Before closing this look at the tenets of materialists' creed, we must consider one other: belief in alien life, a position that follows directly from their origin of life myth. For if life derived from non-life by blind fate on Earth, and the universe is populated with innumerable suns and planetary systems, we would certainly expect life to exist elsewhere in that universe. As Atkins states:

> What happily happened here can happen anywhere with similarly benign and stable conditions, and it is not an unreasonable supposition that the universe teems with life that has stumbled into being and has evolved by natural selection.[59]

If life was actually discovered elsewhere, the find would give the *appearance* that life is a natural product of chemical interactions. As Denton remarks, locating extraterrestrial (ET) life

> would undoubtedly provide powerful circumstantial evidence for the traditional evolutionary scenario, enhancing enormously the credibility of the belief that the route from chemistry to life can be surmounted by simple natural processes wherever the right conditions exist.[60]

Even more than ET life, materialists would love to find ET intelligence (ETI). The reason is that they want to undermine the human race's perception of its own significance, that it is higher than the whole of material creation. If there were intelligent beings elsewhere in the cosmos, we would not be the only ones. Our intelligence would not seem to be the special gift of a benevolent Creator making us in His own image, but just another thing that happened to happen in the cosmic stir pot. It certainly would not seem likely that God would assume a human nature on Earth in order to redeem us from our sins.

ETI would help to reinforce what scientists call the 'Copernican Principle'. The idea is that Copernicus dislodged humans from the top of the cosmic pecking order by moving them away from the centre of the universe and putting the sun in Earth's former place. As we saw in chapter 7, this is a very shallow argument indeed to put forward against human significance.[61] It is certainly not a scientific principle; saying that humanity is insignificant is striking a philosophical position.

Gonzalez and Richards wrote a book-long refutation of the materialistic worldview wrapped in scientific clothing which is the Copernican Principle. In their *The Privileged Planet*, they devote one chapter to SETI, or the search for ETI.[62] They note the quasi-religious aura surrounding belief in alien life; the invasion of popular culture by alien films, books, and magazines; the constant agitprop surrounding SETI in order to reduce human significance. To our day, the least smidgeon of hope that there just might be a living microbe out there is trumpeted with great fanfare by the mass media. Furthermore, just as with life emerging from a lightning-struck pool, communication with an alien race is so easily within the reach of the human imagination that the mind readily accepts it as a plausible idea, without investigating the actual causal forces that would be needed to make it a reality.

Radio astronomer Francis Drake came up with an equation in 1961 whose purpose was to estimate the likelihood of finding an

Inorganic Life

advanced radio communicating civilisation in our Milky Way galaxy. It helped clarify just how many factors are involved in the formation of an environment such as our own, though it was formulated with materialist assumptions. Gonzalez and Richards explain the equation as follows:

$N = N^* \times f_p \times n_e \times f_l \times f_i \times f_c \times f_L$

N, the product of the equation, is the total number of radio-communicating, technological civilizations in the Milky Way at any one time. The answer derives from the total number of stars in the galaxy (N^*) times the fraction of stars with planetary systems (f_p) times the number of habitable planets in each system (n_e—*e* stands for 'Earth-like') times the fraction of habitable planets on which life emerges from inorganic matter or organic precursors (f_l) times the fraction of those planets on which intelligent beings also evolve (f_i) times the fraction of those planets on which sufficient communications technology arises (f_c) times the fraction of the average planetary lifetime during which there is an advanced civilization (f_L).[63]

Carl Sagan, the great atheist propagator of belief in life on other planets, used the Drake equation to estimate 'that there are perhaps one million advanced civilisations in the Milky Way. Little more than a guess, it remains entrenched in both the popular and the scientific imagination.'[64]

The truth is, however, that there are many scientific reasons to believe that we are alone in the universe. Gonzalez and Richards propose their own modified version of the Drake Equation,[65] while indicating all of the concrete scientific reasons that led them to stop believing in extraterrestrial life. Earth is indeed a privileged planet and I leave the reader to review those fascinating and compelling arguments.

Let me just mention here that if it is impossible for life to come by way of abiogenesis, based on our knowledge of life's complexity and requirements, then the entire SETI enterprise is misdirected. The Drake Equation is attempting to calculate the chances of an event that is an impossibility. The only cause proportionate to originating life, whether it be on Earth or somewhere in the universe, is a higher intelligence. Our own intelligence indicates to us as much. Thus, any search for ETI should be conducted in terms of the desires of higher intelligences, not in terms of the chances for abiogenesis somewhere in the universe.

In summary, the abiogenesis worldview necessarily demands
- belief in extraterrestrial life
- belief in the insignificance of Earth
- belief in the meaninglessness of life
- belief in the purposelessness of human existence.

ID arguments

Before I conclude this chapter, I have to make a few notes about the arguments of the Intelligent Design movement, arguments which I support. One reason for broaching this topic is that I am writing as a Thomist philosopher and some Thomists hold that ID views life in a way that is too mechanical. Others confuse ID theorists with creationists. Even Jaki does this to a certain degree in his pamphlet 'Intelligent Design?'. A second reason is to show how ID theory follows a realist epistemology, though its proponents never speak in such terms.

The first thing to be understood is that the ID argument is a scientific one. It makes no reference whatsoever to sacred texts; it allows for the working of secondary causes; it follows the evidence of the senses. It has nothing to say, as such, about the controversies in which the creationists find themselves embroiled.[66]

Secondly, the ID argument is a very specific scientific argument. It wants to establish the causes of events of the past, such as the origin of life or the diversification of species. To do so, it takes as its working premise the principle of uniformitarianism. We have already seen that this principle is necessary for science to take place and matches up with a God is reasonable in His

Inorganic Life

works. Meyer sums up this principle as 'the present is the key to the past', specifically 'that our knowledge of present cause-and-effect relationships should govern how we assess the plausibility of inferences we make about the cause of effects in the past'.[67] In other words, in our explanation of things that happened in the past, we should only make reference to causes that work in the present, and not 'unknown or exotic causes, the effects of which we do not know'.[68]

Now, those scientists who seek to establish the causes of past events work in the 'palaetiological' or historical sciences. Non-historical scientists, on the other hand, seek to discover the general laws of nature that work at all times. Because the two types of scientists have a different object of study, they also make use of different modes of reasoning when establishing their conclusions. Historical scientists use present clues to infer the most likely past causes, a process that is referred to as *abductive* reasoning.[69] Non-historical scientists reason in an *inductive* fashion, taking all of the empirical data presently available and attempting to formulate a general law that fits that data. The chart below clarifies these distinctions.

Table 10.3 *Differences between historical and non-historical sciences*

Distinction of Sciences	Non-historical sciences	Historical or 'Palaetiological' sciences
Object	General laws of nature	Causes that worked in the past
Mode of explanation	Present events are explained by the general laws	Present events are explained by the past causes
Mode of reasoning	Inductive: framing a law that precisely fits all empirical data	Abductive: arguing from present clues back to the most likely past cause

It is precisely Dr Meyer who makes these distinctions in chapter 7 of his *Signature in the Cell*, and it should be clear from them that ID accepts the realist principle of 'different methods of study for different types of objects.'

ID, then, starts with the data of the senses available in the present day, observing the causes now in operation. Then, it gains as much information as possible about the past event that needs to be explained. Finally, it seeks among all of the causes presently in operation for the one which best explains that past event.

There are at least two conditions for a given cause to be a candidate to explain a past effect:

1. **Causal adequacy**—the proposed cause must be capable of producing the effect
2. **Causal existence**—the proposed cause must have been present at the right time and place in order to produce the effect.

One of the ways to show that a cause existed in the past is by proving it is the only one known to produce a certain effect. In this way, it *had* to be present in the past because the effect was produced in the past. In the case of the complexity of life that arose in the past, the only cause that is capable of producing such an effect is an intelligent agent.[70]

Such are the methods and tools of the ID argument. Once they are in place, the argument itself follows directly. Meyer formulates the ID origin of life argument as follows:

> *Premise One:* Despite a thorough search, no material causes have been discovered that demonstrate the power to produce large amounts of specified information.
> *Premise Two:* Intelligent causes have demonstrated the power to produce large amounts of specified information.
> *Conclusion:* Intelligent design constitutes the best, most causally adequate, explanation for the information in the cell.[71]

This argument, in my mind, demonstrates that Meyer and ID in general have a third characteristic of realism: a flexibility in causal explanation or a willingness to consider that causes on both the empiricist side and the idealist side have explanatory legitimacy. Throughout the course of this book, we have seen how minds, captured by one aspect of reality, concentrate on that aspect so heavily that they refuse to see any other aspects. Empiricists wed their minds in a monogamous union with material and efficient causes, idealists with formal and final ones, both to the detriment of their ability to understand reality. With ID, however, we have scientists exploring material and efficient causes as far as possible, finding the boundaries of those causes' explanatory power, being willing to admit the limits of that power, and then using their own scientific historical method to infer another class of causality as the correct explanation for the effect under examination. The point of ID is to show to scientists that their very methods point to final causality.

The attempt to bring final causality back into the realm of science, as it had been for most of human history, has gotten ID theorists into a world of trouble, and it is not for me here to examine those controversies. I will point out, however, that the encouragement for scientists to see the world in more colours than the bland grey of material and efficient causes, is surely a push in the direction of epistemological realism, and therefore in the direction of healing the fragmentation of the mind of modern man.

Having said this, ID is only a step in the right direction, not the entire journey. To make a full return to realism, scientists must acknowledge the existence of formal causes and intrinsic final causes, and permit philosophers of science the freedom to speak in terms of those causes. Without those causes, ID theorists can only argue to intelligence as a *probable* cause of specified complexity in biological forms by *dialectical* reasoning (inference to the best explanation). With those causes, they could provide *demonstrative* reasoning to prove that intelligence is the *certain* cause of specified complexity.

The failure of ID proponents to speak in terms of formal and intrinsic final causes opens them to attacks by Thomists, notably Edward Feser.[72] Until they positively disavow those causes, however, rather than just ignore them, I believe it better to encourage them in the direction of a more integral realism than condemn them for their omissions.[73]

Chapter summary

The universe has a basic order in that all non-living things have a certain configuration that makes them act in a most consistent way. Because of their homogeneous matter, their regularity, and their consistency, human minds are easily able to quantify and measure them. This makes them most apt for the consideration of the exact sciences, specifically physics. In that sense, their material and efficient causality is more evident to us than their final causality. For instance, we cannot say what gravity and quarks are for (final causality), but we can say what they do (efficient causality).

Living things, however, have an additional complexity in that they direct the diverse parts of their bodies, by means of an internal principle, towards the preservation and propagation of their organism, independently of outside causes. This additional complexity, over and above that of non-living things, requires a special explanation, and one that pertains particularly to the realm of final causality. It also makes living things less susceptible to quantification and measurement by the methods of physics.

Despite this fundamental difference, many empiricist scientists today refuse to admit that living things have an internal, immaterial principle which directs them (formal cause, the soul) or that they have any direction at all (final cause). They do not want to grant that there is any knowledge outside that gained by the scientific method.

This refusal on their part leads them to several irrational conclusions:

- they believe that intricate order can come from things that do not possess such order in themselves; that is, they believe that something can come from nothing

- they deny the existence of purpose, purposefully try to convince others that there is no purpose, and find a world without purpose meaningful

- they bend over backwards to explain life's origin scientifically, but in the end have to fall back on non-scientific explanations, such as chance or aliens seeding Earth with life.

The ID movement, on the other hand, consists of a group of scientists who, confronted with the staggering complexity of all life forms, especially the coded language contained and interpreted in every cell, use the very reasoning methods of the historical sciences to conclude that life's origin is best explained as the effect of a designing intelligence. In other words, life is the product of purpose.

In the next chapter, we will conclude our analysis of scientism by considering materialistic explanations for the evolution of life forms and human intelligence.

Notes

[1] See pp. 75–80.
[2] S. Meyer, *Signature in the Cell* (New York: HarperOne, 2009), p. 238.
[3] See E. Gilson, *From Aristotle to Darwin and Back Again* (San Francisco: Ignatius Press, 2009), pp. 3–20.
[4] W. Wallace, *The Modeling of Nature* (Washington DC: The Catholic University of America Press, 1996), p. 109. Microscopes reveal to us that inorganic bodies, like sodium, are not completely homogeneous. Sodium is made up of various components—electrons, protons, and neutrons—and every instance of those components in sodium has its own distinctive properties differentiating it within the sodium atom. For instance, each electron within sodium differs from all the others by a combination of its orbit and spin, allowing it to be 'assigned to a unique state occupied by no other' (Wallace in *Ibid.*, p. 47) and so play a unique role in sodium's makeup. Chemists refer to this law for atoms as the 'Pauli exclusion principle'.
[5] This distinction from the Greek world is the reason why we use the words 'organic' and 'inorganic' to this day to differentiate the matter of living and non-living things. The Greeks referred to heterogeneous parts as 'organs', meaning 'instruments', since the organs worked together to serve the life of their possessor, the 'organism'. Since non-living things, in their homogeneity, do not have such organs, they were referred to as being

'inorganic'. See Wallace, *The Modeling of Nature*, p. 109.
[6] Aristotle, *On the Parts of Animals*, 639–640.
[7] J. Richards, *God and Evolution* (Seattle: Discovery Institute Press, 2010), p. 237.
[8] For more differences between the finality of non-living and living things, see F. Aizpún, *La Quinta Vía y el Diseño Inteligente* (Middletown, Delaware: Organización Internacional para el avance científico del Diseño Inteligente, 2015), pp. 321–326.
[9] See C. Schönborn in Gilson, *From Aristotle to Darwin*, p. xviii.
[10] See p. 39.
[11] On the need for this disambiguation, see Richards, *God and Evolution*, pp. 225–46.
[12] Gilson, *From Aristotle to Darwin*, p. 125.
[13] Cited in G. Kemper, H. Kemper, and C. Luskin, *Discovering Intelligent Design* (Seattle: Discovery Institute Press, 2013), p. 105.
[14] 640a20; translation R. McKeon, *The Basic Works of Aristotle* (New York: Random House, 1941), p. 645.
[15] See pp. 147–149.
[16] D. Ross, *Aristotle* (London: Methuen, 1964), p. 126. See also Richards, *God and Evolution*, pp. 236–243.
[17] See Richards, *God and Evolution*, pp. 247–254; Aizpún, *La Quinta Vía*, p. 294.
[18] See pp. 424–425.
[19] For such an explanation, see D. Bonnette, *Origin of the Human Species* (Ave Maria, Florida: Sapientia Press, 2014), pp. 227–238.
[20] For a primitive example of this argument, see P. Atkins, *On Being* (Oxford: Oxford University Press, 2011), pp. 34, 43–44.
[21] See M. Augros, *Who Designed the Designer?* (San Francisco: Ignatius Press, 2015), pp. 168–179; Aquinas, ST, I, q. 19, a.9.
[22] *The Science Before Science* (Baton Rouge: IAP Press, 2004), pp. 289–290.
[23] *The Edge of Evolution* (New York: Free Press, 2007), p. 237.
[24] Atkins, *On Being*, p. vii.
[25] *A Universe from Nothing* (New York: Atria, 2013), Q&A #3 at back of book.
[26] *Ibid.*, p. xiv.
[27] *On Being*, p. 21.
[28] *Ibid.*, p. 36.
[29] See Aquinas, SCG, III, 2.
[30] G. Gonzalez and J. Richards, *The Privileged Planet* (Washington, DC: Regnery Publishing, 2004), p. 32.
[31] *Ibid.*, pp. 152–153.

Inorganic Life

[32] Ibid., p. 287.
[33] M. Denton, *Evolution: A Theory in Crisis* (Bethseda, Maryland: Adler & Adler, 1986), p. 263.
[34] Ibid., pp. 249–250.
[35] Ibid., p. 261.
[36] Meyer, *Signature in the Cell*, p. 92.
[37] Ibid., pp. 201–213.
[38] Ibid., pp. 122–127.
[39] Ibid., pp. 127–130.
[40] Ibid., p. 134. See also P. Johnson, *Darwin on Trial* (Washington, DC: Regnery Gateway, 1991), p. 105; and T. Bethell, *Darwin's House of Cards* (Seattle: Discovery Institute Press, 2017), p. 182.
[41] Meyer, *Signature in the Cell*, pp. 195–196.
[42] Ibid., p. 212. See Douglas Axe's *Undeniable* (New York: HarperOne, 2016) for a popular presentation of research into the probability of functional proteins arising by chance.
[43] Meyer, *Signature in the Cell*, p. 201.
[44] Ibid., pp. 216–217.
[45] Ibid., p. 218.
[46] Denton, *Evolution: A Theory in Crisis*, p. 268.
[47] Meyer, *Signature in the Cell*, pp. 229–230.
[48] Cited in Johnson, *Darwin on Trial*, p. 104.
[49] Meyer, *Signature in the Cell*, p. 230.
[50] Ibid., pp. 233–237.
[51] See J. Wells, *The Politically Incorrect Guide to Darwinism and Intelligent Design* (Washington, DC: Regnery Publishing, 2006), pp. 96–98.
[52] See Meyer's discussion of Polanyi's work on this question in *Signature in the Cell*, pp. 237–240.
[53] *Signature in the Cell*, p. 252.
[54] *The Greatest Show on Earth* (New York: Free Press, 2009), pp. 235–243.
[55] Ibid., pp. 249–250, emphasis added.
[56] *On Being*, p. 104.
[57] See p. 129.
[58] Cited in E. Burtt, *The Metaphysical Foundations of Modern Science* (Mineola, New York: Dover Publications, 2003), p. 23.
[59] *On Being*, p. 102.
[60] *Evolution: A Theory in Crisis*, p. 251.
[61] See p. 267.
[62] *The Privileged Planet*, pp. 275–292.
[63] Ibid., p. 279.

[64] *Ibid.*, p. 281.
[65] *Ibid.*, pp. 337–342.
[66] See Meyer, *Signature in the Cell*, pp. 441–442.
[67] *Ibid.*, p. 377.
[68] *Ibid.*, p. 160.
[69] This reasoning was first described by C. S. Peirce, who had strong realist tendencies. See Wallace, *The Modeling of Nature*, p. 206.
[70] Meyer, *Signature in the Cell*, pp. 160–168.
[71] *Ibid.*, p. 379, emphasis in original.
[72] See his *Neo-Scholastic Essays* (Notre Dame, Indiana: St. Augustine's Press, 2015), pp. 40–42.
[73] ID theorist Douglas Axe, at least, seems to move in the direction of formal cause, when he says that living things are 'all-or-nothing wholes', that they are 'utterly committed to being what they are', that they are 'each so good that they cannot be other than what they are', and that humans are unable to make things that are so unified. See his *Undeniable* (New York: HarperOne, 2016), pp. 174–178.

11 UNSPECIFIED SPECIES

> *Evolution is a fact. It's a fact which is established as securely and essentially as any other fact that we have in science. It is completely right to say that since the evidence for evolution is so absolutely totally overwhelming, nobody who looks at it could possibly doubt that, if they were sane and not stupid. So, the only remaining possibility is that they're ignorant. Most people who don't believe in evolution are, indeed, ignorant.*
>
> Richard Dawkins

EARLY IN THE morning of Monday, September 24, 2012, I was seated in a Superjet ferry that was taking me from the island of Bacolod in the Philippines to the island of Iloilo. The previous day, I had celebrated Mass on both islands for various groups of faithful, and I was now making my way back to my starting point. The boat had a television screen at the front with speakers above us so that our ears could help make sense of what our eyes were seeing. The first thing that came on was a catchy music video promoting tourist activities in the Philippines, such as visiting the Chocolate Hills of Bohol.

The next thing that came on was *Rise of the Planet of the Apes*. It is an American movie that had been released a year previously and was meant to be a reboot of the famous 1960s *Planet of the Apes* movies that starred Charlton Heston and Linda Harrison. The movie starts off with a day at work for Dr Will Rodman. He is employed at a San Francisco based biotech company that is trying to find a cure for Alzheimer's disease. Rodman has a personal interest in the research, because his own father suffers from the disease.

The research at the company, Gen-Sys, is being conducted on chimpanzees, and consists of developing a series of viral-based drugs and testing their effects on the animals. One such instance of the series, the drug ALZ-112, confers human-like intelligence on a chimp named Bright Eyes. She, however, goes on a rampage in order to protect an infant chimp she had recently given birth to. The workers in the lab kill Bright Eyes, and the team leader, because of the incident, terminates the project and has the chimps euthanised.

Except for one, Bright Eyes' infant. Rodman takes that chimp home, realising it has inherited the intelligence bestowed upon his mother. Rodman names the chimp 'Caesar' and begins giving him a standard grade school education. Caesar has a misunderstanding with the neighbour, which leads him to be placed in a primate shelter, where he receives rough treatment both from his fellow chimps and the chief guard.

At that point, I had to get off the boat, but one could see where the science fiction movie was going. *Wikipedia* told me the rest: Caesar acquires the better drug ALZ-113, confers its rationalising effects on the rest of the chimps in the primate shelter, rallies them as their leader to a rebellion against humans, and starts a battle at the Golden Gate Bridge. The apes break through the human blockades and escape to a redwood forest, after which the credits roll. It was a perfect stopping point for a sequel, which came in 2014, and which I have not seen.

What I did see gave me pause. I had to ask myself (and my students): does Hollywood believe that the mental capacities of apes are separated from those of humans merely by the material conditions of their brains? Does it think that making an ape human is just a question of finding the right chemicals? As portrayed in the movie, the answer to both of these questions was 'yes'. The movie, in effect, was reducing apes and humans to merely material beings whose differences could then only exist at the material level.

To me, this appeared to be a gross oversimplification of the ape and the human species. Being an ape is much more than having an ape body and being a human is much more than having a human body. For the empiricist, however, there is nothing more than the material. Thus, evolving a human from an ape could just be a question of stimulating the ape brain by a powerful drug.

Empiricist origin of species

In chapter 9, we saw how modern empiricists—those who reduce all reality to material causes—attempt to explain the origin of the universe. In chapter 10, we saw how they attempt to explain the origin of life. In this chapter, we will see how they attempt to explain the origin of species of life.

Empiricists wanting to explain the origin of species by means of material causes alone face the same sorts of challenges as when they attempt to explain anything else. They must studiously avoid invoking any power higher than matter. Thus, it is forbidden for them to:

1. Speak in terms of formal causality, that is, to speak of an immaterial principle outside the realm of matter which gives a certain conglomeration of matter to be a single, unified whole. For example, empiricists cannot hold that cats have a certain form, 'catness', which makes all of the material parts of the cat to act in unison and according to the nature of all cats.

2. Speak in terms of final causality, that is, to speak of some goal or purpose beyond the mere material parts of a life form which that life form pursues. For example, empiricists cannot hold that cats *seek* to propagate their kind, which is the equivalent of saying that cats are pursuing a purpose— the continuance of the race of cats—which extends outside the life of the individual cat.

3. Speak of some immaterial principle which confers beauty, functionality, unity, or whatever on life forms. For instance, empiricists cannot hold that some mind has invented the form 'catness' and conferred that nature on cats, as well as given them the power to propagate that nature from generation to generation.

To avoid invoking formal or final causes, empiricists have to observe a most ascetic limitation of their own reason. They must ignore many obvious facts presented to their minds and they must ruthlessly forbid their minds to draw the normal inferences from those facts. Meanwhile, they must convince themselves that some material principle is able to explain everything that they see around them in a completely adequate fashion, such that nothing further is left to be explained.

In the case of the origin of species, the empiricist must find some purely material mechanism which is able to account for the origin of the vast variety of plant and animal species which we observe in the natural world. By all accounts, the best man suited to face this tall empiricist task was Charles Darwin (1809–1882).

Darwin's explanation

Darwin did not invent the theory of evolution, but rather supplied a cause for evolution. For decades before his *On the Origin of Species* appeared, naturalists had discussed with increasing approval the idea that current species evolved from previous ones.[1] They just could not give a naturalistic explanation of how it happened.

Charles Darwin (Image courtesy of Wikimedia Commons)

Darwin himself 'became convinced of the reality of evolution in the late 1830s and the early '40s'.[2] For him, species were not fixed, but mutable. He saw that an able stockbreeder—someone Darwin refers to as 'one in a thousand'[3]—could drastically modify species of dogs, horses, and cattle by selective breeding. This meant that certain forces could act on species, causing them to vary, and that those variations could be passed on to the next generation. It only remained for Darwin to explain how blind, unguided, unintelligent material causes could accomplish these same two things:

- **Modify species positively**—for evolution to happen, species need to undergo variation and at least some of the variations must be beneficial. Beneficial variations enable a species to take on a greater complexity and functionality, thus evolving instead of devolving.

- **Select the positive modifications and eliminate the bad**—for evolution to happen, beneficial variations must win out over deleterious ones. Bad variations must be eliminated and good ones kept such that, over time, species become successively better.

Darwin was convinced that nature, of its own, could account for these two causal activities and, perhaps more importantly, he believed that it was his mission to make the world share his conviction.[4]

With regard to the first aspect—the modification of species—Darwin had plenty of evidence that variations arose of themselves in nature. He has an entire chapter in his *On the Origin of Species* where he details many such variations, 'even in important parts of structure'.[5] To determine how such variations arose, he turned to human modifications of plants and animals. Darwin noted that 'cultivated plants and animals ... generally differ much more from each other, than do the individuals of any one species or variety in a state of nature'.[6] He thought that the greater variation of domesticated plants and animals was 'partly connected with excess of food', but overall 'organic beings must be exposed during several generations to the new conditions of life to cause any appreciable amount of variation'.[7]

Variations arise, then, when plants and animals undergo new conditions of life. Such new conditions can develop spontaneously in nature by, for example, large increases or decreases of rainfall. Thus, nature alone can cause plants and animals to undergo variation. This seems very straightforward, and indeed I am convinced. Whether or not such variations are sufficient to account for the production of new species, however, is another question, which we will leave for later. For now, however, it seems clear that nature alone can cause some changes in species.

A more difficult task for nature is acting in a way similar to a stockbreeder, keeping positive variations in species and eliminating the bad—this is the second aspect. Darwin thought that he found a natural selecting mechanism in an essay on population by the Rev T. R. Malthus. Malthus held that human populations grow continually until they hit a certain threshold which matches the available supply of food. At that point, a competition ensues among humans, with some humans acquiring food and surviving, and others failing to get food and perishing.

Darwin took Malthus's idea for human populations and applied it to all of nature. There are only a limited number of food resources available to plants and animals on this planet, and food resources cannot be shared. As such, there is constant competition among life forms to sustain and propagate life. In such a competition, the stronger and hardier win out and survive. Those who remain have been 'selected' by nature, in that nature, after randomly arranging life conditions, has then proceeded to eliminate life forms unable to survive in those conditions, while retaining those able to survive.

Darwin called this second material force in this theory 'natural selection'; for him, it is nature's blind, undirected way of acting like a stockbreeder.

To speak of natural selection is to speak of nothing if it is not to suggest that everything happens in nature *as if* one saw there the work of a selector, which one knows, however, is not the case.[8]

Random variation and *natural selection*: these are the two material forces which Darwin believed can account for the origin of all biological life forms. Thus, his position may be defined as

> the theory that all life shares common ancestry and evolved through descent with modification, driven by an unguided process of *natural selection* acting upon *random variation*.[9]

Let us take a real life example to illustrate Darwin's theory, the famous Galapagos finches.[10] Finches eat seeds. When a drought sets in, however, there are fewer seeds, and the finches quickly eat all of the seeds that are easy to crack. Once the supply of such seeds is exhausted, finches with small beaks starve. Finches with bigger beaks, on the other hand, live on, for they are able to crack seeds with a tougher shell. Since they are the only ones left, they are the only ones who reproduce, their big beak genetic material is all that gets passed on to the next generation, and so pretty soon the entire finch population sports the bigger beak.

When the process started, there was already variation in the finch population, namely, different beak sizes. Then, a drought hit and a competition for food ensued. Nature then 'selected' the finches with bigger beaks to live on and the ones with small beaks to die out.

Here is how A. G. Cairns-Smith explains the complete process:

> If you have things that are reproducing their kind; *if* there are sometimes random variations, nevertheless, in the offspring; *if* such variations can be inherited; *if* some such variations can sometimes confer an advantage on their owners; *if* there is competition between the reproducing entities;—*if* there is an overproduction so that not all will be able to produce offspring themselves—then these entities will get better at reproducing their kind. Nature acts as a selective breeder in these circumstances.[11]

None of this is controversial and no one should hesitate to admit that *natural selection, in specific cases of variation within species, is a satisfactory explanation of the variations*. Darwin and his successors, however, did not propose natural selection merely as a mechanism for change within species, what is called micro-evolution; they propose it as a mechanism which changes one species into another, or macro-evolution. This is what someone who writes a book *On the Origin of Species*, not *On the Origin of Variations in Species*, has to prove to us that natural selection can do.

On the surface, natural selection seems plausible as having such explanatory power. We can imagine, at least, fishes running out of food in the ocean, some of them crawling onto land, slowly developing legs, surviving, the ones left in the ocean perishing. We would have no problem believing such a story as children; should we not believe it as adults, when the vast majority of the scientific community accepts the story as fact? We should only believe it as adults, if Darwin's theory proves itself not only to be imaginable, but also intelligible and empirically verifiable. It must conform to the data of the senses and the mind in order to be real. Otherwise, we should reject it as modern mythology.

In our examination of natural selection, we will first consider it as a philosophy, wherein it is used as a biological 'theory-of-everything', attempting to explain life forms without having recourse to formal and final causes; then, we will consider it as a scientific theory, in its ability to substantiate macro-evolution as a reality, by use of material and efficient causes.

Natural selection as philosophy

If you travel throughout the great cities of Europe, viewing the imposing buildings with all of their magnificent statuary, you start to notice a pattern developing. It seems as if all the artists agreed that they would only provide pagan deities with a scarf size piece of clothing or less to cover themselves. This fact strikes you as all the more ludicrous if you are walking through the streets in winter time. Here are gods and goddesses, sublime Olympian figures, striking pompous poses, yet they did not even have sufficient fashion foresight to anticipate the rigours of the hibernal season! Compared to them, the fully clothed statued saints seem to be wonders of wisdom.

A similar thing holds true for the doctrine of natural selection. Of itself, it is a small strip of explanation. When it is used to account for a little part of the body of reality, it does a fine job. But when it is stretched in an attempt to cover the whole of reality—when it is divinised—things quickly become ridiculous. It is the very nature of the empiricist enterprise to extend material causes so far beyond their own proper domain that they are trying to cover being itself. That the nakedness of reality remains uncovered by such attempts is all too transparent.

Natural selection, for empiricists, is not just an engine for changes within species. Rather, it is a creative force which, entirely by itself, accounts for *every* facet of biological life. It is put forward by many in the scientific community as capable of providing such total causal explanations, without having recourse to God or an immaterial principle in any way.

This gargantuan task imposed upon natural selection by empiricist science must be carefully kept in mind when the topic of theistic evolution arises. Practically anything becomes possible in the natural order when the power of God is invoked. If a scientist admits that God is involved in 'pre-loading' evolution, he is providing to natural selection—prior to it and above it—an omnipotent cause to assist it in fashioning the biological order. I have argued above that even this is not possible, because God must create directly the major lines of life. Still, this position is intellectually respectable, in that it has God do the heavy lifting in the causal explanation, instead of blind material forces.

Here, we must focus on a natural selection unaided by God or any rational power. This is natural selection used a tool to get rid of God, not as a tool used by God. To consider it in this way, we must not only analyse it as a limited empirical fact, but also in its ability to provide causal explanations of all biological realities, completely on its own. Specifically, we must consider whether it is able to explain the origin of species by material and efficient causes alone, without having any recourse to formal and final causes.

Natural species and biological species

The formal cause is what 'actively determines matter as to its specificity' and so 'determines a thing's nature and places it into its species'.[12] When we link the formal cause to species in this way, we are using 'species' in its philosophical sense. In that sense, it connotes:

- *the essence of an individual*—the species of a thing is the same as its essence, its type of being. As such, any given plant or animal can belong to one and only one species. To belong to two species would be the equivalent of being two beings at once. Species indicates a reality that both makes something be the type of being named by that species and excludes it from belonging to any other type of being.

- *the unity of an individual*—the species of a thing provides unity to its being. Aristotle pointed out that no material component—bird glue, for instance—can do this.[13] The reason is that material components will always be parts. 'Unity' is a reality that goes beyond a mere addition of parts. It is not a question of merely setting a series of things next to one another; rather, unity adds a new reality to that set of things, making them together to be one thing, to be a unified whole. Unity is a reality in addition to this or that collection of material parts, a reality that the parts are not able to give to themselves. Since matter is of its nature particulate, we must have recourse to some immaterial principle if we are to explain why any matter at all is unified. This principle is 'substantial form', the formal cause which makes physical substances to be of a certain species.[14]

- *sameness among multiple individuals*—'species' is a collective word, referring to a set of beings that all possess the same mode of being and the characteristics common to that mode of being, and are distinct from all other modes of being.
- *something fixed*—since a thing's species is the same as its type of being, the species cannot change. To change a thing's species is to change it at the level of the thing's being. Change at the level of a thing's being can only be done in one way: reducing it to non-being, annihilating it. Members of the same species, then, always have the same essential characteristics and are not able to change into new species.

This is the philosophical notion of species, sometimes called 'natural species'.[15] Philosophers use it to distinguish types of beings, and order them in a hierarchy according to inferiority and superiority. Superior beings have species with more powers, inferior beings species with fewer powers. Plants, for instance, are species containing powers of nutrition, growth, and reproduction, but their species are lower than the species of animals, which also possess sentient powers.

Biologists also have a notion of species—biological species—a notion that is different from the philosophical notion of natural species. They distinguish species of life forms, not species of beings. They do so, not on the basis of the essence of a life form, but rather on the basis of its biological characteristics, such as its body shape, its reproductive capacity, or its DNA. In the order of being, these are all *accidental* characteristics. They do not make up the being, but rather derive from the being. They do not, of themselves, set one thing apart from another; they rather manifest that a thing is so set apart.

Table 11.1 Natural and biological species

	Natural species	Biological species
What is distinguished	Types of beings	Types of lifeforms
Basis of distinction	A thing's essence	A thing's biological characteristics
Place in the order of being	Substantial	Accidental
Causality over being	Makes a being distinct	Manifests that a being is distinct

I would like to note here that when I refer to macro-evolution, I am referring to transitions from one natural species to another. Micro-evolution, on the other hand, refers to transitions from one biological species to another. As we will see later, evolution can provide an adequate explanation of changes in biological species, but not in natural species.[16]

Conceptually, the notion of biological species necessarily depends on the notion of natural species. Before anything can be classified as a certain type of living thing, it must first be a thing. It must first have the four substantial characteristics which natural species provides to a being: essence, unity, sameness, and fixity. Only then can we begin to speak of accidental characteristics that derive from those substantial characteristics, the aspects which biologists use to classify living things.

In short, if there is no natural species, there is no biological species. If there is no natural and no biological species, there is no thing. If there is no thing, there is nothing.

Darwin and natural species

The connection between the formal cause and biological species poses enormous problems for the empiricist biologist. By the laws of his epistemology, he cannot have recourse to formal causes in his explanation of life forms. Thus, if he is consistent, he must take up a stand against the very reality of species. *The empiricist biologist must try to find a way to deny that species exist.*

This is exactly what Darwin tried to do. He had a 'profound tendency', says Gilson, 'to destroy species'.[17] This is firstly true of natural species, because Darwin, being an empiricist, excluded formal causes *a priori* from his system. His theory conceptualizes things as not belonging to any species, and then seeks to explain how natural selection led them into different species. He wants species at the end of his explanation, but he does not want it at any time beforehand. While animals are evolving, they are not anything. They are just ontologically amorphous physical bodies waiting to settle on a given mode of being. There was no Creator to confer a mode of being upon them—whether by direct creation or secondary causes—so they are left speciesless. Because they have no species, they are subject to any and all variations. This makes it impossible for us to distinguish them one from another. There are no essential differences between animals, and so they are all essentially the same. Belonging to no species, they all share a negative sameness. They are all nothing.

In trying to make of natural selection a system of total explanation, Darwin seeks to differentiate one thing from another while failing to account for how anything is something. This is like trying to distinguish types of houses by the colour of their brick, without ever giving a reason why houses are houses, that is, why they are not hand grenades, hamsters, hammocks, or anything else. You must first say why a house is a house and not a non-house before you can move to distinguish one type of house from another.[18] But a biologist who denies the existence of formal causes denies any principle making a dolphin a dolphin, then proceeds to tell us what distinguishes dolphins.

Chesterton indicates, with his characteristic verve and pith, this incoherence that results from over-extending the explanatory power of natural selection:

> Evolution is a good example of that modern intelligence which, if it destroys anything, destroys itself. Evolution is either an innocent scientific description of how certain earthly things came about; or, if *it is anything more than this*, it is an attack upon thought itself ... [I]f it means anything more, it means that there is no such thing as an ape to change, and no such thing as a man for him to change into. It means that there is no such thing as a thing. At best, there is only one thing, and that is a flux of everything and anything. This is an attack not upon the faith, but upon the mind; you cannot think if there are no things to think about.[19]

A theory-of-everything evolutionist could try to salvage his position by saying that he is not denying that things are things.

Rather, what he is saying is that there is only one type of being, and we are all that same type of being. This is the pantheistic view wherein all is one. The only differences existing, from such a perspective, are accidental differences.

Such a rescue attempt is really only an act of desperation. If everything is ultimately the same thing, then no thing is essentially higher than any other. People are not higher than pandas are not higher than petunias are not higher than potassium.[20] While such a view is ardently supported by green parties lobbying to endow chimpanzees, flowers, and rivers with personal rights, it runs violently contrary to realist common sense. No person could function in life while assigning an absolute equality to everything existing. And no evolutionist could coherently defend the view that lower life forms are evolving into higher ones.

Darwin and biological species

It turns out that Darwin does not only implicitly deny that things have an essence—a natural species—he also implicitly denies they have a biological species. The reason is that biological species, like natural species, require sameness and fixity.

Species can be defined only as a class of living beings definable by means of characteristics which are not reducible to those of all other classes. Species is thus by definition a strictly defined type. For it to change would be to cease to be what it is, and thus to cease to exist. To say that species are fixed is a tautology; to say that they change is to say that they do not exist.[21]

The Darwinian mechanism of evolution, however, requires there to be no fixity in nature, no sameness. All is variation. Life forms are constantly changing, because of various pressures exerted upon them, especially the pressures involved in surviving. According to Darwin, little changes over long periods of time turn bacteria into whales. For such transformations to take place, nothing can be fixed in the animals undergoing change; nothing can be stable. Animals must not have any inherent boundaries in their beings, confining them to this or that type of life form. They must be willing to be pushed in any direction whatsoever by 'selection pressures' if they are to morph into an endless variety of life forms from a primitive common ancestor. In other words, they must not belong to a biological species.

We saw Darwin's motive for eliminating species back in chapter 7: he wanted to refute what his Protestant background believed to be a Biblical teaching, namely, that the species of all life forms were created directly by God.[22] To prove this wrong, he is going to attempt to show us an *Origin of Species by Means of Natural Selection* (the title of his famous book), not God.

The easiest way to eliminate the need for a special creation of species is to show that species do not exist. But to show us how the species around us got here without God, Darwin must assume that there are species.

> It is quite necessary that there should exist species in the ordinary sense of the term if one wishes to be able to prove that they were not created just as they are from the beginning.[23]

Here we have a catch-22 if there ever was one: prove that species arose without God while denying that any species exists at all. Normally a person would recognise the inherent contradiction in such a project, but Darwin was a scientist and not a philosopher. Thus,

> when Darwin takes leave of the observation and immediate interpretation of facts, wherein he is the master, he displays an intellectual nonchalance and an imprecision in ideas which does not appear in any way tolerable.[24]

Darwin did not recognise the bi-polar nature of his theory and so blithely went forward in a twofold contradictory attempt:

- To prove that species originated by purely material processes
- by saying that there are no species.

Darwin could neither keep the notion of species nor get rid of it. He needed it in order to explain the end result of the development of animal forms (what we see all around us), and he needed to get rid of species to explain how animals are constantly changing into other animals (the process leading up to what we see around us). In the end, he and his disciples tended to treat 'species' as a mere concept, a word that is convenient for speaking about reality, but does not actually correspond to anything really existing outside the mind.

Thus, Dawkins quotes Darwin as saying, 'In a series of forms graduating insensibly from some apelike creature to man as he now exists, it would be impossible to fix on any definite point where the term "man" ought to be used.'[25] In other words, there is nothing in reality which makes a man a man, such that if you don't have that thing, you are not a man, and if you do have it, you are a man. Rather, 'man' is simply a concept which biologists have arbitrarily chosen to assign to a given group of individuals.

If different species do not really exist outside the mind, then the various biological lifeforms are really essentially the same thing. A dog is a bird is a man is a geranium is a cabbage.

Dawkins—faithful acolyte of Darwin that he is—plainly confirms that evolution effectively makes all living things to be of the same species:

> There was no first specimen of any species or any genus or any order or any class or any phylum. Every creature *that has ever been born* would have been classified—had there been a zoologist around to do the classifying—*as belonging to exactly the same species* as its parents and its children. Yet, with the hindsight of modernity, and with the benefit of the fact that most of the links are missing, classification into distinct species, genera, families, orders, classes and phyla becomes possible.[26]

Nature, taken in itself, produces a continuous stream of life forms, without any of them belonging to different species. There are, in reality, no fixed points whatsoever in nature. The only reason that the biologist classifies animals into different species is that time and tide have cut out swaths in that continuous stream—the gaps in the fossil record, the missing links—such that it appears that there were fixed points. Thus, when Dawkins considers anthropologists arguing about whether a fossil belongs to species A or species B, he says to them, 'You are arguing about words, not reality'.[27]

But if you are purporting to explain the origin of species, then surely you are purporting to explain something that exists outside the mind. If species do not exist outside the mind, then they are just words of convenience, without much importance. Evolution would have no interest for us at all if it did not claim to tell us something about reality.

Three things are to be noted in regard to the evolutionists' love-hate relationship with 'species':

- Because of the incompatibility of formal causes with empiricist materialism, Darwinists who deny that species have any reality outside the mind are simply being faithful to their own principles. When they do this, however, they introduce a fundamental incoherence into their explanations of biological species, because while denying species with their lips, they must do biology as if species actually exist.
- Only a powerful ideological faith can move someone to deny all fixity in nature, for such fixity is staring us in the face everywhere.[28] Plants and animals not only belong to a certain kind, but they remain in that kind to such a degree, that there is no known instance of macro-evolution. Evolutionary theory would have all in nature be continuous, when nature actually shows a great discontinuity. We have considered the vast discontinuity between the inorganic and organic in the last chapter, but there is also discontinuity within the organic, such that there are huge voids between biological kinds, that cannot be filled by gradual, adaptive changes, as we will see below.[29]
- The theory of evolution, of itself, need not have these ideological problems. Once a biologist admits the existence of formal causes outside the mind, he can then propose a coherent naturalistic evolutionary process for one life form

changing into another. Such biologists exist and are called 'structuralists'.[30] But because empiricism dominates today, structuralists are very much in the minority and the majority simply lives in and with the empiricist irrationality.

Natural selection and final causality

Aristotle points out in his *Metaphysics* that none of the philosophers preceding him spoke of the final cause as a true cause,[31] and he seemed to be justifiably proud of having introduced its notion as a necessary part of any complete explanation of being. As we saw in chapter 10, just the fact that a given being is determined to one operation over another, is pointing in one direction rather than another, is sufficient to manifest finality or purpose.[32] In Gilson's words, 'Finalism encompasses every doctrine which admits that there are facts in the universe which reveal direction'.[33]

The fact of direction, however, is most manifest in living things. We call them *organic*, because they are *organised*, that is, their bodies consist of many different complicated parts—organs—that serve specific functions. Animal eyes, for instance, are for seeing; ears are for hearing; legs are for walking; wings are for flying. This is as plain to us as the nose on our face. Just as plain is that an intelligent designer is the only cause adequate to explain the existence of purposeful organs. Only intelligence is able to grasp the nature of a given purpose, such as seeing, *as well as* the means necessary to accomplish that purpose—pupil, corona, iris, rods, cones, nerves, and so on.[34] Grasping the nature of means and end, and the relationship between them, intelligence is able to *direct* the one towards the other, for example, to gather the components necessary to achieve seeing, and arrange them in the proper configuration so that seeing takes place. Just as no one could reasonably make use of a camera without grasping that it was designed by an intelligent being, so too one could not make use of one's own eyes without doing the same.

Empiricists, however, being willing to sacrifice reason when there is question of maintaining their epistemology, refuse to *see*

Unspecified Species 451

the eye's design. When Dawkins says that the human eye is 'not just bad design, it's the design of a complete idiot',[35] he is simply executing the empiricist mandate to deny all finality in reality. Darwin understood this mandate and put forward his theory of evolution as a way of accounting for complicated organs such as the eye without having recourse to direction. Natural selection, for him, is an entirely undirected process and is able to explain how functional eyes and ears and noses arose of their own, without having been designed for a purpose.

He admits that it's a tough sell: 'To suppose that the eye... could have been formed by natural selection, seems, I freely confess, absurd in the highest possible degree'.[36] This candour is all the more telling since his knowledge of the eye's complexity was primitive in comparison with current day knowledge.

The question we must ask here, however, is not whether natural selection is sufficient to explain the origin of the eye, but whether it truly does away with final causality, as it claims. We saw that Darwin tried to get rid of species without being able to;[37] was he able to get rid of purpose? Indeed, is anyone with any theory whatsoever able to get rid of purpose?

In the end, Darwin's solution for final causes is the same as his solution for formal ones: get rid of them while keeping them. He will use finality to show that there is no finality.[38] He presents natural selection to us as a mechanism utterly blind, not making choices, not heading in any direction whatsoever, but which then proceeds to strike out on a path so visionary, so well-chosen, so aptly directed that it produced a biological world whose least members vastly exceed in complexity anything human intelligence has ever made.

What Darwin is doing is collapsing the distinction between efficient and final causality. He is taking raw efficient causes—the blind forces of nature—and saying that they are capable of doing the work of seeing, intelligent causes. Things acting without an end, efficient causes, are able of themselves to yield things acting for an end, final causes. Purpose and functionality are not, in effect, realities that are different from and added to mere action.

But in point of fact, Darwin is not really getting rid of finality. He seems to be able to do away with all purposes, save one. He takes that one purpose and makes it the very cornerstone of his natural selection, his mechanism that is supposed to be blind and without purpose. What purpose remains? The pursuit of survival. In Darwin's mind, all of biology is summed up in the natural principle of survival of the fittest. The will to survive, however, is a purposeful resolve and so necessarily falls into the domain of final causality.

David Stove points out that the primacy of the struggle for survival among biological life was only discovered in the modern period. Before the seventeenth century, many other purposes of nature were highlighted by ancient and medieval thinkers, but only Galen (recall his mistakes on blood circulation from chapter 4) discussed the adaptations that organisms make in order to survive as being evidence of design.[39]

The struggle for survival and hence natural selection—to the degree that it exists—being purposive, and so evidence of intelligent design, is the elephant in the room of evolutionary theory. Animals, after all, could make many things besides survival their primary aim: travelling around the world, digging holes in the ground, jumping off of high cliffs, and so on. The resources and effort they invest in surviving indicates a very definite direction, a very definite design. Once we admit that the whole of the biological world is struggling to survive, we are only a step away from saying that someone must have conferred this purpose upon it.

Stove unmasks the finality at the very heart of Darwinism in his typical devastating fashion. His treatment of this question is so apt for *our* purpose that it deserves a long quotation:

> The famous Darwinian 'struggle for life,' on which the whole theory turns, is a struggle *for* something, is it not?: namely, for survival and for leaving descendants. But in that case it is a *purposive* activity on the part of the

individuals which struggle. And in any case, Darwin is always saying things like the following: that 'each organic being is *striving to* increase at a geometrical ratio'; or that 'every single organic being around us may be said to be *striving to the utmost to* increase in numbers.' How could he have ascribed purpose to all organisms more plainly than this? ...

In fact it is precisely the striving of organisms to live, reproduce, and increase which, according to Darwin, *drives* the whole gigantic process of evolution. If organisms were indifferent towards their own survival and reproduction, or if they positively leaned to the Buddhist side of those issues, there would be no struggle for life, hence no natural selection, and hence no evolution, according to Darwinian theory. So very far is that theory, then, from according no causal role in evolution to purpose.

For this same reason, we should not let ourselves be imposed upon by another group of commonplaces: the ones about Darwinism having expelled 'final causes' from biology. If 'final causes' means purposes, or purposive activities, then Darwinism not only does not 'expel' them: it builds them into the very foundation of its explanation of evolution.[40]

Things get worse when Stove applies his analytical powers to the writings of Dawkins. The latter understands clearly his New Atheist task: explain all of reality without God, using only material and efficient causes. Dawkins certainly gets rid of God, and he certainly speaks only in terms of material forces. The problem is that he gives to those material forces the attributes of God. Specifically, he makes genes divine.

Really, that was the only thing to be done. We have seen how empiricists are driven by the laws of their paradigm to explain all of reality by the smallest of its parts: empiricist physicists have the universe derive from the fluctuations of subatomic particles in a quantum vacuum; empiricist origin of life theorists have life come from chemical interactions in a warm pond. Following the same trail, empiricist origin of species theorists have species derive from the interactions of genes. If you are going to explain everything by means of matter, you must start with the lowest common denominator. Moreover, by making that denominator the ultimate first principle of reality, you must ascribe to it the attributes of God.

Dawkins makes genes godlike in three different respects:[41]

1. Genes are capable of manipulating their hosts. We are, Dawkins says, 'robot-vehicles blindly programmed to preserve the selfish molecules known as genes' and are 'manipulated to ensure the survival of [our] genes.' Stove comments:

   According to the Christian religion, human beings and all other created things exist for the greater glory of God; according to sociobiology, human beings and all other living things exist for the benefit of their genes.

2. Genes perform feats beyond the powers of human beings. A certain type of cuckoo places its egg in a reed warbler nest and, once the cuckoo egg hatches together with the warbler chicks, the cuckoo chick's louder cries and more colourful gape induces the warbler parents to feed it more abundantly than their own young. How was this clever strategy conceived and executed? According to Dawkins, the genes of the cuckoo manipulated the reed warblers. Stove comments:

   We cannot build young cuckoos, or breed them, to precise specifications. And no genetic engineer could as yet undertake this particular task with rational confidence of success ... The implication could hardly be plainer: cuckoo genes are more intelligent and capable than human beings. The same presumably holds *a fortiori* for human genes.

3. Genes live forever. The gene, says Dawkins,

   does not grow senile; it is no more likely to die when it is a million years old than when it is only a hundred. It leaps from body to body down the generations, manipulating body after body in its own way and for its own ends, abandoning a succession of mortal bodies before they sink in senility and death. The genes are the immortals...

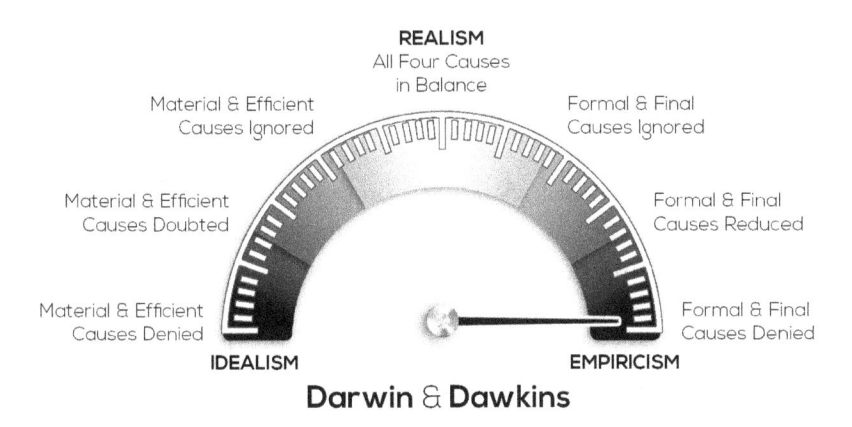

Darwin & Dawkins

Final causality, as I explained in chapter 3, is especially key in religion, which attempts to give an account for the purposes of the universe. What should be our wonder, then, to find that Dawkins, a professed atheist, empiricist, and destroyer of purposes, proposes for our belief that the entire biological world exists to serve the interests of genes? His proposition is not a scientific statement, but a religious one. Dawkins, says Stove, is a polytheist, and shares with believers the fundamental point of all religions, the affirmation of 'the existence of purposive beings of more than human intelligence and power'[42], namely, genes.

In the end, empiricist evolutionists have the same relationship with final causality as they have with formal causality: they can't live with it, and they can't live without it. If they allowed a designing intelligence to play a role in evolution, the difficulty would disappear. Without such an intelligence, the theory must become irrational. It must commit the original sin of the intellect, affirming that a thing is and is not at the same time, that there is no purpose and that everything derives from purpose.

Evolution and empirical evidence

My criticisms of evolutionary theory thus far have only considered its capacity to explain all of reality solely through material and efficient causes—this is empiricist evolutionism. It is evolution extended beyond science to become a theory-of-everything driven by a scientistic epistemology. Evolution in this sense falls into rank irrationality, thus linking arms with the empiricist explanations for the universe and life that we explored in chapters 9 and 10.

I have still left evolution as a scientific theory untouched, that is, evolution in its capacity to explain biological realities in the realm of material and efficient causes. Given that it cannot possibly explain the existence of species and purposes in nature, is it yet able to explain differences in plant and animal bodies? Does empirical evidence show that natural selection has caused, over the history of biological time, marked changes in physical bodies, thus providing a material basis for transitions between natural species?

Allow me first to remark that, if a strictly scientific natural selection had such explanatory capacities, it would in no way detract from the glory of God. As Sertillanges says, 'If the hypothesis of evolution is true, God is proven two times over, once by the world itself and once by evolution, because to create a machine tool of such perfection and power is more difficult than creating an object'.[43] If God did indeed line up the mechanism of natural selection to produce the stunning diversity of biological life, we should be as awed as when considering the fine-tuning of the universe necessary for stars, galaxies, and planets to form.

As it stands, there is strong evidence that, while natural selection has sufficient explanatory power to account for varia-

tions within what we have referred to as biological species, it can in no way account for the production of new natural species. It can account for micro-evolution, but not macro-evolution. At least three pieces of empirical evidence indicate as much:
1. The explosions in the fossil record
2. What evolution must do, but cannot
3. What evolution can do, but leaves undone

Let us consider each of these in turn.

Explosions in the fossil record

Darwinism holds that:
- all life forms derived from a single ancestor in the distant past
- these life forms were differentiated by natural selection acting upon random variation.

The first aspect is referred to as 'common descent' and it makes very specific predictions as to what will be found in the fossil record. It conceives the history of biological life as an inverted pyramid, with all life beginning with the simplest self-replicating life form possible, whose offspring strike out on different paths of evolution, growing in complexity in various ways over the course of biological time, turning into a wide variety of plants and animals.

According to this view, the fossil record should reveal great simplicity and great sameness at first, and then slowly branch out, increasing in complexity and diversity until we come to the richness of the biological world around us.

Recall from your high school biology the standard taxonomic categories that biologists use to classify life forms. The broadest is 'domain', which encompasses the entire biological world in three categories: Archaea, Eukarya, and Bacteria. Each of these divide into different kingdoms. For instance, there are two kingdoms in the domain Eukarya, plants and animals. Then, within the kingdom animal, there are 36 different phyla or body plans. And so it goes down the line, with the members of each category increasing until we reach species, in its biological sense. Biological species, being at the bottom of all of these divisions, has the most members.

Table 11.2 Taxonomic categories

Taxonomic categories from broadest to most specific	Members
Domain	Three: Archaea, Eukarya, and Bacteria
Kingdom	Two in Eukarya, plants and animals
Phylum	Thirty-six in the kingdom animal
Class	
Order	
Family	
Genus	
Species	Millions of members

Darwinism predicts that we will find lowest in the fossil record a single species, which over time branches into several species, whose number increase to the point that they can be grouped in genera, whose number increase in turn until they can be grouped in families, and so on.[44] The progression is supposed to be like the growing of a tree, which begins with a single sprout, then develops twigs, which later turn into branches and subbranches, with leaves, flowers and seeds. The only diagram found in the *Origin of Species* is one representing just such a bottom-up tree of life, wherein the minor classifications (like species and genera) can be made at the beginning or bottom of the tree, and the major classifications (like phyla and kingdoms) only at the end or the top of the tree. Darwin explained that the tree was not just an illustration of common descent, but also showed that higher taxonomic categories would proceed from the lower ones as differences accumulated in evolutionary time.[45] This view is completely consistent with his view that all life forms diversified from a single original life form by slow, gradual steps. It is the opposite of the view that God or some other intelligent beings made life forms in all of their complexity at once.

All scientific theories worth their salt make predictions about what empirical evidence will be discovered in nature. These predictions provide a means for testing whether or not a given theory matches up with a law that actually exists in nature or whether it is just an invention of the mind of the scientist. It makes the theory both falsifiable and verifiable.

In the case of Darwin's theory, the fossil record is decidedly on the side of falsifying the theory. The record even turns his tree of life on its head. Stephen Meyer treats the evidence in his 2013 bestseller *Darwin's Doubt*, which is just as magisterial as his *Signature in the Cell*. He notes that the fossil record is extremely discontinuous, that is, full of great jumps in complexity.[46] Instead of presenting a slow, gradual progression from simple to complex life forms in short steps, the record presents a very sudden appearance of animals that are already diversified into phyla and have nothing even remotely like them preceding them. Meyer quotes the late, great evolutionist Stephen Jay Gould as saying:

> The history of life is not a continuum of development, but a record punctuated by brief, sometimes geologically instantaneous, episodes of mass extinction and subsequent diversification.[47]

The oldest fossils—a type of bacteria—were found in western Australia and have been dated to 3,465 million years ago.[48] For the next 3 billion years, the only fossils to appear are 'single-celled organisms and colonial algae'.[49] Then, there is a sudden jump in complexity in what is called the Ediacarian period, which starts about 635 million years ago (mya). Sponges, worms, and molluscs arose at that time, but getting them from single-celled organisms 'is a little like transforming a spinning top into a bicycle'.[50]

Things get worse when we come to the famous Cambrian explosion. In a geologically short period of 6 million years during the Cambrian period, between 530–525mya, there suddenly appear 'sixteen completely novel phyla and thirty classes'.[51] Meyer notes what great differences these animal forms represent. If we were hiking with him to the Burgess Shale in Canada, where there is a fantastic Cambrian fossil bed, and we saw on the way squirrels, marmots, deer, moose, elk, wolves, mountain goats, horned larks, water pipits, grey-crowned rosy finches, eagles, hawks, dippers, jays, migrating warblers, harlequin ducks—if we were so fortunate as to catch a glimpse of all these animals, we still would only have encountered members of

> a single phylum, Chordata—and even from a single subphylum, Vertebrata. After having feasted your eyes on such animal variety, when you arrive at [the Burgess Shale], it yields not merely dozens of fossilized species from a single subphylum, but wildly disparate creatures from dozens of *phyla*.[52]

This Cambrian explosion presents multiple problems for Darwinism:

- The pattern of the fossil record is the opposite of what Darwin predicted. The record does not manifest a bottom-up order, wherein there is first a single biological species, then there are more species branching off from that single species, making a genus; then multiple genera branching from the single genera, making a family; and so on, until we reach different phyla. Rather, the order of the fossil record is top-down. What appear first are 'individual representatives of the higher taxonomic categories (phyla, subphyla, and classes)' and these 'only later diversify into the lower taxonomic categories (families, genera, and species)'.[53] In the Cambrian explosion, several animals of vast differences, at the level of phyla, suddenly appear in the fossil record. Only later do we find several animals of small differences, at the level of species, within a single phylum, appearing.

- None of the animals from before the Cambrian period—the Precambrian animals—could have been the common ancestor of the Cambrian animals. As Meyer notes:

> All the interesting anatomical novelties that differentiate one phylum from another must arise along the separate lineages branching out from the alleged common ancestor

well after its origin in the fossil record. Heads, jointed limbs, compound eyes, guts, anuses, antennae, notochords, stereoms, lophophores (a tentacled feeding organ), and numerous other distinguishing characteristics of many different animals must come later on many distinct lines of descent. Yet the gradual evolutionary origin of these characteristics is not documented in the Precambrian fossil record. These characteristics do not appear until they arise suddenly in the Cambrian explosion.[54]

- The progression from simple to complex in the fossil record is as Darwin predicted,[55] yet the *suddenness* with which greater complexity appears is not. The six million years of the Cambrian explosion are not nearly enough time for a world of animal forms to evolve by random variation and natural selection. J-Y. Chen puts this duration in the perspective of long term biological time: 'compared with the 3-plus-billion-year history of life on Earth, the period [of the explosion] can be likened to one minute in 24 hours of one day'.[56] This is 0.11 per cent of the Earth's history. To take my own example, it's like an historian investigating the state of technology in the year 1115 and then finding that the following year, it is at the level of the technology of 2016, one year being 0.11 per cent of the years between 1115 and 2016.

- There is strong evidence that the Precambrian fossil record is complete, and so is not hiding some common ancestor of the Cambrian animals. The only animals that appear in the 3,000,000,000 years that make up the Precambrian are one-celled organisms: algae, sponges and so on. These fossils are difficult to preserve, because they are soft-bodied. Thus, scientists were astonished to find in the Precambrian layers even microscopic soft sponges fossilised at an embryonic stage when all of their cells are soft.[57] If any more complex, hard-bodied animals existed during this time, they would have been fossilised, for hard-bodied animals have a much greater chance of being preserved than soft-bodied ones. Moreover, the sponges appeared late in the Precambrian period, at a time when we would most expect to find evolutionary ancestors of the Cambrian animals, animals much more complex than sponges. Thus, while Precambrian layers preserved soft-bodied, microscopic sponges, they 'did not preserve remains of any clearly ancestral or intermediate forms leading to the other main groups of Cambrian animals', when 'some of those animals must have had at least some hard parts as a condition of their viability'.[58]

The fossil record provides strong empirical evidence that the aimless meanderings of random variation coupled with the blind eyes of natural selection were not the causal forces that set off the Cambrian explosion.

Evolution unobserved

Say that evolution was actually able to work the miracle of transforming single-celled organisms into sixteen different animal phyla. What would it have accomplished? What does it take to build a trilobite from a bacterium?

To answer these questions, we must speak about genetics. Darwin, in his day, did not understand how inheritance works, and even had some false ideas in that area.[59] Discoveries in genetics after Darwin's death made it necessary to update his theory. Scientists realised that genes determine the traits of lifeforms and that these genes can be seen as 'discrete units or packets of hereditary information that [can] be independently sorted and shuffled within the chromosome'.[60] If you want to change life forms, then, you need to change genes.

In the 1920s, Hermann Mueller produced many unusual variations of fruit flies by altering their genetic material with X-rays—alterations that he called 'mutations'. Darwinists saw how applicable Mueller's discovery was to the theory of evolution: the random variation component of evolution could be ascribed specifically to gene mutations.[61] These mutations were the exact material upon which natural selection does its work.

This modification of Darwin's theory is referred to as 'neo-Darwinism' and is defined as follows: 'the theory that all life shares common ancestry, and evolved through descent with modification, driven by unguided natural selection *acting upon random genetic mutations in DNA*'.[62] Herein, when we use the term 'Darwinism', we are referring to this updated theory.

To build animals, evolution needs to modify genetic material favourably and get those modifications to the next generation, so that natural selection can 'prefer' them. The genetic material is the code in DNA which contains the commands for building proteins. The code, as mentioned in the last chapter, consists of a sequence of nucleotide bases which are assigned the letters A, C, G, and T by biologists.[63] The cell interprets the *order* in which the nucleotide bases are arranged on the DNA spine, executing all cellular tasks based on the instructions contained in that order.

Mutations in DNA can come through what are called 'typographical errors'.[64] For instance, an 'A' in a given sequence in DNA can be copied wrongly, being changed to a 'T', with the rest of the code remaining the same. This is similar to the English word 'rock' being mistyped as 'rick' or 'uock.'

Darwinists speculate that such mutations are capable of supplying all that is needed to build new animals from old ones. Empirical evidence, however, indicates two reasons why this cannot be the case:

1. Random mutation and natural selection have no direction, but the embryonic development of animals is a process that is carefully choreographed.

2. Random mutation and natural selection have to change animals in the embryonic stage in order to effect major changes, but changes at that stage result either in the destruction of the animal or its impairment.

To grasp these problems facing the evolutionary mechanism, we must look into the stages by which animal embryos develop, starting with strands of DNA and ending with a functional animal body. There are effectively three stages in the process:[65]

1. **DNA (genes) → proteins:** the instructions in DNA are executed to generate a wide variety of proteins.
2. **Proteins → cells:** the proteins are organised into different types of cells, each cell having its own distinctive function and role.
3. **Cells → bodies:** the different cells are organised to form distinctive tissues and organs, each having a specific capability and each occupying a specific place in the body, such that a fully functional animal results from their arrangement.

Thus, in animal reproduction, we begin with a cell containing genes with all of the information necessary to build an animal body. The cell divides, and the two cells head off on different paths, each one having different genes turned on and different ones turned off, which will determine what happens at the next cell division. They divide again and again and again, with genes being turned off and on at each stage, and *differently* for every single cell. When all the stages of the cell division are complete, each cell is in its proper *place* in the animal body and is performing its own specific *function* at that place. The cells now have their final and definitive function: gut cells, pharynx cells, neuron cells, hypodermic cells, germ cells, and so on. A completely functional baby animal body is in place, ready to begin its growth.

The instructions for this complex and amazing choreography are contained in the DNA of the original cell from the very beginning. This means that the DNA 'knows' the final destination of all of the cells to be multiplied, as well as the changes they have to undergo at each stage of the division in order to reach that destination. This empirical fact poses the first of the two immense challenges listed above for the Darwinian account of the origin of species. Random mutation and natural selection are blind processes. Being blind, they cannot look ahead into the future and plan out a series of steps to be accomplished in order to reach a distant destination.

What we see in embryonic development, however, is just such planning. Take, for example, the millimetre long worm *C. elegans*.[66] It has around 1,000 cells,[67] which are the result of 11 cell divisions ($2^{10} = 1,024$). The first 10 of these divisions do not make for a functional organism; they are only steps on the way to the final division, after which each of the 1,024 cells has taken on its very specific place and function in this worm's body.

Natural selection is not able to:

1. plan this series of 11 divisions to arrive at the final differentiation of the cells, because natural selection does not plan;

2. select the various stages of cell division, because those stages do not provide any survival advantage. The purpose of all the cells in stages 1 to 10 is merely to get to the next step of the embryo's development, not to provide function. But natural selection can only select this or that random mutation insofar as it provides a survival advantage, not insofar as it is a stage in a process. Thus, natural selection cannot select for cells to go through the 10 intermediate, non-functional stages.

A second major problem for Darwinians appears when one examines the empirical evidence for what happens when one changes the embryonic building of animals. If you want to take an old animal body plan and build a new animal body plan out of it, then you have to make changes in the genetic code during embryonic development. Such early gene changes, however, result in death or disablement, not more functionality.

Two German geneticists, starting in 1979, executed 'saturation mutagenesis' experiments on fruit flies. What this means is that they isolated 'the small subset of genes that specifically regulate embryonic development'[68] and mutated one or more of those genes in different fruit fly embryos until eventually they had mutated *all of them*. Most of the mutants 'perished as deformed larvae long before achieving reproductive age'.[69] Others survived and had major changes, but all such changes were deleterious—some fruit flies had no eyes, others had legs growing out of their heads, and still others had wings deformed in such a way that they could not fly. None of them turned into a new species with greater functionality.

But, as Meyer points out, we should not expect new and better animals to develop from introducing random mutations into the embryonic development.[70] The reason is that the egg to embryo process is delicate and complex, with every part needing to be in its proper place, at the right time, performing its assigned function, for the result to be correct. If you introduce changes at one stage and do not compensate for that change at the other stages, then you will ruin the entire process. The only way to make a beneficial change would be to accompany that change with corresponding changes at *every* stage. Evolution cannot do this, though, since it works by gradual changes, which is the same as saying that it works by *single* changes.

This situation leads to the 'great Darwinian paradox': animals *do not* tolerate mutations at the *beginning* of their development, but that is the only time that they can be changed substantially; they *do* tolerate mutations *after* they have developed, but such mutations can only induce minor changes.[71] The empirical evidence, then, seems to clearly indicate that large-scale, macro-evolution is impossible.

As if this were not bad enough, Meyer points out that, even if random mutations in embryo development were able to induce major, viable changes, those changes would not be sufficient. The reason is that genes or DNA are not the only player in the building of animals. There are other processes, with their own specified information, that contribute to the construction of animal bodies. These processes and their information are referred to as 'epigenetic' or 'beyond/outside of' the genes. Meyer speaks about their fascinating role in chapter 14 of his book, but suffice it to say here that evolution works only on genes. Epigenetic processes are beyond its reach, and so evolution cannot account for what they do nor can it modify them in order to make new animal body plans.

Evolution observed

Besides evaluating evolution by what it is incapable of doing, we can also evaluate it by looking at the evidence of what it actually does, that is, examples of micro-evolution. This helps indicate to us its limits, or its 'edge', in the language of Michael Behe. How far is the process of natural selection able to go in the modification of life forms? Can it produce new biological species, new genera, new families? How far up the taxonomic scale does its innovative ability reach?

Richard Dawkins, for one, thinks that evolution is able to go all the way to the top, producing new phyla, new kingdoms, and new domains. When I was reading through the 450 pages of his *The Greatest Show on Earth*, I kept waiting for the showstopping argument to appear, that 'sheer weight of evidence' which 'totally, and utterly, sledgehammeringly, overwhelmingly strongly supports the conclusion that evolution is true'.[72] I knew that if such evidence existed in any way, shape, or form, Dawkins would lay it out on the table.

By and large, however, the table was not set with any empirical evidence for macro-evolution and was only decorated with evidence for micro-evolution: lizards from one island getting larger heads, a greater bite force, and a different diet after being transported to another island;[73] certain bacteria, over tens of thousands of generations in a laboratory, adapting to assimilate glucose and citrate, becoming much larger than bacteria not adapting to do so;[74] guppies in ponds with predators losing spots over time and hence becoming less visible to those predators, while guppies in ponds without predators becoming more colourful/visible over time.[75] Whenever larger changes came up, Dawkins had to shift to speculations, metaphors, and his rigged computer programs. In the end, he just expects us to 'take his word for it' that macro-evolution is a fact, since he cannot prove it to us.

To get the actual verdict of empirical science, we have to return to Behe. In his book *The Edge of Evolution*, he makes a careful scientific investigation of exactly what changes random mutations and natural selection are able to effect in nature and what changes they are not.[76] When I say that Behe makes a scientific investigation, I mean that he *quantifies* natural processes based on real empirical evidence and draws his conclusions from the quantification. His conclusion is that evolution's ability to innovate lies somewhere between genera and orders, but it cannot attain to producing new classes of life forms. Let us consider his analysis.

We should note up front that Behe holds, on the basis of empirical evidence, that certain biological components are 'irreducibly complex', meaning that those components have 'multiple interacting parts wherein the removal of any part causes the system to effectively cease functioning'.[77] When all of the parts of a component are needed for it to function, then the parts must be put together at once for it to operate.

Behe's showcase example for a biological component that is irreducibly complex is a part of bacteria called the 'flagellum'. It is 'a tiny rotary engine attached to certain bacteria and functioning as a propeller, like an outboard motor'.[78] The flagellum has many parts, each one of them being necessary. Remove one part and the flagellum will not function.

Given this fact about the flagellum, that all of its parts must be in place for it to function at all, consider what would have been necessary for the first bacterium to develop such a piece of equipment. It would not do for the parts of the flagellum to be added one at a time over generations of bacteria. Having useless non-functional parts attached to your body is not good for your survival. What is necessary, then, is that all of the parts of the flagellum be in place *at once* in a single bacterium for the flagellum to be functional.

Once we realise that the vast majority of the components of biological bodies are irreducibly complex, the question becomes:

can the random mutations to which neo-Darwinism appeals be sufficiently coordinated so as to produce all of the parts of an irreducibly complex system at once?

Behe used his experience working with victims of malaria to assess empirically the degree to which we can expect multiple beneficial random mutations to happen at once and so, hypothetically, produce on the spot a new functional component with multiple, coordinate working parts for some living organism.

Malaria, Behe explains,[79] is a single-celled organism that is carried by mosquitoes. When malaria enters a human through a mosquito bite, it gets into the bloodstream and heads to the liver, where it spends some time multiplying. Then, the amplified malaria posse heads back out into the bloodstream, each parasite digging into a red blood cell, feeding on the haemoglobin therein, making twenty copies of itself, with the successive new posses then leaving the cell they have destroyed and repeating the process with another cell victim. In this way, it can just be a few days before there are a trillion malaria (yes, 1,000,000,000,000 parasites) in the victim's body, drinking up the majority of their host's blood.

What's the best way to drive away this mortal pest? Contract sickle cell disease. Let me explain. Malaria feeds upon haemoglobin, which is a protein with 146 amino acids. Its job is to carry oxygen around the body. Haemoglobin was one of the first proteins that biologists analysed systematically, numbering each amino acid position and identifying which amino acid occupied that space. When the amino acid that is in position 6 is changed by a standard evolutionary random mutation, a person contracts sickle cell disease.[80]

The amino acid change does not affect haemoglobin's ability to carry oxygen, but it does affect its *shape*. Cells with normal haemoglobin, says Behe,[81] take on a 'Lifesaver' or 'doughnut' shape. Sickled cells, however, are no longer round, and have shapes more like that of stars or leaves. Moreover, their modified haemoglobin takes on magnet-like properties, such that all of the haemoglobin in a sickled cell gets stuck together. Biologists believe that this causes traffic jams in the capillaries—and hence sharp pains—and are certain that it causes the spleen to dispose of sickled cells more quickly than normal ones, with the result that the patient becomes anaemic, that is, deficient in blood.[82]

The good news for the sickle cell patient, however, is that the change in his haemoglobin *gives him an immunity to malaria*.[83] When malaria enters a red blood cell that has warped haemoglobin and starts its death-dealing deeds, it is quickly stopped in its tracks. The gelling of the haemoglobin confines the parasite, preventing its activity. Then, the spleen destroys the malaria with the sickled cell. Because the person has sickle cell disease, he does not get malaria.

What are the evolutionary consequences of this dual nature of sickle cell disease, its bad and good side? It causes natural selection to 'identify' sickle cell humans as more fit than healthy ones, in areas where malaria is prevalent. Healthy humans become infected with malaria and die before the age of five. Humans carrying the sickle trait, on the other hand, live on—at least those who have received the sickle cell gene from only one of their parents. Over a long period of time, the sickle cell gene becomes dominant, and an entire population has sickle cell disease, since humans without the sickle trait have died out from malaria. In this case of 'survival of the fittest', the fittest, the ones 'selected' by evolution, are the diseased humans, while the ones eliminated are the healthy humans.

This real example of evolution should cause us to start. It is not evolution but devolution; it is an example of our genetic code deteriorating over time. Dawkins speaks of evolution as an arms race, wherein animals progressively take on greater functionalities over time, due to their efforts to survive against their competitors for food, just as the Soviets and Americans developed better weapons to attack one another during the Cold War. Behe, based on the empirical evidence he puts forward, says that this analogy is not quite correct; the competition is more like trench warfare, with each side performing 'acts of desperate destruction' to themselves in order to gain an advantage over the other side.[84] It is clear that the sickle cell mutation is not an advantage to the human organism and so does not fit into the Darwinian picture of a progressive increase in function over time. Consider two of Behe's take home lessons:

- Both sickle and HbC [another hemoglobin mutation conferring malaria immunity] are quintessentially hurtful mutations because they diminish the functioning of the human body. Both induce anemia and other detrimental effects. In happier times they would never gain a foothold in human populations. But in desperate times, when an invasion threatens the city, it can be better in the short run to burn a bridge to keep the enemy out.

- The mutations are not in the process of joining to build a more complex, interactive biochemical system ... Neither hemoglobin mutation occurs in the immune system, the system that is generally responsible for defending the body from microscopic predators. So the mutations are neither making a new system nor even adding to an established one.[85]

What this means is that the primordial assumption of evolution—that all life forms are in a competition for food and only the fittest survive the competition—is false. Sometimes the more fit survive, and sometimes the less fit. In the end, those who survive are simply those who survive. They cannot be called the fittest, because natural selection sometimes selects the less fit.

Or, if you wish, we can broaden the meaning of the 'fittest' to indicate only a greater ability to produce offspring and not greater health or functionality. Leading Darwinists, realising that it is not necessarily the healthier who survive, have done exactly that. George Gaylord Simpson, for one, expresses this clearly:

> Natural selection favors fitness only if you define fitness as leaving more descendants. In fact geneticists do define it that way, which may be confusing to others. To a geneticist fitness has nothing to do with health, strength, good looks, or anything but effectiveness in breeding.[86]

But if such is the meaning of natural selection, then it tells us nothing; it is tautological, meaning it just says the same thing in different words. It says that those who survive are the ones who were able to survive, that those who have arrived to the present day are the same as those who survived.[87] We don't need a scientific theory to tell us this.

Behe's example also has implications for finding the limits of what natural selection is able to accomplish. The mutation that takes place in haemoglobin to produce sickle cell disease consists in the changing of a single amino acid. The chances of this taking place are very small, because:

1. there are billions of nucleotide components in DNA which can undergo mutation, that is, bases A, C, G, T, which determine which amino acids are used to construct a protein; and

2. 'the cellular machinery that replicates DNA is extremely faithful ... it makes only about one mistake in every hundred million nucleotides of DNA it copies in a generation'.[88]

The typographical error leading to sickle cell disease had to take place in the exact spot on a string of billions of nucleotides in a system where typos hardly ever take place. That mutation, however, did happen, some thousands of years ago.[89] Once the mutation occurred, natural selection started 'favouring' humans with the sickle trait over those without it in malaria-infested areas.

If a single precise mutation is rare, what would it take to get two precise mutations taking place at once? In other words, what if two changes of amino acids taking place at the same time gave an advantage? What are the chances that such a mutation could take place?

It turns out that the malaria parasite underwent a 'two amino acids at once' mutation in the twentieth century, and the double mutation was favourable to its survival. Americans had developed an antimalarial drug called 'chloroquine', having quinine as its active ingredient. The drug did wonders in curing malarial patients for decades, but slowly decreased in its effectiveness until it became useless in the 1980s.[90] The reason its healing ability waned was that malaria was developing resistance to the drug by means of a double random mutation. A change in positions 76 and 220 of one of the 5,300 proteins in malaria, a protein that has 424 amino acids, gives a malaria parasite resistance to chloroquine.[91] (Incidentally, this mutation diminishes malaria's health while enabling it to resist chloroquine, just as the sickle cell mutation causes anaemia while giving malaria resistance.)[92]

Behe estimates that the chances for a specific single mutation in malaria is one in a trillion (10^{12}), while those for a specific double mutation are one in a hundred billion billion (10^{20}).[93] Malaria needs a single mutation to resist a drug called atovaquone and a double mutation to resist chloroquine.

Because there are a trillion parasites in the typical malaria patient, we would expect malarial atovaquone resistance to appear quite frequently and, in fact, it 'can be found in roughly every third sick person'.[94] Once a single malaria parasite gets the right single mutation that gives resistance to atovaquone, natural selection takes over. The mutated atovaquone-resistant malaria reproduces itself a trillion times, while the unmutated malaria dies out.

The double mutation which makes malaria resistant to chloroquine is more difficult. Even with a trillion malaria in the body, busy copying their DNA and sometimes making random mistakes, there is only a one in a hundred million chance for a malaria parasite to get the double mutation ($10^{20} / 10^{12} = 100,000,000$ or 10^{8}). How, then, did malaria happen upon that precise mutation in order to defeat chloroquine? By invading a billion people (10^{9}). That is how many people have malaria, and a trillion malaria pests being in a billion people means that the actual population of the parasites is a trillion times a billion or 10^{21}. This is sufficient to provide all the chances necessary for a double mutation and thus:

> Spontaneous resistance to chloroquine can be found perhaps in every billionth sick person, and since there are usually close to a billion sick people on the planet every

year or so, that means choloroquine resistance is usually waiting to be found in at least one person, somewhere in the world, at any given time.[95]

Such are the chances for malaria to get a simultaneous specific double mutation needed to overcome a drug that kills it. If the human race had to chance on such a double mutation, forget about it. There are just not enough humans around. To get all of the tries necessary for such a mutation, we would have to wait until the number of humans who existed in our entire history reached 10^{20}, and that waiting period is 'many times the age of the universe'. Thus, says Behe, it is reasonable to conclude that 'no mutation that is of the same complexity as chloroquine resistance in malaria arose by Darwinian evolution in the line leading to humans in the past ten million years'.[96]

What are the chances, we may ask, for a quadruple simultaneous specific mutation? They are one in 10^{40}, and if we take the most numerous organism on this Earth—bacteria—we would find that it has almost the 10^{40} rolls of the dice needed to score its quadruple mutation, but not quite. Thus, that is a reasonable place to

> draw a tentative line marking the edge of evolution for all life on earth. We would not expect such an event to happen in all of the organisms that have ever lived over the entire history of life on this planet. So if we do find features of life that would have required a [quadruple mutation] or more, then we can infer that they likely did not arise by a Darwinian process ... [L]ife is bursting with such features.[97]

Evolution relies on randomness up front to introduce changes, and only then can natural selection kick in. For a specific random quadruple mutation to take place, an astronomical number of random iterations is necessary to try all of the combinations possible, more iterations than are possible. Thus, randomness can never generate a quadruple mutation. But life is teeming with features that would have needed a quadruple mutation or more to be generated by random mutation, so that they could then be 'selected' by natural selection. In Behe's mind, no features at the level of the taxonomical category of biological classes could be produced by a mechanism that cannot reach a quadruple mutation.[98] This is the edge of evolution. We cannot, then, reasonably expect that evolution can account for the vast majority of the features of life forms.

Evolution and the origin of the human species

Before I conclude this chapter and section of the book, I must consider evolution's account of the origin of the human species. We have already seen the Darwinian view of reality when evolution is turned into a 'theory-of-everything'. The stark differences that we remark among species are whitewashed such that nature is seen as a homogeneous continuum, where discontinuous divides between life forms do not exist. Instead of being a series of mountains and valleys, where the mountains are the different species and the valleys are the vast differences between them, biological nature is just a level plain that spreads off continuously into the distance from a single starting point. The history of life on Earth is that of an extremely gradual stepwise progression from a single cell to human beings, with no breaks or jumps to be found at any time, no sudden introduction of life forms vastly more complex than previous life forms. Humans cannot be detached from this scheme, and so they too must be a long-term result of a gradual process. As Darwin wrote in one of his notebooks, 'Man in his arrogance thinks himself a great work, worthy the interposition of a deity. More humble and I believe true to consider him created from animals'.

As difficult as it is to maintain the flattened vision of nature when faced with the radical differences among plant and animal species, it is still more difficult to maintain it when confronted with the differences between animals and humans. Empiricist evolutionists have to hold that, deep down, they are really the same. Thus, the radically distinctive characteristics of humans—characteristics such as language, consciousness, and reasoning—must not be seen as being essentially different from the abilities of animals. Animals speak and humans speak; animals are aware and humans are aware; animals think and humans think.

What empiricists are going to attempt to do, then, is erase the lines between animals and humans—or rather, I should say, span the seemingly immense chasm between them. They will try to turn animals into humans and humans into animals.

Animals to humans

For well over a century now, a certain breed of scientists has attacked the idea of human uniqueness by bringing forward evidence they believe shows that animals have intelligence that is not different in kind from that of humans, but only in degree. Darwin himself engaged in this enterprise, as he 'repeatedly adopted [the] strategy of minimizing the difference between the mental powers of humans and animals'.[99]

The truth is that animals only have sense knowledge which, as we saw in chapter one, provides knowledge of the radically particular.[100] Humans, on the other hand, have both sense and intellectual knowledge, that is, knowledge of the particular *and* the universal. Michael Egnor explains this difference as follows:

> Animals think particularly, not abstractly. That is, animals think about particulars (individual things) and about perceptions connected to the particulars, but they are not capable of *abstracting* universal concepts from particulars and contemplating the universal concepts *in isolation from individual things that evoke them*. For example, my dog certainly thinks of my kindness and responds by wagging her tail, but there is no evidence she is capable of contemplating kindness *as a concept*, abstracted from my particular behavior.
>
> That is not to say that animals can't be clever. Animals can be very clever—sometimes more clever than humans. Try

to build a spider web yourself. But animal cleverness is always tied to *particular* things and situations and instincts. A spider builds a very effective web to catch his meals. There is no evidence the spider contemplates the beauty of spider webs or that it understands 'web' as a metaphor for a complex set of associations.[101]

Empiricists, being committed to material causes and sense knowledge alone, do not admit this fundamental distinction between material knowledge of the individual, coming from the body, and spiritual knowledge of the universal, coming from the intellective human soul. Bonnette holds that the failure to distinguish between sense images and immaterial concepts is the primary fallacy of many modern animal researchers who ascribe human intelligence capabilities to animals,[102] and so we must make the distinction carefully.

Sense images, 'being rooted in the individuating, quantifying character of matter', are always 'singular, particular, sensible, concrete, and imaginable'.[103] They are pictures of what is seen or otherwise sensed outside the mind, and carry with them all of the individual characteristics of what is seen. If I look at Socrates, my sense imagination will represent him exactly as he is in all of his individuality. The image, being radically individual, will be incapable of representing all humankind. It corresponds to one human, not all of them.

To know humans as a whole, I need a concept, not an image. I need a universal notion, one that takes all the representatives of a given group, abstracts from whatever sets them apart from one another, and retains whatever is common to them. For instance, the notion 'humanness' is a concept containing certain universal notes—creature, living, sentient, rational—and refers to a certain class of beings, abstracting from their individual characteristics. Unlike Socrates, 'humanness' cannot be imagined. It has no direct connection to matter and quantity, and only material things can be depicted by an image.

According to Austin Woodbury, certain necessary formal effects flow from the human capacity to know universals.[104] These effects open up to humans an entire world of activities not accessible to animals. Two of them are *speech* and *progress*. The failure of animals to be observed performing these activities is strong empirical evidence leading to the conclusion that they do not have the power of abstraction. Let us consider the research.

Can animals speak?

Bonnette has a thirty page chapter on ape-language studies in his book *Origin of the Human Species*. He notes an initial problem for all such studies:

> All ape-language studies presuppose invention of true language by true humans. We then impose this uniquely human invention upon apes. The day apes create their own linguistic system is still the dream of science fiction.[105]

If apes were capable of speech, we would expect them to learn language in the same way that human children do, by grasping the names for things and then constructing sentences using those names. Apes, however, are not interested in learning language:

> Human children, unlike apes, appear to derive intrinsic pleasure from the sheer act of naming ... While apes must be arduously and endlessly drilled to learn signs, small children, once they grasp the game, spontaneously want to learn names for everything in sight ... Chimpanzees brought up in a human family learn no speech. Human children generally do so easily and quickly. Granted, chimpanzees and other apes lack human vocal dexterity. Still, they possess sufficient vocal equipment to enable them to make limited attempts at speech ... Apes attempt nothing of the sort.[106]

Apes, like all other animals, are only interested in the immediate needs of life. Sense knowledge is received by the body, is grasped by the body's organs, and is for the body's needs.[107] It cannot and does not spark interest in any pursuits higher than the sentient life, pursuits such as making money, practising virtue, or having a conversation.

This is why six macaques housed at a zoo in England, when a computer was placed in their cage in 2003, seemed to be most interested in 'defecating and urinating all over the keyboard'.[108] They did produce five pages of text by the end of a month, but it consisted almost entirely of the letter 's' and did not contain a single word.

But, someone may ask, what about apes' ability at sign language? 'Trainers have conditioned apes to associate impressive numbers of signs with objects'.[109] Some claim this means that the apes have language capability.

Such signing, however, is possible for a being possessing only sense knowledge. 'Mere association of images with signs and objects, or even of images with other images, does not constitute evidence of intellective understanding of anything's intrinsic nature'.[110] To demonstrate the possession of human intelligence and language, animals must not only show that they can associate sounds and objects, but also that they can grasp the universal concepts represented by the sounds.

We all have experience of dogs obeying commands, such as 'sit', 'heel', 'stay', and so on. But the dogs do not know what those words mean; they only know the action that corresponds to those sounds. Moreover, their entire focus is on receiving the reward that comes from performing the action.

In all of the attempts by humans to teach animals language, there are three problems which lead researchers to conclude that the animals under their training understand human language when they really do not:[111]

- **unintentional animal cuing**—humans often, without realising it, provide animals with clues when testing their language abilities. The classic case for this was 'Clever Hans', an Arabian stallion in Germany.[112] Hans would tap his foot on the ground so many times to indicate numerical answers to maths problems posed to him. His accuracy was about 90 per cent! The horse was acclaimed to be a 'rational animal'. Psychologist Oskar Pfungst, however, was doubtful. Upon examining the horse closely, he came to the conclusion that Hans only got the right answer when he could see the questioner *and* the questioner knew the right answer. The reason is that Hans was figuring out when to stop tapping his hoof by detecting unintentional changes in the facial expression of his questioner when he arrived at the right number. Hans was indeed clever, but he was not rational.

- **human influence on animals**—'Every experimental method is necessarily a human method and must thus, per se, constitute a human influence on the animal'.[113] The fairest assessment of animal capabilities is made when they are seen in the wild, not having been placed into some artificial environment and context arranged by humans. Animals require enormous coaxing and bribing to participate in lab experiments. This fact indicates that the human world of abstract thought and analysis is utterly foreign to them.

- **anthropomorphic interpretation of data**—researchers who confuse sense images with immaterial concepts are wont to interpret ape actions in the context of humanised experiments as being driven by the same intellectual capabilities that humans possess. What on the surface resembles rational behaviour is really just the result of an association of sense images.

In the end, we must conclude with Bonnette that 'no undisputed evidence exists of ape-language skills that exceed the association of sensible images'.[114]

Do animals make progress?

To manifest progress like that of humans, animals have to show advances on the individual level as well as on the level of their species.

The desire for progress naturally flows from the possession of intellectual knowledge. Humans, by means of their immaterial mind, have self-consciousness, and grasp notions of virtue, goodness, and perfection. This leads them to strive to make progress. 'As intellect naturally seeks universal truth, will seeks infinite good'.[115] Because we know intellectually about the existence of higher goods, our wills naturally desire them, and we cannot be fully content until we obtain them.

The possession of intellect is the reason why

> human beings progress as individuals even in the most primitive societies. Children learn language, arts, complex tribal organization, complex legal systems, and religious rites. Woodbury says, 'Moreover, the lowest of such peoples can be raised by education to very high culture.'[116]

Animals, on the other hand, remain completely content with a sense life from childhood to adulthood, not advancing beyond the confines of that life. They do not progress in virtue, in knowledge of the arts and sciences, in technology.

This is as much true at the level of species as at the level of individual animals. Bee hives, spider webs, and bird nests are amazing constructions, but they have been made in exactly the same way from time immemorial. The animals are pre-programmed to make these artefacts, since they make them without instruction and in the same way that their ancestors made them. They can never make them any differently, because they do not understand what they are making, why they are making it, or the relationship between the means and the end of their activity.

Without abstract knowledge of universals—rational activity—animals will never be able to make progress, either as individuals or as species.

Humans to animals

'Physical anthropology,' says Philip Johnson, 'the study of human origins, is a field that throughout its history has been more heavily influenced by subjective factors than almost any other branch of respectable science.'[117] He goes on to explain the reason: since Darwin's book *The Descent of Man*, scientists have been desperate to show that man descended from apes, because

> the story of human descent from apes is not merely a scientific hypothesis; it is the secular equivalent of the story of Adam and Eve, and a matter of immense cultural importance. Propagating the story requires illustrations, museum exhibits, and television reenactments. It also requires a priesthood, in the form of thousands of researchers, teachers, and artists who provide realistic and imaginative detail and carry the story out to the general public.[118]

In this delicate discussion above all, we must remain realists, committed to being taught by reality instead of imposing a pre-conceived conclusion upon it. It must first be admitted that there are some fossils intermediate between apes and modern men. I list them in the table below, along with some speculated dates for their appearance and their conventional biological classification.

Table 11.3 Human-like species distinguished by palaeontologists

Biological species	Rough date of appearance	Biological affinity
Australopithecus	4,000,000 years ago	Strongly resemble modern apes
Homo habilis	2,000,000 years ago	
Homo erectus	500,000 years ago	
Homo sapiens	300,000 years ago	
Neanderthal man	125,000 to 35,000 years ago	Strongly resemble modern humans
Cro-Magnon man	35,000 to 10,000 years ago	
Modern man	10,000 years ago	

While scientists have identified these different species based on varying body forms, yet the fossils are all incomplete and the record in general is extremely sketchy. To the degree that empirical data is lacking, the science that analyses it becomes less scientific. Grandiose theories get grafted on a mere nub of actual

Unspecified Species

fact. Much of the work of the palaeontologists becomes inventing a human prehistory based on a femur here, a cracked skull there. Such a prehistory cannot be a true history in any sense of the term, as Chesterton points out: 'Strictly speaking of course we know nothing about prehistoric man, for the simple reason that he was prehistoric. The history of prehistoric man is a very obvious contradiction in terms'.[119] And:

> In one sense it is a true paradox that there was history before history. But it is not the irrational paradox implied in prehistoric history; for it is a history we do not know. Very probably it was exceedingly like the history we do know, except in the one detail that we do not know it.[120]

One false assumption, often made, is that the use of tools is an indication of human intelligence and therefore the arrival of humanity can be dated from the arrival of tools. Evolutionists use tool-use as a tool to turn humans into animals. Famous chimpanzee researcher Jane Goodall, for instance, claims that the use of tools 'marked a major step in pre-human evolution' and that 'when, for the first time, an apelike creature made a tool to a 'regular and set pattern' he became, by definition, Man'.[121] She then promptly states that her chimps are able to make tools to a 'regular and set pattern.' For instance, they poke blades of grass into termite mounds, eating the bugs that crawl onto their tool. Eh, voila! Chimps are humans.

What is surprising is how compelling the modern Darwinian mind finds such arguments. As Bonnette points out,[122] no one takes the fact of birds making nests—tools for keeping eggs from dropping to the ground—as evidence of them having more than a 'bird brain.' Many animals use tools and this has long been known. Thus, finding primitive tools next to fossils is no indication that the animal who embodied the fossil was rational:

> Animals lacking intellect, such as Goodall's chimpanzees, can readily fashion and use tools of limited sophistication. Hypothesized use of wooded and bone tools by early

hominids, such as *Australopithecus robustus*, provides no evidence that they must have possessed intellective activity. Even early production of stone tools usually associated with *Homo habilis* need not carry such inference.[123]

If we cannot date the appearance of the first humans according to the appearance of 'regular and set pattern' tools, when should we date it? Clearly, the line should be drawn according to 'what is possible to the purely sentient soul and what must necessarily be attributed to intellect alone'.[124] The intellect alone can produce artistic tools, tools that not only serve a function, but are also visually pleasing.[125] 'Since grasp of artistic symmetry presupposes universal understanding of a geometrical ideal as a good concretely to realise, such tools reflect true intellective activity'.[126] Tools of this nature 'may date to as early as 500,000 years ago'.[127] This would indicate that *Homo erectus* was the first true man, and that the later species in the genus *Homo* actually belong to the same species—their differences were caused by micro-evolution, like the differences among human races today:

> The differences between the human-like members of the genus *Homo* can be explained as the result of micro-evolutionary change. For example, below the neck, *Homo erectus* is extremely similar to modern humans ... Neanderthals are commonly portrayed as bungling, primitive relatives of modern humans. But recent anatomical, genetic, and cultural data have led many scientists to believe Neanderthals were a sub-race that was part of our own species. Not only is their body shape within the range of modern human variation, but anatomical evidence suggests they were capable of speech. Further they have been found associated with signs of art and culture—including the burial of the dead.[128]

One's choice of the evolutionary picture of small, stepwise, gradual changes of apes to humans, or a sudden jump from apes to humans—a certain 'Homo explosion'—will have strong religious implications. The latter scenario favours the Christian doctrine, following an accurate reading of Genesis, that the human race derived from a single set of parents (monogenism). The former view favours the majority evolutionist opinion that we come from several sets of original parents (polygenism).

Perhaps the greatest difficulty that evolutionists face in establishing their gradual, stepwise story of human prehistory is showing how human intelligence can be the product of genetic changes in apes. They have certainly never given the least evidence to show that matter thinks. If, *per impossibile*, they were able to provide such evidence, how could we ever after take our thinking seriously? It would simply be the product of neural impulses, not a conceptualisation of reality rising above the material world. Darwin himself reflected on this difficulty:

> With me the horrid doubt always arises whether the convictions of man's mind, which has been developed from the mind of the lower animals, are of any value or at all trustworthy. Would any one trust in the convictions of a monkey's mind, if there are any convictions in such a mind?[129]

At the end of the day, establishing the precise origins of the human species is beyond the reach of empirical science. To discover where and how humans appeared, science would have to be able to locate a single event that is buried in the remote past and which could not have left a distinct record for scientists to find today. As Bonnette remarks,

> Evolutionary science sees the broad picture of human origins taking place over a time-frame measured in hundreds of thousands, or even millions, of years. It cannot focus on events affecting a single pair of humans at a given point in time.[130]

Moreover, there are substantial indications that 'as far back as we go in palaeontological time evidence of true human beings' presence appears'.[131] This would be sufficient to debunk the evolutionary story of our prehistory, wherein apes gradually turn into humans.

In short, there is very little science and very much tale spinning behind the standard evolutionary account of our origins. For that reason, one offends neither empirical evidence nor right reason in holding a different view on the subject.

Summary of this section (chapters 8–11)

The Middle Ages were realist and the modern age is empiricist. The transition between these epistemologies and their corresponding worldviews began with the decadence of the scholastic era, when arguments about hair-splitting distinctions wearied philosophic minds, leading them to believe that philosophy is not a way to find certitude about reality. The position of nominalism, which holds that our ideas do not correspond to anything real outside the mind, grew in popularity, and was assisted by the radical agnosticism of Protestantism. Realism was no longer the exclusive view to be taken about the ability of humans' minds to know reality; its dominance had been dissolved and the intellectual throne was vacant, waiting for some new occupant who would sweep away all contenders by the force of its evidence, and reign as the epistemology of the Western mind.

The new occupant appeared in the seventeenth century, the century of genius. The discoveries of scientists like Kepler, Galileo, and Newton were novel and compelling. They were accompanied by empirical proofs, proofs based on tangible evidence. Moreover, the proofs showed that Western science had been on the wrong track for a very long time. The fact that these scientists were so convincing *and* that they were overturning previous views on the working of the universe seemed to qualify scientists as having the ultimate say in what we should think about the whole of reality, not just physical bodies.

Kepler, Galileo, and Newton all derived mathematical formulas describing the movements of bodies. These formulas were neat and satisfying for the mind, but in a sense were too attractive. Their scientist discoverers wanted to see them as being more than a description of physical movement. They wanted them to be the only thing to be known about material bodies, and even wanted quantity to be the only thing existing, outside the mind, in the cosmos. Material bodies, in their being, would only be moving extended quantities, and so they would be known completely and exclusively through material causes (the composition of bodies) and efficient causes (the movement of bodies). Formal and final causes, which are only accessible as such to philosophy, would at best be ignored and at worst declared non-existent. Regardless, the field of true knowledge would be shrunk to the confines of a single class of disciplines, the physical sciences.

Scientists thought that adopting empiricism and making exact science the sole domain of real knowledge would be science's salvation. But false epistemologies always lead straight to irrationality, and so empiricism can only harm science, not build it up. It specifically does so in three ways:

1. *It undermines the conceptual foundations of science.* All sciences rely upon concepts taken from reality. The concepts in turn depend on the existence of formal causes. Thus, if there are no formal causes in reality, our concepts cannot correspond to reality in any way. Then principles such as the principles of non-contradiction and of causality—the principles upon which all reasoning is based—are called into doubt. If those principles, however, are called into doubt, the conclusions of modern science must also be called into doubt.

2. *It discredits science.* Those who deny formal and final causes must impose upon themselves a severe 'self-limitation of reason', because our intellects constantly give evidence that natures or essences exist outside the mind (formal causes), as well as direction or purpose (final causes). When such empiricists set out to prove to the world that formal and final causes do not exist, they make themselves look ridiculous to anyone with a minimum of common sense. For

instance, they purposefully set out to prove that there is no purpose, using concepts which they claim are meaningless.

3. *It fosters the science-stifling view of pantheism.* If empirical evidence alone provides true knowledge and material beings are explained exhaustively by means of mathematical formulas, then it would seem that science can explain everything without God. If such is the case, then the material universe is the only thing that exists. The universe is God. If the universe is God, however, it is also incomprehensible, since it is the ultimate source of all explanations, while being inexplicable in itself. Making the universe inexplicable, however, is the same as shutting it off to the pursuits of science.

These three poisonous fruits for science are evident in the areas of modern physics and biology, wherever empiricists are present.

Modern empiricist physicists, following their science-deifying paradigm, have applied the attributes of God to the material universe under their investigation. They have attempted to show that it is infinite, unchanging, homogeneous, unchanged, without a purpose beyond itself. Such a thesis, however:

1. Undermines the conceptual foundations of science—matter, by definition, is limited, finite, changing, determined to an end outside of itself. Pretending that it is otherwise is to denature the notion of matter. It makes matter what it is not while it remains what it is.

2. Discredits science—some scientists have sought desperately to prove that the universe has divine attributes, in the face of clear empirical evidence to the contrary, especially the evidence for the Big Bang. To sidestep this evidence, they have even claimed that the universe and all that is in it comes from nothing. This is a position far more ridiculous than saying that hats produce rabbits, a position which at least provides an actual being as a cause.

3. Fosters a science-stifling viewpoint—if the universe is uncaused, as some empiricists claim, then it is inexplicable. But the purpose of physics is to explain the universe.

Modern empiricist origin-of-life theorists have in turn yielded the same three offspring for their own intellectual discipline, biology. They:

1. Undermine the conceptual foundations of science—such biologists deny the existence of any purpose in life. Without purpose, however, nothing is meaningful. That includes science, which is an activity performed by living human beings.

2. Discredit science—materialists try desperately to account for the incredible complexity of life through material causes, when those causes are utterly inadequate to explain life. This makes them put forward outrageous explanations for life's origins: it came from raw chance, from space aliens, from crystals piggybacking on crystals, and so on.

3. Foster a science-stifling viewpoint—empiricists make matter the only possible source for the origin of life *by definition*. This makes them look *exclusively* in the realm of material causes, and not even consider the *possibility* that life is to be explained by other causes. Thus, empiricism sets scientists on an endless wild good chase, wherein they turn matter over and over, trying to find the *vera causa*, when the true cause is not in matter at all.

Last comes the theory of evolution. Its empiricist version purports to account for the origin of all species of life on Earth without having recourse to formal and final causes, or any power higher than matter. But this leads it to:

1. Undermine the conceptual foundations of science—the notion of species is destroyed by a theory which requires that life forms in nature not have essential differences, the very differences that make for species. At the same time, the theory assumes that species exist. It also requires that

life forms not be headed in any direction, but then assumes that they are headed in the direction of survival. Thus, empiricist evolution both destroys and builds up the conceptual foundations on which its rests.

2. Discredit science—Darwinism is an extremely outdated theory, in that it proposes a clunky, naturalistic mechanism for life systems which we now know are enormously complex. Yet the scientific community clings to Darwinism with a religious devotion. The man on the street is not convinced. Only 14 per cent of the American public thinks that the empiricist evolutionary account is correct.[132] The reason is that 'the public refuses to believe that their most basic perception of living things is an illusion'.[133]

3. Foster a science-stifling viewpoint—billions of dollars and billions of man hours are spent looking for empirical proof of macro-evolution and other confirmations of empiricist Darwinism. Meanwhile, finding and writing about the immense weight of evidence against it, or proposing alternative theories, is not allowed. But having scientists look for something that does not exist and not allowing them to find what really exists is to destroy the scientific endeavour.

Empiricism has been and always will be a huge fail as an epistemology, because it cripples the intellect's abstractive power. It expressly hampers the faculty which separates humans from animals and, in doing so, leads straight to irrationality. Unfortunately, this is exactly where we are at the latest stage of the unfolding of the 'Scientific Revolution'.

A return to realism would be a return to intellectual wellness. But how do you convince a world to change its epistemology?

Notes

[1] D. Stove, *Darwinian Fairytales* (New York: Encounter Books, 1995), p. 22.
[2] *Ibid.*, p. 24.
[3] Cited in E. Gilson, *From Aristotle to Darwin and Back Again* (San Francisco: Ignatius Press, 2009), p. 180.
[4] *Ibid.*, p. 88.
[5] C. Darwin, *The Origin of Species* (Middlesex, England: Penguin Books, 1968), p. 102.
[6] *Ibid.*, p. 71.
[7] *Ibid.*
[8] Gilson, *From Aristotle to Darwin*, p. 90.
[9] G. Kemper, H. Kemper, and C. Luskin, *Discovering Intelligent Design* (Seattle: Discovery Institute Press, 2013), p. 27, emphasis added.
[10] See *Ibid.*, pp. 159–160.
[11] Cited in P. Johnson, *Darwin on Trial* (Washington, DC: Regnery Gateway, 1991), p. 24.
[12] D. Bonnette, *Origin of the Human Species* (Ave Maria, Florida: Sapientia Press, 2014), p. 232.
[13] *Metaphysics*, 1041b11–33.
[14] For a technical philosophical treatment of this subject, see Aquinas, *In Met.*, paragraphs 1672–1680; D. Oderberg, *Real Essentialism* (New York: Routledge, 2007), pp. 66–67.
[15] See Bonnette, *Origin of the Human Species*, chapter 2.
[16] See pp. 468–475.
[17] *From Aristotle to Darwin*, p. 173. See also T. Bethell, *Darwin's House of Cards* (Seattle: Discovery Institute Press, 2017), p. 33, where Darwin is quoted as saying that there is 'no fundamental distinction between species and varieties.'
[18] I am not wanting to imply, by this example, that houses or any other human artifacts have anything more than an accidental unity. I am just using what is clearer for us—our own productions—as a means to understand what is less clear to us, the things of nature.
[19] *Orthodoxy* (London: William Clowes and Sons, 1908), pp. 58–59, emphasis added.
[20] For an example of this view, see R. Dawkins, *The Greatest Show on Earth* (New York: Free Press, 2009). For instance, on pp. 404–405, he says: 'Right up to the middle of the twentieth century, life was thought to be qualitatively beyond physics and chemistry. No longer. The difference between life and non-life is a matter not of substance but of *information*' (emphasis

in original).
21 Gilson, *From Aristotle to Darwin*, pp. 170–171.
22 See pp. 260–261.
23 *Ibid.*, p. 175.
24 *Ibid.*, p. 167.
25 Dawkins, *The Greatest Show*, p. 195.
26 *Ibid.*, emphasis added.
27 *Ibid.*
28 For examples of fixity in the biological world see M. Denton, *Evolution: Still a Theory in Crisis* (Seattle: Discovery Institute Press, 2016), pp. 45–52.
29 See p. 459.
30 The work cited in the previous footnote is a book-long, able defence of structuralism.
31 988b6–16.
32 See pp. 407–408.
33 Gilson, *From Aristotle to Darwin*, p. 156.
34 See Aquinas, SCG, Book II, chapter 24, paragraph 4.
35 Dawkins, *The Greatest Show*, p. 354.
36 Cited in Kemper, *Discovering*, p. 120. Even such a rank atheist as David Hume wrote anent the eye: 'Consider, anatomize the eye; survey its structure and contrivance; and tell me, from your own feeling, whether the idea of a contriver does not immediately flow in upon you with a force like that of sensation' (cited in Stove, *Darwinian Fairytales*, p. 261).
37 See p. 444.
38 See Gilson, *From Aristotle to Darwin*, p. 98.
39 Stove, *Darwinian Fairytales*, pp. 283, 288.
40 *Ibid.*, pp. 285–286, emphasis in original.
41 Material and citations from *Ibid.*, pp. 248–253. A. Flew also critiques the irrationality of Dawkins's *The Selfish Gene* in his *There is a God* (New York: HarperOne, 2007), pp. 79–80.
42 Stove, *Darwinian Fairytales*, p. 266.
43 A. Sertillanges, 'Dialogue sur le problème de Dieu' in *La Vie Intellectuelle*, 1929, my translation.
44 See J. Wells, *The Politically Incorrect Guide to Darwinism and Intelligent Design* (Washington, DC: Regnery Publishing, 2006), pp. 14–16.
45 See S. Meyer, *Darwin's Doubt* (New York: HarperOne, 2013), p. 41.
46 *Ibid.*, p. 15.
47 Cited in *Ibid.*, p. 17.
48 *Ibid.*, p. 58.
49 *Ibid.*, p. 86.

Unspecified Species 493

50 *Ibid.*
51 *Ibid.*, p. 73. We only know of thirty-six animal phyla. Three of them appear in the Precambrian period, twenty of them in the whole of the Cambrian, while nine of them do not appear in the fossil record at all. That means that only four new phyla appear in the fossil record after the Cambrian, which ended 485mya.
52 Meyer, *Darwin's Doubt*, p. 40, emphasis in original.
53 *Ibid.*, p. 74.
54 *Ibid.*, p. 94.
55 See Dawkins, *The Greatest Show*, pp. 99–101.
56 Cited in Meyer, *Darwin's Doubt*, p. 72.
57 *Ibid.*, p. 67.
58 *Ibid.*, pp. 67–68.
59 *Ibid.*, pp. 156–157.
60 *Ibid.*, p. 157.
61 *Ibid.*
62 Kemper, *Discovering Intelligent Design*, p. 28, emphasis added.
63 See p. 412.
64 Meyer, *Darwin's Doubt*, p. 160.
65 See *Ibid.*, p. 257.
66 See Discovery Institute's video clip 'How to Build a Worm' at http://www.evolutionnews.org/2015/05/heads_or_tails096081.html.
67 Meyer, *Darwin's Doubt*, p. 267.
68 *Ibid.*, p. 256.
69 *Ibid.*, p. 257.
70 *Ibid.*, pp. 260–261.
71 *Ibid.*, p. 262.
72 Dawkins cited in Wells, *The Politically Incorrect Guide*, pp. 63–64.
73 Dawkins, *The Greatest Show*, pp. 113–116.
74 *Ibid.*, pp. 116–133.
75 *Ibid.*, pp. 133–138.
76 For Meyer's summary of Behe, see *Darwin's Doubt*, pp. 240–249.
77 Kemper, *Discovering Intelligent Design*, p. 271.
78 T. Bethell, *Darwin's House of Cards* (Seattle: Discovery Institute Press, 2017), p. 186.
79 *The Edge of Evolution* (New York: Free Press, 2007), pp. 17–18.
80 *Ibid.*, p. 22.
81 *Ibid.*
82 *Ibid.*, p. 23.
83 *Ibid.*, p. 25.

84 *Ibid.*, pp. 40–43.
85 *Ibid.*, pp. 33–34.
86 Cited in Johnson, *Darwin on Trial*, p. 20.
87 See Bethell, *Darwin's House of Cards*, pp. 9–15. See also M. Chaberek, *Catholicism and Evolution* (Kettering, Ohio: Angelico Press, 2015), p. 24.
88 Behe, *The Edge*, p. 66.
89 *Ibid.*, p. 25.
90 *Ibid.*, p. 46.
91 *Ibid.*, pp. 48, 50.
92 See *Ibid.*, pp. 50–51.
93 *Ibid.*, p. 57.
94 *Ibid.*
95 *Ibid.*
96 *Ibid.*, p. 61.
97 *Ibid.*, p. 63.
98 Behe summarises his final view in *Ibid.*, pp. 217–220.
99 Bethell, *Darwin's House of Cards*, p. 213.
100 See p. 7.
101 See http://www.evolutionnews.org/2015/12/the_clever_hans101411.html, emphasis in original.
102 *Origin of the Human Species*, p. 100.
103 *Ibid.*
104 Cited in Bonnette, *Origin of the Human Species*, p. 97.
105 *Origin of the Human Species*, p. 80.
106 *Ibid.*, pp. 89, 97–98.
107 See Aquinas, *In Met.*, paragraph 12.
108 Wells, *The Politically Incorrect Guide*, p. 93.
109 Bonnette, *Origin of the Human Species*, p. 85.
110 *Ibid.*
111 *Ibid.*, p. 77.
112 See M. Egnor, http://www.evolutionnews.org/2015/12/the_clever_hans101411.html.
113 Hediger cited in Bonnette, *Origin of the Human Species*, p. 76.
114 *Origin of the Human Species*, p. 83.
115 *Ibid.*, p. 98.
116 *Ibid.*
117 *Darwin on Trial*, p. 80.
118 *Ibid.*, p. 83.
119 *The Everlasting Man* (New York: Dodd, Mead & Company, 1930), p. 28.

[120] *Ibid.*, p. 53.
[121] Cited in Bonnette, *Origin of the Human Species*, p. 156.
[122] *Ibid.*, p. 158.
[123] *Ibid.*, pp. 161–162.
[124] *Ibid.*, p. 164.
[125] See G. K. Chesterton, *The Everlasting Man* (New York: Dodd, Mead & Company, 1930), p. 31: 'A monkey does not draw clumsily and a man cleverly; a monkey does not begin the art of representation and a man carry it to perfection. A monkey does not do it at all; he does not begin to do it at all; he does not begin to begin to do it at all. A line of some kind is crossed before the first faint line can begin.' The entire second chapter of *The Everlasting Man* may be read on this topic of art as a dividing line between man and animals.
[126] Bonnette, *Origin of the Human Species*, p. 164.
[127] *Ibid.*, p. 165.
[128] Kemper, *Discovering Intelligent Design*, p. 186.
[129] Letter of July 3, 1881; C. S. Lewis develops this argument in *Miracles* (Glasgow: William Collins & Sons, 1947), pp. 22–23.
[130] *Origin of the Human Species*, p. 149.
[131] *Ibid.*, p. 204.
[132] Dawkins, *The Greatest Show*, p. 430.
[133] http://www.evolutionnews.org/2016/05/can_evolutionar102886.html.

EPILOGUE

The man who cannot believe his senses,
and the man who cannot believe anything else,
are both insane.

G. K. Chesterton

AT THE START of his *Divine Comedy*, Dante finds himself in a dark wood, disoriented, not knowing how he came there, having wandered by slow degrees from the path of truth. He sees a hill before him, whose top is filled with light from the sun. Moving toward the light, he begins to climb the barren slope, but is hindered by three animals who come one after another, preventing all progress.

The first animal is a leopard, representing incontinence or impurity; the second is a lion, a symbol of violence; and the third is a *lupa* or wolf, a type of the crime of fraud.[1] In their presence, Dante scrambles back down the incline, reversing the little progress he had made. Spying a man, he cries out for help and learns that it is the great Roman poet Virgil approaching. Virgil explains that the animals will not allow him to ascend the 'mountain of delight', atop of which sits 'the origin and cause of every joy'.[2] If he wants to depart that wilderness, Dante must leave by another way. Virgil is willing to guide Dante on the path to the light above the mountain, but they will have to take the long route. They will first have to pass through Hell, the dwelling place of those who have 'lost the good of the intellect'.[3]

The opening cantos of Dante's master epic can serve as a metaphor for human beings and human civilisations without realism. Those who do not adopt a realist epistemology find themselves in an alien place, which appears dark and foreboding. They are off the track of truth, wandering in the obscurity and tangled underbrush of error, different both from what they are and what they are meant to be.

Dwelling in a state of false epistemology, they find it impossible to climb Reality's steep slope. In particular, there are three obstacles blocking their way, three animal tendencies in humans, tendencies which obstruct reason from ascending the causal chain to bask in the light of the truth for which it was made. This is the truth of the First Cause, rightly and precisely understood, a truth which illumines the entire terrain of human truth-seeking.

The first of these tendencies is a leopard-like incontinence, by which humans indulge their senses to excess, filling and overfilling them beyond measure with matter's manifestations. With the sense faculties so sated, the intellect becomes sluggish and flaccid, inert beneath a tsunami of sense impressions, paralysed by the perturbations of the passions. Thus weighed down, reason abandons logical labour, stops at the mountain's foot, and settles for a simplistic worldview, one that sees matter as the ultimate reality, one making God the all and the all God. The pantheistic god, instead of flooding reality with light, overshadows it with an umbrageous cloud, sapping the universe of all causal explanation by reducing it to a brute fact.

Such was the worldview of pre-philosophic cultures and such is today's worldview. The ancient cultures neither understood how to plumb reality nor the laws of the mind which penetrates it. The external world was baffling and inscrutable, full of mystery and mythology. To explain was to tell a story, not to provide a rational cause. The mind was to remain empty and silent in front of the displays produced in imaginations.

We have reverted to this position today, not because we have not understood how to form a realist metaphysics, but because we have rejected it. It is said to be too complex, too religious, or too intellectual. Worst of all, it makes allowance for the intellect to see what cannot be seen, to know what is immaterial. Since what is immaterial cannot be observed and measured, it is said not to be objective, as if aspects of reality unfathomable by the scientific method and so requiring more thoughtful and difficult methods should, for that reason, be ruled out.

To fill in the vast vacuum of explanation left by the removal of formal and final causes, modern materialists tell stories. They say perturbations of nothing configured the universe, that we were born from the stars, that genes wove us from their selfishness, that fish became fowl by turns of fortune. In the end, it is the same magic and mythology of primitive thought, only today's myths do not allow for intelligent agents to enter the story. It is all magic and no magicians. Pagans used myths to give the wrong reasons for everything; scientists today use myths to give no reason for everything. In the first case, the intellect did not possess the truth, but possessed a reason; in the second case, the intellect neither possesses truth nor reasons. The good of the intellect has been lost.

The second tendency of humans which frequently blocks the vision of a realist metaphysics is a lion which seizes upon reason, holding it in its clutches and forbidding it to move freely. That lion is wilfulness. Many persons, infatuated with a single idea, or blinded by their age's ideology, or afraid of the obligations certain knowledge may impose upon them, refuse to allow their intellects to learn further from reality. They have decided what reality is, and will not change their minds, no matter what reality has to say about it.

'The intellect', says Wallace, 'can take the seeming true for being true because its judgement is under the influence of the will, the emotions, and other powers.'[4] In such cases, when assimilating information, reason does not take the time necessary to weigh evidence carefully, to wait for further evidence if that provided is insufficient, to free itself from outside influences before passing to judgement. It jumps to a conclusion straightaway, a conclusion already familiar to it, a pre-determined conclusion, the only conclusion possible because of a decree of a leonine will.

This second defect can proceed from the first. Our laziness can make us want a simplified view of reality that will give us all intellectual success and happiness, without making us do hard work. Do we really have to have God in the picture in order to plumb reality's secrets? Do we really have to make distinction after distinction, carefully separating this from that, making sure at every step that two diverse realities are not being lumped into a single, confused whole? We talk ourselves into believing that 'everything will be alright' if we seize upon our favourite idea, cease investigating and reasoning about reality, and declare that idea to be all that is. The rest of the candidates for realness we will define out of existence, the shortest possible way of dealing intellectually with a thing. But reality has a way of getting its revenge, by leaving us in a state of mental impairment, unable to see past our own artificial paradigm.

In our historical survey, we have seen how often not just individuals, but entire civilisations can become gripped by an ideology, some master key of interpretation for all of reality, a key that does not unlock reality, but is rather wielded as a hammer to beat reality into the ideology's shape. This is done most characteristically by religious believers who conceive their God as being entirely wilful and arbitrary, and who expresses that will in a certain text. Turning aside from God's reality and the mind that God has endowed upon them to know it, they think to find all knowledge in disconnected propositions from their sacred text. They fill their minds with these 'truths', though they are not able to make sense of them or harmonise them with reality as presented by the senses.

Once believers are locked into the template of such an interpretative key, their minds no longer have the freedom to infer proper causal knowledge from the extramental world. They continue to ingest sense data, but the data is swallowed by the will, not the intellect. The lion's paw has such a firm grip on reality's mouth, that it cannot speak in its proper voice. Whenever the intellect makes an inference in contradiction to the divinely-ordained ideology, the will pounces on it, stifling the realist inference by the idealist construct. Like the God they have fashioned, such believers are more wilful than reasonable.

Ironically, today's empirical science has become today's religious ideology. Modern empiricism is an idealism, in that many academics have taken certain fascinating but extremely limited scientific discoveries, constructed on top of them a theory-of-everything, and imposed that theory back upon the reality from which they initially derived their discoveries. The theory-of-everything has no basis in science, yet is used to say that science knows all that can be known. It is used, in other words, to say that science knows about reality even what it does not know and can never know.

Once such believers and such scientists have formed their ideology and have wilfully chosen it as the only possible explanation for all that is, reality loses its ability to speak to the intellect, and so the intellect is unable to access its true good, the truth.

The third tendency by which humans all too easily compromise realism is the wolf of fraud. Everyone of us is created a realist and lives as a realist. It is our birthright, and the endowment of the human race. All true knowledge that has been achieved in human history and will be achieved in the future has been acquired by thinking as realists.

Because realism is hard-wired into the very constitution of our being, we cheat ourselves when we artificially adopt, in certain mental exercises, the unhuman epistemologies of empiricism or idealism. This self-defrauding happens in two ways.

When thinking as non-realists, firstly, we prevent our mind from matching up with our life. In our daily activities, coffee and communication, being and bananas, seeing and saying, living and loving, are all blended together in a harmonious whole, our persons connecting with reality in all of its manifestations, by means of our senses and intellect, without a shadow of difficulty.

It is only by second-guessing ourselves, denying the obvious, or embracing the unthinkable that we are able to be, even briefly, an empiricist or idealist. A materialist, for instance, may claim that nothing is certain beyond what can be sensed, but as soon as you steal his car, he will immediately be demanding the fulfilment of that abstract concept 'justice'. As for the idealist, he will boldly cling to the notion that sense data is illusory, until his house is set on fire.

Another way of expressing this is by saying that empiricism and idealism are existential hazards. They are injurious to human physical and mental health. To the degree that a human adopts a false epistemology, he renders himself incompatible with reality. The more he separates himself from reality, the more he puts his life and lucidity in danger. We humans are so constructed that we cannot survive without the real. Because we are made for what is and not for what is not, there is something suicidal in denying one's knowing faculties their connection with reality.

The second species of fraud that one exercises upon oneself by refusing realism is the cheating of the mind. An idealist or empiricist cannot be consistent in his thinking; he cannot maintain an integral coherence among the positions he takes. We have seen this time and time again in the course of our investigation.

The Muslim occasionalist Al-Ghazali made an ardent attempt to prove that philosophy is useless, by arguing philosophically. The Muslim philosopher Averroes seemed content to keep two sets of contradictory propositions in his mind, one for religion and one for philosophy, both of which he held to be true. The Catholic monk William of Occam argued that our ideas do not correspond to reality, but used ideas taken from reality as the basis of his arguments. The former monk Martin Luther reasoned against reason, held that God does everything in man's salvation and that man does something, and encouraged people to do good while saying that it is impossible for us to do good.

But it is not just idealists who inevitably fall into contradiction; it is the empiricists as well. Some modern physicists hold that nothing is something, that disorder is the cause of order, that what has no causal power is the cause of all. Some modern biologists claim that humans are a mere conglomeration of matter, without purpose, and purposefully set out to convince other people units of their belief. Some modern evolutionists assert that the ultimate reason why species developed is that there are no species, and that a purposeless process of purposeful striving for survival caused a vast variety of complex biological forms to come into being.

In the end, if a human's epistemology does not match up with reality, then he cannot think or speak coherently and consistently about it, and this is a cheating of his own mind.

We owe it to ourselves to be what we are, to live up to what we are. We are realists. Thus, we must live as realists, reason as realists, embrace conclusions as realists, argue as realists. Only then can we provide to our own reason its full rights, assimilate reality's rich texture to our full capacity, and reach maximal agreement with our fellow human beings, realist as they are. Our own age, in its anti-human bent, has invested immense effort into making empiricists out of us all. But it can no more do so than it can re-create reality or re-engineer the human race. It will always have 'being' in general and 'human being' in particular standing in the way of its mind-numbing efforts.

At the same time, the vast propaganda machine advocating, with great logical inconsistency, the materialist worldview, holds a certain sway over the general populace, overshadowing and confusing their innate realism and its commonsense conclusions. How many today, for instance, think that 'there is no absolute truth', not realising that the very statement is an attempt to state an absolute truth?

We are today confused as a civilisation, alien, as it were, to our own rational powers. We are disoriented, in a dark wood, our senses overloaded, our wills shutting off rational deliberation, our reason and life cheated of their proper relation to reality. We are in desperate need of a Virgil-like guide to lead us out of our obscurity, back into reality's full light, lest we lose the good of the intellect for good.

Epistemological realism is our Virgil, and it has no need to lead us the long way to reality's heights. We have only to calibrate our epistedometer to a perfectly balanced realism, cast our animal tendencies aside, and then start climbing.

Notes

[1] W. Cook and R. Herzman, *Dante's Divine Comedy* (Chantilly, Virginia: The Teaching Company, 2001) audio course, lecture 5.
[2] *Inferno*, I, 77–78; translation A. Mandelbaum (New York: Bantam Books, 1982), p. 7.
[3] *Inferno*, III, 18; translation A. Mandelbaum (New York: Bantam Books, 1982), p. 21.
[4] *The Modeling of Nature* (Washington DC: The Catholic University of America Press, 1996), p. 153.

BIBLIOGRAPHY

Adler, M. *Aristotle for Everybody*. New York: Simon & Schuster, 1978.

Aizpún, F. *La Quinta Vía y el Diseño Inteligente*. Middletown, Delaware: Organización Internacional para el avance científico del Diseño Inteligente, 2015.

Arber, Cabbibo, and Soronado. *Scientific Insights into the Evolution of the Universe and of Life*. Vatican City: Pontifical Academy of Sciences, 2009.

Atkins, P. *On Being*. Oxford: Oxford University Press, 2011.

Augros, M. *Who Designed the Designer?*. San Francisco: Ignatius Press, 2015.

Axe, D. *Undeniable*. New York: HarperOne, 2016.

Behe, M. *Darwin's Black Box*. New York: Simon & Schuster, Inc., 1996.

____. *The Edge of Evolution*. New York: Free Press, 2007.

Bethell, T. *Darwin's House of Cards*. Seattle: Discovery Institute Press, 2017.

Blackwell, R. & Spath, R. & Thirlkel, W. 1995. *Commentary on Aristotle's* Metaphysics. Notre Dame, Indiana: Dumb Ox Books.

Bonnette, D. *Origin of the Human Species*. Ave Maria, Florida: Sapientia Press, 2014.

Brown, W. *In the Beginning*. Phoenix: Center for Scientific Creation, 1995.

Burtt, E. *The Metaphysical Foundations of Modern Science*. Mineola, New York: Dover Publications, 1932.

Chaberek, M. *Catholicism and Evolution*. Kettering, Ohio: Angelico Press, 2015.

Chesterton, G.K. *Orthodoxy*. London: William Clowes and Sons, 1908.

____. *What's Wrong with the World*. London: Cassell and Company, 1910.

____. *The Everlasting Man*. New York: Dodd, Mead & Company, 1930.

____. *St. Thomas Aquinas*. London: Hodder & Stoughton Limited, 1933.

Copleston, F. *Aquinas*. Harmondsworth, Middlesex: Penguin Books, Ltd., 1955.

Craig, W. *The Cosmological Argument from Plato to Leibniz*. Eugene, Oregon: Wipf and Stock Publishers, 1980.

Dales, R. *The Scientific Achievement of the Middle Ages*. Philadelphia: University of Pennsylvania Press, 1973.

Dalrymple, B. *Ancient Earth, Ancient Skies*. Stanford, California: Stanford University Press, 2004.

Darwin, C. *The Origin of Species*. Middlesex, England: Penguin Books, 1968.

Dawkins, R. *The Greatest Show on Earth*. New York: Free Press, 2009.

Denton, M. *Evolution: A Theory in Crisis*. Bethesda, Maryland: Adler & Adler, 1986.

Denzinger, H. & Hünermann, P. *Compendium of Creeds, Definitions, and Declarations on Matters of Faith and Morals*. San Francisco: Ignatius Press, 2012.

Feser, E. *The Last Superstition*. South Bend, Indiana: St. Augustine's Press, 2008.

____. *Scholastic Metaphysics*. Heusenstamm, Germany: Editiones Scholasticae, 2014.

____. *Neo-Scholastic Essays*. South Bend, Indiana: St. Augustine's Press, 2015.

____. *Five Proofs of the Existence of God*. San Francisco: Ignatius Press, 2017.

Fowler, H. *Plato's Euthyphro, Apology, Crito, Phaedo, Phaedrus*. Cambridge, Massachusetts: Harvard University Press, 1914.

Garrigou-Lagrange, R. *God, His Existence, and His Nature*, vol. 1. St. Louis: B. Herder Book Co., 1939.

Gigot, F. *Special Introduction to the Study of the Old Testament*, vol. 1. New York: Benziger Brothers, 2nd ed., 1903.

Gilson, E. *Methodical Realism*. San Francisco: Ignatius Press, 1935.

____. *The Unity of Philosophical Experience*. London: Sheed and Ward, 1938.

Bibliography 507

_____. *The Spirit of Medieval Philosophy.* New York: Charles Scribner's Sons, 1940.

_____. *God and Philosophy.* New Haven: Yale University Press, 2nd ed., 1941.

_____. *History of Christian Philosophy in the Middle Ages.* New York: Random House, 1955.

_____. *From Aristotle to Darwin and Back Again.* San Francisco: Ignatius Press, 1971.

Gonzalez, G. & Richards, J. *The Privileged Planet.* Washington, DC: Regnery Publishing, 2004.

Grant, E. *The Foundations of Modern Science in the Middle Ages.* Cambridge: Cambridge University Press, 1996.

Grisar, H. *Luther.* St. Louis: B. Herder, 2nd ed., 1914.

Haffner, P. *The Mystery of Reason.* Leominster, Herefordshire: Gracewing, 2001.

_____. *Creation and Scientific Creativity.* Leominster, Herefordshire: Gracewing, 2nd ed., 2009.

Hankins, B. (editor) *Evangelicalism and Fundamentalism, A Documentary Reader.* New York: New York University Press, 2009.

Hannam, J. *The Genesis of Science.* Washington, DC: Regnery Publishing, 2011.

Heller, M. *Ultimate Explanations of the Universe.* Berlin: Springer-Verlag, 2009.

Jaki, S. *The Paradox of Olbers' Paradox.* Pinckney, MI: Real View Books, 2nd ed., 2000.

_____. *Science and Creation.* New York: Science History Publications, 1974.

_____. 'The Physics of Impetus and the Impetus of the Koran'. In *Modern Age* (Spring, 1985), 153–159.

_____. 'Socrates or the Baby and the Bathwater'. In *Faith and Reason* (Spring, 1990).

_____. *Scientist and Catholic: Pierre Duhem.* Front Royal, Virginia: Christendom Press, 1991.

_____. *Reluctant Heroine: The Life and Work of Hélène Duhem.* Edinburgh: Scottish Academic Press, 1992.

_____. *Bible and Science.* Grand Rapids, Michigan: William Eerdmans Publishing Company, 1996.

_____. *God and the Cosmologists.* Fraser, Michigan: Real View Books, 1998.

_____. *Genesis 1 Through the Ages.* Edinburgh: Scottish Academic Press, 2nd ed., 1998.

_____. *Means to Message.* Grand Rapids, Michigan: William Eerdmans Publishing Company, 1999.

_____. *Miracles and Physics.* Front Royal, Virginia: Christendom Press, 2nd ed., 1999.

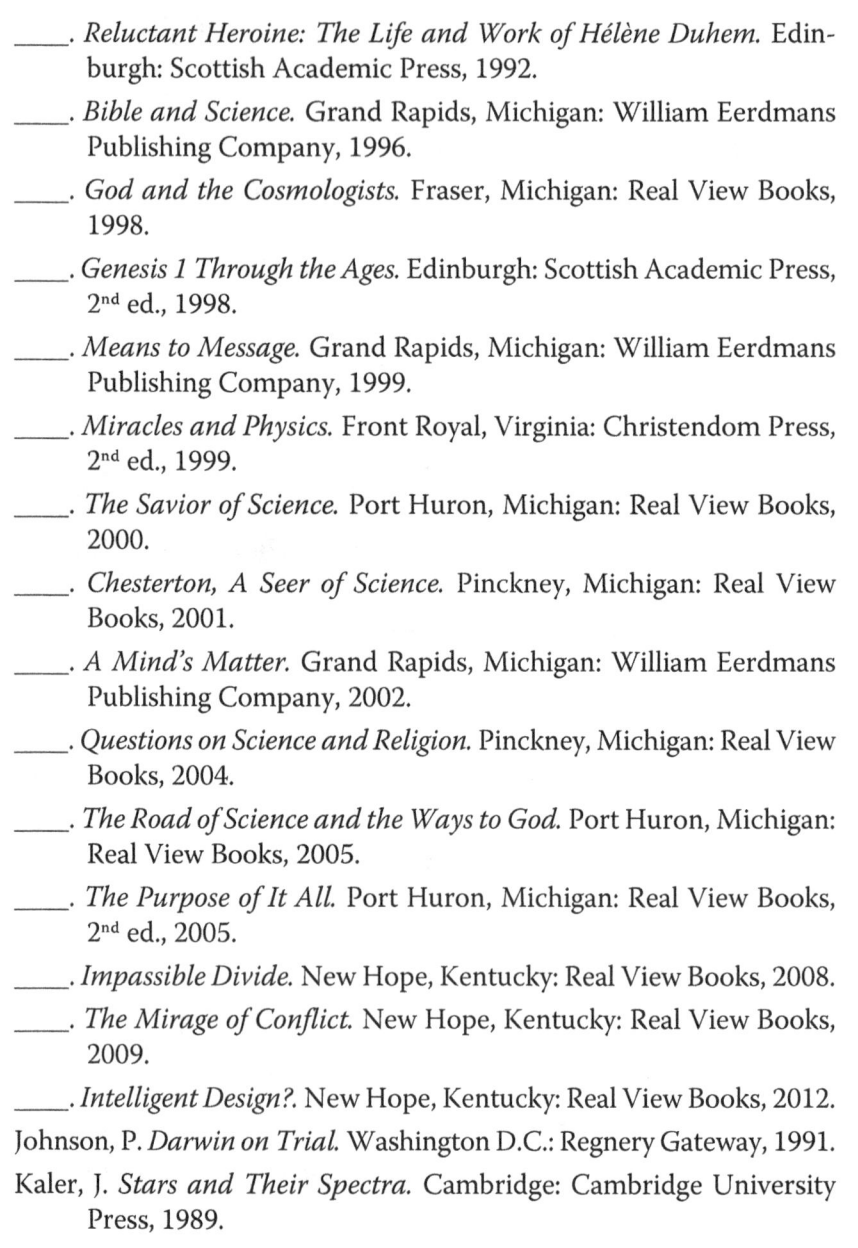

_____. *The Savior of Science.* Port Huron, Michigan: Real View Books, 2000.

_____. *Chesterton, A Seer of Science.* Pinckney, Michigan: Real View Books, 2001.

_____. *A Mind's Matter.* Grand Rapids, Michigan: William Eerdmans Publishing Company, 2002.

_____. *Questions on Science and Religion.* Pinckney, Michigan: Real View Books, 2004.

_____. *The Road of Science and the Ways to God.* Port Huron, Michigan: Real View Books, 2005.

_____. *The Purpose of It All.* Port Huron, Michigan: Real View Books, 2nd ed., 2005.

_____. *Impassible Divide.* New Hope, Kentucky: Real View Books, 2008.

_____. *The Mirage of Conflict.* New Hope, Kentucky: Real View Books, 2009.

_____. *Intelligent Design?.* New Hope, Kentucky: Real View Books, 2012.

Johnson, P. *Darwin on Trial.* Washington D.C.: Regnery Gateway, 1991.

Kaler, J. *Stars and Their Spectra.* Cambridge: Cambridge University Press, 1989.

Kemper, G., Kemper, H. and Luskin, C. *Discovering Intelligent Design.* Seattle: Discovery Institute Press, 2013.

Bibliography

Krauss, L. *A Universe from Nothing.* New York: Atria, 2013 paperback ed.

Koestler, A. *The Sleepwalkers.* London: Penguin Classics, 1959.

Lewis, C. S. *Miracles.* Glasgow: William Collins & Sons, 1947.

____. *The Discarded Image.* Cambridge: Cambridge University Press, 1964.

____. *God in the Dock.* Glasgow: William Collins & Sons, 1979.

Machamer, P. (editor). *Cambridge Companion to Galileo.* Cambridge: Cambridge University Press, 1998.

Maritain, J. *An Introduction to Philosophy.* London: Sheed and Ward, 1930.

____. *Three Reformers.* London: Sheed & Ward, 1944.

McKeon, R. *The Basic Works of Aristotle.* New York: Random House, 1941.

Meyer, S. *Signature in the Cell.* New York: HarperOne, 2009.

____. *Darwin's Doubt.* New York: HarperOne, 2013.

Neill, T. *Makers of the Modern Mind.* Milwaukee: The Bruce Publishing Company, 1949.

Oderberg, D. *Real Essentialism.* New York: Routledge, 2007.

Owens, J. *An Elementary Christian Metaphysics.* Houston: Center for Thomistic Studies, 1963.

Pieper, J. *Leisure, the Basis of Culture.* Indianapolis: Liberty Fund, 1952.

Relja, H. *Il Realismo di S. L. Jaki.* Rome: Ateneo Pontificio Regina Apostolorum, 2008.

Richards, J. *God and Evolution.* Seattle: Discovery Institute Press, 2010.

Rizzi, A. *The Science Before Science.* Baton Rouge: IAP Press, 2004.

Ross, D. *Aristotle.* London: Methuen, 5th ed., 1964.

Ruffini, E. *The Theory of Evolution Judged by Reason and Faith.* New York: Joseph Wagner, Inc., 1959.

Sheen, F. *God and Intelligence in Modern Philosophy.* New York: Longmans, Green and Co., 1925.

Stove, D. *Darwinian Fairytales.* New York: Encounter Books, 1995.

Taylor, A. *Plato.* London: University Paperbacks, 1960.

Trasancos, S. *Science Was Born of Christianity.* The Habitation of Chimham Publishing Co., 2014.

Trefil, J. *Space Atlas.* Washington, DC: The National Geographic Society, 2012.

Wallace, W. *Causality and Scientific Explanation.* Ann Arbor: University of Michigan Press, 2 vols., 1972 and 1974.

____. *The Modeling of Nature.* Washington, DC: The Catholic University of America Press, 1996.

Waterfield, R. *The First Philosophers.* Oxford: Oxford University Press, 2000.

Webb, J. (editor) *Nothing.* New York: The Experiment, 2013.

Wells, J. *The Politically Incorrect Guide to Darwinism and Intelligent Design.* Washington, DC: Regnery Publishing, 2006.

Whitcomb & Morris. *The Genesis Flood.* Phillipsburg, New Jersey: Presbyterian and Reformed Publishing Company, 2011.

Wiker & Witt. *A Meaningful World.* Downers Grove, Illinois: IVP Academic, 2006.

Winter, T. (editor). *The Cambridge Companion to Classical Islamic Theology.* Cambridge: Cambridge University Press, 2008.

Wolfson, R. *Einstein's Relativity and the Quantum Revolution: Modern Physics for Non-Scientists* Course Guidebook. Chantilly, Virginia: The Great Courses, 2nd ed., 2000.

Wuellner, B. *Dictionary of Scholastic Philosophy.* Fitzwilliam, New Hampshire: Loreto Publications, 2012.

INDEX OF NAMES

Bold indicates sections which are specifically about the person named.
Underlining indicates references to pages of notes.

Adam, 268, 278, 482
Adler, M., 67, 68
Aizpún, F., 430
Alfarabi, 209, **214–215**, 216, 219, 228
Alpher, R., 371
Anaxagoras, 127
Anaximenes, 127
Anselm, St, 176
Aquinas, St Thomas, 3, 6, 7, 25, 31, 32, 35, 49, 51–52, 68, 69, 76, 102, 109–110, 126, 128, 133, 145, 153, 164, 170, 194, 195, **175–182**, 191–195, 203, 216, 220, 229, 235, 250, 256–257, 260, 296, 301–302, 346, 358, 361, 364, 430
Aristotle, 3, 12, 15, 26, 31, 32, 33, 35–37, 42, 53–54, 68, 75, 85–86, 90, 93, 96, 108, 109, 114, 127–128, **135–150**, 152, 155–164, 171–194, 201, 216–217, 220–223, 228–229, 236, 295–298, 312, 315, 317–318, 328, 330, 338, 397–400, 402–403, 406, 411, 416, 442, 450
Ash'ari, al-, 207–212, 220, 227, 310
Atkins, P., 406, 419, 421, 430
Augros, M., 17, 430
Augustine of Hippo, St, 168, 176, 228, 250–252, 255–256

Averroes, 209, **218–222,** 229, 502
Avicenna, 172, 186, 209, **215–219,** 224, 229
Axe, D., 432

Behe, M., 405, 467–475
Bellarmine, R., St, 283–284
Belloc, H., 349
Benedict XV, Pope, 277
Benedict XVI, Pope, 199–200
Benignus, Brother, 32
Bentley, R., 359–360
Berkeley, G., 333
Bessel, F., 281
Bethell, T., 493–494
Bonaventure, St, 174, **222–223**
Bondi, H., 364
Bonnette, D., 69, 430, 477–480, 483, 485, 491, 495
Brahe, T., 315
Brown, W., 268–273, 275
Buddha, 119
Buridan, J., 187–194, 215, 229, 264, 284, 297
Burrell, D., 230
Burtt, E., 314–322, 337–339, 347

Cairns-Smith, A., 439
Calvin, J., **244–245,** 262–263, 265
Chaberek, M., 250, 301
Chen, J-Y., 461

Chesterton, G. K., xviii–xviii, xxi, 3, 7, 11–12, 22, 28, 40, 52, 68, 151, 177, 180–182, 209, 267, 301, 356, 379, 390, 445, 483, 497
Clarke, 67, 68
Craig, W., 231, 301, 389–390
Copernicus, N., 194, 264, 284, 315, 422
Copleston, F., 21, 197
Crick, F., 393

da Vinci, L., 194
Dales, R., 154, 185, 197
Dalrymple, B., 285–290
Damascene, St John, 176
Dante Alighieri, 196, 497
Darrow, C., 71
Darwin, C., 89, 260–262, **436–440**, 444–462, 475–490
Dauvillier, L., 117
Davies, P., 380–381
Dawkins, R., xvii, 390, 393–395, 402, 418–419, 433, 448–455, 467, 470
Democritus, 125, 365
Dennett, D., 393
Denton, M., 410, 421, 431
Descartes, R., 89, 194, 198, 297, 333, 338–339
Dingle, H., 366
Diogenes, 127
Dixon, T., 260
Drake, F., 422
Driscoll, J., 110
Duhem, H., 156, 190
Duhem, P., 154, **155–156**, 190, 194, 197, 391
Duns Scotus, Blessed J., 223

Egnor, M., 476
Einstein, A., 180, 310, 352, 362
Empedocles, 127, 403

Feser, E., 31, 68, 108–109, 198, 323, 328, 389–390, 427

Galen, 113, 452
Galileo, 189, 191, 194, **282–284**, 297, **320–323**, 325, 328–329, 335, 486
Garrigou-Lagrange, R., 68
Ghazali, al-, 210, 213, 227, 230, 310, 376, 502
Gilson, E., 3, 28, 31, 32, 67, 108, 135, 138, 142, 154, 171, 175, 177, 189–190, 195–198, 207, 213, 219–221, 223, 226, 261, 229, 231, 334, 429–430, 444, 450, 491–492
Gonzalez, G., 303, 389, 422–423, 430
Goodall, J., 483
Gould, S., 459
Grant, E., 153–154, 165–171, 183–184, 194, 196–198, 209, 211–212, 229–232, 302
Gregory IX, Pope, 175
Grisar, H., 235, 300
Grosseteste, Bishop R., 185

Haffner, P., xi, 204–205, 467
Halley, E., 360–361
Ham, K., 233–234
Hankins, B., 274
Hannam, J., 108–109, 153, 198
Hartle, J., 377
Harvey, W., 103

Index of Names

Hawking, S., 377
Heisenberg, W., 384–385
Heller, M., 109
Heraclitus, 127
Heller, M., 388, 390
Hesiod, 32
Hippasus, 127
Hippocrates, 113
Hoyle, F., 352, 365–367, 374, 415
Hubble, E., 349–351, 353, 365, 370
Hume, D., xx, 50, 492

Innocent IV, Pope, 175

Jackson, P., 51
Jaki, S., xx–xxii, 3, 8, 31, 32, 78, 89–90, 101, 104, 108–109, 110, 113, 115–116, 119–120, 122, 125, 148, 151, 152–154, 161–162, 165, 179, 189–190, 195–198, 201–205, 215–216, 230–232, 254–255, 258, 262, 282, 285, 302–305, 317, 345–347, 358, 360, 383, 385–386, 388–391, 424,
Jastrow, R., 353–354
Jesus Christ, 96, 103, 165–166, 170, 180–181, 205
Johnson, P., 481–482

Kaler, J., 304
Kant, E., xx–xxi, 342, 361
Kelvin, Lord, 362
Kemper, G., 388, 430, 491
Kenyon, D., 415–416
Kepler, J., 277, **315–321**, 486
Koestler, A., 282–283, 345
Koyré, A., 265

Krauss, L., 374–380, 388–389, 406
Kuhn, T., 326

Lazarus, 103
Leavitt, H., 349–350
Leibniz, G., 52, 333
Lemaître, G., 352–353, 370
Leo XIII, Pope, 255–257, 277
Lewis, C. S., 155, 345
Luskin, C., 233
Luther, M., 233, **235–244**, 258, 265, 298, 310, 502
Lyell, C., 271

MacMillan, W., 362
Maimonides, M., 211
Maldamé, J.-M., 204
Malthus, T., 438
Manuel II Paleologus, 199
Maritain, J., 31, 116, 152, 198, 300
Marx, K., 89
Maugham, S., 101
Mayer, R., 71
McGrath, A., 390
McNamara, P., 244
Melanchthon, P., 265
Meyer, S., xviii, 389, 397, 411–417, 424–425, 459–460, 466
Mill, J. S., 50, 101
Mohammed, 205, 214
Moses, 118, 255, 263
Mueller, H., 462
Myers, P., 393

Neill, T., 237, 244–245
Newton, I., 180, 189, 255, 297, **334–342**, 357, 359–360, 486

Nietzsche, F., 89
Nye, B., 233–235

Occam, W. of, **223–228, 235–241**, 273, 298, 300, 310, 502
Oderberg, D., 109, 110
Olbers, W., 361
Orage, A., xxi
Oresme, Bishop N,. 169, 264
Owens, J., 68

Pfungst, O., 480
Philoponus, J., 186
Pieper, J., 10, 109
Pierce, C., 431
Pirandello, L., 52
Pius XII, Pope, 277
Plato, 25, 130, **135–137**, 150, 170–171, 180, 201, 295
Plotinos, 170
Pope, A., 334
Popper, K., 326
Protagoras, 129, 419–420
Pythagoras, 127, 318

Ramon of Sauvetat, Bishop, 172
Relja, H., 108, 109, 195
Renié, R., 255, 273
Ricci, M., 123, 126
Richards, J., 303, 389, 422–423, 430
Richardt, A., 303
Rizzi, A., 6, 88, 108, 405
Ross, D., 154, 430
Ruffini, E., 253, 301
Ruse, M., 393–394
Russell, B., 21, 50, 362, 389, 420–421

Sagan, C., 423
Scopes, J. T., 71
Sertillanges, A., 456
Shakespeare, W., 310
Sheen, F. J., 32
Simpson, G., 471
Slipher, V., 349–350
Smith, G., 231
Socrates, **129–137**, 150, 180, 182, 294–295, 312
Stein, B., 393–395
Stenger, V., 199
Stove, D., 326, 452–455, 491
Sungenis, R., 266–268

Taylor, A., 135
Thales, 126–127, 130
Tolkien, J. R. R., 51–52
Trasancos, S., 124, 198
Trefil, J., 388, 390

Vigouroux, F., 278, 291, 305

Waismann, F., 385
Wallace, W., 31, 68, 108–109, 151, 153, 325, 327, 429, 432, 499
Waterfield, R., 77, 128
Webb, J., 380
Wells, J., 108, 390, 431, 492, 494
Whitcomb, J., 273–275, 291, 303–304
Wiker, B., 109
Wilson, J., 303
Witt, J., 109
Wolfson, R., 385, 390
Woodbury, A., 478
Wuellner, B., 7

GENERAL INDEX

abiogenesis 408, 423–424
act, first and second 42–44, 56, 88
age
  of the Earth 268–273, 276, 278, 279, 285–291, 299, 410
  of the universe 234, 251, 256, 277, 299, 366–367, 409
aliens 395–396, 421–424, 429, 489
Allah 199, 202–207, 209–213, 214, 215, 227–229, 230, 241, 264, 297, 298
amino acids 41, 411–416, 469, 472–473
Ancient Earth, Ancient Skies 285
angels 186, 188, 237, 405
animism 135
anthropology 449, 481–486
antimatter 372–374
ape-language studies 478–480
apologetics 95, 97, 167, 170
argumentation
  abductive 425
  a posteriori 34, 140, 142, 150, 190, 295
  a priori 34, 127, 142, 148, 190, 444
  demonstrative 17, 54, 55, 84, 86, 218, 283, 314, 324–326, 374, 427
  'demonstrative regress' 325–326
  God of the gaps (see 'God, of the gaps')
  hypothetic-deductive 326
  method of Catholicism 95–97
  three modes of 86

probabilistic 54, 95–96, 297, 299, 324–327, 427
Aristotle 3, 12, 15, 25, 32, 33, 35–37, 42, 53, 54, 67, 75, 86, 90, 96, 114, 127, 135, 136, 153, 155, 160, 162, 163, 164, 180, 191, 192, 214, 236, 312, 317, 318, 320, 324, 328, 330, 338, 339, 397, 398, 399, 400, 402, 403, 404, 411, 416, 442, 450
  as first professional realist 35, 137, 312
  assessment of his achievement 156–159, 170–173
  Catholic reception of 174–182, 193–194, 221–223, 228–229, 295–296
  errors in physical science 114, 145–149, 182, 186, 312
  limitations in metaphysics 140–144, 156–157
  Muslim reception of 216–220, 296–298
  over-emphasis of final causes 147–149, 150, 320, 328, 400, 404
  view on life 403–404
archaeology 79–80
assumptions, false xvii–xviii
astronomy 79–80, 249, 279–282
Augustinians 236, 244, 298
authority 5, 11, 14, 15, 21, 65, 73, 91, 92, 94, 95, 97, 104, 107, 168, 169, 177, 227, 234, 239, 242, 243, 245, 258, 296, 339

Babylonians 115
'being'
  as outside the scope of science 87–89, 336, 342–343
  concept of 9–10, 176–177, 214, 317–318, 327, 328, 330, 446, 487, 503
  in connection with causes 36–49, 51–53, 55–65, 69, 91, 102, 106, 117, 125, 127, 134, 140–141, 142, 145, 150, 158, 160–163, 164, 214–217, 223–224, 231, 252, 279, 296, 301, 328, 331, 340–341, 353, 365, 374, 378–379, 386, 399, 404, 405, 408, 421, 441, 442–445, 450
  in connection with realism 23–26, 27, 105, 317
  of God 358, 363, 364, 374
belief 54, 86, 93
Bell Telephone Lab 371
Bible
  in general 28, 72, 153, 216, 292, 297, 302, 365
  as impeding science ('biblicism') 234–235, 243–246, 258–276, 282–284, 287, 298–299, 303, 447
  as not impeding science 158–162, 167–169, 176, 202, 204, 247–257, 277–278
Bible and Science xxv
Biblical catastrophism 272, 303
Big Bang 86, 234, 352–353, 366–367, 370–374, 376, 409, 414, 488
biology 79–80, 148, 261, 374, 396–406, 449–475, 488–489
bodies, study of physical 73–89, 90, 92, 107, 109, 114, 127, 130, 184, 186–191, 192, 227, 294, 296, 297, 298, 312, 321–323, 324–326, 331, 334, 338, 360, 372, 397–398, 402, 428, 429, 456, 486–487
Buddhism 119, 260, 453
Burgess Shale 459

Cambrian explosion 459–462, 492
Catholicism
  and the Bible 167–169, 202, 249–258, 276–278
  and realism 170–173
  as originating modern science 174–191
  as cautious about miracles 104–105
  mode of arguing dogmas 95–97
causality, principle of
  definition 20, 203
  denial of 225–226, 228, 380, 382, 383–386, 387, 415, 428, 487
causes in general
  definition 35
  acceptance of all by the realist 74
  all are needed to explain material beings 35–39, 161, 399
  causal chains 41–47
  essentially and accidentally ordered 44–45, 106
  four types 35–40, 106, 161, 162, 179, 192, 222, 397, 399
  hierarchy in reality 42
  immediate vs. ultimate 90
  primary and secondary causation 55–65, 99–100, 106, 140–141, 150–151, 160, 164, 179, 183, 209–211, 215, 223, 240, 271, 328–329, 332, 341
  proper cause 49–50
cause, efficient

General Index 517

meaning 36, 38, 39, 90, 106, 161
  clearer in life sciences 83–85, 397
  obscure in inorganic bodies 80, 82–83
  of being and becoming 43–44
  as over-emphasised by empiricists 98–100, 184, 327, 329–330, 398, 402, 426–427, 442–456, 487
  primary and secondary 56, 59–61, 92, 141, 160, 211, 216, 217, 328, 329
  as reduced by idealists 107, 133–134, 135, 141, 144, 150–151
cause, final
  meaning 36, 38, 90, 106, 161, 327
  and Intelligent Design 426–427
  as most important cause 133
  as object of religion 92
  as over-emphasised in science 132–134, 147–148, 192, 320
  as clearer in life sciences 83–85, 397, 399–400, 428
  as denied by empiricists 98–99, 192, 240, 312, 327–329, 331, 406–407, 435–436, 451–456, 487–490
  inaccessible to senses 98
  intrinsic 369, 398–399, 401, 404, 427
  Unmoved Mover as 142–144, 159
  present in all beings 399, 407–408
cause, formal
  meaning 35–36, 39, 90, 106, 161, 324, 404, 417, 428, 435, 442–443
  as law of nature 102
  as over-emphasised 132–135, 150, 427
  clearer in inorganic bodies 80, 82–85, 194, 296, 397, 400

denied by empiricists 98–100, 107, 192, 224, 324, 327, 329, 331, 356, 398, 435–436, 444–445, 449, 487–490
  inaccessible to senses 98
  extrinsic or exemplar 399, 401, 404
  needed for demonstration 324
cause, material
  meaning 35–36, 38, 39, 90, 106, 161, 327
  as reduced by idealists 133, 145, 147, 150, 180, 312
  at bottom of reality 42
  clearer in inorganic bodies 82–85, 397
  new appreciation in Middle Ages 180–182, 194
  over-emphasis by empiricists 98–100, 126–127, 130, 313–314, 355–367, 374–386, 396, 435
century of genius 313, 320, 326, 334, 486
certainty
  absence of 225, 236, 238, 342, 376, 384–386
  demonstrative 17, 35, 55, 271, 301
  of the first principles 27
  of religion 93–97, 167
  of science 267–268, 299, 324–327
  Aristotelian degrees of 53–54, 85–86, 324
chance 267, 353, 369, 382–383, 393, 403, 413–415, 423–424, 429, 431, 472–474, 489
chemistry 79–83, 148, 246, 347, 421, 491
China xxiv, 115, 119, 122–125, 128, 149, 164, 178, 202, 293–294
Clever Hans 479–480

Cold War 470
'The Commentator' see 'Averroes'
common descent 457–458, 463
complexity 78, 185, 279, 304, 331, 373–376, 397–399, 401, 404, 407–411, 416–418, 423, 428, 437, 451, 457–462, 461–466, 471, 474, 475, 489, 490, 503
  irreducible 468–469
  mere and specified 368–370, 411, 417, 426–427
Confucianism 122
contingency 34, 106, 179, 180, 214–215, 217, 296, 353, 364, 369, 387
  definition 34, 161, 369
Copenhagen school 385
Cosmic Microwave Background Radiation (CMBR) 370–373
'Cosmic Origins' (documentary) 394
cosmological constant 373
Creation and Scientific Creativity xxv
creation, doctrine of
  as encouraging realism 157–165, 222
creationism xxv, 233, 262–276, 278, 287, 291, 292, 299, 303, 305, 332, 419, 424
  definition 234
  progressive 252–253
creatures
  as contingent 37–40, 50, 51, 55, 67, 160–161, 176, 179, 217, 296
  their causation 62–65, 100, 106, 162, 183, 222, 259, 263
  their causation denied (see 'occasionalism')

credibility, motives of 95–97, 167, 243
cycles
  eternal 113, 116–125, 127–128, 131, 145, 293, 363
  non-eternal 163–164, 282, 291, 350, 366, 400, 409
cults 93

Darwin's Doubt xviii, 459
Darwinism 71–72, 452–453, 457–458, 460, 463, 469, 490
dating, radioactive 286–291
De Ente et Essentia 177
The Descent of Man 482
design, intelligent see 'Intelligent Design'
dialectics 54, 86, 133, 218, 427
dialogue 130, 132, 199
directed panspermia 395
DNA 412–417, 443, 463–466, 472–473
Dominicans 198, 235
Drake Equation 422–424

The Edge of Evolution 468
effects
  being and becoming 42
  used to infer causes 55
Egyptians 115
emanationism 216, 223
empiricism xxi, 18–19
  as denying formal and final causes 98–101
  as denying primary causality 58
  as irrational 20–21
  as using same method for all reality 73–74

General Index

in ancient peoples 121, 123–124, 130, 403
in Catholics 191–192
in the century of genius 315–343
in modern scientists 356–386, 393–396, 402–403, 406–424, 435–441, 444–486
The Enlightenment 190, 386
epigenetic processes 466–467
epistedometer 15, 29, 33, 73, 129, 211, 503
    explained 13–14
    types of 99–101
epistemologies 25, 26, 30, 89, 100–101, 487, 501
epistemology 16, 19, 21, 22, 23, 25, 26, 34, 65, 99, 139, 144, 179, 180, 192, 424, 444, 450, 456, 486, 490
    definition 4
    e. of ancient cultures 115–125, 149
    e. of Islam 202–220
    formation of 15–16
    grounds for a realist e. 25–29, 87, 106
    relation to Christianity, creation and realism 157–159, 165, 193
    relation to modern science 314–344
    relationship between e. and truth and logic, and irrationality 156, 417–419, 497–503
essence and existence 51, 141, 150, 153, 173, 214, 296
Everest, Mount 3, 15, 33, 35, 74, 115, 292
evidence, eyewitness xvii
evolution
    and time 285, 410
    chemical 372, 409–410

of non-life to life 410–424
macro- and micro- 405, 440, 444, 449, 457, 467, 484, 490
Expelled 393
experimentation xvii, 75, 77, 82, 85, 109, 114, 148, 185, 190, 194, 226, 283, 323, 326, 335–336, 338, 343, 354, 465, 480

fideism or 'blind faith' 92–93, 97, 226, 208, 361, 381, 417–418
fine-tuning, cosmic 371–375, 382, 456
firmament 248, 251, 254, 255, 263
first principles 19, 27, 28, 51, 123, 149, 228, 380, 387
fossil record 449, 457–462, 492
Franciscans 222, 223, 228, 260

Genesis, book of 158, 162–164, 177, 234, 248–249, 251–258, 260–261, 268, 273–275, 277, 301, 485
The Genesis Flood 274
geocentrism 264, 266–268, 277, 279–285, 303, 304
geology 79–80, 274, 275
God xix
    and annihilation 102
    attributes 357–358, 363, 374
    as efficient cause of creation 159–160, 328
    as emanating cause 216–218
    as First Cause 48–65, 101–102, 106, 126, 160, 216, 222, 226, 258–260, 279, 285, 301, 354, 383, 498

as First Unmoved Mover 137–144, 146, 150–151, 153, 160, 216, 295
as mechanical inventor 319, 328–330, 331–332, 340–343
as object of religion 92
as pure act of existence 175–178
as reasonable 162, 203
as unable to change laws of nature 102
as voluntarist 204–207, 209, 213, 224, 240–241, 244–245, 298
certainty of His existence 53–55, 91, 106
characteristics of His causation 59–62, 159–162, 271
of the gaps 259–260, 268–270, 299, 304, 341–342, 347
proof of His existence 48–53
Great Period 123
Greeks xxiv, 125–149, 171, 223, 294–296, 429
The Greatest Show on Earth xvii, 418, 467

heliocentrism 264, 267, 279–285, 291, 292, 305, 315
hexameron 164
Hinduism 119–121, 124
Hollywood 434

idealism xxi, 16–17
 definition 9
 as denying material and efficient causes 98–101
 as irrational 17–18, 21–22, 26
 in ancient peoples 121, 124, 132–136, 142–149
 in Islam 209–220
 in Catholics 220–227
 in Protestantism 235–246, 258–276
identity, principle of 19, 203
ignorance xvii
immaterial 11, 23, 25, 36, 77, 78, 98, 108, 142, 143, 164, 295, 330, 331, 333, 346, 357, 399, 410, 416, 428, 435, 441, 442, 477, 480, 481, 498
immorality 129
impetus see 'movement, impetus theory'
Incans 116
India xxiv, 115, 119–121, 124, 127, 149, 164, 178, 293
individualism 21
inertia, existential 328
inertia, law of see 'movement, law of inertia'
infinity material vs. immaterial 357–358
intellect 4–8, 11–15, 22, 23, 25, 26–29, 40, 51, 53, 54, 57, 65–66, 73, 74, 77, 87, 89, 91, 92, 93, 97–107, 127, 133, 139, 140, 161, 174, 183, 224, 293–295, 311, 327, 334, 354, 368, 417, 418, 477, 479, 481, 483–484, 497–501
 and empiricism 18–21, 489–490
 and idealism 16–18
 connection with formal and final causes 98
 doubting the i. 116–118, 123–124
 and Islam 199, 204–222, 297, 310
 Luther and the i. 233–244, 310
 Occam and the i. 224–241, 310
 operation of judgement 9–10, 27–29, 65, 91, 93, 97, 104,

Index of Names

107, 162–164, 238, 243, 298, 499
type of knowledge attained 8, 476–481, 484
unable to think contradiction 51
Intelligent Design (ID) xviii, 71–72, 368, 393–396, 402, 404, 424–427, 429, 432
'Intelligent Design?' (booklet) 424
'The Invisible Man' (short story) xviii
Ionians 127, 130, 312
Islam xxiv, 164, 168, 169, 199–220, 227–229, 232, 297–298

Jesuits 123, 198, 325
John, Gospel of 158, 160, 162
Judaism 116, 118

kalam cosmological argument 376
Kentucky 233, 234
knowledge
  definition 4
  dependence on reality 6
  faculties of 5
  human way of knowing 34, 57
  of animals 476–481, 483–484
  starting point 6
Koran
  as contradictory 199, 227, 245
  as incarnation of Allah 205–206, 227
  as supporting a Creator God 214–215
  as supporting a voluntarist God 202–207, 209, 213, 220, 297

logic 91, 123, 124, 125, 139, 150, 156, 157, 203, 325
logos 126, 178

Lord Gifford and his Lectures xxv

malaria 405, 469–474
materialism 18, 20, 58, 131, 135, 182, 353–354, 363, 413, 418–424, 429, 449, 489, 499, 501, 503
  definition 355
  using only one method of study 396
mathematics
  as metaphysics 315–320, 327–332, 333, 339–340
matter 23, 35, 38, 39, 42, 75–76, 78, 79, 81, 87, 89, 98–99, 107, 132, 149, 161, 180, 183, 190, 216, 217, 295, 296, 297, 312, 323, 328, 329, 330, 333, 344, 353, 358, 360, 363, 365, 370–372, 377, 383–386, 394, 396–401, 407, 416, 417, 418, 423, 428, 429 n.4, 435, 442, 454, 477, 485, 488, 489, 498, 502
Mayans 115
measurement 77, 81–85, 109, 113–114, 217, 272, 282, 289–290, 336, 346, 349–350, 367, 384, 428
mechanism 135, 183, 398, 400, 402, 406–418
mentalities xxi
Messenger from the Stars 320
Metaphysics 15, 42, 318, 450
metaphysics 40, 66, 89, 98, 117, 122, 123, 126, 135, 136, 140, 150, 151, 156, 160, 170, 172, 175, 177, 179, 193, 208, 214, 216, 217, 222, 228, 242, 295, 296, 298, 301, 312, 315, 316,

319, 320, 328, 334, 336–342, 344, 354, 498–499
   definition 40
methods
   definition 72
   different for different objects 73, 79–80, 84, 107, 148, 169, 184, 318, 333, 396, 399, 425
   error of using a single method 73–74, 246, 318, 322–323, 333, 336, 338, 386, 487, 498–499
   of physical sciences 81–83, 399–401
   of life sciences 83–85, 396–401
   scientific 75–87, 98, 102, 148, 182–185, 197, 285, 322, 323, 325, 335–337, 340, 343, 396, 398, 406, 416, 419, 428, 499
A Mind's Matter xxv
The Merchant of Venice 310
The Metaphysical Foundations of Modern Science 314
miracles 63, 96, 101–105, 271–272, 292
misologist 131
The Modeling of Nature 325
monogenism
   definition 485
   as not conflicting with science 249, 485–486
movement
   as explained by empiricists 329–330
   as explained by final causes 132, 182, 187
   impetus theory 186–191
   law of inertia 189, 198
   of heavenly bodies 117–118, 143–144, 164, 188–189, 214–215, 279–285, 349–352

'whatever is moved is moved by another' 137–140
multiverse 86, 109, 382–383
Muslim, see 'Islam'
mutazilites 206–207
mythology 118–119, 122, 126–127, 134, 141, 149, 178, 294, 440, 498, 499
The Mystery of Reason 204
mythos 126, 178

natural selection 72, 394, 405, 418, 421, 440–442, 444–445, 450–456, 457, 461–465, 467–475
   meaning 438–439
nature, laws of 89, 103, 115, 179, 184, 263, 270–272, 274, 276, 285, 293, 299
   not broken by miracles 102–104
Nature 380
Neanderthals 484
New Atheists 301, 374, 394–395, 419, 453
New Scientist 380
nominalism 192, 224–225, 486
non-contradiction, principle of
   definition 19
   denial of 20, 51, 55, 163, 294, 365, 456, 487
nothing
   as not a cause 118, 123, 125, 365
   as a cause 365, 376–381
Nothing 380

object
   definition 72
   relation to knowledge 73
   of biology's study 75, 396

Index of Names 523

of chemistry's study 75
of philosophy's study 90–91
of physics' study 75, 396
of religion 92
of science's study 90
specificity in scientific fields 79–80
universe as o. of study 183–184
occasionalism (and occasionalist) 56–58, 98, 104, 208, 210, 223–224, 228, 269, 332, 502
On the Heavens 147
On the Origin of Species 261, 436, 437, 440, 447, 458
On the Parts of Animals 398, 403
opinion 53–54, 86
Origin of the Human Species 478

panteleologism 147
pantheism 149–151, 216, 229, 293–295, 298, 312, 339, 374, 488
  definition 116
  crass 116–125, 374
  elaborate 125–136, 374
  in modern science 355–387, 445–446, 453–454, 498–499
The Paradox of Olbers' Paradox 360
paradox, Darwinian 466
paradoxes, stellar 359–362
parallax, stellar see 'stars, measurement of'
particle accelerators 384
Pauli exclusion principle 429
Phaedo 130, 131
Philippines 433
philosopher(s) 257, 279, 294, 296, 309, 342, 359, 384, 427, 450
philosophism
  definition 208

in Catholicism 220–222, 229
in Islam 208–209, 213–220, 227–229, 297–298, 502
in Protestantism 262
of empiricists 300, 314, 333–334, 344
philosophy 22, 28, 71, 79, 87, 88–92, 94, 85, 115, 126, 128–137, 145, 149, 150, 151, 158, 165–178, 182–185, 202, 212–220, 221, 226, 236–237, 267, 299, 339, 343, 386, 405, 421, 440–442
  as judge of everything 91
  as necessary for human beings 89–90, 336
  in relation to religion 91, 94
  role in human knowing 92
  science without philosophy 311–313, 319–320, 326, 335–337, 361, 486
phyla, animal 448, 457–460, 462, 467, 492
Physics 187
Planet of the Apes 434
polygenism 485
positivism 320, 329, 336, 385
Posterior Analytics 75
Pre-Socratics 127–128
Precambrian period 460–462, 492
presuppositions (see 'assumptions')
Primum Mobile 143
Principia 359
principle, Copernican 303, 422
principles, first 19–20, 51, 55
The Privileged Planet 373, 422
propositions, self-evident 19, 86

Protestantism 71, 98, 168, 169, 229, 233–246, 258–276, 277–278, 292, 298–300, 301, 343, 447, 486
Protrepticus 90
Psalms 160, 264, 302, 345

quality
  as over-emphasised 134, 182, 217
  as part of science's study 81, 109, 323, 346
  primary and secondary 319, 321–322, 326, 338
quantity 76–79, 81, 87, 88, 114, 134, 217, 292, 319–320, 322–323, 339, 343, 344, 358–361, 477, 487
  as alone knowable 315–323, 324, 327, 330–332, 339, 343
  as known via quality 323–324

random mutation 463–466, 467–475
real (see also 'reality mentality', 'realism', 'realist' and 'epistemologies')
reality mentality xix, xx, xxi, xxiv, 4, 14, 226, 295, 320
realism xvii, xix–xxiv, 4, 41, 49, 58–66, 86, 92, 98, 116, 124, 149, 259, 285, 293, 299, 311, 314, 326, 333, 334, 336, 355, 361, 362, 381, 387, 420, 426, 427, 486, 490, 497, 501–503
  definition xx
  ability to account for reality 89
  Aquinas's r. 179–182
  Aristotle's r. 36–37, 136–139, 148, 150, 156–157, 295

  as balancing the four causes 99, 311–312, 329, 399, 401
  Catholic r. 158–165, 170–173, 183, 193–195 296
  defence of 23–26, 57, 105–106
  Islam and r. 204, 207, 208, 221, 297–298
  principles 5, 6, 10,11–22, 27–28, 40, 132, 137
  as human xix, xxiii, 22–23, 27–28, 105–106, 150, 334, 501–503
  as rejecting occasionalism 57
  the Reformation and r. 258–260, 278, 298–299
  religion needs r. 107–108
  science needs r. 87–89, 107–108, 297, 311–314, 327
  weakening of r. 191–192, 226, 334–343
realist (the r.) 6, 12, 13, 14, 26, 28–29, 51, 58, 66, 73–74, 89, 93, 99, 102, 104, 106, 148, 161, 163, 164, 222, 330, 334, 335, 401, 402, 404, 501–503
  contrasted with the idealist 17
  contrasted with the biblicist 258–262, 365
regress, demonstrative see 'argumentation'
reincarnation 25, 32, 119, 131
religion
  and intellectual progress xxiii
  as influencing worldviews xix, 91, 115, 158
  conflict with science 98–101, 107
  harmony with science 97–98, 179–191
  irrational or wrong xxi
  need to be realist 97, 107
  rational foundation xxi, xxiii

General Index 525

test of reasonableness 92–97
text-based vs. institution-based 168–169, 202, 258
revelation 95, 140, 163, 165, 205–207, 208, 221, 234, 254, 263, 296, 332, 417
rhetoric 54, 86, 93, 128, 324
Rise of the Planet of the Apes 434
The Road of Science and the Ways to God xxv

saturation mutagenesis 465
The Savior of Science 125, 165
scholasticism, scholastics
  positive contributions of 16, 151, 172–173, 175, 179, 184–191, 194, 246, 254, 321, 386
  decline of 226–227, 236, 241, 343, 486
Science and Creation 115, 125
The Science before Science 6
science
  its assumptions 87, 89, 107, 128, 271, 276, 285, 299, 342–343, 347, 364, 381, 424–425
  its dependence on philosophy 87–89, 311
  exact 76–79, 81, 116, 145, 150, 151, 179, 189, 194, 201, 217, 220–221, 229, 285, 344, 400, 428, 487
  its autonomy in the Middle Ages 165–167, 184, 193
  gradation in sciences 79–80
  hindered by pantheism 115–149, 339, 367
  its understanding of causes 80–86, 102
  modern meaning 75
  philosophical meaning 35, 53, 75, 128, 227, 324, 326
  pseudo- 86

sciences
  physical 75–83, 85, 396, 399–401, 487
  palaetiological 425
scientific method, see 'methods, scientific'
Scientific Revolution xxiv, 191, 314, 324, 490
Search for Extraterrestrial Intelligence (SETI) 422–424
senses 5–8, 9–14, 57, 66, 73–74, 77, 89, 90, 91, 103–107, 222, 251, 264, 275, 284, 295, 298, 315, 319, 322, 323, 329, 330–331, 334, 355, 357, 398, 404, 405, 417, 424, 425, 440, 497, 498, 500, 501, 503
  as used by philosophers 90–92
  as used by scientists 75, 77, 84, 85, 190, 323
  definition and list 4–5
  Aristotle on the s. 137, 140
  Christian philosophy and the s. 182, 194, 256
  connection with material and efficient causes 85, 98
  distrust of the s. 14–22, 99–100, 116–120, 133, 149–150
  Occam and the s. 224–226
  position in hierarchy of knowledge 86–89
  starting point of knowledge 6, 22–27, 34–35, 40, 65, 132
  type of knowledge attained 7–8, 34, 476–481
  unable to see God 355, 375
Signature in the Cell 411, 425, 459
The Sleepwalkers 282
sola Scriptura 243–244
solipsism (and solipsist) 4–6

Sophists 128–130, 133–134, 294–295
soul 4, 8, 13, 23, 96, 105, 131, 164, 174, 177, 181, 200, 240, 330, 333, 344, 398, 399, 404, 428, 477, 484
species
  biological 443–444, 446–450
  evolution as cause of 261, 435–486
  human 98, 434, 475–486
  God as cause of 260, 261, 447
  natural 442–446
stars, measurement of 280–282, 305, 349–352
Steady-State Theory 364–367, 370
sufficient reason, principle of 20, 52, 162
Summa Theologiae 175, 178
supernova 409
superstition
  definition 379
  of atheists 271, 311, 379–380, 386, 415, 499
survival of the fittest 89, 452–454, 465, 468–472, 490, 503
syllogism 7, 16, 17, 139
Système du Monde 156

Taoism 122–124
tautology 446, 472
taxonomy 457–458, 460, 467, 475
telos 99, 130, 133, 322, 402
theologism
  definition 208
  in Catholicism 222–227
  in Islam 208, 209–213, 220, 227–228, 297
  in Protestantism 235–246, 262–276, 298–300

of empiricists 314, 333–334, 344
theology
  in general 170–171, 178, 184, 191, 195
  natural xxii, 93–94, 107, 140–141, 145, 148, 172, 193, 226, 245, 298, 339
Theory of Relativity 352, 362
thermodynamics 361
Thomism 177, 180, 235, 238
truth
  definition 9
  absolute 20, 27, 271, 325, 503
  double 163, 174, 175, 229, 250, 299
  oneness 162–163

Uncertainty Principle 376, 384–386
Undeniable: Evolution and the Science of Creation 235
uniformitarianism 271–272, 276, 285, 364, 424
  as necessary assumption for science 105, 271, 276, 285, 364, 424
  as rejected by creationists 272, 274–275
union, hypostatic 96
The Unity of the Philosophic Experience 334
universe
  definition 87, 161
  as assumed by science 87, 107, 263, 271
  as conceived by Catholics 158–165, 179–184, 190–193, 228, 251–253, 256–257, 277, 296

General Index

as conceived by creationists 234, 243, 258–260, 264, 266–271, 282, 283, 299, 303
as conceived by empiricists 58, 98, 314, 319, 322, 327–331, 336–343, 354–387, 406, 408–410, 420–424, 435, 453, 456, 488–489, 499
as conceived by Muslims 208–218, 223, 224, 229, 297–298, 395, 396
as conceived by pantheists 116–127, 130, 135, 138, 139–150, 171, 293–296, 404, 498
as dependent on God 52, 56, 101, 102, 104, 106, 203, 208, 228, 231, 285
as infinite 357–362
as specific 367–374
Universe Creating Machine 373, 374, 382
A Universe from Nothing 378

voluntarism see 'God, as voluntarist'

water
as cause of wetness 55, 211, 324
as explaining everything 126
as purposeful 83, 407–408
in the Flood 274–275 291–292
in the Hebraic view of the world 248, 255, 263, 265, 275
its nature 85–86
will, free xix
worldview xix, 109, 115, 119, 135, 158, 180, 185, 192, 193, 194, 195, 202, 207, 226, 233, 235, 238, 242, 243, 293, 295, 296, 314, 315, 327, 331, 338, 343, 355, 356, 381, 386, 387, 420, 422, 424, 498, 503
how it is formed 91–92
of realists 107, 179, 311–312

Yin and Yang 122–123, 294

CPSIA information can be obtained
at www.ICGtesting.com
Printed in the USA
JSHW021950080722
27724JS00001B/1

9 780852 449226